SSSP

Springer
Series in
Social
Psychology

SSSP

Joel Brockner
Jeffrey Z. Rubin

Entrapment in Escalating Conflicts

A Social
Psychological Analysis

Springer-Verlag
New York Berlin Heidelberg Tokyo

Joel Brockner
Graduate School of Business
Columbia University
Uris Hall
New York, NY 10027
U.S.A.

Jeffrey Z. Rubin
Department of Psychology
Tufts University
Medford, MA 02155
U.S.A.

With 3 Illustrations

Library of Congress Cataloging in Publication Data
Brockner, Joel.
   Entrapment in escalating conflicts.
   (Springer series in social psychology)
   Bibliography: p.
   Includes index.
   1. Interpersonal conflict.   2. Social psychology.
3. Social conflict.   I. Rubin, Jeffrey Z.   II. Title.
III. Series.
HM291.B77   1985   303.6   84-23645

Typeset by Ampersand Publisher Services, Inc., Rutland, Vermont.
Printed and bound by R.R. Donnelley & Sons, Harrisonburg, Virginia.
Printed in the United States of America.

9 8 7 6 5 4 3 2 1

ISBN 0-387-96089-9 Springer-Verlag New York Berlin Heidelberg Tokyo
ISBN 3-540-96089-9 Springer-Verlag Berlin Heidelberg New York Tokyo

Preface

It was just over 12 years ago that we first sat down together to talk about psychological traps. In the relative calm of late afternoons, feet draped casually over the seedy furnishings of the Tufts psychology department, we entertained each other with personal anecdotes about old cars, times spent lost on hold, and the Shakespearean concerns of Rosencrantz and Guildenstern, Lord and Lady Macbeth, and other notables. Eventually, informed by our many illustrations and the excitement that their repeated telling engendered in the two of us, we began to move more formally into trap analysis. How do you know a trap when you see one? What are the shared characteristics of all psychological traps, regardless of origin, scope, or complexity? What are the key conceptual elements in any effort to differentiate among the traps of the world? What factors make us more or less apt to fall prey to entrapment? These were some of the questions that arose during these initial meetings.

A series of weekly meetings stretched over the ensuing years—interrupted temporarily by various exigencies—and led eventually to a research program that grew to involve a number of students and faculty colleagues. At the time, of course, we did not regard our work as a "research program"; rather, even as our experiments proceeded to answer two burning questions at a time, they managed to raise three or four new issues that we had not anticipated before. Aided by the generous support of the National Science Foundation, our research continued to lead us down new—and for us interesting—pathways, until we decided that the time had come to pause and take stock of where we had come from, and how far we had yet to go. Our reflection and reconnoitering has led to this book—a much needed opportunity to take a close look at the empirical evidence bearing on entrapment, to pose questions of these data that are not typically acceptable in the standard psychological journals, and to organize some integrating themes and concerns. In short, this book has made it possible for us to chronicle what is known, and is yet to be discovered, about the phenomenon that we have dubbed entrapment.

The book's 11 chapters have been organized to reflect our own special slant on the material of entrapment. Chapter 1 uses a number of everyday illustrations to introduce the concept of entrapment. We advance the defining criteria of entrapment, and in so doing attempt to specify those phenomena that are to be included and excluded from the subsequent analysis.

Chapter 2 introduces the reader to the half-dozen research paradigms that have been developed over the last decade or so for the study of entrapping behavior. Only by having some reasonable degree of familiarity with the tools of research in this area, we believe, is it possible to make sense of the areas of convergent and divergent experimental evidence that have emerged.

Chapter 3 argues for the robustness of the entrapment phenomenon. Drawing upon the work of three major research efforts to study entrapment, we develop evidence in support of the phenomenon's ubiquity, as well as researchers' ability to study it under controlled laboratory conditions.

In Chapters 4 through 6 we turn to the task of documenting the set of factors that have been found to influence the degree of entrapment. All of these factors seem to fall into one of two broad categories: nonsocial versus social considerations. Included in the nonsocial category are factors pertaining to the economic feasibility of continuing to invest one's resources, the matter in which such investments are made, and so forth. These and other nonsocial considerations are addressed in Chapter 4. Chapters 5 and 6, in turn, examine the more extensive body of work that is pertinent to social considerations: whether investments are made by individuals or groups, the effects of competing against nature versus another person, the attributes of this other person, the effects of an observing audience, the role of modeling in entrapment, and so forth.

Having charted much of the research terrain by this point in the book, we move away in Chapter 7 from a listing of antecedent and dependent considerations to a more thorough exploration of the entrapment process per se. One of the hallmarks of entrapping situations, we argue, is that they are constantly changing; problems that seem eminently soluble in the present have a nasty way of shifting beneath one's feet, becoming far more difficult to solve with each passing moment or expenditure of additional resources. Since entrapment ultimately must be analyzed and understood as a process, Chapter 7 provides the necessary exploration of these dynamic considerations.

Chapter 8 deals with the impact of individual difference variables on entrapment behavior. Are some people more prone to entrapment than others? What is the effect of person–situation interactions on escalation of commitment decisions? Is it possible to "explain" the large within-condition variability in entrapment behavior typically found in the experiments reported in earlier chapters? These are some of the issues addressed in this chapter.

Chapter 9 focuses on the reduction of entrapment. On the basis of research conducted by our colleagues and ourselves, we use this chapter to indicate and discuss those factors that bear on people's ability to avoid entrapment to begin with, and to escape entrapment once they have been caught.

Given the initial premise with which our joint exploration of entrapment began—namely, the assumption that entrapment is a phenomenon that pervades everyday life—it is only fitting that we turn our attention to the possible practical applications of entrapment theory and research. This is the focus of Chapter 10, an effort to spin out some of the implications of our work and that of our associates for the analysis and reduction of entrapment in interpersonal, organizational, and even international settings.

Chapter 11 concludes our exploration of entrapment, not by offering a recitation of what has already been presented elsewhere in the book, but by suggesting a few of the areas that warrant further thought and development. Some of the major assumptions that have guided entrapment research arc highlighted in this chapter, and analysis of these assumptions is presented in the service of tying entrapment more closely to some of its conceptual and ideological brethren.

Acknowledgments

Numerous individuals made significant contributions to the writing of this book. Several professional colleagues—Max Bazerman and Gerrit Wolf in particular, as well as Barry Staw—provided very insightful comments on earlier versions of the manuscript. Alan Teger stimulated much of our thinking, both by participating in research meetings and by writing his book, *Too Much Invested to Quit*. Many of our students contributed mightily to our research efforts, most notably Sinaia Nathanson and Bob Houser. Others lending a hand included Gregg Birnbaum, Dan Brenner, Martin Countryman, Janet Deitcher, Clotilde Didomenico, Judy Fine, Alan Friend, Tom Hamilton, John Harbeck, Elaine Lang, Kathy Lloyd, Mary Lloyd, Laurie Losen, Bill McKersie, Maritere Mendez, Kiki Olivera, Charles Samuelson, Susan Small-Weil, Bud Shaw, Barbara Thomas, Beth Turetsky, Karen Wilner, and Julie Wolf.

We are also indebted to the staff of Springer-Verlag New York for greatly facilitating the completion of this project. The National Science Foundation generously supported much of our research, and The University of Arizona provided a fertile environment in which several of the book's chapters were written. In addition, we thank Dolly Hernandez, Jean Intoppa, and Gail Shulman for their careful preparation of the manuscript.

Several other very special individuals provided much-needed support, love, and inspiration during the writing of this book. The first author's mother, Helen Brockner, passed away while the book was in progress. She would have been proud and pleased to see this work in its current form. The first author's mother-in-law, Esther Jacobs, who also recently passed away, offered frequent encouragement for the "ensnarement book." We are saddened that she too cannot share in this moment. Finally, our wives, Audrey Jacobs Brockner and Carol Rubin, provided the love, caring, and nurturance needed to see the project through to its successful completion. We are delighted to dedicate this book to them with love and affection.

New York, NY   JOEL BROCKNER
Medford, MA   JEFFREY Z. RUBIN
January 1985

Contents

Chapter 1
Introduction

Some of the most prominent lines of social-psychological inquiry have stemmed from researchers' observations of significant (indeed, sometimes shocking) real-life occurrences. Consider, for example, the substantial research attention directed to an area that has since come to be known as "bystander intervention." Kitty Genovese was murdered late one night in 1964 as she returned to her New York City apartment. Although at least 38 individuals witnessed the crime, not one person did so much as call the police to inform them that a murder was in progress. The collective inaction of the 38 observers spurred many studies, focused on the conditions under which people will and will not aid victims in emergency situations (e.g., Latane & Darley, 1970). Similarly, the research by Milgram (1974) on obedience to authority was derived from his observations of Nazi war criminals, who were able to commit heinous crimes perhaps because they believed that they were only following the orders of their commanding officers.

Our research on entrapment was also stimulated by observation of real-life events. Unlike the previous examples, however, our attention was not caught by any one particular earthshaking incident. Rather, we were struck by the wide variety of situations in which decision makers persist in a conflictual, failing course of action in order to justify prior commitments made in pursuit of some goal. Consider the following illustrations:

1. Suppose you have been waiting 15 minutes for a bus to take you someplace to which you could have just as easily walked. As you continue to wait, you begin to experience an interesting kind of conflict. On the one hand, you want to start walking; you feel impatient, even foolish, about not starting to walk immediately. On the other hand, you also feel compelled to continue waiting for a number of reasons. First, you believe (probably accurately) that the longer you wait the more likely the bus is to arrive. Second, and of greater relevance to the concept of entrapment, you may feel that the 15 minutes you have already waited will have been spent in vain if you were to start walking.

Against your better wishes you continue to wait, in large part to rationalize the correctness or appropriateness of the time already invested.

2. Lately your old car has been breaking down with great frequency. Rather than heeding your spouse's call to buy an affordable new car, you decide to invest a considerable sum of money repairing the old one. Having already spent hundreds of dollars replacing the transmission, exhaust system, tires, and shocks, you are likely to feel that you have "too much invested to quit" now that the brakes require immediate action.

3. You are dissatisfied with your current job or career, and are contemplating switching to another line of work. However, you then begin to contemplate all that you have invested to put yourself into your current work situation (e.g., years of studying, thousands of dollars in training and schooling, etc.). You decide to remain with your current employment position, hoping that things will change for the better, and that all of your prior effort will not have gone for naught.

4. You are a student enjoying a between-semester break. You have completed two years of study in pursuit of an academic degree (e.g., B.S., Ph.D.). The program requires a commitment of at least several additional years. Your interest in the subject under study has waned. Moreover, you are no longer certain that you want, or will be able, to procure a job in your field of study after graduation. Nevertheless, having already devoted so much time and money to your education, you return to school in September as always, ready to face the hardships of another academic year.

5. You have been involved in a "serious" romantic relationship for 3 years. Recently, things between you and your partner have gone sour. You fight constantly, and rarely spend enjoyable time together anymore. You would like to terminate the relationship. However, you decide to "stick it out" because you feel that if you were to break up after 3 years together, then all of that time would have been spent in vain.

6. The workers at a manufacturing plant have been on strike for 15 days. During this time production has been at a standstill. As a result, both labor and management have suffered tremendous financial hardships. For economic reasons, both parties would like very much to end the dispute. Nevertheless, as the length of the impasse increases, both sides become less conciliatory. When asked to explain its unwillingness to negotiate, each side states that it cannot make concessions, after having suffered so long to this point. Thus the strike and further hardship continue.

7. A business organization has hired a new worker who has been put through an extensive employee training program. The company has invested a considerable amount of human energy, time, and money preparing the new employee for his or her position. Much to management's dismay, however, the employee's first 6 months of job performance is well below par. Though it is costly to do so (given this individual's poor work performance), the organization decides to keep the employee in the present position, in order to "reap the

benefits" of all that it has invested in this person's development within the organization.

8. A national government has been engaged in a costly war. During the past 3 years of fighting, there has been a considerable loss of lives, money, and "national honor." The government must decide whether to make additional economic allocations to the war effort. Top-level policy makers decide to follow the advice of the military, who argue that the government must escalate its commitment so that the prior loss of life will have not been for naught.

In each of the preceding examples, as in all entrapment situations, the individual makes investments in the hope of achieving some goal. The process of goal attainment, however, requires the individual to make repeated investments over time. Thus, it is not uncommon for people to discover, somewhere during the course of this process, that they are in a "decisional no man's land," in which they have made a substantial investment but have not yet achieved their goal. At this point individuals are apt to experience considerable conflict about the prospect of making continued investments. On the one hand, they may not want to continue investing, because the goal may no longer be seen as either readily attainable or worthy of additional costs. On the other hand, the individual may feel a strong need to continue investing, at least in part to justify the expenditures that have already been made. To the extent that they do continue investing in order to justify prior commitments, they are said to be entrapped. When taken to an extreme, the choice to escalate commitment to a chosen course of action can produce irrational behavior with disastrous consequences.

The variety of cited examples should make two points apparent. First, although all decision makers in entrapment situations must make some investment, the precise nature of that investment can vary. The person waiting for the bus invests time, the individual with the faulty auto spends money, the partners in a romantic relationship "invest" human emotion, while the warring government's commitment, among other things, is one of "national honor." Of course, in certain entrapment situations an individual's investment can occur simultaneously in two or more of these domains. Thus, if people waiting for the bus to take them to work are paid on an hourly basis, they may be losing money as well as time as they continue to wait. Second, entrapment situations range greatly in scope. The conflict can arise at the intrapersonal, interpersonal, intergroup, organizational, or even international level.

Toward Some Generalizations

Obviously, there are many differences among the various entrapment situations cited above. The process of deciding to continue waiting for a bus, for example, is clearly different from the decision-making process that leads to an escalation of military commitment. Nevertheless, we believe that there are common strands running through these and all entrapment situations. It may be useful at this point to highlight these points of convergence.

There are two ways to discuss the defining properties of entrapment. First, one needs to consider the common elements inherent in the decision-making situation itself. Second, there are similarities in the decision makers' psychological and behavioral reactions to this situation.

Situational Characteristics

1. The decision makers' investments in the pursuit of the goal can also be interpreted as an irretrievable expense, depending upon the perceiver's perspective. For example, a prolonged wait for a bus can be viewed as an investment, to the extent that it is associated with an increase in the perceived likelihood of the bus' arrival. It can also be seen as an expense, to the extent that it is viewed in relation to the costs already incurred by having continued to wait.

2. The decision maker must be able to choose between entering and remaining in the entrapping situation, or not. The decision of whether to continue investing in an entrapment situation is conflictual. If the person has no choice, however, there cannot be any conflict. If, for example, the owner of an old car does not have the funds to buy a new car, and instead *must* repair the old one, the decision to spend additional funds for the car is not a manifestation of entrapment. The person is apt to "feel" badly about having to spend more money on the car; this negative feeling, however, is not the same as the experience of entrapment.

3. It is never entirely certain that the decision maker's goal will, in fact, be realized. Thus, an entrapment situation is an example of the more general category of situations dealing with decision making under uncertainty. For example, no matter how long the romantically involved couple tries to mend its relationship, this "repair work" may never be done to the couple's mutual satisfaction.

4. In order to achieve their objective, decision makers must make investments *repeatedly*. In all entrapment situations, individuals allocate resources and subsequently receive feedback suggesting that this initial resource allocation will not be sufficient for goal attainment. Thus, entrapment situations require individuals to make continual, rather than "one-shot," decisions about whether to escalate their commitment or withdraw.

Response Characteristics

1. As the entrapped individuals' investments mount, so does their conflict about whether to make continued investments. This is due to the fact that the pressures to both withdraw from and remain in the situation heighten over time.

To use Lewin's (1938) distinction between "driving" and "restraining" forces, there is an increase in the impact of the force restraining one against continued involvement (i.e., the ever-increasing financial, emotional, or temporal cost). However, the strength of the driving force(s) toward escalation (e.g., avoiding the cost associated with having "given up" on one's investment) is also enhanced.

2. Perhaps most fundamental to the process of entrapment, there is an important shift in the decision makers' definition of their involvement in the entrapment situation as their degree of commitment escalates. At the outset the individuals have clear (usually economic or material) reasons for investing. For example, the owner of the old car simply wants a smoothly functioning automobile. Or, the person waiting for the bus merely wishes to arrive at his or her destination without having to walk. As their degree of commitment deepens, however, the individuals are less motivated by these "rational" reasons. Rather, there is a greater degree of "emotional" involvement. Thus, in the later stages of an entrapping conflict, people may wish to achieve their goal(s) simply for the psychological sake of achievement. Or, they will experience the need to continue investing in order to justify the appropriateness of already sunk costs. Or, people may feel the desire to save face in the eyes of others present, to show them that by continuing to invest they are strong-willed individuals who are not easily deterred. Put more simply, the entraped decision makers' motives shift over time, from the rational to the rationalizing.

3. In addition to producing cognitive and/or affective consequences, the state of entrapment induces certain behavioral tendencies. Most important, entrapment is self-perpetuating, begetting even further degrees of commitment. This is not to say that entrapment *always* engenders further entrapment. We know that people do eventually stop waiting at bus stops, sell their old cars, and terminate unsatisfying relationships. In fact, Chapter 9 analyzes some of the conditions under which a person can be led to withdraw from an entrapping conflict. Yet, at least up to a certain point, the more individuals invest their resources in an entrapping dilemma, the more likely they are to remain committed to the chosen course of action.

These situational and response similarities form the essence of entrapping conflicts. Entrapment refers to a particular behavior pattern (response characteristics) when certain prerequisite conditions (situational characteristics) have been met. Any conceptual analysis of the nature of entrapment must consider both sets of characteristics. Entrapment does not merely reside in situations; it is the decision makers' *reactions to* those conflictual situations that sets the stage for entrapment. More succinctly, *entrapment is a decision making process whereby individuals escalate their commitment to a previously chosen, though failing, course of action in order to justify or "make good on" prior investments.*

Now that the concept of entrapment has been introduced, it would seem important to distinguish between it and other related terms or concepts. First, there is a legal usage of the term entrapment, referring to a process by which law enforcement agencies or other individuals use unlawful tactics as a means to provoke a secretly monitored other into illegal behavior (e.g., Lingle, Brock, & Cialdini, 1977). The work described in this book is completely unrelated to that concept.

Second, it is not identical to escalation, or even conflict escalation. Rather, it is a particular type of conflict escalation, based on the individuals' need to feel that their past commitment to a chosen course of action was not made in vain. There are undoubtedly situations in which people escalate their degree of commitment, but are not entrapped. For example, if medical students have completed 2 years of medical school, and love every minute of it, then their decision to escalate commitment (i.e., complete the third and fourth years) is not at all reflective of entrapment.

Third, entrapment does not simply refer to being caught or trapped in a particular course of action. Entrapment refers to *a particular process* by which individuals become stuck or caught in dysfunctional behavioral patterns. It is entirely possible for individuals to become trapped in a course of action through processes other than entrapment. It is tempting, for example, to note the similarities between entrapment and Platt's (1973) analysis of "social traps." Social traps are defined as "situations in society that contain traps formally like a fish trap, where men or organizations or whole societies get themselves started in some direction or some set of relationships that later prove to be unpleasant or lethal and that they see no easy way to back out or to avoid." At first blush this definition seems to have much in common with our description of entrapment. However, there are at least two fundamental ways in which entrapment differs from social traps:

1. *Level of analysis*. The process which leads to trapped behavior is different in the social trap analysis from the position espoused in entrapment. Platt utilizes a reinforcement or Skinnerian perspective, noting that behavior more often is shaped by its immediate than its long-term consequences. Thus, individuals persist with trapping behavior, such as smoking cigarettes or overeating because the reinforcements to be gained are proximal, whereas the negative consequences are distal. It is possible, we suppose, to analyze some entrapment situations from a reinforcement perspective, but to do so would add little explanatory value.

2. *Social consequences*. A central theme in the social trap definition is that individuals embark upon courses of action that are rewarding to that individual in the short run, but which produce very negative consequences for the collective and/or society in the longer haul. It is possible that some entrapment situations contain this property, but it is not a defining characteristic of them.

To reiterate, entrapment situations are but one exemplar of a broader array of situations in which decision makers act and/or feel trapped. The reader interested in a more general analysis of traps may find the work of Rubin (1985) to be of value.

Finally, while entrapment behavior describes a *process* in which decision makers *rationalize* the appropriateness of past investments, it is not necessarily the case that the decision to escalate, that is, the behavioral *outcome* of this process, is *irrational*. Central to the entrapment construct is the process of justifying past investments made to a failing course of action. Clearly, such a process will *often* lead to irrational decision making (i.e., escalating commitment, when deescalation or withdrawal is the wiser course of action). Indeed, what makes the process of entrapment even more interesting is when it results in decision making that is illogical according to some external standard. For example, in the next chapter we will describe a laboratory simulation of an entrapment situation in which decision makers regularly spend $3–5 to "buy" a $1 prize. However, we should emphasize that the process of entrapment will not *always* lead to irrational decision making. That is, there may be some conditions under which the objective expected value of persisting with the previously chosen course of action is favorable to the decision maker. If decision makers escalate their commitment under such conditions, are they entrapped? Perhaps. To the extent that their escalated commitment stems from their felt need to justify past resource allocations (rather than from a prospective cost–benefit analysis suggesting that escalation is appropriate), they are considered to be entrapped. To reemphasize, entrapment refers to a decision making *process*, and not (necessarily) the outcome of that process. Entrapment can and often does lead to irrational decision making; moreover, it is precisely when entrapment does produce irrational or suboptimal decision making that it becomes crucial to understand better this process. Strictly speaking, however, irrational decisional outcomes are not a necessary result of the entrapment process.

Summary

The purpose of this chapter has been to introduce the concept of entrapment, a ubiquitous form of conflict escalation that can arise within and between individuals, groups, and organizations. Some common elements of entrapment were described, both in terms of situational similarities, and the responses evoked by these situational factors. After having described what entrapment is, we deemed it necessary to discuss what it is not. Chapter 2 lays the groundwork for subsequent empirical research, by describing some of the methodological procedures that have been used to explore the intriguing process of entrapment.

Chapter 2
Experimental Research Methods

The contents of this book are based largely on data. In most reports of empirical research, the author introduces the topic area of inquiry, describes the method used to test hypotheses, and then presents and interprets the major findings of interest. A similar, though more expanded, approach will be adopted in this monograph. Rather than report the results of one or two studies, we shall discuss in subsequent chapters the major findings uncovered in the burgeoning area of entrapment research. Following journal format, we will now describe the various experimental methodologies that researchers have employed. This chapter, then, is a collective method section, in which the different experimental procedures will be described in some detail.

The procedures to be described are all laboratory simulations of entrapping conflicts. The skeptic concerned with the external validity or "relevance" of results may believe that it is inappropriate to study entrapment under such artificial conditions. After all, if entrapment is so ubiquitous in everyday life, why not study it in naturalistic settings? Indeed, this is hardly the first time that experimental social psychologists have been called upon to defend the validity of their most widely used empirical approach—the laboratory study.

We heartily agree with the notion that more field studies on entrapment are needed. The fact that this is so, however, does not detract from the fact that laboratory paradigms offer several key virtues. First, when studying complex processes (like entrapment), researchers typically need to simplify the phenomena to a certain extent. Once a firm understanding of the process is gained at a relatively elemental level, it becomes more appropriate to explore the process at more sophisticated or complex levels. The study of entrapment is only in its fledgling years; consequently, the laboratory procedure which typically simplifies complex processes is an especially useful research tool at this juncture.

Second, and at a more theoretical level, we are especially interested in *why* entrapment occurs. What factors cause people to escalate their commitment to, or withdraw from, a conflictual course of action? Laboratory procedures, in which subjects are randomly assigned to different experimental conditions, are particularly well suited for delineating causal relationships between (independent and dependent) variables.

The research described in this book—virtually all of which was done using laboratory methodologies—represents an important *first step* in furthering our knowledge of entrapment. It is *now* important to test the external validity of some of the laboratory findings, which can be achieved by studying entrapment in naturalistic settings.

Three other points concerning the relationship beween laboratory and field research should be mentioned. First, regardless of the location of the study, it is important for the procedure to have experimental realism (Carlsmith, Ellsworth, & Aronson, 1976); that is, for the subjects to be psychologically involved in the task at hand. It is not clear that all field methodologies possess greater experimental realism than laboratory procedures. Second, it is not even certain that the results of field research are any more externally generalizable to field settings (other than the one utilized) than are the findings derived from laboratory experimentation under controlled conditions.

Third, most laboratory procedures mentioned in this chapter were derived from everyday life entrapment situations. In fact, in describing these procedures we will also discuss the real-life episode(s) from which the laboratory procedure originated. Moreover, the variety of real-life examples of entrapping situations that ultimately led to the development of an experimental scenario should further attest to the ubiquity of entrapment in everyday life. In general, then, it is important to remember that the various experimental procedures were carefully constructed to capture the necessary ingredients of *all* entrapment situations discussed in the first chapter—namely that (1) subjects engage in some goal-directed behavior; (2) they are unsuccessful in their initial attempt to attain the goal, and must therefore escalate their commitment in order to achieve their desired endpoints; (3) they experience conflict about the prudence of escalating their commitment (perhaps because the goal is no longer seen as attainable or even worthwhile); (4) they have a choice about whether to escalate their commitment; and (5) the probability of goal attainment is uncertain.

The Dollar Auction Game

In his interesting and insightful book, *Too Much Invested to Quit*, Teger (1980) has described the Dollar Auction game as well as a set of experiments based on this procedure. This paradigm, originally developed by Shubik (1971), is an extremely effective demonstration of entrapment in the laboratory, the classroom, or even at a cocktail party. The rules of the game are simple. The auctioneer announces to an audience of two or more persons that a $1.00 bill is about to be sold. As in a typical auction, the person who makes the highest bid is the recipient of the dollar, and must pay the auctioneer the amount bid in return.

The primary way in which this procedure differs from a regular auction, would-be bidders are told, is that the person who finishes as the second highest bidder must also pay the auctioneer the amount bid—but receives nothing in return. The audience is further told that there cannot be any form of communication between bidders, such as threats, promises, or attempts at coalition formation against the (soon to be richer) auctioneer, other than making bids. Moreover, the bidders are told the minimum amount of their opening bid and subsequent bid investments (e.g., 5 cents).

Perhaps because the procedure seems like a novel, fun way to earn money, individuals are often willing to start bidding. If there is a relatively large audience, as in a classroom, many people make low bids such as 5 cents, 15 cents, etc. If the auction is being performed under controlled experimental conditions with only two subjects bidding, the subjects are typically willing to start bidding. As the bidding nears $1.00 there are invariably two bidders remaining, neither of whom wishes to be the second highest bidder. Indeed, it is the second highest bidder who is entrapped in the Dollar Auction; he or she has made an irretrievable investment without achieving the goal, and must escalate the bidding in order to do so.

Given that the two bidders alternate being second highest (and therefore feeling entrapped), it becomes easy to understand why the bidding frequently goes well past $1.00. "Winning" bids of $3.00–5.00 are not uncommon. In one of our more compelling classroom demonstrations, the *auctioneer* had to terminate the bidding when the two entrapped decision makers had made bids of $24.95 and $25.00, respectively. (Fortunately for the bidders, they were not subsequently required to pay the auctioneer.) As Teger (1980) writes:

> The classroom experiments showed that first, and most importantly, the phenomenon was real. The students who were still bidding as the bids approached one dollar knew that they were in a difficult conflict situation, and felt emotionally aroused. They sweated, cried, looked around at their classmates for reassurance, and removed their wallets and checked to see if they had enough money with which to bid. After the auction, they attempted to apologize for their own irrational behavior. One indicated that he had been drinking, as if to explain away his behavior as that of an irrational drunk. Several were unusually embarrassed that they had lost money—indicating that they were students at the business school, and that such behavior was inexcusable for them.

In Dollar Auctions conducted in the laboratory, subjects typically are given a small amount of money which they are to treat as their own. In fact, subjects are explicitly told that they can quit the experiment without making a single bid if they so desire, and thus keep the money. If they do wish to take part in the auction, they are pitted against a real or simulated opponent. The chief behavioral dependent measure of entrapment is usually the amount of money bid in the Dollar Auction.

The Counter Game

We have used this methodology in many of the studies to be discussed in later chapters. It has elements of both everyday life gambling and waiting situations, each of which can produce considerable entrapment. In this procedure subjects enter the laboratory for a study of "decision making" and are provided an initial stake of money in cash (usually $5.00). It is emphasized that this money is theirs to keep; it is their payment simply for reading through the instructions. If they wish to leave the experiment after the study has been explained, they are free to do so and retain the $5.00 initial stake. They are told, however, that by proceeding further they may be able to earn even more money.

Specifically, subjects are placed in front of an electronically controlled counter and told that the counter will increase by units of one at a rate of approximately one unit per second. They are also told that a computer has randomly generated a winning number, such that when that number appears on the counter, a buzzer will sound, indicating that they have "hit the jackpot." The jackpot is typically worth $3.00. Subjects are further instructed that they will have to pay 1 cent for each unit expired on the counter in order to purchase the jackpot. For example, if the winning number is 50, subjects will have to pay 50 cents, and will receive the $3.00 jackpot in return. Thus, provided that the winning number is less than 300, subjects stand to earn additional money by participating. In all versions of the counter game subjects are led to believe that it is likely but by no means certain that the winning number will be reached if they let the counter increase long enough. (This characteristic is consistent with the defining element of entrapping situations mentioned earlier—that the probability of goal attainment is uncertain.) However, the winning number could be greater than 300, in which case it would cost more than $3.00 to win the $3.00 jackpot. Moreover, they are instructed that it is entirely possible, though not likely, that the winning number may never be reached. For example, in several studies subjects were informed that the winning number was between 1 and 600. They were told that if the counter reached 500 and the winning number had not been reached, the experimenter would stop the proceedings and require them to pay $5.00 for the 500 units "bought" on the counter. Of course, in this instance they received no money in return. Thus, regardless of when (or whether) the winning number was reached, participants had to pay 1 cent for each unit expired on the counter. In other versions of the counter game subjects were not told the range of the winning numbers, only that it was "very likely but not a certainty" that the winning number would be reached if they waited long enough.

Subjects were told that if they attempted to win the jackpot, they were free to quit at any point. They merely had to inform the experimenter that they no longer wished to let the counter increase. By quitting, subjects could retain a portion of their initial stake. For example, if a person quit at 100, he or she paid the experimenter $1.00 and left with $4.00. In reality, there was no winning number. Thus, once having decided to try to win the jackpot, subjects either allowed the counter to increase until they quit, or until the counter reached 500. To increase the credibility of the existence of a "winning number," the experimenter had subjects complete a practice trial, during which the winning number was supposedly preset at 25. The experimenter started the counter and allowed it to increase until it had reached 25. At this point he surreptitiously pressed a button which caused a buzzer-like noise to emanate from a speaker. The experimenter then adjusted several dials on some nearby bogus electronic equipment, and casually mentioned that he was randomly generating a new winning number for the upcoming trial, of which even he was unaware.

Consider the plight of the person in the counter game who has watched the counter increase to 150, without having reached the winning number. Like the second highest bidder in the Dollar Auction game, the individual has made an irretrievable investment, has not yet achieved the goal, and is likely to be experiencing some conflict about whether it would be wise to continue. On the one hand, the person may want to quit, and retain the $3.50 remaining from his initial stake. Alternatively, as any amateur gambler knows, the person may believe that he or she has a chance to "make it all back" by letting the counter increase for just a little while longer. The primary behavioral measure of entrapment in the counter game, then, is the amount of money subjects invest— or rather, lose—from their initial stake.

The Jigsaw Puzzle Procedure

All of us have had the experience of embarking upon some enjoyable activity but then persisting beyond the point of diminishing returns. For example, we might begin reading a 300-page murder mystery supposedly for pleasure, only to discover after reading 150 pages that the book is no longer enjoyable. What do we typically do in such situations? On the one hand, we would like nothing better than to stop reading this now tedious book. On the other hand, we may feel entrapped by a commitment to stay to the end in order to discover "whodunit." A similar conflict is felt by people who have watched the first hour of a movie that is turning increasingly distasteful. Will they stop watching the movie, and not continue to waste time? Or, will they feel that they must see the entire movie, in order to learn how the plot turned out? (When making decisions about whether to continue reading a bad book, a colleague recently suggested, people should stop reading and wait until the bad book has been made into a bad movie. Then, he argued, they can learn whodunit by watching the movie, for a period of time usually much shorter than would be needed to finish the remainder of the book!)

Attempting to solve lengthy puzzles, such as crossword or jigsaw puzzles, can also produce entrapment. At the outset these activities are usually pleasurable. However, after people have solved part of the puzzle, and are no longer enjoying the task at hand, they may feel entrapped. They would like to quit, either because they are pessimistic about being able to solve the puzzle, or because the act of trying to find the solution simply is no longer intrinsically interesting. Nevertheless, having worked on the puzzle for a substantial period of time, the problem solvers are also likely to feel that they have too much invested to quit.

Relying on the fact that jigsaw puzzles can be quite entrapping, we devised a laboratory analogue. Subjects were given an initial stake of money (e.g., $4) which was to be viewed as their own. As before, they were not required to take part in the jigsaw phase of the experiment. If they wished, they could exit the experiment at the outset and retain their initial stake. By solving the jigsaw puzzle within a certain number of minutes, they were told, they would be able to win an additional sum of money (e.g., $10). However, if they were unable to solve the puzzle, they would have to pay a certain amount (e.g., 5 cents) for each piece that they requested.

Subjects were allowed to request a maximum of 10 pieces at a time from the experimenter, but they could make as many requests as needed in order to obtain all of the pieces. For example, if they requested all of the pieces and were able to complete the puzzle within the allotted time, they lost no money from the initial stake, and won the additional amount of money in the jackpot. If they requested 25 pieces, and then wanted to quit (which, as always, was a possible option), they were required to forfeit a portion of the initial stake (typically at a rate of 5 cents per piece). In the example just cited, then, subjects would have had to pay $1.25, and receive nothing in return.

The puzzle was designed to be very difficult to solve in the time provided. As a result, it was our surmise that after having requested a portion of the pieces, people would experience the conflict inherent to entrapment. Although the decision makers may wish to quit, they may also feel compelled to continue in order to justify the time and money already expended on the task. In this procedure, then, the dependent measure of entrapment was the number of puzzle pieces subjects requested before they were forced to quit, by virtue of not being able to solve the puzzle in the allotted time.

The Carnival Game

Have you ever tried your hand tossing baseballs at milk bottles at a carnival midway? If so, you have embarked on a potentially entrapping course of action. According to a CBS *60 Minutes* documentary, the traveling carnival is a multibillion-dollar-per-year industry. Commentator Morley Safer suggested that a sizable portion of that money is spent by customers lured by the prospect of winning a teddy bear or television set in a so-called game of skill.

A particularly entrapping, and illegal, carnival game is known as the "razzle." In this game the proprietor entices customers to try to win some valued prize by charging very little money for the first few attempts. Moreover, the customers learn that they have initially made considerable progress toward attaining the goal. For example, if the individuals must earn a total of 1000 points in order to win the prize, they learn that they have amassed 750 points on the first few trials. Having drawn customers into this course of action, the operator then introduces certain features that prove frustrating and costly. First, a performance feedback chart constructed by the proprietor informs the customers that while they are approaching the goal, they never quite manage to attain it. Second, unlike the first few attempts to win points, the later trials become quite costly. As a result, Safer reports, people have lost as much as $95,000 at razzles. An investigator for the California Attorney General who has made a career out of arresting operators of illegal carnival games summarized this little scam this way: "They razzle and dazzle the poor victim. He doesn't know what is happening. The victim is left with the feeling that if he plays it just one more time, he's got to win it. He's gained all these points. There's no way he can lose" (*thinks* the victim).

In our laboratory analogue of "razzle" subjects are first provided with an initial stake of money (e.g., $3.50). They can either quit the experiment at that point or attempt to win even more money by performing a "perceptual task." Specifically, participants are shown a series of 5½ × 8½ white cards upon which black geometric figures are mounted. The subjects' task is to estimate the percentage of the white card that is covered by the black geometric figure. They are further told that by accumulating a certain number of points they can win a jackpot cash prize. However, it costs money to attempt each trial. As in the actual carnival razzle, although subjects are required to pay very little money at first, the cost of participating in later trials (as goal proximity is presumably heightening), is greatly increased. In all instances, however, as in actual razzles, subjects never amass enough points to win the jackpot. Thus, the dependent variable is task persistence, operationally defined as the number of trials that subjects fruitlessly work at the task before they either quit or are forced to quit by virtue of having exhausted all of their money.

The Waiting Game

Waiting situations have the potential to be extremely entrapping. In Chapter 1 we described the conflictual plight of commuters waiting for a bus to take them to a destination that could have also been reached by walking. Or consider the dilemma confronting people who have called a telephone operator for some needed information, and have been placed on hold. As the caller continues to wait, the entrapping conflict heightens. On the one hand, the caller may wish to hang up and try to acquire the information later. Alternatively, the caller might reason that the operator is sure to return at any moment. Even more germane to entrapment, they may believe that because they have already waited so long, it would be foolish not to continue waiting just a little longer. The image that emerges is one of the telephone callers who are holding the telephone closer and closer to their ears as they simultaneously move toward hanging up.

Based on this notion that waiting situations can prove to be quite entrapping, we have devised several experimental analogues in which the main dependent variable is the amount of time subjects wait for some important resource. For example, in a study to be discussed in Chapter 7, subjects were told upon their arrival in the laboratory that the experimenter had not yet arrived. Unbeknownst to the participants, the experimenter for whom they were waiting did not exist. The purpose was to determine if certain variables affected how long subjects would continue to wait. In another experiment, to be described in more detail in Chapter 3, subjects had to wait in line to obtain a resource that *potentially* could enable them to earn a relatively large sum of money. As they continued to wait, however, they were losing *actual* money from their initial stake. In reality, no such resource existed. The purpose of the study was to delineate several factors affecting the length of time that decision makers were willing to wait.

Role-Playing Simulations

In each of the aforementioned experimental procedures, subjects take part in *actual* entrapment situations, although admittedly, such situations tend to be low in mundane realism. The final technique to be described makes use of a role-playing methodology. The participants, who have typically been business students, are presented with an investment scenario in which they have to allocate funds for a particular project. They are then told that this initial allocation failed to achieve the company's goals, and the participants are given an additional opportunity to invest more money in the chosen course of action.

An example of a role-playing simulation of entrapment research has been presented by Staw (1976), who used a financial decision case describing a hypothetical corporation in the year 1967. As Staw (1976) writes:

> The case depicts the financial history (including 10 prior years of sales and earnings data) of the "Adams & Smith" company, and a scenario is presented in which the subject is asked to play a major role in financial decision-making. As stated in the case, the profitability of the A & S Company has started to decline over several preceding years, and the directors of the company have agreed that one of the major reasons for the decline in corporate earnings lay in some aspect of the firm's program of research and development. The case further states that the company's directors have concluded that 10 million dollars of additional R & D funds should be made available to its major operating divisions, but, that for the time being, the extra funding should be invested in only *one* of the corporation's *two* largest divisions. The subject is then asked to act in the role of Financial Vice President in determining which of the two corporate divisions, Consumer Products or Industrial Products, should receive the additional R & D funding. A brief description of each corporate division is included in the case material, and the subject is asked to make the financial investment decision on the basis of the potential benefit that R & D funding will have on the future earnings of the divisions.

After completing the above section of the case and turning it in to the experimenter, subjects were administered a second section of the case which necessitated another financial investment decision. Part II of the Financial Decision Case presents the subject with the condition of Adams & Smith in 1972, five years after the initial allocation of research and development funds. As stated in Part II, the R & D program of Adams & Smith is again up for re-evaluation, and the management of the company is convinced that there is an even greater need for expenditure on research and development. In fact, 20 million dollars has been made available from a capital reserve for R & D funding, and the subject, as Financial Vice President, is again asked to decide upon its proper allocation. This, time, however, the subject is allowed to divide the R & D money in any way he wishes among the two major corporate divisions.

The financial data (e.g., sales and earnings) provided for each of the 5 years since the initial allocation decision reveal that the chosen course of action has produced negative outcomes. That is, there is a deepening decline in the profitability of the chosen division but an improvement in the unchosen division. The primary dependent variable, therefore, is the amount of money subjects allocate on the second funding decision to the corporate division chosen earlier.

Closing Comments

All of the preceding experimental paradigms are similar in that they include the necessary elements of entrapping situations. Nonetheless, there are at least four important differences among them, which may limit the external generalizability of results obtained with the use of any particular procedure.

1. *Interpersonal competitiveness*. The Dollar Auction entails interpersonal competition, whereas each of the other methodologies does not. In that sense the Dollar Auction poses a more complex problem for decision makers. They must deal not only with all of the exigencies associated with entrapping conflicts, but also with those produced by having to compete against another person. In Chapter 5 it will be shown that the presence or absence of interpersonal competition influences entrapment behavior.

2. *Skillfulness required to perform the task*. In some of the experimental procedures the participants' goal-directed behavior is perceived to be the result of personal accomplishment, typically stemming from some personal skill. In other situations, movement toward the goal is not the result of any skill-related behavior. For example, in the Jigsaw Puzzle and Carnival Game, subjects believe that their movement toward the goal is a result of their own personal accomplishment. By contrast, in the Counter Game and the Waiting Game, they are much less apt to believe that increased goal proximity is due to their skill. The extent to which the procedure is perceived to tap skillful behavior may

be a significant determinant of resource allocation behavior. This issue is given some attention in Chapter 6.

3. *Decision making: actual vs. role-playing.* Except for the procedures employed by Staw and his colleagues, all of the methodologies require subjects to make decisions from a "live," rather than a role-playing, perspective. None of the experiments reported in this book studies the effect of this variable on entrapment. However, there is much theory and research in the social-psychological literature (e.g., Holmes & Bennett, 1974) to suggest that individuals respond differently as a function of whether they are actually placed in the situation, or are merely asked to imagine how they would respond if they were in that situation. For entrapment to occur, the process of increasing expenditures accompanied by negative feedback must truly be *experienced*. Role-playing methodologies may produce the experience of entrapment to some extent, but probably not as much as those which confront decision makers with an actual dilemma. Said differently, the role-playing methodologies are probably lower in experimental realism than are its alternatives.

In several role-playing experiments (e.g., Bazerman, Giuliano, & Appleman, in press; Staw, 1976) relatively large samples had to be studied in order to yield statistically significant results. Why were large samples necessary? One possible explanation is that the low experimental realism of a role-playing procedure invited extremely large within-condition variability.

4. *Number and type of decision option.* In some of the procedures (i.e., Counter Game, Carnival Game, and Waiting Game) subjects had to make a binary choice—whether to escalate their commitment or withdraw—at various decision points. The other three methodologies (Dollar Auction, Jigsaw Puzzle, Role-Playing) included this binary choice *and* a different type of problem for those who decided to persist: the *extent* to which they wished to escalate their commitment. These different decisional requirements may be noteworthy in two respects. First, the initial binary decision—that is, to persist or withdraw—could be affected by whether or not the latter type of decision must also be made. Second, for the procedures requiring both decisions, it is possible for certain factors to have differential impact on the two types of decisions. For example, in Chapter 7 a study is described (Levi, 1982) in which an independent variable had no impact on the binary choice of whether to persist or withdraw. However, for those who persisted this variable did affect the extent to which they escalated their commitment.

Finally, several other methodological comments are in order. First, based on our experience with these procedures, we are confident that most possess at least a moderate degree of experimental realism. During the postexperimental interviews most subjects reported experiencing the entrapping conflict that we tried to create. Second, the fact that such a wide variety of experimental procedures has been utilized is, as always, a double-edged sword. Whenever discrepant results emerge between two different research paradigms, it is unclear whether they are due to substantive theoretical or less important methodological factors. To circumvent this problem, some research programs have used the same experimental procedure. For example, most of Byrne's (1971) voluminous work on attitude similarity and attraction was performed using one methodology. Teger's (1980) research monograph on entrapment was based solely on experimental findings using the Dollar Auction game.

The great virtue of resorting to multiple methodologies, of course, is that as consistent results emerge across different experimental techniques, one gains increased confidence in their generality or external validity. Stated differently, the major problem with using only one research procedure is that methodological aspects of the procedure begin to have as much importance as the theoretical issues under study. We wish to avoid a research orientation that is too narrow; as a consequence, we have devised different entrapment procedures to study different questions. Moreover, as the subsequent chapters will reveal, there are important behavioral similarities among decision makers taking part in very different entrapping dilemmas, lending support to the major advantage of a multiple-methods approach.

This concludes the discussion of the experimental research methods that have been employed to study entrapment. In describing research findings in subsequent chapters, we will provide a brief overview of the method in order to refresh readers' memories; typically, though not always, the method will be one of those discussed in this chapter. Thus, readers familiar with the intricacies of the various methods described herein may wish to skim the method overviews provided in the following chapters.

Chapter 3

Preliminary Experimental Analyses
of Entrapment

In this chapter we shall describe the earliest attempts to study entrapment under controlled conditions. The entrapment phenomenon has been investigated programmatically in three research laboratories in the past 10 years: by Barry Staw and his colleagues (Fox & Staw, 1979; Staw, 1976; Staw & Ross, 1978), by Allan Teger and his students (Teger, 1980), and by the present authors and our students. Interestingly, the three research programs have operated in relative ignorance of one another. In fact, a major reason why we wrote this book was to provide an *integrative* push to these diverse research programs.

The three studies to be discussed—the initial efforts in what later proved to be systematic series of experiments—raised different questions and employed very different methodologies. Taken together, however, the results of these initial studies illustrate the central theme of this chapter, namely that the entrapment process can be recreated, and therefore critically studied, under controlled laboratory conditions.

Overview

The first study to be described (Teger, 1980) was nonexperimental. All subjects took part in the same entrapping task. By requiring all subjects to take part in the same task, Teger was able to discover "baseline" information concerning decision makers' propensities toward entrapment. This baseline information was especially important in Teger's research program, given that he relied upon the same experimental procedure throughout.

The second study (Staw, 1976) explored the effect of a very basic determinant of entrapment: whether individuals were personally responsible for the previous decision which had yielded the negative feedback. If escalated commitment is the result of a self-justification process than entrapment should be heightened when decision makers perceive that they, rather than another person, were responsible for the prior resource allocation. In the third study

(Rubin & Brockner, 1975) all subjects were personally responsible for the prior resource allocation. The purpose of this experiment was to delineate the effects of several independent variables on degree of entrapment.

Teger (1980—Study I)

In this study college students participated in dyads in a version of the Dollar Auction Game. Upon entering the laboratory, subjects sat across a table from one another in order to take part in a study on "Decision Making." More specifically, subjects were allocated a certain number of points with which to alternate making bids. They were told that because the points would later be converted into money, it would be to their advantage to leave the experiment having amassed as many points as possible. Supposedly at random, all participants received 975 points which they could use in attempting to win a 500-point prize. Subjects were aware of the number of points that they possessed, but were not aware of their opponent's number of points. All subjects were informed that the higher bidder would pay the amount bid in return for the 500-point prize. The lower bidder also had to pay the auctioneer the amount bid, but received nothing in return. Moreover, subjects were free to quit the bidding at any point.

No independent variables were studied in this initial demonstration; rather, all participants were tested under identical conditions. Teger observed that subjects exhibited one of two distinctive behavioral patterns. Some dyads (58%) invested little of their initial stake, quitting at or before the bidding had reached the value of the prize (500 points). The other modal response exhibited by 42% of the participants was to invest more than 500 points (that is, more than the value of the prize). What was most noteworthy about this latter group was that very few quit at a point in between the 500-point mark and the value of their initial stake (975 points). Thus, the 500-point level was a critical point for participants. Once having escalated their bidding beyond this point, they were very likely to spend all of their money. In fact, fully 90% of the subjects who bid beyond 500 points invested virtually all of their resources.

Teger (1980) also noticed several other behavioral changes once the bidding had exceeded the 500-point level. He writes,

> Once the bids had passed the value of the prize, the escalation seemed to acquire a new character. The bidders took longer to decide their next bid, their pattern of bid increases changed (some subjects greatly increased the magnitude of their bid increments, whereas others did just the opposite), and they continued to bid until they were broke. These results appear to indicate that there are at least 2 stages involved in such an escalation. (p. 25)

We shall return to this "stage" analysis of entrapping dilemmas in Chapter 7. For now, suffice it to say that a substantial number of the subjects in Teger's initial demonstration manifested signs of entrapment.

Staw (1976)

Using the role-playing methodology described in Chapter 2, Staw measured subsequent commitment to a chosen course of action by asking undergraduate business students to decide how much money they were willing to allocate to a division of their corporation. Specifically, in 1972 (i.e., the time of the second decision) subjects learned the outcome of the first decision—the choice to allocate in 1967 a large sum of money ($10 million) to one of a hypothetical corporation's two largest divisions (Consumer Products or Industrial Products). Thus, all participants were well aware of the fact that the company had already invested a large amount of money in that division.

The effects of two independent variables were tested. At the second decision point half of the subjects learned that the prior commitment of funds had proved to be financially successful to the corporation (Success condition). That is, subjects in the Success condition received financial data showing that the chosen division had returned to profitable levels while the unchosen division had continued to decline. The remaining half of the subjects (i.e., those in the Failure condition) received the opposite feedback. The other independent variable was the identity of the individual responsible for the earlier decision. In the High Personal Responsibility condition it was the subject (as financial Vice President) who had made the prior investment in 1967. In the Low Personal Responsibility cell the decision was made by another financial officer of the company. Thus, unlike the subjects in the High Responsibility condition, who had to make two investment decisions (in 1967 and 1972, respectively), those in the Low Responsibility condition had to make only one decision (the 1972 one). Identical subsidiary information (i.e., sales and earnings data from years 1967–1972) was presented to subjects in both conditions except for the fact that the case's scenario began in 1972 rather than 1967 in the Low Responsibility Condition.

The entrapment process could have occurred only in the Failure condition; that is, the decision to persist with the previously chosen decision in the Success Condition could be more easily construed as a prudent investment than as an act of "throwing good money after bad." Moreover, the self-justification process upon which the entrapment phenomenon is predicated should be more salient when subjects are personally responsible for the earlier decision than when they are not. Simply put, individuals should have a stronger need to justify the appropriateness of their own decisions than those of someone else. The results of Staw's study, depicted in Table 3-1, yielded a significant interaction between the Outcome and Responsibility variables, $F(1,275) = 5.56, p < .05$. As predicted, subjects were much more persistent when they, rather than others, were responsible for the prior decision in the Failure condition. The effect of the Responsibility variable was trivial in the Success condition.

As in Teger's demonstration, some subjects displayed escalated commitment to an already chosen course of action. Of even greater significance, subjects were most apt to escalate their commitment in the condition in which the self-

Table 3-1. Amount of Money (in Millions) Allocated to Previously Chosen Alternative as a Function of Personal Responsibility and Outcomes (Source: Staw [1976])

	Personal Responsibility	
Outcomes	High	Low
Success	9.18	8.35
Failure	13.01	9.44

Note: Scores could range from 0 to 20, with higher scores reflecting greater entrapment.

justification motive underlying entrapment should have been strongest: the Failure–High Personal Responsibility cell.

The role-playing methdology, like the Dollar Auction game, thus appears capable of operationalizing the entrapment process. Moreover, the results of the Staw (1976) study suggest that the entrapment process may be an especially potent mediator of escalated commitment. Note that conventional reinforcement theory predicts that subjects should have allocated more resources in the Success than in the Failure condition, particularly if they felt personally responsible for the success. After all, if individuals' decisions produce a positive outcome, then they should be quite likely to persist in that decision. The results showed, however, that negative outcomes stemming from a decision for which subjects felt personally responsible produced much more escalation than that observed in all other conditions.

Rubin & Brockner (1975)

In this study all subjects were personally responsible for previous decisions yielding negative feedback. The experiment was designed to delineate the effects of several factors on degree of entrapment: reward value, awareness of costs, and goal proximity.

Upon their arrival at the laboratory, subjects were ushered into individual cubicles and were seated at a table, on top of which lay $2.40 in cash, a set of written instructions, and a stopwatch. Subjects were led to believe that the three others in their group (none of whom actually existed) had arrived earlier and were already seated in three adjacent cubicles.

The instructions began by informing subjects that they would be taking part in a study concerned with "how groups go about solving problems, especially when the resources necessary for doing so are scarce . . . and how familiarity among group members affects this process." Subjects were told that other groups of subjects would be permitted to meet and speak with one another before engaging in a problem-solving task, but that no such interaction was possible in the subjects' own group. The instructions then continued:

> You are one in a group of four people, who will each be given an identical task.
> In a few minutes we will ask each of you to attempt to solve the same crossword
> puzzle. As soon as you have finished reading the instructions you may take the

$2.40 on your desk. This is *your* money, and we will refer to it as your INITIAL STAKE. Whether you get to keep all of it, go home with less, or as much as a grand total of $8.00 will depend entirely upon your performance in the experiment. In a few minutes you will be given a crossword puzzle to solve, which contains 10 words. The amount of money that you will make will be determined by: (1) the number of words you solve, and (2) the amount of time you take to solve them.

 If you are able to solve *at least eight of the ten words in three minutes* or less, you will win a total of $8.00. We will refer to this $8.00 prize as the JACKPOT. However, in order for you to be eligible for the jackpot, or any portion of it, you must correctly solve *at least eight* of the ten words in your puzzle.

Assuming that they were able to solve at least eight words, and were therefore eligible for the jackpot, subjects were told that the amount of money they would win would be determined by the amount of time taken. If they were unable to solve at least eight words they would be ineligible for the jackpot, and their pay would be based on the initial stake as well as the amount of time that they had spent in the experiment. For each minute beyond the first three, they would lose an additional 10% from their $2.40 initial stake (e.g., winning $2.16 before the end of minute 4, $1.92 before the end of minute 5, etc.)

Value of reward. In Chapter 1 it was suggested that entrapment is a self-perpetuating process, at least up to a point. In order to make quitting a more viable option—that is, in order to heighten decision makers' conflict about whether to persist or withdraw— the value of the reward was programmed to decrease over time. For economic reasons, if the magnitude of the sought-after goal declines, the strength of the decision maker's goal-directed behavior should also lessen. Moreover, it stands to reason that the greater the decline in the value of the goal, the more likely the decision maker is to exhibit reduced goal-directed behavior. For half of the participants, the rate of decrement was low (Low Decrement condition), whereas for the other half it was high (High Decrement condition). It was predicted that entrapment would be greater in the former than latter condition.

 Operationally, those in the Low Decrement condition were told beforehand that for each minute taken to solve eight words beyond the first 3 minutes the value of the jackpot would decrease at a rate of 10% from its initial $8.00 level. For example, if subjects solved eight words in five minutes, they would leave the experiment with $8.00 minus 2 times $.80, or $6.40.

 In the High Decrement condition subjects were told that for each minute beyond the initial three they would lose an increasing 10% not from the initial $8.00, but from the *remainder* of the $8.00. For example, by solving eight words before the end of the fourth minute, they stood to earn 90% of $8.00 (just as they would in the Low Decrement condition). If they needed 5 minutes, however, they would earn 80% of the $7.20 remainder, or $5.75. Thus, by the end of the fifth minute the value of the jackpot was lower in the High than in the Low Decrement condition. Thereafter, the spread in values increased between these two conditions (see Table 3-2).

The High Decrement condition contained another interesting feature. If the participants could not solve the puzzle before the end of the eighth minute, they could actually earn more money by quitting and retaining the amount left in their initial stake than by solving eight words and winning the jackpot. Based on Teger's (1980) results however, we surmised that a substantial number of subjects would remain in the experiment for a period longer than that which was economically feasible. Furthermore, based on Teger's results it was predicted that High Decrement participants who persisted beyond the critical point (i.e., the eight minute, when the value of their initial stake surpassed the amount of money in the jackpot) would continue to work on the puzzle until the very end (i.e., the 13th minute).

Awareness of costs. One particularly diabolical aspect of many investment situations that later prove entrapping is that at the outset the decision maker is unaware of, or inattentive to, the costs associated with a possible long-term commitment of resources. Upon deciding to wait for the bus, for example, people typically do not think about the amount of time they may feel compelled to wait if the bus does not arrive within the first few minutes. Similarly, when automobile owners make their initial set of repairs, they may ignore the fact that the car could become increasingly costly over time. Several important questions follow from the prospect that people are initially inattentive to the possible costs associated with continued investments.

First, why is it that people are not more vigilant? Why have they not learned from previous entrapment-type situations to anticipate the potentially negative long-term consequences that can arise if their immediate actions do not produce the desired short-run effects? To speculate, it may be that people fail to appreciate the generality of the entrapment process. That is, perhaps it is not obvious that the process by which people come to wait too long at bus stops is similar to the process that causes them to persist too long in souring relationships. By failing to see the relatedness of these various situations, people become less apt to learn from their previous experiences.

Another, more motivational, reason for decision makers' reluctance to ponder the costs associated with becoming committed is that costs after all, are often perceived as aversive. As a result, decision makers may not like to dwell on the amount of time, money, and effort they have spent (and will continue to spend) by continuing in a chosen course of action.

There is an important, empirically testable hypothesis stemming from the notion that entrapment is due to decision makers' initial lack of attention to costs: namely, if people are forced to focus on information pertaining to costs, they should be less apt to become entrapped. Note that financial costs existed for participants in two ways in this study (see Table 3-2): as they spent more time in the experiment the magnitude of their (actual) initial stake and (potential) rewards both decreased. If these costs were made more salient, we hypothesized, subjects should be less likely to exhibit entrapment.

Table 3-2. Jackpot Values as a Function of Time

	Low Decrement Condition			High Decrement Condition	
End of Minute	Initial Stake	Jackpot	End of Minute	Initial Stake	Jackpot
3	$2.40	$8.00	3	$2.40	$8.00
4	2.16	7.20	4	2.16	7.20
5	1.92	6.40	5	1.92	5.75
6	1.68	5.60	6	1.68	4.00
7	1.44	4.80	7	1.44	2.40
8	1.20	4.00	8	1.20	1.20
9	0.96	3.20	9	0.96	0.72
10	0.72	2.40	10	0.72	0.50
11	0.48	1.60	11	0.48	0.10
12	0.24	0.80	12	0.24	0.01
13	0.00	0.00	13	0.00	0.00

To manipulate subjects' cost awareness, we provided half of the participants with a copy of the chart shown in Table 3-2 (High Salience condition). These subjects were told the following:

> In order to make it easier for you to understand the amount of money you can win as time passes in the experiment, we have constructed a chart which shows your potential earnings at the end of each minute. This chart is located on the wall next to your desk. Take a moment now to familiarize yourself with it. You may refer to it at any time during the experiment.

Subjects in the Low Salience condition did not receive this chart. Entrapment was expected to be greater in the Low than High Salience condition. The instructions then continued:

> Because some of the words are more difficult than others, you may want to make use of a crossword puzzle dictionary which the experimenter has available. This dictionary contains the answers to all of the words used in constructing your puzzle. However, because we are interested in studying group problem solving when resources are scarce, there will be one, and only one dictionary available for the four of you to use.

In order to obtain the dictionary from the experimenter, subjects were told to move the switch on their table into the "On" position. If the dictionary was not currently being used by one of the group members, the experimenter would hand it to them at once, and they could then use the dictionary for as little or as much time as they wished. The instructions then continued:*

---

*From Rubin & Brockner, "Factors affecting entrapment in waiting situations: The rosencrantz and guildenstern effect," JPSP, 31. Copyright 1975 by the American Psychological Association. Reprinted by permission of the publisher and authors.

If, however, the dictionary is being used by someone else at the point that you request, the experimenter will hand you a card with a number on it (either a 1, 2, or 3), indicating your place in line. For example, if you receive a card with the number 1 on it, this means that the dictionary is in use by a member of your group, and that you are next in line to get it as soon as he is through. If the dictionary is not available when you request it, and the experimenter hands you a card indicating your number in line, he will ask you to hand him your puzzle, while you wait. Thus, you cannot wait for the dictionary and continue to work on your puzzle at the same time. If you decide that you would prefer not to wait any longer, or that you would like to continue working on your puzzle, simply ask the experimenter for your puzzle. The experimenter will return your puzzle and take back the card he has given you. This means, of course, that you will lose your place in line for the dictionary.

Proximity to goal. All subjects were presented with the identical puzzle, deliberately constructed to be so difficult that eight or more words could not be solved without the use of the dictionary. Indeed, none of the participants were able to solve eight words. Moreover, there was in reality no crossword puzzle dictionary. Thus, subjects had been placed in a situation in which they could choose to wait for a valuable, necessary resource which never became available. Subjects had been led to believe that attaining the dictionary would enable them to solve the puzzle, because the dictionary reportedly contained all of the needed answers. Probably because of this, and because of the fact that subjects were unable to solve the puzzle on their own, most of them (83%) requested the use of the (nonexistent) dictionary within the first few minutes after they had started to solve the puzzle. It was at this point that the third independent variable was manipulated. All subjects learned that they had to wait for the dictionary. Half of them were given a card telling them that they were first in line for the use of the dictionary (High Proximity condition), whereas the other half were given a card suggesting that they were third in line (Low Proximity condition). Subjects were expected to exhibit greater entrapment (i.e., wait longer) in the High than in the Low Proximity conditions.

All subjects then proceeded to work on the crossword puzzle. The experiment ended when subjects decided to quit (that is, before 13 minutes had elapsed) or when 13 minutes had passed, at which point the experimenter notified subjects that they had exhausted their entire stake. A postexperimental questionnaire was then administered to all participants.

The results on the chief dependent measure of entrapment—the amount of time subjects spent in the experiment, measured inversely by the amount of the initial stake remaining when the experiment ended—are presented in Table 3-3. The average earning was $1.04 (out of a maximum of $2.40). The three independent variables yielded main (but no interaction) effects. As predicted, subjects quit the experiment later: (1) in the Low Decrement ($M = \$0.82$) than in the High Decrement conditions ($M = \$1.25$; $F(1,64) = 4.24, p < .05$), (2) in the Low Salience ($M = \$0.70$) than in the High Salience condition ($M = \$1.37$; $F(1,64) = 10.16$, $p < .005$), and (3) in the High Proximity

Table 3-3. Mean Amount of Money Remaining from Initial Stake as a Function of Decrement, Salience, and Proximity to Goal (Source: Rubin & Brockner, "Factors affecting entrapment in waiting situations: The rosencrantz and guildenstern effect," JPSP, 31. Copyright 1975 by the American Psychological Association. Reprinted by permission of the publisher and authors.)

Rate of Decrement	Cost Salience	Perceived Goal Proximity	
		High	Low
High	High	$1.44	$1.77
	Low	$0.77	$1.07
Low	High	$0.75	$1.57
	Low	$0.40	$0.58

Note: Scores could range from $0.00 to $2.40, with lower scores reflecting greater entrapment.

($M = \$0.84$) than in the Low Proximity condition ($M = \$1.21$; $F(1,64) = 3.65$, $p < .07$).

A related dependent variable was the amount of time that subjects spent waiting for the dictionary. On the average, subjects spent slightly more time than 4 minutes (out of a maximum of 13) doing so. As expected, subjects waited significantly longer in the Low Salience than in the High Salience condition ($Ms = 248.84$ vs. 202.49 seconds; $F(1,64) = 4.02$, $p < .05$), and in the High Proximity than Low Proximity conditions ($Ms = 330.89$ vs. 158.72 seconds; $F(1,64) = 17.04$, $p < .001$). The means in the Low vs. High Decrement conditions were in the predicted direction (260.00 and 228.11 seconds, respectively) but did not differ significantly.

It is also noteworthy that across conditions, as in the Teger (1980) study, almost all subjects manifested one of two very different kinds of game behavior. As can be seen in Table 3-4, from the end of minutes 3 through 9, a steady stream of subjects quit the experiment. However, once the decision makers had persisted beyond the ninth minute, they were very likely to remain until all, or nearly all, of their initial stake had been spent.

Postexperimental questionnaire. All participants completed a questionnaire subsequent to working on the puzzle. They were asked to rate the importance of various reasons for their decision to wait as long (or as short) as they did for the dictionary. Two of the reasons were designed to measure mediating processes presumably influenced by the Cost Awareness and Proximity variables. Specifically, to evaluate whether they were less attentive to costs (and therefore perhaps more prone to entrapment) in the Low Cost than High Cost Salience condition, subjects indicated the extent to which they agreed with the following statement: "I did not realize how much money I had lost. If I had, I surely would have quit sooner." A three-factor analysis of variance revealed only a

Table 3-4. Frequency Distribution of Quitting Points (Source: Rubin & Brockner, "Factors affecting entrapment in waiting situations: The rosencrantz and guildenstern effect," JPSP, 31. Copyright 1975 by the American Psychological Association. Reprinted by permission of the publisher and authors.)

By the end of minute:	Number of subjects who quit:
1	0
2	0
3	9
4	5
5	6
6	4
7	3
8	2
9	7
10	2
11	4
12	0
13	30

significant Salience effect, ($p < .01$). As predicted, subjects in the Low Salience condition rated this reason as much more self-descriptive than did those in the High Salience condition.

It was also predicted that subjects would become more entrapped in the High than in the Low Proximity condition because of the former group's greater confidence that they would soon receive the dictionary. Accordingly, subjects rated the self-relevance of the following item: "As time went by, I felt increasingly confident that I would get the dictionary soon." The only significant finding was the Proximity main effect. Subjects were much more likely to endorse this statement if they had been in the High than in the Low Proximity condition, ($p < .001$).

Finally, all participants completed a measure of subjectively experienced entrapment: "I had already waited so long, it would have been foolish not to wait a little longer." Importantly, there were parallel findings on the behavioral and self-report measures of entrapment. As in the analysis of the dictionary waiting-time measure, the only significant findings were the Salience and Proximity main effects. Subjects rated the reason as more self-descriptive in the (1) Low than in the High Salience condition ($p < .01$), and (2) High than in the Low Proximity condition ($p < .05$). Thus, subjects who waited longer for the dictionary also reported feeling more entrapped.

Summary

The results of the three studies reported in this chapter provide preliminary evidence that the entrapment process can be captured under controlled laboratory conditions. Although the purposes and procedures varied greatly across the three studies, several basic findings emerged: (1) A substantial portion of participants escalated their commitment to a previously chosen course of action, even when such escalation was no longer economically prudent. (2) Escalated commitment occurred most often under the conditions predicted by an entrapment analysis. For example, Staw (1976) demonstrated that negative feedback about the earlier decision produced heightened commitment only when subjects felt personally responsible for the prior decision. This finding, coupled with some of the questionnaire data found by Rubin and Brockner (1975), suggested that decision makers escalated their commitment in the service of justifying previous investments. (3) The decisions made by those who were personally responsible for prior investments were susceptible to influence by a host of other variables (Rubin & Brockner [1975]).

Another noteworthy commonality was that in each study there was a large degree of within-condition variability in entrapment behavior. For instance, the subjects in Teger's (1980) study tended to quit either relatively early or very late in the bidding process. Staw's (1976) findings were based on cell sample sizes of approximately 60, necessary in order to overcome the large within-cell variability. Similarly, the within-cell variablity in the Rubin and Brockner (1975) study was considerable. In fact, in many of the studies reported in later chapters, there was a great deal of within- as well as between-condition variability in behavior.

What are some possible explanations for the relatively large within-condition variability? First, it may be that people vary greatly in their susceptibility to entrapment. We shall return to this possibility in Chapter 8, which deals exclusively with the effects of individual difference variables on entrapment behavior. Second, entrapment situations present a great deal of conflict and ambiguity to most decision makers. Indeed, the very definition of entrapment includes uncertainty about the costs needed to achieve one's goals, as well as uncertainty about the likelihood of goal attainment.

Faced with this ambiguity, individuals attempt to impose some structure by investing a certain portion of their resources. Moreover, as Schelling (1960) has pointed out in a different context, the amounts invested tend not to be normally distributed. Rather, socially defined "prominent" points are used as decisional anchors. For example, in the Dollar Auction simulation, 500 points served as a prominent decision point in that it (1) represented the value of the prize, (2) was equal to approximately one-half of the subject's total point allocation, and, (3) was a "round" number. Other prominent points included 0 points and 975 points. In the Staw role-playing simulation subjects had to allocate anywhere from 0 to 20 million dollars. Many participants chose amounts of $0, or $10, or $20 million, corresponding to the prominent points of none, half, and all of their resources, respectively.

One effect of the decision makers' reliance on prominent points is that it increased within-condition variability in behavior. For example, in the Dollar Auction subjects, in theory, were free to quit when the bidding had reached 673; or, in the Staw role-playing situation, to spend $6½ million. In actuality, however, they never did, perhaps because these amounts were not psychologically prominent.

It should be noted that the large degree of variability shown by participants in these initial studies is probably not an artifact of the experimental procedures. Behavior in everyday life entrapment situations, both across and within individuals, tends not be distributed along normal or even continuous distributions. As in Teger's (1980) study, some people probably avoid entrapment situations altogether, or perhaps invest little of their resources (e.g., people who rarely bet or gamble). On the other hand, there are individuals who are prone to extreme entrapment (e.g., people who have lost $1000 at the gambling casino, when they only "intended" to spend $500). Our "prominent point" analysis of entrapment situations suggests that once the latter group of decision makers has invested more than some critical amount, it may well manifest an extreme degree of escalated commitment.

Subsequent chapters will describe experimental research on particular antecedents of entrapment. The focus primarily will be on between-condition differences in behavior. The preceding discussion suggests that it may also be worthwhile to attend to (1) overall, or across conditions, patterns of decision making, and/or (2) within condition variability in entrapment.

Chapter 4

Some Nonsocial Antecedents of Entrapment

In the next several chapters we will attempt to synthesize the experimental research on entrapment. In practically every experiment to be described, the researchers have sought to delineate the antecedents of entrapment. Accordingly, they have tested the effect(s) of one or more independent variables on decision-makers' willingness to persist in, or withdraw from, an entrapping dilemma.

Although the independent variables have differed greatly across studies, all of them can be subsumed under two broad situational categories: nonsocial and social aspects of the decision environment. In Chapters 5 and 6 the impact of various social-psychological forces on entrapment will be discussed. In the present chapter we shall consider several nonsocial determinants of entrapment.

More specifically, the determinants of entrapment to be presented in this chapter have been organized into two classes of variables:

1. *Expectancy value, or economically based factors.* Rational theories of human choice behavior suggest that individuals will choose those behavioral alternatives which maximize their subjective expected utility (SEU). SEU, in turn is influenced by two factors: (a) the extent to which the behavior is perceived to increase the likelihood of goal attainment, and (b) the extent to which the goal is valued.

In Chapter 1 it was suggested that the process of entrapment does not necessarily yield irrational outcomes. Implicit in this notion is that decision making in entrapment situations may be influenced by a host of factors rooted in expectancy value theory (cf. Rubin & Brockner, 1975). The basic proposition in all of these studies is that decision makers will be more apt to escalate their commitment to an entrapping course of action to the extent that the likelihood of goal attainment (and/or the perceived value of the goal) is high rather than low.

2. *Decision structure variables*. Recent research in the cognitive sciences has demonstrated that the manner in which the decision is structured can have a marked impact on choice behavior. In the second half of this chapter we describe the results of several studies in which the effects of two such structural variables were explored.

Expectancy Value Antecedents

The effect of several "expectancy value" variables on entrapment has been investigated in one or more studies. The fairly straightforward prediction in all of these studies is that decision makers will seek to maximize their economic outcomes. Stated differently, they will do whatever best enables them to gain maximum rewards at minimum cost.

Value of Goal

In one study (described in detail in Chapter 3) subjects persisted in their goal-directed (albeit entrapping) behavior as long as they perceived their goal as valuable (Rubin & Brockner, 1975). In a related experiment Rubin (1978a) also demonstrated that the value of the goal influenced decision makers' degree of entrapment. Subjects in this experiment had responded to an ad placed in Boston newspapers which read, "Take part in a scientific study of game-playing behavior. Make money. Phone for details." Several hundred Boston area residents made phone contact with us and were told that the study involved game playing. They were also told that they would be given $5 for coming to the experiment, and would have the opportunity to win even more money by playing the game. A total of 118 subjects (60 male, 58 female) completed the experiment.

When subjects arrived they were handed $5 in cash, ushered into a small research cubicle, and given instructions for the Counter Game procedure described in detail in Chapter 2. Placed on top of the subject's desk was the counter and an intercom system with which they could communicate with the experimenter, who was in an adjacent room. The study supposedly was "designed to understand better the decision making process that underlies people's willingness to take risks, make bets, and attempts to solve a variety of problems."

To reiterate the basic procedure of the counter game, subjects were told that the counter increased by units of 1 from 000 to 500. A randomly selected number between 1 and 600 was chosen as the winning number. If and when subjects reached that number, a light would flash on the counter, indicating that they had won the jackpot. If the winning number was between 501–600, the counter would stop automatically at 500. Thus, subjects were led to believe that there was a good chance (500/600, or 83%) that they would win the jackpot by playing the game. Of course, it cost them 1 cent for each unit increment on the counter, regardless of outcome. Subjects were also told that they were free not to start playing the game, or to quit at any point if they did decide to begin. If they did wish to start investing, the counter would increase continuously until they either hit the jackpot or decided to quit. In reality, no "winning number" existed. Thus, the primary concern was the amount of money subjects spent in attempting to win the jackpot.

Subjects were randomly assigned to one of seven conditions, in which the jackpot was worth either $2, $4, $6, $8, $10, $15, or $20; their initial stake was fixed at $5 in all instances. Most of the participants (84%) invested some of their $5 initial stake. Of the 19 who did not, most (16) were in three conditions having the lowest jackpot value (i.e., $2, $4, or $6). A two-factor (Sex of the Subject $\times$ Value of Goal) unweighted-means analysis revealed a significant value of goal main effect, $F(6,104) = 7.06$, $p < .001$. As expected, participants spent the largest amount of money in the $20 condition, and the least amount in the $2 condition. Interestingly, as can be see in Table 4-1, there was not a monotonic increase in expenditures as the jackpot increased from $2 to $15.

The Sex of Subject $\times$ Value of Goal interaction was marginally significant, $F(6,104) = 1.94$, $p < .10$. This interaction revealed an important difference in the entrapment behavior of men and women: with one exception, men showed a linear increase in their expenditures as the value of the goal increased. (The only reversal occurred in the $10 and $15 conditions.) Women were far less consistent in this regard. Although they spent the most money in the $20 condition, they did not spend the next highest amount in the $15 (or even in the $10) condition. Furthermore, women did not spend the least amount in the $2 (or even in the $4) condition.

Value of Costs

The preceding experiment showed that subjects (especially males) generally spent more of their initial stake as the magnitude of the possible reward to be gained increased. From an expectancy value perspective, it also stands to reason that individuals will be more likely to invest their resources if the costs associated with doing so are low rather than high.

In the following experiment (Rubin, 1978b) we varied the perceived value of the cost of investing. Unlike the previous experiment, the nature of this manipulation was more psychological rather than economic. In virtually all of the entrapment experiments in which the participants' investments are in the form of money the experimenter provides them with an initial stake. To increase realism, subjects are told to treat the money as their own. In fact, they do not even have to invest any of their initial stake if they so desire. Nevertheless, participants have often remarked that they do not completely experience a sense

Table 4-1. Amount of Money Invested as a Function of Sex of Subject and Size of Jackpot (Source: Rubin [1978a])

Sex of Subject	Size of Jackpot (in dollars)						
	2	4	6	8	10	15	20
Male	$0.83	$2.87	$3.91	$4.24	$4.62	$4.38	$5.00
Female	$2.38	$3.34	$2.07	$4.41	$3.02	$4.17	$5.00
Overall	$1.61	$3.11	$2.99	$4.33	$3.82	$4.28	$5.00

Note: Scores could range from $0.00 to $5.00, with higher scores reflecting greater entrapment.

of ownership of the money. During postexperimental debriefings some commented that they might have exhibited less entrapment had they invested money which they had brought to the experiment, rather than money which had been given to them.

It seemed important to evaluate this hypothesis for several reasons: First, if subjects actually did become less entrapped when the money being invested was that which they had brought with them, rather than that provided by the experimenter, it would support the general notion that heightened costs leads to reduced entrapment. Second, if significant differences were obtained then it could have considerable implications for the external validity of the findings in those studies in which money is provided to subjects. That is, the effect of certain independent variables on entrapment may differ, depending upon the original source of the money. Third, it seemed important to determine whether subjects were accurate in their postexperimental assertion that they would have spent less if the money originally came from their own, rather than the experimenter's, pocket. After all, many subjects who made this claim had just lost a considerable portion (if not all) of their money. Consequently, in saying that they would have acted differently had the money originally been their own, they may be justifying their lost money *after the fact* by adopting an "easy come, easy go" attitude.

The 36 subjects (14 male, 22 female) in this experiment were drawn from an introductory psychology course at Tufts University. They received required credit for taking part in the study. The procedure of the Counter Game used in the prior experiment was carefully repeated, with one major exception: instead of being given an initial stake participants were required to pay with whatever they had brought with them to the lab. Also, all subjects were studied in the condition in which the jackpot was worth $10. In the subsequent analyses, we compared the behavior of males and females run in that condition in the previous study (see Table 4-1) to that of the present participants.

A somewhat greater proportion of subjects (11 out of 36, or 30%) refused to spend any of their money in this experiment than in the $10 condition of the previous experiment (1 out of 16, or 6%). (The difference between proportions was marginally significant, $F(1,50) = 3.80$, $p < .06$, according to an analysis of variance of dichotomous data.) A 2×2 (Sex $\times$ Condition) unweighted-means

Table 4-2. Mean Amount of Money Invested as a Function of Sex of Subject and Source of Money (Source: Rubin [1978b])

Sex of Subject	Source of Money	
	Experimenter	Subject
Male	$4.62	$3.40
Female	$3.02	$1.37

Note: Higher scores reflect greater entrapment.

analysis of amount invested (only for those participants who did spend money) revealed two significant main effects. As shown in Table 4-2, male subjects spent significantly more money than did female participants, $F(1,48) = 10.48$, $p < .01$. Moreover, subjects became less entrapped in this study than in the previous experiment (in which they had been given an initial stake), $F(1,48) = 6.55, p < .025$. The interaction effect was trivial, $F < 1$.

Of course, it is always difficult to draw inferences on the basis of comparisons between studies. By examining two different samples, we did not randomly assign subjects to different experimental conditions. Thus, we cannot evaluate the *causal* effect of the chief independent variable—whether subjects invested money that had or had not been given to them—on degree of entrapment. Nevertheless, we can tentatively propose that the value of costs in particular— and economic considerations more generally—affect decision makers' persistence with a previous chosen, though failing course of action.

Before concluding this section, we should mention that the results of several experiments have failed to support the hypothesis that heightened costs reduce entrapment. In one study (Teger, 1980) subjects participated in a Dollar Auction against a simulated opponent who made either a very large (250 points) or rather small (25 points) opening bid. Teger's expectation was that subjects would be more reluctant to get involved in the condition requiring them to make a counterbid of more than 250 points than of 25 points. In another experiment (Brockner, 1977), Dollar Auction subjects bid against a simulated other whose first bid and three subsequent counterbids were either relatively large ($\bar{x} = 12.5$ cents) or small ($\bar{x} = 3$ cents). The prediction was that subjects would be less willing to get involved in the former than in the latter condition. In both experiments, however, it was observed that the size of the opponent's opening bids had absolutely no effect on the decision-makers' willingness to become involved in the bidding or on the size of their ultimate final bid. Rather, over 90% of the subjects in both conditions at least started to bid.

Several factors could account for the fact that the Initial Cost of Bidding variable produced no effect in these two studies. First, the manipulation of cost may not have been powerful enough. It could be reasonably argued that in both conditions in both studies, subjects did not have to invest much of their resources to get started. For example, in the Brockner (1977) study, the opponent's opening bids were only 10 cents greater in the large than in the small condition. Second, it may have been that the participants' opponent who opened with large bids aroused subjects' competitive spirit, making subjects equally willing to start bidding in the large and the small bid conditions.

Third, the tendency for virtually all participants to start bidding may in itself be the result of a self-justification process! Subjects had already invested some time and effort in order to arrive at the experiment. If it can be assumed that at least most people were curious about the nature of the experiment, then they may have been reluctant to quit at the very outset after having expended energy to take part in the study. Fourth, the decision makers may have felt some pressure to start bidding due to demand characteristics and/or some tacit equity norm. They may have inferred that the researcher was interested in studying their bidding behavior. In order to "help them out," they perceived it appropriate to exhibit some bidding behavior. Or, they could have reasoned that because the experimenter had given them some money, it was only "fair" for them to bid at least some of it.

Although each of the explanations may have some merit (and is empirically testable) we wish to devote some attention to the demand characteristics analysis. In its most general form, the demand characteristics interpretation suggests that certain cues in the experimental environment caused subjects to start investing. If so, then there is less of a reason to expect decision makers to be influenced by the magnitude of the opponent's bids. In addition, the demand characteristics hypothesis can account for a related finding, consistently shown in the experiments (and to be discussed in subsequent chapters): in particular, very few participants fail to start investing even though economic analyses of the decision situation suggest that it would be prudent for them to "take the money and run."

Demand characteristics often are treated as a methodological nuisance by experimental social psychologists (cf. Carlsmith, Ellsworth, & Aronson, 1976). Indeed, the presence of demand characteristics may interfere with the effects of certain independent variables in experimental studies of entrapment. However, in several ways, the pressure of demand characteristics to start investing may not be entirely problematical in entrapment studies. First, demands to invest resources are probably most influential at the beginning, rather than during the latter stages of the entrapment situation; that is, demand characteristics may explain why individuals start to invest, but not why they persist.

Second, and perhaps even more important, we suspect that demand characteristics to "get started" may well be present in many situations in everyday life that ultimately prove to be entrapping. Said differently, as decision makers we may be "seduced" into courses of action whose entrapping qualities are not apparent at the outset. Those external cues are not responsible for our continued commitment, but they may well be the cause of our being in the situation in the first place. For example, we may initially choose to wait for the bus because of the presence of others at the bus stop; or, we may make an initial repair on our old car because it seemed like the most economically feasible thing to do at the time. In short, demand characteristics to start investing may pose some problems in experimental studies of entrapment. However, the presence of this factor in the experimental situation may be analagous to the factor(s) that cause decision makers in everyday life to embark upon courses of action that subsequently prove entrapping.

In any event, and to return to the studies that stimulated this discussion, a myriad of factors (including demand characteristics) may have been active at the outset of the Dollar Auction game, which rendered subjects equally likely to compete initially, independent of perceived costs.

One criticism of the "expectancy value" studies is that they produced results that were not terribly surprising. After all, is it not "common sense" that entrapment will be greater to the extent that the perceived likelihood of goal attainment and/or value of the goal is high? Perhaps. What is less obvious, however, are the host of factors (besides economic variables) that may affect decision makers' perceived probability of goal attainment and/or goal value. Delineating such factors will enable us to understand the conditions under which entrapment is more or less apt to occur. For example, Tropper (1972) observed that subjects were more likely to persist in an entrapping dilemma similar to the Dollar Auction when they believed that it would be more (rather than less) costly for their opponent to persist than it would be for they themselves. A plausible interpretation of this finding is that the participants inferred that their opponent was more likely to quit when it was costly to continue. Stated differently, the perceived likelihood of being able to outlast their opponent was probably enhanced by the fact that it was more costly for the opponent to persist.

Attribution Processes and Entrapment

The causal attribution(s) that individuals make for the outcome of their prior decisions in entrapping situations may also affect the decision makers' perceived likelihood of goal achievement. Before describing how this may occur, it may be useful to place attribution research in a broader context.

The past 15–20 years have witnessed a veritable explosion of research on the role of attribution processes in social interaction. The seminal works of Heider (1958), Jones and Davis (1965), and Kelley (1967) suggested that people are motivated to explain the causes of their own and others' behavior. The basis of this motivation presumably is to attach meaning to behavior. According to these theorists, locus of causality is the crucial dimension along which attributions are made. A person's behavior, such as friendliness at a cocktail party, can be seen as caused by factors internal or external to the individual. Internal dimensions include the person's abilities, traits, effort, and moods. External factors included luck, social norms prescribing behavior, and the difficulty of the behavior being performed. Thus, the same friendliness at the cocktail party can mean very different things, depending on whether it is attributed to internal or external factors.

Further conceptual advances, primarily in the domain of achievement motivation, have suggested that other dimensions besides locus of causality are psychologically meaningful. Weiner (1974) added the notion of stability, suggesting that in some instances individuals perceive that they have succeeded or failed because of persistent factors (i.e., those likely to remain present over time), whereas in other cases the same outcome is attributed to transitory or unstable causes. Learned helplessness theorists (Abramson, Seligman, & Teasdale, 1978; Miller & Norman, 1979) added the dimension of generality or globality. They posited that individuals faced with the inability to control their fates will respond very differently, depending upon whether the cause of their lack of control is due to global factors (i.e., those likely to remain present in different situations) or specific causes (those limited to that particular instance of lack of control).

Several experiments have tested for the effect of causal attributions for the negative setback on subsequent escalation decisions. The basic thesis is that individuals, when deciding upon the magnitude of further allocations to the chosen course of action, will ask themselves why the previous commitment was unsuccessful. Abramson et al. (1978) have pointed out, though in a different context, that decision makers should be less likely to persist following failure to the extent that the failure is attributed to stable, rather than unstable causes, and/or to global rather than specific causes. *It is in this sense that attributions presumably influence decision makers' expectations about the likelihood of goal attainment. The more immutable (stable and/or global) is the perceived cause of the setback, the more pessimistic should the decision maker be about the likelihood of goal attainment.* Said differently, entrapment should be less apt to occur under such conditions.

This hypothesis has some empirical backing. Staw and Ross (1978) demonstrated that subjects escalated their commitment to a failing course of action to a lesser extent when the cause of the earlier setback was due to a persistent (i.e., stable) rather than unstable factor. Conlon and Wolf (1980) observed a similar finding, but only for some of their subjects (the "non-calculators"). From an attributional perspective, one problem with both of these studies is that the investigators (intentionally) confounded the stability variable with the foreseeability of the problem. The persistent (stable) cause was always foreseeable, whereas the nonpersistent (unstable) cause was always unforeseeable. Obviously, this confounding clouds any attributional interpretation of the results.

This difficulty was eliminated in a study by Levi (1982). Like Staw and Ross (1978) and Conlon and Wolf (1980), Levi used a role-playing methodology in which respondents learned that their earlier commitment had met with failure. Half of the subjects were led to believe that a purely stable factor caused the setback, while half were led to attribute the failure to purely unstable factors. As predicted, subjects' subsequent allocations were significantly smaller in the Stable than in the Unstable attribution condition. Although the decision makers' perceptions of the likelihood of goal attainment were not measured in this study, it seems highly likely that such expectations were far more negative in the Stable than in the Unstable condition.

Attribution and entrapment: some speculations. In short, attributions for prior setbacks do seem to affect subsequent escalation decisions. However, there is ample room for future research. For example, further work is needed to specify the conditions under which attributions will affect entrapment. As Wortman and Dintzer (1978) have pointed out, causal attributions may not be nearly as psychologically salient to the decision maker as attribution theorists have assumed; that is, entrapped decision makers may not always (or even often) ask themselves the "why question." If so, then attributional accounts of escalated commitment may be misleading.

Furthermore, we need to determine the joint effects of various attributional dimensions (i.e., locus of control, stability, globality, intentionality) on escalation of commitment. The three studies cited to this point only explored the effect of the stability factor, and in two of these studies it was confounded with another dimension. In addition, researchers have hitherto studied the effect of attributions for *one's own* behavior on subsequent escalation decisions. In interpersonally competitive entrapment situations, however, decision makers may make attributions about the causes of *the other party's* actions, and plan their own behavior accordingly. For example, if the opponent's escalation appears to be due to his or her reckless, irrational personality then one may wish to avoid competing with this person, and thereby not become entrapped (Schelling, 1960).

When studying the effects of attribution on entrapment, future researchers also need to specify the precise aspect of behavior for which the decision maker is engaged in the attribution process. Is the decision maker trying to determine what caused the *outcome* of the target's behavior? Or is the individual trying to determine why the target decided *to embark upon the failing course of action?* Locus of control research (Rotter, 1966; Seligman, 1975) deals with behavior–outcome relationships. Research on intrinsic and extrinsic motivation (Deci, 1975) focuses on the effect of viewing the cause of the behavior itself (and not necessarily the outcome) as internal or external. The attribution/entrapment experiments performed to date seem to have focused more on behavior–outcome linkages. However, research is also needed which studies the effects of attributions that individuals make for why they even decided to enter the potentially entrapping situation (or why they decided to remain, once having entered).

One factor that could influence this attribution process is volition, that is, the extent to which individuals believe that they acted out of their own free will. In a fine piece, Salancik (1977) has written about the processes by which individuals become committed (to organizations). He posits that individuals are likely to feel more committed if their behavioral choice is perceived to be self, rather than externally imposed. If it can be assumed that commitment and entrapment are related psychological processes, then it stands to reason that factors affecting commitment may also influence entrapment. It can be predicted, therefore, that the more individuals perceive that they embarked upon a course of action that later proves entrapping out of their own free will, the more likely they are to become entrapped.

Moreover, according to Kiesler (1971), a variety of subtle factors can influence perceived volition. For instance, in one study it was shown that subjects felt more commited to a soft drink (as measured by the amount that they drank) when they made their selection from among four rather than two alternative choices (Reibstein, Youngblood, & Fromkin, 1975). Presumably, by having a wider selection than those in the two-alternative condition, subjects in the four-alternative condition inferred that they must have truly liked their chosen drink.

How can these results be applied to an entrapment situation? Suppose subjects were given a choice of participating in a number of experimental tasks, all of which were designed to study entrapment. Our hunch is that these subjects would be more likely to become committed to (i.e., entrapped in) the experimental task than would subjects upon whom the experimental task was externally imposed. Other aspects of the experimental situation could be varied to influence attribution, commitment, and entrapment. For example, in most of the laboratory tasks subjects receive an initial stake of money; it is emphasized that they do not have to invest any of that money. These instructions were introduced in order to make the experimental situation analogous to everyday-life entrapment scenarios, in which decision makers must perceive choice about whether to enter (and/or remain in) the potentially entrapping conflict. What would happen, we wonder, if the salience of perceived choice was experimentally varied? Suppose that some subjects were reminded shortly before investing about the fact that they were free to do whatever they wished (as in the typical study), whereas others were not. It seems plausible that the former subjects who do decide to invest their resources will make more self-attributions for doing so, and will thus become more committed to (or entrapped in) a failing course of action than will subjects for whom choice was not made salient.

Decision Structure Antecedents

Other nonsocial determinants of entrapment do not focus on expectancy value antecedents, but on structural characteristics or decision rules. One variable that we find to be particularly important, although subtle in form, is whether the continued investments are the result of an "active" or "passive" decision. In "passive" or "self-sustaining" investment situations, the decision makers' degree of commitment to the previously chosen course of action increases automatically *unless* they deliberately decide to terminate their involvement. Waiting for a bus, or remaining in an unsatisfying relationship or job can be considered examples of passively escalated commitment. Once people decide to wait for a bus, an important component of their commitment (i.e., time) increases continuously and automatically unless they decide to stop waiting. Similarly, by failing to take the conscious step to remove themselves from souring romantic relationships, people have made a decision, however passively, to continue their commitment.

In other escalating conflicts, however, the process of resource allocation is more "active" or "self-terminating." Unlike the investments made in passive situations, continued investments in active conflicts do not accrue automatically. Rather, they are the result of an active decision to continue allocating one's resources. Consider the plight of the owner of an old car that continues to require repair. The owner can escalate his or her commitment only after making an active, intentional decision to do so. Unlike people waiting for the bus, who literally have to "do nothing" in order to increase their degree of entrapment, the car owner must reach into his wallet and pay the mechanic each time that the car needs repair. Another example of "active" entrapment is the United States' military escalation in Vietnam. In order to increase the U.S.' degree of commitment, it was necessary for the United States' policy makers to decide consciously and deliberately to do so. At the conflict's outset, there was no specification that the U.S. would automatically increase its degree of commitment if its objectives had not been reached within a certain time period.

The crux of the active–passive distinction, then, is this: In passive situations, it is necessary for decision makers to take an active step in order to alter their behavior if they no longer wish to escalate their degree of commitment. In active situations, it is necessary for decision makers to take an active step in order to increase their commitment (typically by allocating more of the same resources that have already been expended). By not taking this active step, they are tacitly withdrawing from the situation.

There are several reasons to expect decision makers to become more entrapped in Passive than in Active situations. In the Passive situation escalation can occur in the absence of any activity. In the Active situation escalation is typically *dependent* upon some form of active thinking and behavior. Based on the assumption that it is physically and/or psychologically "easier" for the decision maker to do nothing than to take action, we expected subjects to become more entrapped in Passive than in Active situations. In addition, in the Active situation the very fact that decision makers must make deliberate decisions to increase their commitment may also sensitize them to the costs associated with each increase. If such costs are rendered more psychologically salient, then the individual may be more likely to quit than to persist (Rubin & Brockner, 1975). The effect of the active–passive Resource Allocation variable was studied in the following three experiments.

Brockner, Shaw, and Rubin (1979)

Eighty-one (38 female, 43 male) undergraduates volunteered to take part in the experiment. When recruited to participate, subjects were told that they had an opportunity to earn some money. However they were informed that the exact amount would depend upon what happened during the experiment. All subjects took part in the Counter Game procedure described in detail in Chapter 2.

Subjects were seated in front of the counter and were provided instructions for a "decision-making" study. They were given $4 in single dollar bills, and told that they had the opportunity to win an additional amount of money (the jackpot), which was worth $2. The rules of the counter procedure were then explained. To summarize, they were told that

1. The counter was operated manually by the experimenter, and increased by units of 1 up to 500.
2. A winning number between 1 and 500 had been randomly selected. If and when that number was reached on the counter, a tone would sound indicating that they had won the jackpot.
3. Each unit on the counter cost subjects 1 cent, regardless of whether or not they actually "hit" the jackpot.
4. Subjects could not invest more than their $4 initial stake in order to win the jackpot. If the winning number had not been reached when the counter reached 400 (i.e., if the winning number were between 401 and 500) they would be forced to quit and forfeit their initial stake.
5. Subjects were free not to invest any of their $4 initial stake, and to quit once having started investing.

All subjects were then informed about the counter's operation:

> If you decide to go for the jackpot, the experimenter will set the counter in motion until it reaches the number 20, or until the tone sounds—whichever comes first. If the tone has not sounded by the time the counter reaches 20, there will be a short pause and decision point. During this time you must decide what you would like to do.

In the Self-sustaining, or Passive, condition subjects were told the following:

> If you want to go on for the jackpot, *do not say anything. If you want to quit, announce out loud the word STOP. Unless you say STOP, the experimenter will re-start the counter*, and set it in motion until it reaches the number 40, or until the tone sounds—whichever comes first. The same procedure will be followed as before if the tone has not sounded by this point.

In the Self-terminating, or Active, condition subjects were told:

> If you want to go on for the jackpot, *you must announce out loud the words GO ON. Unless you say GO ON, the experimenter will not re-start the counter, and you will be forced to quit at that point.* If you do say GO ON, the experimenter will set the counter in motion until it reaches the number 40, or until the tone sounds—whichever comes first. The same procedure will be followed as before if the tone has not sounded by this point.

The tone never did sound in either condition. Hence, subjects were faced with a decision point every 20 units (20, 40, 60, . . . 380) until they had either decided to stop investing or had invested their entire initial stake.

Table 4-3. Frequency Distribution of Amount Invested (Source: Brockner, Shaw, & Rubin [1979])

Amount	Number of Subjects Investing That Amount
$0.00	11
$0.20	1
$0.40	4
$0.60	2
$0.80	2
$1.00	15
$1.20	0
$1.40	1
$1.60	4
$1.80	1
$2.00	13
$2.20	2
$2.40	1
$2.60	2
$2.80	0
$3.00	9
$3.20	0
$3.40	1
$3.60	1
$3.80	1
$4.00	10

All subjects were then asked if they wanted to try for the jackpot. The major dependent variable was the amount of money that subjects chose to invest.

Table 4-3 reveals the overall distribution. A small percentage (14%) of subjects chose not to invest any of their resources. Given that subjects had only a 40% likelihood of increasing their earnings beyond the amount contained in their intial stake (that is, if the winning number were between 1 and 200), it is surprising that so few participants quit at the outset. As discussed previously, however (see pages 37–39), there are a variety of noneconomic factors (e.g., demand characteristics) that could have motivated participants to start investing. Slightly more than half (53%) of the subjects invested some of their money, but were not willing to spend more than $2 in order to win a $2 jackpot. The remaining third of the subjects spent more than $2, with approximately 12% of the sample spending their entire $4 initial stake. The overall distribution is thus quite similar to Rubin and Brockner's (1975) and Teger's (1980) initial findings, even though the Counter Game procedure is quite different from the methodologies employed in those studies.

A t-test on the effect of the Resource Allocation variable revealed, as predicted, that subjects became more entrapped in the Passive ($M = 2.11) than in the Active ($M = 1.46) condition, $t(79) = 2.32, p < .025$, two-tailed. Unexpectedly, this significant effect was partially attributable to the tendency for subjects in the Active condition to be less willing to start bidding. Out of the 11 participants who retained their entire $4 initial stake, 9 were in the Active condition, $\chi^2(1) = 3.96$, $p < .05$. When the data of these 11 subjects were excluded there was no longer a significant effect of the Resource Allocation variable ($t(68) = 1.22$, $p > .05$), although the means in the Active and Passive conditions ($2.22 and $1.88) were still in the predicted direction.

Questionnaire data. After the counter procedure was completed the 70 subjects who invested at least some of their initial stake rated the importance of several explanations for their behavior (along 41-point dotted continuum scales). These include (a) "I wanted to minimize the amount I would lose from my initial stake," (b) "I had already invested so much, it seemed foolish not to continue," (c) "As the counter increased I became more and more confident that I would win the jackpot," and (d) "I did not want to spend more than the amount of the jackpot to win the jackpot." There were no differences in ratings as a function of the Resource Allocation variable.

A series of internal analyses showed, however, that across conditions subjects ascribed differential importance to these reasons, in relation to the amount of money they had invested. Specifically, the responses of those who spent more than the value of the jackpot (High Investors) were compared to those who had not invested not more than the jackpot value (Low Investors). The Low Investors rated reasons (a) and (d) as more important than did the High Investors (both p values $<.001$). The High Investors, however, rated reasons (b) and (c) as more important causes of their behavior than did the Low Investors (reason (b): $p < .001$; reason (c): $p < .02$). Reason (b) is particularly noteworthy, in that it was designed to be a self-report measure of entrapment. Thus, just as in the Rubin and Brockner (1975) study, there was evidence that participants who were more entrapped *behaviorally* reported *experiencing* entrapment to a greater degree than did those who invested less of their resources.

In sum, the Resource Allocation variable produced a significant effect on degree of entrapment. Those in the Passive condition invested more money than their Active-condition counterparts. This was in large part due to the fact that more participants refused to get involved in the latter than in the former condition. The greater tendency for Active subjects to avoid bidding could have been a chance finding or it could have been of theoretical importance; that is, Active-condition subjects were expected to be more aware of the costs associated with remaining in the situation as a result of being called upon to make repeated "active" decisions to continue. However, a greater proportion of Active subjects quit before they had ever reached the decision points (which was the time during which cost salience was expected to increase). How can this apparent ambiguity be resolved? The Resource Allocation variable was initially manipulated during the instructions and a "practice trial," when subjects read about and then were exposed to the different rules in the Active and Passive conditions. Thus, it may have been the mere *anticipation* of having to take part in an Active entrapment situation which rendered the associated costs more salient.

In any event, the Resource Allocation effect was ambiguous although statistically significant. The effect of this factor was therefore retested in each of the following two studies.

Rubin, Brockner, Small-Weil, and Nathanson (1980, Experiment I)

The subjects were 43 male and 46 female Boston area residents who were recruited through a newspaper advertisement inviting participants in a study of decision making. When subjects responded to the advertisement they were told that they would be paid $5.00 for coming to the laboratory and reading a set of instructions.

Upon their arrival at the laboratory, subjects were seated at a table in a private cubicle. They were given $5 in cash and instructions for the Counter Game. The basic procedure employed in the Brockner, Shaw, and Rubin (1979) study was used. There were, however, a number of modifications. First, the financial parameters were altered. Instead of receiving a $4 initial stake with which to bid for a $2 jackpot, the initial stake and jackpot were set at $5.00 and $3.00, respectively. Second, the experimeter was not in the same room as the subjects. Rather, he communicated with them by use of an intercom system and headphones. Third, subjects were not told the range of the randomly chosen winning number; instead, their chances were simply said "to be good" if they remained in the situation long enough. Fourth, the decision points occurred every 25, rather than 20, units. Those in the Active condition were required to press a button on their intercom within 5 seconds, to indicate their desire to continue; if they wished to quit they were to do nothing during this period and the study would automatically end. Passive-condition subjects were told that if they wished to remain in the experiment, they should "do nothing" during the 5-second decision period—the counter would pause for 5 seconds and then automatically continue to increase; if they wished to quit, subjects had to press the button on their intercom during the 5-second decision period.

The results yielded no significant effects for the various analyses. Although subjects spent more money in the Passive ($M = \$2.08$) than in the Active ($M = \$2.03$) condition, this effect did not approach significance ($t < 1$). A greater percentage of participants than in the preceding study (26/89 or 29%) refused to invest any of their resources. This percentage was slightly higher in the Active (14/44 or 32%) than in the Passive condition (12/45 or 27%), but the difference did not attain significance, $\chi^2 < 1$. Finally, contrary to the order of means in Experiment 1, there was a slight, though clearly nonsignificant, tendency for subjects to spend more money in the Active than in the Passive condition when the data of only those subjects who had invested some of their initial stake were analyzed ($Ms = \$2.98$ vs. $\$2.84$, $t < 1$).

The findings of this study were disappointing. Nevertheless, it seemed important to study the effect of the Passive–Active variable again, for a variety of reasons. First, the results of the initial investigation suggested that this factor could have a significant effect on entrapment. Whenever inconsistent results emerge (as was the case in these two experiments), a host of factors could be influential. For example, the sample studied in the second experiment was drawn from a considerably more heterogeneous population than the college student group who served as subjects in the first study. The "noise" due to this heterogeneity could have masked any "signal" attributable to the Passive–Active variable. Several statistical tests showed that the subjects' entrapment behavior was, in fact, more variable in the second than in the first experiment. Specifically, the F_{max} statistic was significant within and across the Passive and Active conditions, with the amount of money invested more variable in the second than in the first experiment in all analyses (all p values $< .01$). Furthermore, whereas the subjects in Study 1 were highly consistent in at least starting to invest (over 86% did so), the participants in the second experiment were considerably more variable in their initial decision to risk their initial stake (only 71% invested some of their money). Statistical analysis revealed that a greater proportion of subjects failed to invest any of their initial stake in the second than in the first experiment, $\chi^2(1) = 5.20$, $p < .025$; this means that participants in the latter study as a group were more variable in their behavior upon deciding whether to invest any of their resources.

The fact that there was a relatively large amount of individual variability in behavior in the second study is related to an additional reason to study once again the effect of the Passive–Active variable. In both experiments the operationalization of the variable was rather subtle. The only procedural differences between the two conditions were what subjects were instructed to do or say during the decision points, and it could be argued that even these procedural differences were slight. In spite of its subtlety, the Resource Allocation variable had an effect on the behavior of the first sample, which was more homogeneous in nature. When a sample is heterogeneous, however, as in the second experiment, it may be necessary to employ a more powerful experimental manipulation. Thus, in order to give the Resource Allocation variable another test we deliberately (1) introduced a more powerful manipulation and (2) studied a more homogeneous sample.

Rubin, Brockner, Small-Weil, and Nathanson (Experiment II)

The participants were 45 Tufts University undergraduates of both sexes who volunteered for a study of puzzle solving in exchange for extra class credit. Upon arriving at the laboratory, subjects were seated in individual cubicles containing a clock, desk, intercom, an initial stake of $2.50 in cash, and a set of written instructions. The counter game was eschewed in favor of the crossword puzzle procedure employed by Rubin and Brockner (1975). As in that study, subjects could win a jackpot (this time worth $10) by correctly solving 8 or more of the 10 words within 3 minutes. If at the end of the 3 minutes they had not solved at least 8 words, 25 cents were to be subtracted from their initial stake for each additional minute taken. Also, a crossword-puzzle dictionary was supposedly available on a first-come, first-served basis. In reality, this dictionary did not exist. The puzzle was so difficult that none of the subjects could solve it. Whenever they requested the dictionary (as 89% did) they were told: "It is not available right now. What do you wish to do?" The subjects' choices were to wait for the dictionary or continue working on the puzzle; they could not do both simultaneously. Unlike in the Rubin and Brockner (1975) experiment, the value of the jackpot remained fixed (at $10) for the entire testing period.

In the Passive condition subjects were told, "In order to quit, simply press the call button and tell the experimenter that you wish to stop the experiment." Thus, in the absence of doing anything, Passive subjects' degree of commitment automatically heightened. Subjects in the Active condition were given the preceding instruction as well as the following: "In addition, the experimenter will contact you every 3 minutes to ask you if you wish to continue." Once subjects in the Passive condition started to work on the puzzle they were not interrupted. Thus, all of them either quit before 13 minutes had passed (at which point some of their initial stake remained), or were forced to quit at the 13-minute mark. In the Active condition the experimenter interrupted the subjects every 3 minutes and asked, "Do you wish to continue with the experiment?" In order for Active subjects to remain eligible for the jackpot, they had to make an affirmative decision to do so every 3 minutes (by responding "Yes" to the experimenter's query). By contrast, those in the Passive condition literally had to "do nothing" in order to remain in the situation.

The results revealed an unequivocal effect of the Resource Allocation variable. When the data of all subjects were included, it was shown that Passive participants remained in the entrapping situation longer than Active subjects. Specifically, those in the former condition subjects spent an average of $1.70 from their initial stake, whereas those in the latter spent an average of only $0.76 ($t(43) = 4.03$, $p < .001$). A total of 8 subjects did not remain in the experiment beyond the third minute. (These participants can be considered analogous to those who were unwilling to invest and thus lose any of their initial stake in the counter game.) Interestingly, as in the first experiment in this series, most of the 8 participants were in the Active ($N = 7$) rather than the Passive condition ($N = 1$; $\chi^2(1) = 3.03$, $p < .10$). Unlike the initial experiment, though, the Resource Allocation effect was still significant even when the results of these 8 subjects were excluded; that is, the remaining 20 subjects in the Passive condition spent an average of $1.79 of their initial stake, whereas the 17 remaining Active condition participants lost an average of only $1.07 ($t(35) = 3.05$, $p < .01$).

Discussion of all three experiments. Taken together the results of all three studies suggest that the Resource Allocation variable could be an important determinant of entrapment behavior. Moreover, (and this was not predicted), this variable apparently begins to exert influence on decision makers *before* they have even started to invest their resources. A greater proportion of participants refused to invest in the Active than in the Passive condition in the Brockner, Shaw, and Rubin (1979) study. In the first of the two experiments performed by

Rubin et al. (1980), slightly (though not significantly) more subjects retained their entire initial stake in the Active condition and in the second study the between-condition difference in dropout rate was marginally significant. It is also noteworthy that this similarity in dropout rates across studies occurred in spite of the fact that different experimental procedures and operationalizations of the Resource Allocation variable were employed. Across all three experiments, 30 out of 108 (28%) subjects in the Active conditions did not invest any of their resources, whereas in the Passive conditions the corresponding rate was only 14% (15 out of 107). Importantly, the difference between these two proportions is statistically significant, $\chi^2(1) = 5.35$, $p < .025$.

Why might individuals be more reluctant to invest any of their resources in Active situations? Although we can only speculate, it may be that the costs associated with escalated commitment become more salient as the procedure for making repeated investments is described. If decision makers are told beforehand that they must take some kind of action in order to continue investing, they may begin to consider whether they should make any investments at all. The Active decision structure may have implied to individuals that it is not a foregone conclusion that they will automatically wish to escalate their degree of commitment. Rather, the implication is that there are potentially important reasons, most notably the associated costs, why people may *not* wish to continue; no such message is conveyed to decision makers under Passive conditions.

Furthermore, the process by which people escalate their commitment may seem more psychologically "difficult" in the Active condition. After all, they are being told that in order to continue they will have to make a conscious choice to do so at each decision point; those in the Passive condition, however, receive no such forewarning. In short, it may have been that two factors—increased cost salience and greater awareness of the difficulty of the decision task—made decision makers more apt to avoid the Active than Passive entrapment situations.

It also seems important to explain why the magnitude of the Resource Allocation effect varied across the three experiments. Clearly, the strongest effect was obtained in the last experiment in the series, the weakest in the second study, while an effect of intermediate strength was found in the first experiment. At least two factors could have contributed to the differences.

1. The strength of the manipulation. It was expected that subjects would become more entrapped in the Passive than in the Active condition for two reasons: First, cost salience was expected to be lower in the Passive condition. Second, for a variety of reasons (one to be discussed below), it would be more psychologically difficult to quit in the Passive than in the Active condition. The way in which the Resource Allocation variable was operationalized may have indirectly affected these two underlying processes.

   The manipulation of Active and Passive conditions was extremely subtle in the second of these three experiments, so much so that the conditions may have appeared virtually indistinguishable to subjects. In both conditions a set of decision points existed during which subjects were to decide whether to continue investing. Their choice was communicated either by pressing an intercom button during each decision period to signal a desire to continue (Active condition), or by pressing the intercom button only when they wished to stop (Passive condition). In retrospect, it appears that cost salience and/or degree of effort needed to continue was not differentially manipulated in the two conditions, or at least not very powerfully.

   In contrast, consider the circumstances in the Brockner et al. (1979) study, in which the effect of intermediate strength was obtained. Here subjects were required to indicate their decision not by nonverbally signalling the experimenter but by calling out either the words "Go on" or "Stop" to an experimenter who was in the same room. In both conditions subjects may have inferred that the experimenter wished them to take part in the study, in which case they may have experienced the experimenter's presence as a source of pressure. If they did wish to quit, they could do so far more easily in the Active condition, by simply saying nothing during the decision period; in the Passive condition subjects had to say "Stop" to the experiment's face—an act requiring greater psychological effort. Hence, it may have been this situationally induced constraint against quitting in the Passive condition that contributed to the stronger finding obtained in Brockner et al. (1979) than in the initial study of Rubin et al. (1980).

   It was in the final experiment that the manipulation of Active and Passive conditions was perhaps most striking. Subjects in this Passive condition were left entirely alone. There were no decision periods for them, and there was no intrusion by the experimenter. Thus, the participants were placed in a situation devoid of any obvious remainders of the costs incurred. In the Active condition, however, there were decision periods; every 3 minutes the experimenter stopped the proceedings and directly inquired of the subjects whether they wished to continue. Consequently, Active subjects were constantly reminded of the fact that another period of time had elapsed, and that additional costs had therefore been incurred without their having reached the goal.

2. The heterogeneity of the sample. The subjects for which the significant Active–Passive effects were obtained were drawn from introductory psychology classes at Tufts University. Although there is obviously considerable individual variability even within these groups, the sample as a whole should have been far more homogeneous than the Boston area volunteers who served as participants in the study in which the Active–Passive effect was nonsignificant. In analysis of variance terminology, an independent variable should be most likely to produce a significant effect when (a) a powerful manipulation is employed and/

or (b) a more homogeneous sample is studied. Viewed from this perspective, it becomes more understandable why the Resource Allocation effects were ordered in magnitude as they were. In listing the effects in ascending order of significance with regard to the Resource Allocation variable, one observes the following pattern:

1. weakest manipulation, heterogeneous sample (Rubin et al., Experiment 1),
2. intermediate manipulation, homogeneous sample (Brockner et al.), and
3. strongest manipulation, homogeneous sample (Rubin et al., Experiment 2).

Framing and Entrapment

Another decision structure variable which could affect entrapment decisions is the manner in which the dilemma is "framed" (Kahneman & Tversky, 1979). To understand what is meant by framing, consider the following example:

> The U.S. is preparing for the outbreak of an unusual Asian disease which is expected to kill 600 people. Two alternative programs are being considered. Which would you favor?
> 1. If Program A is adopted, 200 people will be saved.
> 2. If Program B is adopted, there is a one-third probability that all will be saved and a two-thirds probability that none will be saved.

From expectancy value theory these two alternatives yield identical payoffs (i.e., 200 saved lives). However, 70% of 158 respondents chose Program A rather than B. Apparently, these subjects were risk-averse; they took the "sure thing," rather than a risky prospect of equal expected value.

> Another group of subjects received the following choices:
> 1. If Program A is adopted, 400 people will die.
> 2. If Program B is adopted, there is a one-third probability that that no one will die and a two-thirds probability that 600 people will die.

Once again, these two choices have equal expected value. In addition, the expected value of these two choices is identical to that of the previous two choices (i.e., 200 saved lives). Interestingly, however, the vast majority (87%) of the 169 respondents in the second group chose Program B. Unlike the previous group, these participants were risk-seeking, choosing the high payoff, uncertain prospect over the sure thing.

In discussing these and similar results, Kahneman and Tversky have proposed that decision makers are risk-averse when the decision environment is framed positively (e.g., when evaluating gains), but risk-seeking when that same situation is framed negatively (e.g., when evaluating losses). This "prospect theory" may be of relevance to entrapment, because the decision situation facing the entrapped decision maker is almost always framed negatively. The entrapped decision maker typically is evaluating a losing proposition, and must decide whether to accept the sure loss (i.e., to not invest further), or to try to recoup all that has been expended (i.e., to allocate additional resources). The fact that many decision makers choose to escalate their commitment to the failing course of action is thus consistent with the prediction offered by prospect theory, if it can be assumed that the decision to escalate commitment is riskier than the decision to withdraw.

A recent study by Arkes and Hackett (1984) nicely demonstrates that entrapment situations are negatively framed. Subjects were given the following problem:

> As a business person, assume that you have to choose between these two options.
> *Option 1*: If you choose this option your company will definitely lose $9000.
> *Option 2*: If you choose this option, there is a 95% chance that your company will lose $10,000 but a 5% chance that your company will lose nothing.

Over 90% of the subjects chose the latter option (even though its expected value was equal to the former option.)

Arkes and Hackett then translated these parameters into the context of an entrapment situation:

> As an electronics manufacturer, you have already invested $9000 of your company's funds to design a device that greatly improves TV reception in the home. Now that your production is 90% done, a competitor begins selling a product similar to your product, except the competitor's product works much better and sells for a lower price than your product will. The question is: should you spend the remaining $1000 to finish production of your TV reception device. Your chief financial analyst informs you that if you do invest the remaining $1000, there is a 95% chance that you'll lose the total investment of $10,000 (the $9000 already spent plus the $1000 to finish production). However, if you spend the remaining $1000 there is a 5% chance that your company will lose no money because you will be able to regain the $10,000 by selling a limited number of these devices. (It is absolutely impossible for you to regain more than your $10,000 investment.) Of course, if you don't invest the $1000, production stops immediately, the devices are not completed, and you lose the $9000 investment you've made so far. What do you decide? Should you invest the entire $1000 or not?

Arkes and Hackett found that 75% of the respondents opted to allocate the additional $1000, a finding consistent with prospect theory.

One implication of prospect theory is that the tendency to remain entrapped may be reduced if the decision situation can be framed positively rather than negatively. How can entrapment situations be framed positively? After all, entrapment refers to escalating commitment to a *failing* course of action. It may not be possible to frame the situation positively (at least in an absolute sense). However, it may be possible to frame the same unfavorable feedback more or less negatively.

Note the (somewhat paradoxical) prediction that prospect theory would make: if the unfavorable feedback concerning the previous investment is framed negatively, then decision makers should be more risk-taking (i.e., they should be more likely to persist with the failing course of action) than if the feedback is framed positively (or at least less negatively). The paradox lies in the fact that reinforcement theory would make the opposite prediction: namely, that the more favorable (less unfavorable) the feedback, the greater the likelihood of persistence.

Brockner, Bazerman, and Rubin (1984) recently performed a study to test this logic. Thirty undergraduates at Tufts University were asked to assume the role of "financial vice president at ABC university." In that capacity they were to allocate $40 million of limited existing funds for investment purposes to increase the university's endowment. Subjects were given some facts about two possible ventures (computers and oil exploration), and asked to choose one. They were then told that 3 years had now passed, and feedback about the initial investment was provided. In all conditions subjects were informed that the $40 million investment was now worth only $20 million. In other words, the venture had not gone well in an absolute sense.

However, this feedback was presented differently in the two framing conditions. In the Negative Frame condition subjects were informed:

> As of now, it is fair to say that your initial investment was a disaster. The stock value which was once worth more three years ago, is now worth only $20 million today. It is important for you to keep several things in mind. First, you have lost fully half ($20 million) of your initial investment. Second, investments fared well across the country during this three-year period. For example, had you invested in the (unchosen) firm, you would have considerably more than $20 million left. *So taking all these factors into account it appears that you did relatively poorly with your investment.*

In the Positive Frame condition subjects were told:

> As of now it is fair to say that your initial investment worked relatively well. True, the stock value which was worth $40 million three years ago is now worth $20 million today. But, it is also important for you to keep several things in mind. First, a substantial amount of money ($20 million) is *still* remaining from your investment. Second, in general investments fared poorly across the country during this three-year period. For example, had you invested in the (unchosen) firm, you would have even less than $20 million left. *So, taking all these factors into account, it appears that you did relatively well with your investment.*

Subjects in both conditions were told that, "the present investment situation is uncertain; things may get better or they may not." Subjects had to decide whether they wanted to continue their investment in the previously chosen firm. The options in the Negative Frame condition were:

1. Accept a loss of $20 million by not continuing your investment in this firm, or,

2. Risk the remaining $20 million by continuing your investment in this firm, with a 50% chance of losing $0 from the entire original $40 million, and a 50% chance of losing the entire original $40 million.

Note that these two alternatives have equal expected values.

The choices were phrased slightly differently in the Positive Frame condition:

1. Save the remaining $20 million by not continuing your investment in this firm.

2. Risk the remaining $20 million by continuing your investment in the firm, with a 50% of chance of saving the entire original $40 million, and 50% chance of saving $0 from the original $40 million.

The expected values of these two alternatives are equal to one another, and to the two choices in the Negative Frame condition.

Results. Manipulation check data revealed that the feedback showing a $20 million decline was perceived to be more unfavorable in the Negative than Positive Frame condition ($p < .001$). Of greater importance were subjects' decisions about whether to persist with, or withdraw from, the failing investment. Eleven out of the 15 (73%) of the participants chose to persist with the investment in the Negative Frame condition. The corresponding proportion in the Positive Frame condition was only 33% (25 out of 15). An analysis of variance of dichotomous data (Winer, 1971) revealed that these two proportions were significantly different from one another, $F(1,28) = 5.38$, $p < .03$.

These data provide preliminary evidence that Kahneman and Tversky's (1979) prospect theory is relevant to the process of entrapment. Most entrapped decision makers probably experience the decision structure to be negatively framed; individuals are aware of what they have lost, or said differently, the focus is on the proverbial "glass that is half empty." It is precisely under these conditions, according to prospect theory, that risk-seeking behavior (i.e., escalated commitment) is bound to occur. If, however, entrapped decision makers can be reoriented to perceive the situation from a positive frame (i.e., if they can see the glass as half full, rather than half empty) then they may become risk-averse, and thus not become further entrapped.

Further research is warranted to establish the conceptual and empirical links between prospect theory and entrapment. The possibility that framing is manipulable, for example, has implications for the reduction of entrapment, a topic that is covered in Chapter 9. More generally, further research along these lines will place the entrapment phenomenon within the context of "behavioral decision theory"—a burgeoning area of experimentation in the cognitive sciences (cf. Kahneman, Slovic, & Tversky, 1982).

Summary

This chapter has focused on some nonsocial antecedents of entrapment. The results of several experiments revealed that "expectancy value" variables that account for a substantial portion of human choice behavior in nonentrapment situations also influence the actions of entrapped decision makers. Thus, individuals can be expected to commit more of their resources when the value of the goal is relatively high, when costs are low, and/or when the perceived likelihood of goal attainment is high.

While such results are not particularly surprising, they may serve to stimulate research on less obvious social and/or psychological determinants of "perceived likelihood of goal attainment" and/or "perceived goal value." For example, it has been shown that the causal attributions that individuals make for the negative feedback about their prior investments may have a marked effect on subsequent resource allocation behavior, presumably by affecting the perceived likelihood of future goal attainment.

Finally, we discussed the impact of several (relatively subtle) decision structure variables on degree of entrapment. One variable of particular importance is whether continued investments are made automatically and "passively," or as the result of a more conscious, deliberate, and "active" process. Across three experiments the Passive decision structure was found to be more entrapping than its Active counterpart, largely because of decision makers' greater reluctance to begin investing in the latter type of situation. A second factor derived from prospect theory (Kahneman & Tversky, 1979) refers to the manner in which the decision problem is framed. We have suggested that most entrapment situations are framed negatively, which may account for risk-taking behavior in the form of escalated commitment. In a positively framed entrapment situation, however, the likelihood of risk-averse behavior (i.e., withdrawal) should be increased. The results of a preliminary study were consistent with this conjecture.

Chapter 5

Social Influence and Entrapment

Taken together, the results described in the previous two chapters provide a useful first step in identifying some antecedents of entrapment. A more complete analysis, however, should consider the interpersonal factors that affect such escalation decisions. Note that in most entrapment situations there exist or could exist a "cast of characters," each of whom may influence the decision makers' degree of entrapment. For instance, in some entrapment situations decision makers must compete against another person or group in order to reach their objectives, while in other circumstances decision makers must "compete" against a nonsocial entity (e.g., chance). Is entrapment more apt to occur under one condition rather than the other?

In addition, a large body of social-psychological research has studied the effects on decision making of models (e.g., Bandura, 1977) and groups (e.g., Dion, Baron & Miller, 1970). Is entrapment heightened by the presence of models whose behavior suggest that they are entrapped? Furthermore, in all of the experiments discussed to this point, decisions about whether to persist were made by individuals. What would happen if such decisions were made by groups?

The purpose of this chapter is to examine the effects of various sources of social influence on the extent to which decision makers escalate their commitment to a failing course of action. Notice the complexity of the problem. Sometimes groups may become more entrapped than individuals, whereas sometimes the opposite is bound to be true. Similarly, the presence of an entrapped model may increase *or* decrease entrapment, depending upon a host of variables. Also, it is possible to imagine that a social opponent can lead to greater or lesser entrapment than a "nonsocial" opponent. In short, the effects on entrapment of the various sources of social influence are not unidirectional. The scholar seeking "quick" answers to the relative efficacy of social-psychological variables in the entrapment process may find the research state of affairs frustrating, albeit exciting.

This chapter is organized into five main sections. First, we shall discuss the effects of competing against a social versus nonsocial opponent. The second part grew out of an unexpected, but consistent, finding observed in the first section: the tendency for men and women to be differently influenced by the social/nonsocial variable. Possible reasons for this sex difference are considered, giving rise to a study that investigated the effect of a sex-linked individual difference variable on entrapment.

Third, in most entrapment situations in which the decision maker must compete against another person (rather than a nonsocial entity) it is quite possible that characteristics of the other party (e.g., perceived similarity) may influence the decision makers' resource allocation behavior. The results of several pertinent experiments are discussed at this point. Fourth, the effects of modeling processes on entrapment are considered. Fifth (and finally), the impact of group versus individual decision making on entrapment is presented. Relevant empirical research will be presented in each section. It will become apparent that "contingency theories" are needed to specify the conditions under which these various sources of social influence increase or decrease the likelihood of entrapment. Put differently, in making predictions about the effects on entrapment of a social (vs. nonsocial) opponent, a model, or a fellow decision maker, one needs to consider the effects of other relevant situational and/or dispositional factors.

Social Versus Nonsocial Entrapment

As stated in Chapter 2, some laboratory procedures require subjects to compete against another person for a valuable prize, whereas others do not. This distinction is *not* an artifact of the laboratory procedure. Rather, practically all real-life entrapment situations can be classified as either social or nonsocial. Commuters waiting for a bus, people waiting on the telephone, slot machine gamblers, and individuals trying to salvage an old jalopy are clearly not competing against another person while in pursuit of their goal. However, a protracted labor–management dispute, a runaway arms race, or an international conflict such as the Vietnam War are examples of socially competitive entrapment situations.

It is important to note that the crux of the social/nonsocial distinction is based on the presence or absence of a *competitive* interpersonal relationship. Thus, even in what are being labeled the "nonsocial" situations, it is possible for other people to be present or interacting with the decision maker in some capacity. However, for the situation to be classified as nonsocial the other person(s) must not be competing with the decision maker for the valued prize. Although there are other people involved in the examples of the commuters waiting for the bus, telephone callers lost on hold, and people attempting to repair their old car (i.e., the bus driver, the telephone operator, and the mechanic), these others have no known intention of competing with the entrapped decision maker. Their actions may have the effect of preventing the decision makers from achieving their goals, but presumably not for intentionally competitive reasons.

In general, decision makers should become more entrapped in social than in nonsocial entrapment situations. In a preceding chapter we described the driving forces that motivate individuals to persist in an entrapping dilemma: (1) the reward associated with the goal, (2) the presumed increasing proximity of the goal, and (3) the cost associated with giving up on one's investment. In theory, all of these factors should be present in both social and nonsocial conditions. Only in the social condition, however, does an additional driving force exist: the competitive motive to defeat one's opponent. Stated differently, the last of the three driving forces mentioned above may be heightened in the social condition, in that there are additional (interpersonal) costs associated with giving up on one's investment—that is, the loss of face related to being defeated by another.

Let us now turn to the research. In each of three experiments half of the participants were competing against another person in their quest for a valued prize (Social condition), whereas the remaining half were not (Nonsocial condition). The decision-making process was expected to be more competitive in the Social than in the Nonsocial situation, engendering greater entrapment in the former than in the latter condition.

Teger (1980)

In the first of the relevant experiments, Teger required half of the subjects to bid against a programmed other person in the Dollar Auction (Social condition), and half of them to bid against a deck of cards in a nonsocial variant of this procedure (Nonsocial condition). All subjects had been given 975 points with which to bid for a 500 point prize. They were told that the points they had won would later be converted to money, but the conversion ratio was left unspecified.

In the Social condition subjects were isolated in small rooms and used an intercom to inform the experimenter of their bids. These subjects never actually met the "other" person; rather, they were told that the experimenter would relay all bids between the opponent and them. In reality, no other person existed. The experimenter programmed the opponent to increase the subject's bid by an average of 30 points. To avoid arousing suspicion, the opponent's increases were not always exactly 30 points; instead, the increases ranged from 20 to 40 points, in multiples of 5. Of course, subjects were free not to start bidding, and to quit at any point if they did begin to bid. The "opponent" never did quit; thus, the auction continued either until subjects had decided to quit or had exhausted their 975-point initial stake.

In the Nonsocial condition the subject sat facing a deck of cards on the table, while the experimenter, seated nearby, unobtrusively watched. To simulate the Dollar Auction, but in a nonsocial fashion, subjects were told:

> For every 5 points you invest, you will be permitted to draw one card from the deck. These playing cards have new numbers written on them, and some have a star. (Subjects were shown examples of a star in the deck, and of the new numbers which ranged in multiples of 5 from 20 to 40, in order to simulate the bids of the other person in the Social condition). If you draw a card with a star you will have achieved the goal and will then get 500 points. If you do not draw the card with a star, then you can make another investment. For example, let's say that you invested 25 points. You get to draw one card for every 5 points that you invested, so for an investment of 25 points you get to draw 5 cards. (p. 28)

Other rules and procedures were included so that the Nonsocial and Social conditions would be as similar as possible, except for the key component of the manipulation—the nature of the subject's opposition. Thus, by making large bids and drawing more cards, subjects probably believed that they could increase their chances of getting a star and winning. (Presumably in the Social condition the "other" person would be perceived as more likely to quit if subjects' own previous bid had been larger.) In addition, the participants' subsequent investment had to exceed the sum of their own last investment and the number on the last card that they drew. Let us say that they had invested 25 points and the last drawn card showed 30; if so, then their next investment began at 55 (i.e., 25 plus 30). Suppose further that the subject then bid another 25 points at this juncture. This would mean that if the winning card were not in the five additional cards drawn, the bidding level had reached 80—plus whatever was the value of the last card. This rule, as in the Social condition, allowed the subject and the deck of cards to alternate making bids. Finally, as in the Social condition, subjects' investments were irrevocable; moreover, the subject never outbid the "opponent" (i.e., there was actually no winning card in the deck).

The results of the experiment are presented in Figure 5-1. Although no statistical tests of those data are reported, Teger does say that "the two conditions are very different." In the Social condition subjects behaved much like the participants in Teger's initial Dollar Auction study (see Chapter 3). Some people quit at the outset, or, if they did bid, did not exceed the value of the goal (500 points). A sizable portion bid beyond 500 points, and of those the vast majority (80%) bid their entire 975-point stake. In the Nonsocial condition the *average* level of entrapment was considerably lower; in addition, overall *variability* in behavior appears to be lower in the Nonsocial than Social condition. Note that Teger's (1980) "end effect"—that is, the tendency to invest all of one's resources once having invested beyond a critical point, such as 500 points—does not appear in the Nonsocial condition: a much smaller proportion exceeded the 500 point level, and those who did were more likely to quit at a point in between 500 and 800 than to bid their entire 975 points. Moreover, of the few people who refused to bid ($N = 4$), none was in the Nonsocial condition. In sum, this study provided firm empirical support for the prediction that Social (competitive) investment conditions engender greater entrapment than Nonsocial circumstances.

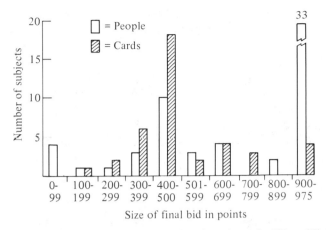

Figure 5-1. Distribution of final bids against cards and people. (*Note*: Higher bids reflect greater entrapment.) Source: Teger (1980).

The following two experiments were designed to replicate, extend, and help clarify the nature of this effect. Different entrapment procedures were utilized in these experiments. Moreover, unlike the Teger experiment, in which only male participants were tested, subjects of both sexes were studied.

Although there were no compelling reasons (a priori) to expect sex differences in entrapment as a function of the Social-Nonsocial variable, it seemed useful to test this notion directly. On the one hand, there is ample evidence in the bargaining literature (e.g., Rubin & Brown, 1975) that men and women often behave differently in experimental games. On the other hand, if no sex difference should emerge (and if Teger's results were replicated) then the external generalizability of the previous finding would be considerably enhanced.

Rubin, Brockner, Small-Weil, and Nathanson (Experiment 1, 1980)

The method of this experiment is described in considerable detail in Chapter 4 (p. 47), and will not be reiterated here. The effect of the Active-Passive variable was tested in that study. A second independent variable, manipulated orthogonally to the first, was whether subjects competed against another person (Social condition) or took part in a game of chance (Nonsocial condition). All subjects were given a $5 initial stake and then took part in the Counter Game procedure. They were told that by participating in the experiment they would have a chance to win a $3 jackpot, either by reaching a random number that had been generated by a computer (Nonsocial condition) or by remaining in the study longer than an adversary who was supposedly seated in the next cubicle (Social condition). As in Teger's (1980) experiment, subjects in this study never met the "other person." Consequently, they were unaware of that individual's sex, race, age, attractiveness, or other characteristics that could have influenced their behavior. Nonsocial condition subjects were told that, just prior to the beginning of the experiment, a winning number would be randomly generated. If and only if subjects remained in the experiment long enough to reach this number would they be awarded the jackpot. Moreover, although the chances of winning the jackpot were said to be good, there was also a possibility that the winning number would not be a number in the 0–500 range, in which case no jackpot would be awarded.

In the Social condition, subjects were told that if one person decided to stop participating in the study, both the subject's and the opponent's counters would stop automatically, and the person who did not quit would be declared the winner of the jackpot. Like those in the Nonsocial condition, subjects in the Social condition were told that they had a "good chance of winning," although this would supposedly depend on what the other person decided to do. If the players should tie—either by both quitting at exactly the same decision point in the experiment (including the beginning) or by remaining in the experiment to the end (when the counter reached 500)—neither would win the jackpot.

A 2×2 (Sex $\times$ Social–Nonsocial) unweighted-means analysis of variance revealed a main effect for the Social–Nonsocial variable. As predicted, subjects become more entrapped under Social than under Nonsocial investment conditions ($F(1,85) = 6.11, p < .025$). Although there was no Sex main effect, there was a significant interaction effect ($F(1,85) = 5.03, p < .05$). As shown in Table 5-1, the Social–Nonsocial main effect was entirely attributable to the male subjects. Simple effect analyses revealed that men became much more entrapped in the Social than in the Nonsocial condition ($F(1,85) = 11.12$, $p < .005$). This comparison thus replicates the finding obtained by Teger (1980), who studied only male subjects. There was no difference between conditions for female participants ($F < 1$). To state this interaction effect differently, there was no difference between the sexes in the Nonsocial condition ($F < 1$); in the social condition, however, men became more entrapped than women ($F(1,85) = 6.74, p < .02$).

Rubin et al. (Experiment 2)

The tendency for males to become more entrapped in the Social than in the Nonsocial condition replicated the finding of Teger (1980); however, this effect was not obtained for females. Since this interaction effect was not predicted, we considered it important to replicate this effect, this time using an entirely different entrapment paradigm.

This third experiment was also designed to elucidate the nature of the Social–Nonsocial effect. As mentioned earlier, the conceptual key to the distinction is whether decision makers perceive themselves to be competing against another person or against some nonsocial entity (e.g., fate). However, the manner in which the variable was operationalized in the two previous experiments may have produced a confounding of several social-psychological processes with the manipulation of interpersonal competition.

Table 5-1. Mean Amount Invested as a Function of Sex of Subject and Type of Opponent (Source: Rubin, Brockner, Small-Weil, & Nathanson, "Factors affecting entry into psychological traps," *Journal of Conflict Resolution*, 24 [1980], Experiment 1. Copyright © 1980 by Sage Publications, Inc. Reprinted by permission of Sage Publications, Inc.)

Type of Opponent	Sex of Subject	
	Male	Female
Social	$3.24	$1.80
Non-social	$1.39	$1.71

Note: Scores could range from $0.00 to $5.00, with higher scores reflecting greater entrapment.

More specifically, the effect of the Social–Nonsocial variable could have been mediated by social facilitation and/or modeling/social comparison processes. A social facilitation theorist (e.g., Geen & Gange, 1977; Zajonc, 1965) could argue that the dominant response of men in these investment situations is to become entrapped, or at least more than women. Under Social conditions—that is, in the presumed presence of another—a decision maker should be even more likely to emit the dominant response. As a result, men in the Social condition should become more entrapped than (1) men in the Nonsocial condition, and (2) women in the Social condition. Simple effect analyses revealed that both of these comparisons were statistically significant. The major difficulty with this line of reasoning is its assumption that the dominant response of males (more than females) is to become entrapped. If that were the case, then men should have shown a relatively high degree of entrapment in the Nonsocial condition (which was then heightened even further in the Social condition). However, the least degree of entrapment was exhibited in the Male-Nonsocial condition.

A combination of both modeling and social comparison processes also could have mediated the Social–Nonsocial effect in the previous two studies. Subjects in the Social condition may have used the information provided by the other person's degree of entrapment as a cue to guide their own behavior. Given that Social subjects were always exposed to a persistent model who would not quit, they may have deemed it appropriate to escalate their own degree of commitment. Although this analysis provides a reasonable interpretation of the males' tendency to become more entrapped in the Social than in the Nonsocial condition, it does not explain why females did not exhibit the same tendency.

Thus, for men, at least, the possibility remains that modeling rather than some aspect of interpersonal competition mediated the effect of the Social–Nonsocial variable. In order to evaluate these two hypotheses, all subjects in this experiment participated in the presence of another person who remained entrapped. For half of the subjects this other person competed with them for the valued prize, just as in the Social condition of previous experiments (Competitive condition). For the remaining half of the subjects, the other person's persistence in the entrapping dilemma was in no way related to the subjects' own outcome (Noncompetitive condition). If the previous finding that (particularly male) subjects became more entrapped under Social conditions were mediated by interpersonal competition, then the effect should be replicated in the Competitive, but not in the Noncompetitive, condition of the present experiment. If, however, the (males') previous results were due to modeling, then there should be no differences in their behavior in the two conditions.

The procedure utilized in this experiment has been described in considerable detail in Chapter 4 on pp. 48–49 of Rubin et al. (1980), Experiment 2 and thus will only briefly be repeated here. Subjects were given an initial stake and were required to solve a difficult crossword puzzle. If they solved the puzzle within 3 minutes they stood to earn a sizable jackpot. All participants were led to believe that both they and another subject simultaneously were attempting to solve the puzzle. (In reality, no such person existed, although the experimenter did a considerable amount of stage setting to convince the subjects of the "other person's" existence.) Through written instructions given before they started working on the puzzle, subjects' perceived relationship with the other was experimentally varied. In the Competitive condition subjects were informed that they and the other person were competing for the jackpot. ("The first person to corectly solve the words will win the jackpot while the other will not.") In the Noncompetitive condition the instructions stated instead: "You and another participant are taking part in the experiment simultaneously. You can each win a jackpot by correctly solving the words."

The puzzle was made so difficult that no one could solve it. After subjects had continued to work on the puzzle for longer than 3 minutes they began to lose money from their initial stake of $2.50 (at a rate of 25 cents per minute). All subjects either quit before they had lost their entire initial stake or were forced to quit after 13 minutes (at which point their initial stake had been exhausted). The major measure of entrapment was the amount of money spent from the initial stake at the end of their participation.

A Sex × Competitive–Noncompetitive unweighted-means analysis did not reveal any significant main effects (contrary to the previous experiment, in which a main effect for the Social–Nonsocial variable was obtained). However, there was a significant interaction effect, $F(1,41) = 7.44$, $p < .01$. Table 5-2 reveals that, as in the previous experiments, only male subjects became more entrapped under Competitive than under Noncompetitive conditions (simple effect: $F(1,41) = 4.38$, $p < .05$). Females showed a marginal tendency to become more entrapped in the Noncompetitive condition than in the Competitive (simple effect: $F(1,41) = 3.11$, $p < .10$).

The interaction was basically similar to the Sex × Social/Nonsocial interaction effect obtained in the previous experiment. In both studies males exhibited significantly greater entrapment in the Competitive (Social) than Noncompetitive (Nonsocial) condition; females' behavior was unaffected by this factor. There were, however, some differences in the two sets of results that should at least be noted. In both studies: (1) men became more entrapped than women under Competitive (Social) conditions, and (2) women were more

Table 5-2. Mean Amount Invested as a Function of Sex of Subject and Relationship with Other Person (Source: Rubin, Brockner, Small-Weil, & Nathanson, "Factors affecting entry into psychological traps," *Journal of Conflict Resolution*, 24 [1980], Experiment 2. Copyright © 1980 by Sage Publications, Inc. Reprinted by permission of Sage Publications, Inc.)

Relationship with Other Person	Sex of Subject	
	Male	Female
Competitive	$1.35	$1.08
Non-competitive	$0.60	$1.71

Note: Scores could range from $0.00 to $2.50, with higher scores reflecting greater entrapment.

entrapped than men under Noncompetitive (Nonsocial) conditions. In the earlier study the former comparison was statistically significant while the latter was not. In the present experiment males did not spend significantly more than females in the Competitive condition ($F < 1$); however, females did become significantly more entrapped than males in the Noncompetitive condition ($F(1,41) = 9.57, p < .01$).

Sex Differences

Although the Sex of subject variable was not expected to interact with the Social variable, it nevertheless appears to be a highly reliable effect. In the three studies reported thus far it was found that the socially competitive decision structure caused only males to exhibit a high degree of entrapment. Specifically, in three out of three instances (Rubin et al., 1980, Experiments 1 and 2; Teger, 1980) male decision makers became significantly more entrapped in the Social (Competitive) than in the Nonsocial (Noncompetitive) condition. In the two instances in which such comparisons were possible (Rubin et al, 1980, Experiments 1 and 2) the degree of entrapment of females did not differ significantly as a function of the Social–Nonsocial variable. Moreover, in both of the studies by Rubin et al., men became more entrapped than did women under Social conditions, although this difference was not significant in the second study.

The results of several other studies by Teger (1980)—primarily designed to address other empirical issues—are also germane. In two studies he included conditions in which the behavior of individual (rather than teams of) males was compared to that of individual female decision makers in the Dollar Auction game (which is obviously a social type of entrapment situation). Based on the data that were just reported, one would expect males to become significantly more entrapped than females. This is precisely what occurred.

Finally, the comparison of men and women under Nonsocial conditions has yielded more ambiguous results. In the two studies performed by Rubin et al., women invested more money than men in the Nonsocial or Noncompetitive condition, and in one of these instances the difference was significant. However, in other studies using Nonsocial methodologies (e.g., the counter game) no sex differences have emerged (e.g., Brockner, Shaw, & Rubin, 1979). Moreover, in one of the Counter Game studies reported in the previous chapter (i.e., in which subjects had to invest with money that they had brought with them to the laboratory, rather than with an initial stake) men became *more* entrapped than did women.

While the Sex × Social–Nonsocial interaction appears to be statistically reliable, the important question is whether it is psychologically or theoretically significant; *why* is the behavior of men, but not women, influenced by the Social–Nonsocial variable? One possibility is that these results are due to sex differences in interpersonal competitiveness. Many writers (e.g., Frost & Wilmot, 1978) have commented that men, more than women, are socialized to compete with others. Theoretically, the males' competitive orientation should be manifested by their greater entrapment in Social (Competitive) than in Nonsocial (Noncompetitive) conditions. The results of one of Teger's (1980) studies are consistent with this reasoning. Teger observed not only that males become more entrapped than females *on the average* when playing the Dollar Auction game, but also that males, but not females, exhibit the "end effect." In other research, Teger has shown that the end effect is largely motivated by decision makers' competitive strivings directed against their opponent.

Other research, however, suggests that it would be misleading simply to explain the results as due to sex differences in competitive orientation. In their exhaustive reviews of sex differences in competition and cooperation, Maccoby and Jacklin (1974) and Rubin and Brown (1975) have concluded that there is little consistency in the studies germane to this issue. In the bargaining literature, in which most of the adult studies of competition and cooperation have been conducted, there have been literally dozens of studies showing (1) men to be more competitive than women, (2) women to be more competitive than men, and (3) no sex differences in competitiveness (Rubin & Brown, 1975).

Before attempting to extrapolate from the voluminous results obtained in bargaining studies to the process of entrapment, we should make explicit that the choices available to decision makers are not exactly equivalent in bargaining methodologies and social entrapment paradigms. To be sure, individuals in both situations have the option to compete (by deciding to maximize their own gains at the expense of the other in the bargaining setting, and by escalating their degree of commitment in the entrapment context). However, the only other option available to individuals is quite different in the two situations. Bargainers have the opportunity to cooperate with one another, whereas participants in a social entrapment situation do not. By choosing to cooperate, bargainers can ensure that both they and the other person can (1) *win*, and (2) win *comparable amounts*. By contrast, there is always a winner and a loser in social entrapment studies. Moreover, it is theoretically possible but in actuality very unlikely, that decision makers' will obtain equal outcomes in an entrapment situation. If their outcomes are equal (such as in the case of two bidders who are willing to invest $2 and $1, respectively, for a dollar bill) they will be negative rather than positive. Whereas bargainers have the opportunity to compete or cooperate, entrapped decision makers have the option of either competing or withdrawing. In short, we are suggesting that the decisional structure of Social entrapment situations—but not bargaining paradigms—renders the former particularly appropriate to the measurement of interpersonal aggression, in which the individual deliberately intends to harm another.

The possibility that Social entrapment situations may be construed more appropriately as measures of aggression, rather than competition versus cooperating, is not trivial. Although sex differences are not consistently obtained on measures of competition/cooperation, it has been shown across a wide variety of settings and measures that men are generally more aggressive than women (Maccoby & Jacklin, 1974). In short, we are speculating that the tendency for males to become more entrapped than females in the Social (but not Nonsocial) entrapment situation is a manifestation of a more general tendency for males to behave more aggressively than females.

This speculation stimulates two related questions; first, what is the more precise nature of this aggression? Aggression scholars (e.g., Bandura, 1973) have noted that aggressive behavior can have a variety of underlying motivations. In some instances aggression stems from the aggressor's intent to inflict harm on another for its own sake. In other situations aggression may be *instrumental* in helping the aggressor to achieve some desired outcome. It is our conjecture that the competitiveness exhibited by males in Social entrapment situations is an example of instrumental aggression, rather than aggression for its own sake. Consistent with this conjecture, Maccoby & Jacklin (1974) have noted: "In view of what is known about sex differences in aggression, we would expect men to be more competitive than women in those situations in which aggression toward the opponent plays an especially strong role" (in producing positive outcomes for the competitor).

Second, if males' greater escalation in Social entrapment situations is a manifestation of instrumental aggression, what are the mediating processes? In many potentially conflictual social encounters the disputants' behavior may be influenced by two classes of variables: (1) as discussed in Chapter 4, variables related to maximizing financial or material outcomes clearly can affect behavior; (2) as pointed out in this chapter, a variety of interpersonal factors, quite independent of material payoffs, can also be influential.

This distinction between task or material versus interpersonal cues as determinants of social behavior may be quite useful in explaining why males' degree of entrapment was influenced to a greater extent by the Social/ Nonsocial variable than females'. Deaux (1976), Rubin and Brown (1975), Strodtbeck and Mann (1956), and others have pointed out that men and women are differentially sensitive to these cues. In particular, males more than females tend to be interested in, and responsive to, variables pertaining to maximizing their material outcomes. The bargaining literature lends considerable support to this conjecture. When it is to the bargainer's material advantage to cooperate rather than to compete (such as in most versions of the Prisoner's Dilemma game), males behave more cooperatively than do females. Just the opposite occurs, however, when it is materially wise to compete rather than cooperate (Rubin & Brown, 1975). This greater tendency of males to act in an outcome-maximizing manner was also found in entrapment research described in the previous chapter (Rubin, 1978a). Specifically, as the value of the jackpot increased in the Counter Game procedure, the males' degree of entrapment showed a nearly perfect monotonic increase. The behavior of women, however, was far less predictable as a function of the value of the goal.

Females are more influenced than are males by the nonmaterial, interpersonal cues—an assertion that is once again lent support by the bargaining literature. Kahn, Hottes, and Davis (1971) reported that women, but not men, bargained more cooperatively when their opposite sex opponent was physically attractive rather than unattractive. In another study, Hottes and Kahn (1974) had their same sex partners meet and talk with each other after they had bargained for some time. Content analyses of these conversations were consistent with the present position. Men typically discussed their bargaining strategies, and how to maximize better their joint outcomes; as a result, their joint payoffs subsequent to the conversation increased. Women rarely discussed strategy. Instead, they talked of non-game-related issues (e.g., roommates) or their general level of interest or disinterest in the bargaining procedure. Consequently, they showed little change in their game behavior.

We suspect that the tendency for males, but not females, to be differentially responsive in the Social and Nonsocial conditions is related to the males' greater sensitivity to task or materialistic rather than interpersonal cues. Note that in the Nonsocial versions of the experimental paradigm for entrapment, it is not a "good bet" to start investing. For example, in the Rubin et al. (1980) Counter Game procedure, the initial stake was worth $5 and the jackpot was set at $3. The probability of goal attainment was simply described as "good," but no further details were provided that would enable decision makers to calculate the likelihood of winning the jackpot. Under these conditions, subjects attentive to economic considerations probably reasoned that it was not wise to invest much. In order for the expected value of investing to be positive, the actual probability of goal attainment had to be slightly more than 80%. (This was calculated as follows. Let us suppose that the probability of winning the $3.00 jackpot was set at 5/6 or 83%. If so, then the expected value of the jackpot payoff is equal to 5/6 times ($3.00) or $2.50. Subjects were only allowed to "buy" 500 units on the counter. So, if the jackpot was hit, then in theory it should "hit" at 250, i.e., the point halfway in between 0 and 500. At this (break-even) point subjects would have to pay $2.50 to win a prize whose expected value was also $2.50. Thus, it would be economically sound to start investing in the Counter Game only if the perceived probability of hitting the jackpot was at least 5/6.) If the decision makers perceived that the likelihood of hitting the jackpot was less than 5/6, as many probably did, then they should have concluded that it was not appropriate to invest, or least not to invest much of their resources.

In the Social versions of the entrapment paradigms, however, the expected values are even more difficult to estimate. This is because under such conditions the likelihood of goal attainment does not depend on objective laws of probability. Rather, it depends solely on the perceived likelihood of being able to invest more than the other person. Male, but not female, subjects may have believed that the best or only way to maximize their outcomes in the Social entrapment situations was to invest their resources. After all, they may have reasoned, if their opponent backs down, they stand to be the "winner." Moreover, they might have inferred that their opponent was quite likely to quit if they did not. Thus, we are suggesting that the high degree of commitment shown by males (but not females) in the Social conditions was not the result of aggressing against or punishing their opponent *for its own sake*. Rather, the males' highly variable behavior between the Social and Nonsocial conditions may have reflected their differential beliefs about the actions that were necessary for them to take in order to win money in the two conditions. It is in this sense that their game behavior was *instrumentally* aggressive.

The above analysis assumes that men and women differ in the cues to which they are most responsive in entrapment (and other kinds of decision making) situations. While this may be true in general, it is also undoubtedly true that there is variability in the extent to which individuals (particularly college students) subscribe to these cultural sex-role stereotypes. That is, contrary to the stereotype, some men may be more attentive to the interpersonal environment than to the economics of the decision-making task. Also contrary to the stereotype, some women may be more likely to adopt the stereotypically "masculine" mindset of responsiveness to task rather than to social characteristics.

In the past decade psychologists have conceptualized about the causes and consequences of individual differences in sex-role orientation. To facilitate empirical research on these issues, several individual difference measures of sex-role orientation have made their way into the literature (e.g., Bem, 1974; Spence & Helmreich, 1972). By classifying individuals on these dimensions, researchers have shown that male and female variations in behavior formerly attributed to the amorphous construct of "sex differences" can be more clearly explained by a psychological difference: sex-role orientation (e.g., Bem & Lenney, 1976). Thus, an individual who subscribes to a cross-sex, rather than same-sex, orientation should exhibit behavioral manifestations more consistent with cross, rather than same, sex.

In the present studies, males may have varied their entrapment behavior as a function of the Social–Nonsocial variable because of their greater responsivity to task/economic cues than to interpersonal cues. If so, then two implications follow: (1) males more attentive to interpersonal cues should *not* be affected by the Social–Nonsocial variable, just as females in general were not, and (2) females more concerned with task cues *should* be more influenced by the

Social–Nonsocial variable, just as males in general were. In order to evaluate these possibilities, we administered the Interpersonal Orientation Scale developed by Swap and Rubin (1983) to participants in the first experiment performed by Rubin et al. (1980).

Interpersonal Orientation

Interpersonal Orientation (IO) was originally proposed by Rubin and Brown (1975) as an individual difference factor that could help explain a set of seemingly inconsistent findings in the bargaining literature. According to Rubin and Brown (1975), the person who is located near the upper end of the dimension is an individual "who is, first and foremost, responsive to the interpersonal aspects of his relationship with the other. He is both interested in, and reactive to, variations in the other's behavior" (p. 158). In contrast, the low IO individual "is characterized, first and foremost, by a nonresponsiveness to interpersonal aspects of his relationship with the other. His interest is neither in cooperating nor competing with the other, but rather in maximizing his own gain—pretty much regardless of how the other fares" (p. 159).

The IO scale has two major components: (1) *Responsivity*, that is, 13 items measuring the extent to which a person responds emotionally and/or behaviorally to another's actions which directly affect the subject ("I am very sensitive to criticism"; "The more other people reveal about themselves, the more inclined I feel to reveal things about myself"; "I can be strongly affected by someone smiling or frowning at me"), and (2) *Interpersonal Interest*, that is, 10 items measuring interest in what other people are like (e.g., "I am interested in what makes people tick"; "Sitting on a bus or subway, I sometimes imagine what the person sitting next to me does for a living").

Swap and Rubin (1983) report a consistent, highly significant sex difference in IO, with women scoring higher than men. The relevance of IO to sex differences in entrapment should be clear. Most men should score low in IO, and thus be affected by the Social–Nonsocial variable for the economic reasons discussed previously. Most women should fall high on the dimension; because maximizing outcomes is of lesser concern to them, the Social–Nonsocial variable should have little effect on their behavior. Finally, the remaining minority of individuals (whose IO is "incongruent" with their sex) should respond like those of the opposite sex.

The sex difference in IO was also observed in the present study, $t(87) = 2.44$, $p < .025$. Closer analysis revealed, however, that this difference was due to the items measuring Responsivity rather than Interpersonal Interest. (The t-test on the Responsivity subscale was significant $[t(87) = 2.37$, $p < .025]$, whereas it did not even approach significance on the Interest subscale $[t < 1]$.) Given that our theoretical analysis of sex differences in entrapment behavior necessitates that the sexes differ along the underlying dimension, we only employed subjects' ratings on the Responsivity subscale in subsequent analyses.

Table 5-3. Mean Amount Invested as a Function of Subject Sex, Subject Responsivity, and Type of Opponent (Source: Rubin, Brockner, Small-Weil, & Nathanson, "Factors affecting entry into psychological traps," *Journal of Conflict Resolution*, 24 [1980], Experiment 1. Copyright © 1980 by Sage Publications, Inc. Reprinted by permission of Sage Publications, Inc.)

		Sex of Subject	
Subject Responsivity	Type of Opponent	Male	Female
High	Social	$2.11	$2.23
	Non-social	$1.83	$1.70
Low	Social	$3.96	$1.03
	Non-social	$1.02	$1.75

Note: Scores could range from $0.00 to $5.00, with higher scores reflecting greater entrapment.

A median split was used to classify subjects as high or low in Responsivity. A three-factor (Responsivity $\times$ Sex $\times$ Social–Nonsocial) unweighted-means analysis was then performed on the mean amount invested by condition. Of course, the already reported main effect for the Social–Nonsocial variable and the Sex $\times$ Social–Nonsocial interaction were significant. Of greatest importance was the significant triple interaction effect, $F(1,81) = 6.05$, $p < .025$. As can be seen in Table 5-3, it was the Low Responsivity males who were most influenced by the Social–Nonsocial variable. The men who were also high in Responsivity—i.e., the ones whose Responsivity scores were sex-incongruent—did not show differential entrapment in the two conditions. A simple interaction effect for the males, comparing the effect of the Social–Nonsocial variable on these two groups, was statistically significant, $F(1,81) = 5.60$, $p < .025$. The females' behavior, in contrast, did not differ as a function of the Responsivity and Social–Nonsocial variables (simple interaction $F(1,81) = 1.24$). To state the triple interaction effect differently, for those subjects (63%) whose responsivity scores were "congruent" with their sex, the Sex $\times$ Social–Nonsocial interaction was significant, $F(1,81) = 4.60$, $p < .05$. For the remaining subjects, however, the interaction was not significant, $F < 1$.

In sum, there is some support for the notion that sex differences in response to the Social–Nonsocial variable may be mediated by the extent to which the decision maker is responsive to interpersonal or task cues. Only those men who were less attentive to social cues (and thus, we assume, more responsive to task qualities) were more entrapped in the Social than in the Nonsocial conditions.

What still needs to be explained, however, is why Low Responsivity females did not respond like Low Responsivity males. First, it may be that there were not enough Low Responsivity females to give the hypothesis a fair test. Only 33% (15 out of 46) of the women were so classified. Furthermore, the Responsivity scores of these few women were somewhat, though not significantly ($p < .20$), higher than of the men classified as low in Responsivity. (The mean Responsivity scores of the two sexes who scored high on the dimension were practically identical.) Second, it may be necessary, as the present results suggest, to explore the joint or interactive effects of sex and sex-role orientation on behavior. For example, a male's low Responsivity may mean something that is very different from a female's low Responsivity. There certainly is an abundance of evidence in the person-perception literature (e.g., Deaux, 1976) that sex-linked traits and behaviors are not judged by absolute standards, but *in relation to* the sex of the target person. Thus a female's dependency may be perceived differently than a male's, or a male's tendency to self-disclose may be viewed differently from a female's.

Finally, it may also be that taking sex-role orientation into account will eliminate some, but not all, of the differences in behavior of men and women. More specifically, Swap and Rubin (1983) studied reward allocation patterns of men and women. Previous research showed that when sex differences had been obtained, men divided rewards according to equity principles (in which outcomes were allocated in proportion to inputs) whereas women used equality principles (in which each person's reward was equal, independent of inputs). Swap and Rubin replicated the procedure of previous research by including IO as an additional independent variable, and expected to find that IO would account for the previously obtained sex difference. In fact, low IOs were more guided by equity than were high IOs, regardless of sex. However, there was still a significant sex effect, consistent with the previous research. Moveover, sex and IO operated in an additive rather than interactive fashion, so that low-IO males behaved most equitably and high-IO females most equally. Clearly, further research is needed to delineate the effects of sex and interpersonal orientation on entrapment behavior.

Attraction, Aggression, and Entrapment

The studies just discussed demonstrated that decision makers' level of entrapment was significantly influenced by the Social/Nonsocial variable. This finding gives rise to a related question: given that an entrapment situation is social, will attributes of the opposing party influence decision maker' actions? The purpose of this section is to discuss the handful of experiments that have explored the effect of opponents' characteristics on entrapment.

The independent variables in all of these studies were factors that probably affected subjects' liking for their opponent. For example, Teger (1980) reported that subjects became more entrapped in the Dollar Auction when participating against an opponent who was dissimilar rather than similar to themselves. In two experiments, subjects were characterized along a dimension that was particularly salient to college students at the time that the study was conducted (in the early 1970s). More specifically, subjects were rated by the experimenter along a "freak–jock" dimension. "Freaks" were more likely to wear long hair and faded jeans, whereas "jocks" were more apt to wear short hair and to dress conservatively. In one study freaks exhibited greater entrapment, whereas in a second study, jocks showed greater entrapment. In the former study, however, the confederate opponent was a jock, whereas in the latter he was a freak. These results suggest that personal similarity with (and perhaps liking for) one's opponent is inversely related to entrapment.

The effect of the similarity variable was only correlational in these studies, in that subjects were not randomly assigned to compete against a similar or dissimilar opponent. In a related study, Teger (1980) did experimentally vary the opponent's characteristics, in a manner that probably influenced subjects' liking for the opponent. Before bidding in a Dollar Auction against their confederate opponent, (male) subjects took part in a modified Prisoner's Dilemma game with the confederate. In half of the cases the confederate behaved exploitatively; that is, his choices enabled him to win only a little more money than he would have won if he had behaved cooperatively, while simultaneously costing the subject a relatively large amount of money (Instigation condition). The other half of the subjects participated against a noninstigating confederate (No Instigation condition). Subjects were much more likely to compete against the confederate in the subsequent Dollar Auction (and as a result, became much more entrapped) in the Instigation than in the No Instigation condition.

It is interesting to note that the effect of the Instigation manipulation was significantly reduced when, prior to its occurrence, subjects performed a vigorous, bicycle-pedaling exercise. By way of explanation, Teger suggests that subjects who had performed the exercise may have (1) been distracted by the exercise from their instigation-produced annoyance with the confederate, and/ or (2) attributed their instigation-produced arousal to the exercise, and as a result felt less annoyed by the instigation.

The fact that the exercise-produced arousal reduced the effect of the confederate's instigation is consistent with our earlier speculation that social entrapment situations may operationalize aggressive behavior. In the aggression literature, it has been shown that instigation-produced anger (and subsequent aggression) can be reduced by leading individuals to attribute their arousal to a nonemotionally laden source. For example, Younger and Doob (1978) had subjects ingest placebo pills shortly before they were emotionally provoked by (i.e., instigated to aggress against) the confederate. Half of the subjects were led to believe that the pill would increase their level of physiological arousal (Arousal condition), whereas the other half were led to believe that it would relax them (Relaxation condition). In essence, subjects in the Arousal condition were led to believe that the pill would produce physiological symptoms similar to those caused by the anger instigation, whereas those in the Relaxation condition were led to believe that the pill-produced symptoms would be directly contrary to those caused by the instigation. Thus, subjects in the former condition should have been much more primed to misattribute the cause of their instigation-produced arousal to the placebo. In fact, subjects behaved much less aggressively toward the instigating confederate in the Arousal than in the Relaxation condition.

Note the similarities between the Younger and Doob (1978) and Teger (1980) experiments. In both instances subjects were provided with a non-emotional alternative explanation for their arousal (i.e., exercise, placebo pills). In the Younger and Doob experiment this had the effect of reducing aggression. In the Teger study it had the effect of reducing escalation in the Dollar Auction. Thus, at least under certain circumstances (e.g., following a prior instigation), social-entrapment situations may provide vehicles through which decision makers can express aggressive behavior.

A third study performed in our own laboratory (Rubin & Samuelson, 1980) further suggests that attraction toward one's opponent can affect the decision maker's degree of entrapment. In this study male and female subjects received false personality feedback about their confederate opponent before bidding in a Dollar Auction against the confederate. Both the subject and confederate had completed a "Personal Opinion Survey," which consisted of a subset of items from the Mach V scale developed by Christie and Geis (1970). They were then asked to exchange their responses before the Dollar Auction began. In the Attractive condition the confederate described himself in a likeable fashion. He agreed with statements like, "To help oneself is good; to help others, even better," and "Honesty is the best policy in all cases," and disagreed with statements like, "Barnum was right when he said there's a sucker born every minute," and "There are very few people in the world worth caring about." In the Unattractive condition the confederate presented himself more negatively, responding to the statements in the exact opposite fashion relative to the Attractive condition.

Post-experimental questionnaire results revealed that the confederate was, in fact, perceived much more negatively in the Unattractive than in the Attractive condition. Specifically, subjects rated the confederate as significantly more competitive, intimidating, aggressive, confident, angry, unfriendly, and determined in the former than in the latter condition. In the Dollar Auction, subjects also invested much more of their resources against the Unattractive than Attractive opponent ($p < .01$).

Taken together, the results of these three studies suggest that decision makers' attitude toward their opponents may well affect their degree of commitment in Social entrapment situations. Subjects invested more when they were personally dissimilar to their opponent, when the opponent provoked them by behaving competitively in a prior encounter, and when the opponent appeared to have a manipulative (machiavellian) outlook on life. Future research should delineate the effects of the other's characteristics, as well as the nature of the relationship between the decision maker and opponent, on escalating commitment in Social entrapment situations. If, as the present studies suggest, liking decreases entrapment while anger increases it, then useful leads for further research may be found in the vast social-psychological literature on interpersonal attraction and aggression. For example, what effect does the presence or absence of anticipated future interaction with one's opponent (e.g., Tyler & Sears, 1977) have on entrapment? Will decision makers become more entrapped against an opponent who has instigated them to aggress, and who, in other, more subtle ways, has become associated with aggression-eliciting stimuli (e.g., Berkowitz & LePage, 1967)? These are some of the many questions which should be addressed by further research.

Modeling and Entrapment

A point emphasized throughout this book is that entrapped decision makers experience considerable conflict about whether to persist in or withdraw from their previously chosen course of action. Several factors contribute to their conflictual state. In Chapter 1, for example, we spoke of the "driving" forces toward persistence versus the restraining forces toward withdrawal with which the entrapped individual must simultaneously cope. As also mentioned in Chapter 1, in all entrapment situations it is uncertain if and when individuals will be able to achieve their goal. Thus, not only is conflict produced by the opposition of driving versus restraining forces, but also by the person's sense of not knowing whether persistence or withdrawal is the wiser course of action. When faced with these types of uncertainty, and when there are no clear objective guidelines to be followed, what can the decision maker do? According to social comparison theory (Festinger, 1954) it is precisely under such conditions of uncertainty that people will regard the behavior of others as a guide to how they themselves should behave (Gerard & Rabbie, 1961).

Social comparison theory further posits that observers should be most attentive to the actions taken by others who are facing (or have faced) the same predicament as the observers. Thus, owners of old cars that too frequently need repair may seek the advice of trusted friends or colleagues who have owned old jalopies themselves. If other people have junked their cars, then observers may be more likely to get rid of theirs. Or, a company that has "too much invested to quit" in a failing product or service may wish to observe the actions taken by its competitors. If the competition abandons that product or service, then the company may be more likely to follow suit.

The research described in this section attempts to determine the extent to which the presence or absence of an entrapped other affects one's own degree of entrapment by serving as a model for "correct" behavior. Of course, the notion that individuals often imitate another's behavior is hardly novel; it has served as a cornerstone for much research in social, developmental, and organizational psychology (e.g., Bandura, 1977; Manz & Sims, 1981). Indeed, it is the very pervasiveness of modeling that led us to speculate about its importance as a social determinant of entrapment. Given that the most appropriate course of action in an entrapment situation is often ambiguous at best, and that people are most apt to engage in social comparison when faced with this type of uncertainty, entrapping conflict situations may provide particularly fertile ground for modeling effects.

Five studies are presented. The first three studies were designed to demonstrate that modeling effects can in fact occur in entrapping conflicts. Experiments 4 and 5 sought to determine possible boundary conditions for such modeling effects. In Experiment 4 the notion was explored that observers will not only attend to the model's behavior, but also to the model's labels or perceptions of his or her behavior. A model who acts in a certain manner, but expresses remorse in doing so, may produce a "reverse" modeling effect, in which the observer behaves in a manner directly contrary to the model's behavior. In Experiment 5 it was hypothesized that decision makers would be more apt to imitate the actions taken by an attractive, likeable model than an unattractive one. It is important to keep in mind that these experiments are not primarily concerned with modeling per se, but rather with modeling processes as a vehicle for better understanding the social psychology of the entrapped decision maker.

Experiment 1

The first experiment was designed to test the hypothesis that the presence of an entrapped model can increase a decision maker's degree of entrapment. In order to test this modeling hypothesis, it is of course necessary for some subjects to participate in a condition in the absence of an entrapped model. Thus, subjects took part in an entrapping conflict either in the absence (Alone condition) or presence of a model who became (and remained) entrapped. Half of the subjects in the Present conditions were led to believe that their and the model's outcomes were independent (Model condition). The remaining half were told that only one person could win the valued prize (Competitive condition). It was expected that subjects would become more entrapped in the Model than in the Alone condition. A subsidiary hypothesis, based upon the results presented earlier in this chapter, is that the male subjects in the Competitive condition would also exhibit a high degree of entrapment, relative to females.

Method. Subjects were 84 male and female undergraduate volunteers at Tufts University, who were randomly assigned to one of the six experimental conditions in this 3×2 factorial design (Experimental Condition $\times$ Sex of Subject). The Jigsaw Puzzle paradigm described in Chapter 2 was employed. Upon their arrival at the laboratory subjects were seated at a table in a cubicle, either alone or in the presence of a male confederate. On the table lay a set of written instructions and $4, which was the subject's pay for agreeing to read through the instructions. The experiment was described as a study of jigsaw puzzle problem solving, in which it would be possible to win a $10 jackpot.

In the Alone condition subjects were told that this jackpot would be awarded if the jigsaw puzzle could be completely solved in 15 minutes or less. Subjects in the Model and Competitive conditions were told that the two people in the room (the subject and confederate) had been given different, though equally difficult, jigsaw puzzles to solve; in addition, Model condition subjects were told that one person's winning the jackpot, by solving the puzzle within 15 minutes, would have no effect on how well the other could do. Competitive condition subjects were told that only the *first* person to solve the puzzle in 15 minutes would win the jackpot.

All subjects (and whenever appropriate, the confederate) were given the completed outline of the puzzle in order to give them some idea of the task before them. They were told that they could ask for as many of the (40) missing puzzle pieces as often as they liked, and that it would cost them nothing to obtain these pieces *provided that they managed to complete the puzzle in 15 minutes.* If they failed to complete the puzzle, however, either because time expired or because they decided to quit the experiment (something that they could do at any time), they would be asked to pay 10 cents for each piece that they had requested.

During the 15-minute session, the confederate was instructed to follow an identical program in the Model and Competitive conditions, requesting several pieces initially, and 10 additional pieces every 30 seconds until, at the end of the fourth minute, he asked for all of the remaining pieces. The puzzle itself was designed to be too difficult for people to solve in 15 minutes.

How can this experimental situation be characterized as entrapping? Note that subjects had to pay for the puzzle pieces that they requested if (and only if) they could not complete the puzzle within 15 minutes. Also, the puzzle had been deliberately made very difficult. By quitting after requesting some, but not all, of the pieces (which they were always free to do) they could retain the remaining portion of their initial stake. For example, take the case of individuals who have requested 20 pieces, but of course have not yet completed the puzzle. What is the nature of their conflict? On the one hand they may be motivated to withdraw and keep the $2.00 remaining in their initial stake, especially if they do not believe that they can complete the puzzle in time. On the other hand, by quitting they will automatically lose the $2.00 that they have already spent, as well as any opportunity to win the jackpot.

Results. The primary measure of entrapment was the total amount of money subjects spent from their $4.00 initial stake. This amount was determined by multiplying 10 cents times the number of pieces that the subject had requested. The overall mean ($3.67) was quite high, suggesting that subjects were very involved with the task. A two factor (Condition $\times$ Sex) unweighted means analysis revealed only a marginally significant Treatment effect, $F(2,78) = 2.95$, $p < .06$. As shown in Table 5-4, subjects were least entrapped in the Alone condition, relative to the Model and Competitive conditions. The degree of entrapment in the latter two conditions was practically identical.

In sum, this experiment provided initial evidence that the presence of an entrapped model can enhance a decision maker's own degree of entrapment. Several unexpected findings did emerge, however. The Competitive condition did not produce an entrapment effect beyond that which was obtained in the Model condition. Given that the results of the studies in the preceding section

Table 5-4. Mean Amount Invested by Condition (Source: Brockner, Nathanson, et al. [1984], Experiment 1)

Alone (29)	Model (25)	Competitive (30)
$3.42	$3.82	$3.78

Note: Scores could range from $0.00 to $4.00, with higher scores reflecting greater entrapment. Cell Ns are in parentheses.

showed that men become more entrapped than women under Competitive than Noncompetitive conditions, this (non-) effect appears surprising. Perhaps a "ceiling effect" analysis may most parsimoniously account for the failure of the Competitive structure to enhance further the males' degree of entrapment. Even in the Alone condition, subjects spent a large percentage of their initial stake. The Model condition produced a significant increment in entrapment, but there was little room for a further significant increase in the Competitive condition.

The other unpredicted result was that most subjects, regardless of condition, invested all of their initial stake. Thus, the modeling effect was a bit weak, especially given that (1) nearly 30 subjects were run in each of the three treatment conditions, and (2) a significance level of only .06 was obtained.

Experiment 2

In order to strengthen the modeling manipulation, several procedural modifications were introduced in the second experiment. First, as opposed to subjects being exposed to an entrapped model or not, as in the previous experiment, all subjects were put in the presence of a model. For half of the subjects the model escalated her degree of commitment (Increasing Commitment condition), whereas for the other half she steadily deescalated her commitment and ultimately terminated her involvement in the situation (Decreasing Commitment condition). Second, it may have been that subjects in general spent most of their initial stake because the value of the jackpot was relatively high ($10). In previous experimentation (Rubin, 1978a), for example, it was shown that decision makers were more likely to commit their resources in direct proportion to the value of the goal. If most subjects in the first study tended to be "drawn" by the attractive jackpot, then the modeling manipulation would have had less of a chance to exert influence on their behavior. Therefore, in the second experiment the value of the goal was set at a relatively low level ($2.00). Also, in order to increase the range of the dependent variable, a puzzle with 84 rather than 40 pieces was employed.

Method. Subjects were 42 undergraduate students (23 male, 19 female) from an introductory psychology class who received course credit for participating. In most respects the procedure employed was virtually identical to the Model condition of Experiment 1. Subjects were given the same initial stake of $4, were seated at a table (this time) with a female confederate, and were given written instructions that described the jigsaw puzzle problem-solving task.

Subjects were given 15 minutes to solve the jigsaw puzzle, and were told that they would be charged 5 cents (rather than 10 cents) for each of the puzzle pieces they requested—unless they managed to complete the puzzle within the time limit. As in Experiment 1, if they quit they would pay for the number of pieces purchased and retain the remaining portion of their initial stake. As in the Model condition of the preceding experiment, subjects were told:

> You will each be given a different jigsaw puzzle to solve, so that whether you win the $2 jackpot or not will have no effect on how well the other person does, and vice versa. You can both win, you can both lose, or one can lose the jackpot while the other does not.

In both the Increasing and Decreasing commitment condition the confederate requested 10 puzzle pieces at the outset and 15 additional pieces after 1 minute had elapsed. At this point the two conditions diverged. In the Increasing commitment condition the confederate requested 10, then 15, and then 15 more pieces after lapses of 1 minute each, before requesting all of the remaining pieces. Conversely, in the Decreasing commitment condition the confederate asked for 5, then 5 more, and yet another 5 pieces before finally announcing that she had decided to quit the experiment. At this point the confederate was asked to complete a postexperimental questionnaire and to wait quietly until the subject had finished. The subject, in turn, upon finishing the puzzle or announcing a decision to quit, was asked to complete a questionnaire that asked for a series of ratings on 9-point bipolar scales. These questions tapped (among other things) their perceptions of the other person.

Results. The data of the two subjects who quit at the outset, and thus were not exposed to the Model manipulation, were not included in any of the analyses. There were two important behavioral dependent variables. As in Experiment 1, the primary measure of entrapment was the total amount of money spent. This figure was determined by multiplying the number of pieces that the subject had requested times 5 cents. Thus, scores could range from $0 to $4.20. Second, unlike in Experiment 1 we recorded the mean number of jigsaw puzzle pieces subjects requested each time that they asked the experimenter for additional pieces. If subjects exhibit a modeling effect, then they should ask for more pieces per request in the Increasing Commitment condition, in which the model's requests grew larger, than in the Decreasing Commitment condition, in which the magnitude of her requests decreased over time.

The modeling hypothesis received firm support on both behavioral measures. A two-factor (Sex $\times$ Model's Commitment) unweighted means analysis revealed a main effect for the Modeling variable, $F(1,38) = 5.38$, $p < .05$. As predicted, subjects became more entrapped in the Increasing ($M = \$3.77$) than in the Decreasing ($M = \$3.10$) condition. The Sex main effect and the interaction effect were trivial (both $Fs < 1$).

The mean amount that subjects invested is an outcome measure. As the modeling hypothesis predicted, subjects exposed to a model who increased her degree of commitment and remained entrapped to the end engendered greater entrapment than did the model who gradually decreased her degree of commitment and ultimately withdrew from the situation. The outcome measure, however, revealed nothing about the *process* by which subjects came to be entrapped or not. In theory, it was possible for subjects to request all of the puzzle pieces at the outset and then work on the puzzle for the 15-minute duration. Very few participants ($N = 3$) chose this option, perhaps because the model asked for her pieces sequentially, rather than all at once.

The remaining 39 participants made two or more requests for puzzle pieces, after being exposed to the model's requests. It is thus important to know if the magnitude of these 39 subjects' requests was influenced by the size of the model's. For all participants, we computed the mean number of pieces for which they had asked on each request. A Sex $\times$ Model Commitment analysis of variance revealed a highly significant Modeling effect, $F(1,35) = 8.84, p < .01$. As expected, subjects asked for more pieces per request in the Increasing ($M = 17.47$) than in the Decreasing Condition ($M = 11.03$). The sex main effect was not significant ($F < 1$). The interaction effect was marginally significant, $F(1,35) = 3.62, p < .07$, such that the modeling effect was somewhat stronger for male, rather than female subjects.

Questionnaire data. As in most studies subjects completed a postexperimental questionnaire; in particular, they were asked to make a number of self- and other ratings after working on the jigsaw puzzle. A number of Model Commitment main effects were obtained. Specifically it was found that subjects in the Increasing Commitment condition rated the confederate as more confident ($p < .001$) and more competitive ($p < .05$) than did those in the Decreasing condition. Moreover, Increasing condition subjects rated themselves as more interested in the performance of the "other participant" while they were working on the jigsaw puzzle ($p < .025$), and reported feeling that they were being 'watched/observed by the experimenter to a greater extent ($p < .025$) than did their Decreasing Condition counterparts. These findings suggest that although the subject and confederate were in fact told that their outcomes were independent, those in the Increasing Model Commitment condition may have felt like they were in a competitive relationship, replete with special interest in their adversary's behavior and the belief that their own (competitive?) behavior was under the experimenter's evaluative scrutiny.

If this conjecture is accurate, then it may provide another interpretation of our failure to obtain behavioral differences in the Model and Competitive conditions in the previous experiment (in which the confederate always showed increasing commitment). It had been suggested previously that the Competitive condition could not produce a further increase beyond that obtained in the Model condition because of a ceiling effect. An alternative possibility is that subjects may have felt some degree of competition even in the Model condition, in which the subjects' and confederate's outcomes were defined as independent. Thus, the "modeling" effect discussed in the preceding experiment, in which subjects became more entrapped in the Model and Competitive conditions than in the Alone treatment, may have also been, at least in part, a "competition" effect. The resolution of this ambiguity must await further research.

Experiment 3

The questionnaire data from Experiment 2 implied that subjects in the Increasing Model Commitment condition may have experienced some degree of competition with the other person, even though their financial outcomes were actually independent. Thus, the behavioral outcome—that decision makers became more entrapped in the Increasing than in the Decreasing condition— may have been due to modeling and/or interpersonal competition. There was a clear matching effect on the process measure of investment; subjects' requests for puzzle pieces were larger in the Increasing than in the Decreasing condition.

It should be mentioned that modeling-based and competition-based explanations of entrapped decision makers' behavior are not mutually exclusive. That is, individuals may exhibit greater entrapment in Social rather than Nonsocial due to the effect of interpersonal competition; however, within this context, modeling could still serve as the entrapment-engendering process. Said differently, even if the entrapping conflict were Social or Competitive rather than Nonsocial or Noncompetitive, individuals may model one another in the process of becoming entrapped. For example, in the arms race (a clear instance of a socially competitive entrapment situation), the United States and the Soviet Union probably study each other's moves, and escalate their own degree of military commitment in proportion to the perceived magnitude of the opponent's increments. To test the notion that modeling can occur even in clearly competitive entrapment situations, subjects participated in a Dollar Auction against a simulated opponent (Brockner, 1977).

Method. Subjects ($N = 109$) were female undergraduates who volunteered to participate in a study on "auction behavior." Pairs of subjects were first brought together in order to receive instructions on how to bid. They were then isolated in individual cubicles, in which they were given (supposedly at random) an initial stake of $2.05 with which to bid for the $1 prize. Subjects were not told the amount of money possessed by their opponent. In order to "minimize face-to-face contact with their opponent," subjects were instructed to bid by written communication. In reality, all subjects were participating against a programmed bidding schedule, in which the "opponent" never quit. This enabled the experimenter to control the magnitude of the bidding increments which the subject received from the opponent.

The effects of two independent variables—Early Bids Size and Late Bids Size—were studied simultaneously. The opponent always made the opening bid. In the Low Early Bids condition "she" (i.e., the program) made an initial bid of 1 cent. In the High Early Bids condition the program's first bid was 15 cents. In the Low Early Bids condition the program continued to make small increments, increasing the subjects' bids by 5 cents, 5 cents, and 1 cent on its next three turns. In the High Early Bids condition the program's subsequent three increments were 10 cents, 10 cents, and 15 cents, respectively. The Late Bids variable was initially manipulated on the program's fifth bid. In the Low Late Bids condition the program's bid was 1 cent, and it continued to make increments of either 1 cent or 5 cents until subjects either quit or had bid away all of their initial stake. In the High Late Bids condition the program made an increment of 15 cents over the subjects' previous bid. From that point until the end of the auction, the program's increments were either 10 cents or 15 cents in the High Late Bids condition. Thus, subjects participated against a programmed opponent who utilized one of four bidding strategies: (1) Low–Low (the opponent's increments were always low), (2) Low–High (the opponent's first four bids were low, but then all of her subsequent increments were high), (3) High–Low (the opponents first four bids were high, but all of her later increments were low), and (4) High–High (in which the opponent always made relatively large increments).

Results. As in Experiment 2, both outcome and process measures of entrapment were collected. Subjects' overall degree of entrapment was very high ($M = \$1.69$), and did not differ as a function of experimental condition. One possible reason that entrapment was high across all conditions was that even in the Low Late Bids condition the "other person" never quit the experiment. By contrast, in Experiment 2 the Decreasing Commitment Model not only made similar and smaller requests for pieces, but also ultimately withdraw from the conflict.

The process measure of entrapment, as in Study II, revealed pronounced modeling effects. Subjects' bidding investments in response to the opponent's first four bids were significantly greater in the High Early Bids ($M = 8.67$ cents) than in the Low Early Bids condition ($M = 5.75$; $t(107) = 3.54$, $p < .001$). All subjects' mean investments on the remaining trials were then computed (i.e., on those bidding turns after the Late Bid manipulation had occurred). Unexpectedly, there were no condition differences as a function of the magnitude of the opponent's Early or Late Bids. Nevertheless, visual inspection of the data suggested that the vast majority of subjects tended to match their opponent, even during the later stages of the bidding. The nonsignificant effect of the magnitude of the opponent's Late Bids was due to a few aberrant subjects in the Low Late Bid condition. These individuals greatly escalated the bidding on several trials, perhaps in an effort to drive out their low-bidding opponent. Not only were such data contrary to the modeling hypothesis, but they also introduced a great deal of within-cell variability into the analysis of variance.

A nonparametric analysis showed that most subjects matched the magnitude of their opponent's increments during both the early and the late stages of

Table 5-5. Number and Percentage of Ss Increasing Bid Increments in the Four Bidding Conditions (Source: Brockner [1977])

Bid Condition	Number of Ss Increasing Increments	Number of Ss Decreasing Increments	Percentage of Ss Increasing Increments
Low-Low	14	13	52%
Low-High	21	5	81%
High-Low	9	18	33%
High-High	13	11	54%

$\chi^2 = 12.2$, $df = 3$, $p < .01$.

the bidding. For each subject we determined whether their mean Late Bid increment was larger or smaller than their mean Early Bid increment. The summary data are reported in Table 5-5. When the magnitude of the increments showed no change (the Low–Low or High–High conditions), subjects were fairly evenly divided into those increasing and those decreasing their level of commitment. When the opponent's increments were Low-High, 81% of the subjects also increased their degree of commitment. Only 33%, however, showed an increase upon exposure to a High–Low opponent. The chi-square comparing the four proportions was highly significant, $\chi^2(3) = 12.2$, $p < .01$).

Experiment 4

This study was designed to replicate and extend the modeling effect, utilizing yet another experimental paradigm. In many potentially entrapping situations, the decision makers are exposed to models who *concurrently* face the same dilemma. Such was the case for subjects in Experiments 1–3. Perhaps just as often, however, decision makers gain information about the behavior of a relevant model *prior* to entering the potential entrapment situation. For example, upon trying to describe whether to spend more money on an additional repair of their old car, decision makers may be influenced by the actions taken by an appropriate model who *has already been through* that dilemma. If that model escalated his or her commitment, observers may be more likely to do so as well. In Experiment 4 all subjects participated in a potentially entrapping investment situation *after* having witnessed the behavior of a model who had just gone through the same situation. It was expected under certain conditions (described below) that this "prior exposure" type of model would also produce imitative behavior.

A second major purpose of Experiment 4 was to delineate some of the conditions under which the modeling effect could be eliminated or even reversed. When prospective decision makers observe a model, they may attend not only to the model's behavior, but also to the model's attitude toward or labeling of the behavior. In some instances models may remark that they are pleased about their chosen course of action, whereas in other instances they may let it be known that they are regretful about their already performed behavior.

Whether the observer imitates the model may well depend upon the model's attitude toward their chosen behavior. If the model's attitude toward their own behavior was positive, rather than negative, then the observer should be more likely to mimic the model's behavior. Why? Research exploring the effects of modeling on aggression (Bandura, 1973) and altruism (Hornstein, 1970) has shown that the extent to which an observer imitates a model's behavior depends upon the perceived consequences for the model of performing that behavior. If the model's consequences are positive (e.g., the model is rewarded) then the observer is more likely to imitate than if the model is punished. By extension, if models label their behavior positively, they are implying that others stand to gain the same positive consequences (i.e., whatever it was that caused them to react favorably) by performing the same behavior. Alternatively, observers either may fail to imitate, or perhaps do just the opposite of models who express negative attitudes toward their behavior.

Optimally, observers should try to learn from the model's mistakes. There are several ways by which the observer may come to view the model's behavior as a mistake. If the observer clearly can see the negative consequences that have befallen the model, then imitative behavior should be less likely to occur. For example, it may have been that the U.S. President and Congress "learned" from their predecessors in the entrapping international conflict in Vietnam not to embark upon a similar course of action in Angola in the mid-1970s. Or, the observer may interpret the model's behavior as a mistake if the model personally labeled it as inappropriate.

A 2×2 (Model's Behavior $\times$ Model's Label of Behavior) factorial design was employed in Experiment 4 in order to test the above notions. Subjects witnessed a model who either became entrapped (High Entrapment Model condition) or not (Low Entrapment Model condition). Furthermore, the model either expressed pleasure (Glad condition) or displeasure (Regret condition) over his chosen course of action. A modeling effect was predicted in the Glad condition, such that subjects should become more entrapped in the High Entrapment than in the Low Entrapment Model condition. In the Regret condition, however, the modeling effect was expected to be significantly reduced or even reversed.

Method. Fifty-two undergraduates (38 female, 14 male) from an introductory psychology class at Tufts University received extra course credit for participating in a study on "Decision Making." (No sex effects were obtained on the dependent variable; thus, this factor will not be considered further.)

In order to verify that the modeling effects obtained in the previous experiments were not dependent upon the use of specific methodologies, a third technique was employed in this and in the subsequent experiment. Upon their arrival at the laboratory, subjects were seated at a table in a research cubicle, opposite to a male confederate, and given instructions for the Counter Game procedure. As in previous experiments, their initial stake and the jackpot values were set at $5.00 and $3.00, respectively. Both the confederate and subject were seated in front of their own counters, which, they were told, were not connected to each other. After the experimenter fully explained the procedure to the two of them, she said, "I've noticed that when I run subjects together in this experiment they tend to influence one another's decisions. So, I'd like to run you one at a time, so that this does not occur. As long as you (pointing to the confederate) were here first, I'll let you go first."

The subject then watched the confederate take part at the task. Under no circumstances did the model win the jackpot. In the High Entrapment Model condition the confederate continued to invest until the counter reached 500. At this point the experimenter reminded him that he had lost all of his initial stake, and thus would have to quit. In the Low Entrapment Model condition the confederate quit when the counter reached 50.

The Model Labeling variable was manipulated immediately thereafter in all conditions. The experimenter asked the confederate to respond verbally (so that subjects could hear) to the following questions (scores could range from 1 to 10, such that higher scores represented more affirmative responses to the questions): (1) To what extent do you think you made the right decision in remaining in the situation for as long (or as short) as you did. (2) To what extent did you feel foolish letting the counter tick for as long as it did? In the Glad condition the confederate responded "9" to the initial question and "2" to the second one. In the Regret condition his responses were "2" and "9," respectively. To strengthen this manipulation, all confederates were then verbally asked a more open-ended question: Would you enter a situation like this again? In the High Entrapment–Glad condition the confederate said, "Yes. It seemed like a good bet and I thought that I had a good chance of winning." In the High Entrapment–Regret condition his response was, "No, I should have quit much earlier. It was a mistake to stay in." In the Low Entrapment–Glad condition the model's response was, "No, I've seen this happen before and I know not to get involved with it." In the Low Entrapment–Regret condition the confederate said, "Yes, I quit too early. I think I could have won if I had stayed longer."

At this point the experimenter dismissed the confederate and asked subjects if they wished to begin. For those who responded affirmatively, the counter was set in motion. The dependent measure, of course, was the amount of the initial stake that subjects were willing to invest.

Results. A 2×2 unweighted-means analysis revealed nonsignificant main effects for both independent variables ($Fs < 1$). There was, however, a highly significant interaction effect, $F(1,48) = 25.81$, $p < .001$. As predicted, and as shown in Table 5-6, there was a markedly pronounced modeling effect within the Glad condition, with decision makers becoming much more entrapped in the High Entrapment than in the Low Entrapment Model condition (simple effect: $F(1,48) = 11.76$, $p < .005$). In the Regret condition, however, a slightly more powerful "reverse modeling" effect was obtained, with decision makers becoming more entrapped in the Low Entrapment than in the High Entrapment

Table 5-6. Mean Amount Invested as a Function of Model's Behavior and Attitude Toward Behavior (Source: Brockner, Nathanson, et al. [1984], Experiment 3)

Model's Degree of Entrapment	Model's Attitude	
	Glad	Regret
High	M = $3.59 SD = 1.47	M = $1.36 SD = 1.36
Low	M = $1.71 SD = 1.16	M = $3.42 SD = 1.55

Note: Scores could range from $0.00 to $5.00, with higher scores reflecting greater entrapment.

Model condition, $F(1,48) = 14.10$, $p < .001$. To state this interaction effect differently, within the High Entrapment condition, individuals invested significantly more of their resources in the Glad than in the Regret condition ($F(1,48) = 16.56, p < .001$). Just the opposite effect was obtained, however, in the Low Entrapment condition ($F(1,48) = 9.70, p < .01$).

Several other aspects of the data are worthy of mention. First, all three subjects who quit at the outset were in the High Entrapment–Regret condition. Unlike in Experiments 1 and 2, it was appropriate to include their results in the statistical analyses because they had been exposed to both of the Modeling manipulations. Perhaps these subjects learned from the mistake of the model by avoiding the entrapping conflict altogether. Second, unlike in almost all entrapment experiments, within-cell variability was quite low. For example, within each of the two conditions in which subjects' degree of entrapment was expected to be relatively low (Low Entrapment–Glad and High Entrapment–Regret) only one subject invested all of his initial stake. The next highest investments in these two conditions were $2.50 and $3.00, respectively. There was also a similar degree of within-cell homogeneity in the two conditions in which subjects tended to become entrapped (High Entrapment–Glad and Low Entrapment–Regret). Apparently, the joint effect of the Model's Behavior and Model's Attitude toward that behavior is quite powerful.

Experiment 5

The results of Experiment 4 clearly suggest one boundary condition for the straightforward modeling effects obtained in Experiments 1–3. Subjects only imitated the model when they perceived that the model was pleased with his behavior in the entrapping dilemma. In fact, they did just the opposite of what the model had done if the model showed remorse over his or her chosen course of action. Experiment 5, like its predecessor, was generally concerned with establishing the conditions under which imitative behavior will and will not be exhibited.

More specifically, modeling effects should be more apt to occur if observers judge the model to be an appropriate comparison person for their own behavior.

Theoretically, a variety of factors can influence the extent to which the model is perceived as a relevant other. For example, social comparison theory (Festinger, 1954) posits that similar (rather than dissimilar) others are more appropriate models. The results of many studies, including one by Hornstein, Fisch, and Holmes (1968) in which the dependent variable was altruism rather than entrapment, lend support to this conjecture. In that study, as in Experiment 4, all subjects witnessed the behavior of a model who held either positive or negative feelings about his altruistic behavior. Like the participants in the previous experiment, subjects only matched the model's behavior if his attitude was positive. Moreover, this finding was in turn moderated by the model's and observer's degree of similarity. That is, the above effect did not emerge when subjects had been led to believe that the model was quite dissimilar to themselves.

Characteristics of the model's personality should also affect his or her status as a relevant target for social comparison. Specifically, if the model is portrayed to be a rather unlikeable, obnoxious individual, then observers may conclude that the model is not an appropriate person to imitate. In essence, observers may reason that they do not wish to be or act like the obnoxious model. In Experiment 4 subjects were given no information about the model's personality. However, they had no reason to think that the model was not an appropriate other for comparison. After all, this person was, like themselves, a college student at the same university that they were attending.

In Experiment 5, the same person was employed as the model. However, we went to great lengths to portray this person as a very unlikeable (and somewhat ignorant) individual. As in Experiment 4, all subjects watched the model become either very entrapped (High Entrapment Model condition) or not at all entrapped (Low Entrapment Model condition) before taking part in the same situation. Moreover, in all instances the Model indicated that he or she was glad, rather than regretful about the chosen course of action. No modeling effect was predicted in this study. If anything, a negative or reverse modeling effect was expected, such that subjects would do just the opposite of what they had observed the model to do. Whether no (or a reverse) modeling effect was observed, it was expected that there would be significantly less of a modeling effect than was obtained in the Glad condition of Experiment 4, in which subjects had no reason to think that the model was not an appropriate comparison person.

Method. Fifteen male and female Tufts University undergraduates were drawn from the same pool as in Experiment 4. None of them had taken part in the previous experiment.

The procedure was designed to be identical to the Glad condition of the previous experiment. The main difference was that the model presented the image of a very unappealing individual (very unlikeable and moderately unintelligent). The methods by which the impression was fostered are described below.

Upon entering the laboratory, subjects encountered a male confederate who had already arrived and who was completing a "Personal Opinion Survey." This scale consisted of a subset of items drawn from the Machiavellianism scale devised by Christie and Geis (1970) (see page 74 of this chapter for a more detailed discussion of this procedure). The experimenter told subjects that they would also be filling out the same questionnaire, but that she had left the subject's copy in another part of the building. When the confederate "completed" his copy the experimenter said to him: "Would you mind if the other person (i.e., the real subject) has a look at your questionnaire while I go out and get his (hers)?" The confederate answered affirmatively, though in a testy tone of voice. The experimenter handed the confederate's Personal Opinion Survey to subjects and said to them: "Please familiarize yourself with all the items so that when I bring your questionnaire out, it won't take you too long to complete. Please do not talk to each other while I'm out of the room."

Upon reading the questionnaire, the subjects were initially exposed to information about the confederate's personality. He answered all of the items in a fashion that made him appear maximally undesirable. For example, he strongly agreed with statements like, "There are very few people in the world worth caring about" and strongly disagreed with items such as, "To help oneself is good; to help others is even better," and "Most people are basically good and kind."

While the experimenter was next explaining the rules of the counter procedure, the confederate continued to present himself in a socially undesirable fashion. He argued with the experimenter, expressed sarcasm to her, was uncooperative, and furthermore did not appear to understand the procedure for making investments very well. For instance, when asked if he wished to start investing, the confederate said in an annoyed tone, "To tell you the truth, I don't give a damn. I really don't understand the game but I suppose you want me to play so I will. Sure!"

With that, the subject observed the confederate invest either all of his initial stake ($5.00) or little of it ($.50), as in the High and Low Entrapment conditions of the previous experiment. When asked how he felt about what he had just done, the confederate expressed that he was quite pleased and did not at all feel foolish (in the same manner used in the Glad condition of Experiment 4).

At that point the confederate exited, and the subject next performed the counter procedure. After that part was completed subjects were asked to rate the confederate on a variety of scales (nasty–nice; unintelligent–intelligent; unfriendly–friendly). Subjects were then debriefed and dismissed.

Results. All of the 15 subjects in this experiment invested at least some of their initial stake. As expected, no modeling effect was obtained. Subjects became slightly, though not significantly, more entrapped in the Low ($M = \$3.34$) than in the High Entrapment Model condition ($M = \$3.11$; $t < 1$). The results of the present study were then compared in several ways to those obtained in the Glad condition in Experiment 4. First, a 2×2 unweighted-means analysis was

Table 5-7. Mean Amount of Money Invested as a Function of Model's Behavior and Model's Personality (Source: Brockner, Nathanson, et al. [1984], Experiment 4)

| | Model's Personality | |
Model's Degree of Entrapment	Unlikeable	No Information
High	M = $3.10 SD = 2.03	M = $3.59 SD = 1.47
Low	M = $3.34 SD = 1.96	M = $1.71 SD = 1.16

Notes: Scores could range from $0.00 to $5.00, with higher scores reflecting greater entrapment. The No Information condition was taken from the Glad condition of the preceding experiment.

performed, in which the independent variables were Model's Degree of Entrapment (High or Low) and Model's Disposition (Unlikeable or Not). Both main effects were nonsignificant. Of greater importance, there was a significant interaction effect, $F(1,37) = 4.16$, $p < .05$. As predicted, the powerful modeling effect obtained in the Glad condition of Experiment 4, when no information about the model's personality was provided, was significantly reduced in Experiment 5, in which the model was portrayed as rather unappealing.

Additional evidence of the strength of the modeling effect in the previous experiment was the relatively low within-condition variability. By contrast, the within-cell standard deviations (see Table 5-7) were larger in Experiment 5. In order to compare statistically the within-condition variability between the two studies, we computed for each subject an absolute difference score between the amount that he or she invested and the condition mean. Subjects in the previous experiment deviated on the average from their respective condition means by $1.10, whereas the corresponding difference score in Experiment 5 was $1.69. The difference between these two means reached significance at the .025 level, according to the results of a t-test.

In sum, analyses performed on measures of both central tendency and variability demonstrated that the model had a much more pronounced effect on subjects' behavior in the Glad condition of Experiment 4 than in Experiment 5. We should mention that subjects in these two experiments were drawn from similar populations (i.e., male and female introductory students during the same academic year at Tufts Unviersity who completed the experiment for course credit). Thus, it is reasonable to speculate that the different results obtained in the Unlikeable model condition (Experiment 5) and the Glad condition in Experiment 4 in which no information was provided about the model's disposition, were not due to sample differences. Nevertheless, subjects were not randomly assigned to the Unlikeable Model and No Information Model condition. Therefore, any statement about the effect of this variable must be viewed as correlational rather than causal. In any event, what is not ambiguous is the lack of a modeling effect within the Unlikeable Model condition.

Questionnaire data. The interpersonal judgments that subjects made about the model in Experiment 5 further suggest that he was not viewed as a useful reference person for social-comparison purposes. Across conditions, the mean ratings on the nasty–nice (3.67), unintelligent–intelligent (4.40), and unfriendly–friendly (3.67) dimensions were all on the negative side of the midpoint (5.5) of the 11-point scale. Unexpectedly, the model was rated more negatively on all three dimensions in the Low than in the High Entrapment condition, although only the statistical comparison on the nasty–nice dimension attained significance. (No interpersonal judgments of the model were made by subjects in Experiment 4; thus no between-study comparisons can be made.)

Discussion of the Modeling Experiments

Taken together, the results of these five experiments suggest that the actions taken by an appropriate model may be an extremely important social determinant of entrapment. Experiments 1–4 demonstrated with considerable generality that modeling processes can affect the entrapped decision maker. The tendency for observers to imitate the model's degree of entrapment was obtained (1) for observers and models of both sexes, (2) on measures of both process and outcome, (3) across three very different paradigms for the experimental study of entrapment, and (4) when the model was viewed both during and before the point in time at which observers were required to make their decisions.

The results of Experiments 4 and 5 further specified some of the conditions under which the model's actions will not affect the observer's behavior. If the model expressed regret over his or her behavior in the entrapping dilemma, or if the model was not viewed as a relevant comparison other, then subjects either ignored the model's behavior or acted in a manner directly opposite to the model. Interestingly, the same two boundary conditions on modeling effects were also obtained by Hornstein et al. (1968), though in a context not related to entrapment.

Like much of the research described in this book, the modeling experiments should be viewed as an important first step. Future research on the modeling– entrapment relationship may fruitfully proceed in a number of directions. First, given the ambiguity of appropriate behavior in an entrapping conflict, observers are potentially quite susceptible to be influenced by a model's behavior. It is important to specify the conditions under which models will and will not be imitated. Toward that end, researchers may draw from theoretical and empirical bases in the abundant modeling literature in social psychology. There are at least three broad categories of factors that have been shown (in investigations of other social behaviors, such as aggression) to influence the magnitude of modeling effects: (1) the observed consequences for the model of engaging in that behavior, (2) the relevance of the model as a target for social comparison, and (3) the observer's degree of certainty, independent of the model, about the most appropriate course of action to follow. Each of these broad categories of factors could moderate the effects of models. Moreover, many situational and/or dispositional variables can be subsumed under these broader categories. For example, the consequences factor can be operationalized by having the observer watch the model receive either positive or negative "feedback" for performing the target behavior.

The effect of the comparison-relevance variable also can be assessed in numerous ways. For example, the degree of similarity between observer and model appears to be an important determinant of modeling (e.g., Hornstein et al., 1968). Similarity, in turn, is a multifaceted concept, lending itself to a variety of manipulations. Other variables related to the comparison-relevance factor include the attractiveness and credibility of the model.

The effect of the certainty variable also can be put to experimental test through a number of techniques. In some instances the most prudent course of action should be quite clear to the decision maker in the entrapping conflict. For example, if the value of the goal and/or the probability of goal attainment is relatively high, then it should be relatively clear that escalation of commitment rather than withdrawal is the wiser thing to do. Under such conditions, the behavior of an even relevant model should be less influential. Consistent with this logic, in Experiment 1 the value of the goal ($10) was much higher than in the other four experiments; in that study the modeling effect was found to be only marginally significant. Personality characteristics of the observer can also effect their degree of certainty. For instance, low-self-esteem observers, lacking in confidence in their own beliefs about appropriate behavior, may be particularly susceptible to modeling processes in entrapping conflicts (Weiss, 1977).

More generally, dispositional qualities of the observer may influence the magnitude of modeling effects. In one recent study (Ankuta, 1981) subjects were placed in an entrapping waiting situation in the presence of a model who either continued to wait, or departed from the situation. No overall modeling effect was obtained in this experiment. Rather, individuals who were dispositionally more sensitive to social processes and/or less attentive to their own internal state (i.e., those scoring high on the public self-consciousness and/or low on the private self-consciousness dimensions developed by Fenigstein, Scheier, & Buss, 1975) were very much influenced by the model's behavior, waiting longer in the presence than in the absence of the entrapped model. The degree of entrapment of all other participants, however, was not affected by the model's actions. We shall consider the role of individual differences, as well as the interaction between individual differences and situational variables, in greater detail in Chapter 8.

Another important task for future research is to determine whether the relationship between modeling and entrapment is, as we suspect, bidirectional. More specifically, in the present studies the model's behavior was the independent variable and the subject's degree of entrapment was the major dependent variable. It seems entirely possible that observers' degree of entrapment may also influence the extent to which they will rely upon a model as a guide for further behavior. On the one hand, for example, there is evidence that decision makers become increasingly conflicted about whether to persist as their degree of entrapment heightens (Teger, 1980). If so, then they may be more attentive to, and manipulable by, the behavior of an appropriate model as their degree of entrapment increases. In fact, questionnaire data from Experiment 2 are consistent with this conjecture. Participants in the Increasing Model Commitment condition, who were more entrapped, reported that they were significantly more interested in the performance of the other person while they were working on the jigsaw puzzle than were those in the Decreasing Model condition, who were less entrapped.

On the other hand, it may be that under certain conditions decision makers can get so "caught up" in a self-justificatory process of escalation that they literally become immune to the actions taken by an appropriate model. This reasoning suggests that heightened entrapment may *decrease* the observing decision maker's susceptibility to model-produced influence. Whether observers are more or less susceptible to model influence as they become increasingly entrapped may depend upon the specific nature of their psychological discomfort. If their conflict stems from the rational question of not knowing whether persistence or withdrawal is the wiser course of action, then they may become more affected by the model. Alternatively, if their internal discomfort can be better described as cognitive dissonance, then they may become increasingly immune to the actions taken by a model. Festinger (1964) distinguishes between conflict and dissonance in terms of their temporal relation to the decision point. When faced with making a choice between two relatively equally attractive alternatives, individuals experience conflict; they literally do not know what to do. It is at this point, we suspect, that models can effectively influence the observer.

Once the individuals have made their decision, however, they are no longer experiencing conflict; rather, their psychological state is one of dissonance. The nature of the dissonance is that the decision makers are wondering whether they chose the proper alternative. It is at this "after the decisional fact" point that they may be less susceptible to model influence. There are at least two techniques that they can use in order to reduce the dissonance: they can attend to information consistent with their behavior and/or ignore information that is inconsistent. What impact, then, should a modeling manipulation have? If the observer is entrapped and exposed to an entrapped model, he or she may take solace in the social support offered by the model, and thus remain entrapped. However, the effect of a model who quit the entrapping dilemma may not decrease the likelihood of further entrapment. According to the dissonance analysis, the inconsistent information (i.e., the model who quit) will be discounted or ignored. If entrapped observers in a state of conflict are more prone to a model's influence than are entrapped observers in a state of dissonance, it then is important to determine the conditions under which the observers' entrapment elicits these two different psychological states.

Finally, it would seem important to explore the practical implications of the fact that the actions taken by entrapped decision makers may be influenced by models. Consider, for example, the process of gambling, which is laden with entrapping qualities. To increase their revenue, the owners of casinos and other gambling establishments may well be advised to use "shills" at the gambling table who repeatedly make investments in order to "recoup" previous losses. In a more optimistic vein, however, members of Gamblers' Anonymous and other self-help groups may find it useful to be exposed to peer models who have quit the entrapping gambling process, so that they too may find it easier to stop "throwing good money after bad."

Group Decision Making and Entrapment

The social-psychological analysis presented to this point has shown that an individual's decision to persist in or withdraw from an entrapping dilemma can be affected by the social or nonsocial nature of the opponent, characteristics of a social opponent, or the behavior of models. Whether or not actions are taken individually or in groups could represent an additional rich source of social influence upon decision makers. Indeed, for purely "ecological validity" reasons it would be important to study group effects on entrapment. As group theorists have pointed out, many political, economic, and social decisions in everyday life are made by groups rather than individuals. Much basic and applied research is thus needed in order to describe, explain, and improve group decision making in real-world situations.

The past 20 years have witnessed a flurry of research activity by social psychologists on the vitally important topic of group decision making. In 1962, James Stoner described the "risky shift," that is, the tendency for groups to make decisions more risky than those made by individuals acting alone. A search for the best explanation for the risky shift has revealed that it is in fact one example of a more general group shift, namely, the tendency for groups to make more *extreme* decisions than individuals (Baron & Byrne, 1981). In his book, *Victims of Groupthink*, Janis (1982; see also 1st ed., 1972) has added an extremely provocative and important concept to the group decision making literature. According to Janis, Groupthink refers to "a mode of thinking that people engage in when they are deeply involved in a cohesive in-group, when the members' strivings for unanimity override their motivation to realistically appraise alternative courses of action." Taken together, the group shift and groupthink literatures suggest that a variety of dynamics are present in group situations that simply do not exist within individuals. In general, these group dynamics may have a profound effect on decision making. Later, we will discuss more specifically how group dynamics may affect decision makers' degree of entrapment.

As of this writing, very little research has explored group decision making in entrapping dilemmas. Our literature search has revealed only two relevant studies. One was designed to replicate Staw's (1976) demonstration of the escalation phenomenon and extend that finding to groups (Bazerman, Giuliano, & Appleman, in press). In this role-playing study all participants (183 male undergraduates at the University of Texas) were asked to commit additional resources (ranging from $0 to $20 million) to a previously chosen but failing course of action. Two independent variables were manipulated in a 2×2 design. As in the Staw experiment, half of the subjects were personally responsible for the previous decision, whereas half were not. In addition, half of the subjects made the subsequent allocation (and in the High Responsibility condition, the earlier) decisions individually, while the other half made them in four-person groups. Group members were instructed to discuss the matter for approximately 20 minutes, and then to reach a group consensus.

The analysis of variance yielded a highly significant Responsibility main effect ($F(1,71) = 15.45$, $p < .001$). Replicating the results of Staw (1976), it was found that subjects escalated commitment to a greater extent when they, rather than another person, were responsible for the previous decision that had produced negative consequences. The Group variable produced no significant effects. Given the absence of any Group effect, Bazerman et al. merely concluded that entrapment may be exhibited by groups as well as individual decision makers.

The more interesting research task, of course, is to specify *the conditions under which* the behavior of groups will differ from that shown by individual decision makers in entrapping dilemmas. Moreover, there are firm theoretical reasons for predicting group versus individual differences. Specifically, Staw (1976) has shown that decision makers' sense of personal responsibility for a negative setback has a direct effect on their subsequent tendency to escalate their commitment to the chosen course of action. Accordingly, factors affecting one's sense of personal responsibility should affect escalation. Studies of group behavior (Darley & Latané, 1968; Mynatt & Sherman, 1975; Zimbardo, 1970) have demonstrated repeatedly that group members feel less personally responsible for the group's behavior than they do for their own individual behavior.

This analysis suggests an additional way to conceptualize the logic underlying the Bazerman et al. in press) experiment. Perhaps both of their independent variables influenced the decision makers' sense of personal responsibility for the earlier decision. Obviously, subjects should have felt more personally responsible in the High than in the Low Responsibility condition. Furthermore, they should have perceived more responsibility in the Individual than in the Group condition. Thus, subjects should have escalated the most in the High Responsibility–Individual condition and the least in the Low Responsibility–Group condition. The amount of escalation in the "hybrid" conditions—High Responsibility–Group and Low Responsibility–Individual—should fall in-between these two extremes.

An inspection of means (see Table 5-8) revealed that this, in fact, was the case. We then performed a one-way analysis of variance (rather than a two-factor ANOVA) coupled with multiple comparisons to test for differences between the four groups. (Our sincere thanks go to Toni Giuliano for making these

Table 5-8. Mean Amount of Funds Allocated to Previously Chosen Division (in millions of dollars) (Source: Bazerman, Giuliano, & Appleman [1984])

High Responsibility, Individual	High Responsibility, Group	Low Responsibility, Individual	Low Responsibility, Group
13.42	13.19	10.77	7.81

Note: Scores could range from 0 to 20, with higher scores reflecting greater entrapment.

data available.) As expected, the one-way ANOVA produced a highly significant effect ($F(3,71) = 6.57$, $p < .001$). The Newman-Keuls multiple comparison revealed that (1) the condition in which subjects should have felt least personally responsible for the earlier decision—the Low Responsibility–Group cell—engendered significantly less entrapment than each of the remaining conditions, and (2) the degree of escalation in the Low Responsibility–Individual condition was marginally ($p < .10$) less than that observed in the High Responsibility–Individual condition. Thus, the reanalyses of the Bazerman et al. data suggest that under certain conditions groups may be less prone to entrapment, because the members' sense of personal responsibility for the earlier setback should be less than that of individual decision makers.

A study performed by Teger (1980) revealed that groups can become more *or* less entrapped than individuals acting alone, depending upon other factors. In this study subjects (undergraduates at the University of Pennsylvania) were given an initial stake of $2.00 with which to bid against a simulated opponent in the Dollar Auction game. The independent variables in this 2×2 design were Sex and Social Unit—subjects bid either alone or in a team with another person of the same sex. Subjects (or pairs of subjects) called in their bids to an experimenter, who supposedly relayed them to the opponent. In reality, subjects participated against a preprogrammed opponent who never quit. Although subjects had no information about their opponent they were told to assume that he or she was similar to themselves. The dependent variable was the amount of money (out of the $2.00) that subjects invested.

Both main effects were nonsignificant. However, a highly significant interaction effect emerged ($F(1,194) = 9.19$, $p < .005$). As can be seen in Table 5-9 male groups became less entrapped than male individuals. Female participants, on the other hand, spent considerable more money in the group than in the individual condition. Put another way, males were more entrapped than females in the individual condition, a finding that was reported earlier in this chapter. However, females became more entrapped than males in the group condition.

How might this rather interesting pattern of data be explained? Teger's speculation also centers on the diffusion of responsibility notion, although in a manner different from how it has been presented to this point. Teger argues that males are socialized to behave more competitively or aggressively than females; that is why males became more entrapped in the individual condition. However,

Table 5-9. Mean Amount Invested as a Function of Sex of Subject and Individual vs. Team Bidding (Source: Teger [1980])

| | Sex of Subject | |
Type of Bidding	Male	Female
Individual	$1.24	$0.77
Team	$0.84	$1.19

Note: Scores could range from $0.00 to $2.00, with higher scores reflecting greater entrapment.

in the presence of group members individuals feel less personally responsible for acting in a manner consistent with socialized rules. As Teger puts it, groups "as opposed to individuals, give the subject social support for defying the norms which they see as operating in this situation." Thus, males in groups are free to deviate from the macho, tough guy image, whereas female teams are released from their socialized inhibitions against aggressive behavior.

Although Teger's results (and account of the results) are highly intriguing, they are inconsistent with other bodies of data in social psychology. Specifically, Lamm and Myers (1978) have reported an impressive array of findings suggesting that group discussions usually have a polarizing effect on decisions made by individuals. It is relatively rare, as in the Teger study, for groups to make decisions that actually *reverse* those made by individuals. Nevertheless, Teger's diffusion of responsibility from social norms explanation is worthy of further study. The critical task is for researchers to specify *a priori* those aspects of the decision making situation for which group members feel less personally responsible than individuals. Staw (1976) suggested that those who feel more personally responsible for *the decision producing the negative setback* will be more likely to escalate. Teger's analysis implies that those who feel more personally responsible *to adhere to the norm for appropriate behavior* can become more or less entrapped (depending upon the behavior prescribed by the norm). In short, if felt responsibility affects entrapment then it is critical to identify precisely what it is for which the decision maker feels responsible. Having specified the specific nature of the felt responsibility, researchers will be much better equipped to predict group-based (or even individually-produced) degree of entrapment.

Group Decision Making and Entrapment: Some Speculations

Much theoretical and empirical work on the group bases of entrapment is needed. For example, how does the concept of entrapment relate to Janis' (1982; see also 1st ed., 1972) formulation of Groupthink? What factors (besides the sex of the decision makers) cause groups to behave differently from individuals in entrapping conflicts? Once pertinent moderator variables have been identified, how may their effects be explained? Will group effects on entrapment decisions fit into the more general framework proposed by polarization theorists (e.g., Myers, 1978)?

In particular, let us consider the relationship between groupthink and entrapment. Janis proposed that cohesive groups have a number of characteristics that render them prone to engage in a variety of faulty decision-making processes. For example, victims of groupthink become very rigid in their cognitive appraisal of the situation. They believe that their plan of action is indisputably moral and invulnerable to failure. They hold oversimplified, stereotypical views of outgroups. They fail to examine critically the specific information which points to the fallacies in their plans. They do not work out contingency plans if the original course of action goes astray, probably because they do not seriously entertain the prospect that the original plan could go awry.

How, then, are groupthink and entrapment related? One (but by no means the only) way in which cohesive groups make bad decisions is by engaging in the self-justification process underlying entrapment. We and others (Staw, 1976; Teger, 1980) have suggested that a self-justification process at least partially mediated the Johnson Administration's decision(s) to escalate the U.S.' military involvement in Vietnam. Interestingly, Janis (1982) has chosen this policy as one in which the decision makers of a cohesive group were victims of groupthink. It may be useful at this point to discuss the conceptual links between groupthink and entrapment. We shall do this by selecting excerpts from Janis' analysis of the escalation of the Vietnam War. One cannot help but notice the striking similarities between the processes underlying entrapment and the groupthink tendencies that produced the Vietnam fiasco. First, according to the reports of those who observed the Johnson policy makers from inside as well as outside the group, the necessary precondition for groupthink—group cohesiveness—existed within the inner circle. Next, consider the following quotations from Janis' groupthink analysis:

Bill Moyers, an articulate member of Johnson's in-group, admitted: "With but rare exceptions we always seemed to be calculating the short term consequences of each alternative at every step of the policymaking process, but not the long term consequences. And with each succeeding short-range consequence we became more deeply a prisoner of the process." Indeed, Moyers appears to be describing the psychological perspective of the entrapped decision maker.

"The escalation decision was made despite strong warnings from intelligence experts within the U.S. government as well as leaders of the United Nations, from practically all of America's allies, and from influential sectors of the American public." Widespread opposition to a policy can serve as a watershed. On the one hand, it might make policy makers less apt to adopt the controversial plan. On the other hand, as the results of the Fox and Staw (1979) study suggest, if decision makers adopt a policy *in spite of* initial resistance to it, then they will be even more motivated to justify the appropriateness of the plan if it produces undesirable results in the short run; entrapment is particularly likely to occur under these conditions.

James Thomson, a historian who was a member of the White House staff, explains the poor quality of the escalation decision in the following way:

> The men in Johnson's inner circle convinced themselves that the Vietnam War was of crucial significance for America's future—a conviction that grew directly out of their own explanations and justifications . . . Instead of reevaluating their policy in response to clear-cut setbacks, their energetic proselytizing led them to engage in 'rhetorical escalation' that matched the military escalation.

Janis similarly explains the escalation by saying the following:

> We know that most individuals become heavily ego-involved in maintaining their commitment to any important decision for which they feel at least partly responsible. Once a decision-maker has publicly announced the course of action he has selected, he is inclined to avoid looking at evidence of the unfavorable consequences. He tries to reinterpret setbacks as victories, to invent new arguments to convince himself and others that he made the right decision, clinging stubbornly to unsuccessful policies long after everyone else can see that a change is needed. Each policy-maker, whether he has made the crucial decisions by himself or as a member of a group is thus motivated to perpetuate his past errors.

Janis is suggesting that groups, like individuals, are prone to escalate their commitment following a setback for which they feel personally responsible (a notion consistent with the Bazerman, Giuliano & Appleman [in press] results). What makes the conceptual links between groupthink and entrapment even clearer is Janis' notion that two factors may affect the extent to which groups will become entrapped: (1) group cohesiveness—the quintessential antecedent of groupthink, and (2) group norms. Small group research (Shaw, 1976) has shown that highly cohesive groups are more likely to exert pressure on their members to adhere to group norms or standards. Thus, the fact that Johnson's staff was highly cohesive was not sufficient in and of itself to produce entrapment in Vietnam. According to Janis, cohesive groups also can be *un*likely candidates for entrapment if the group norm is one of "open minded scrutiny of new evidence and willingness to admit errors (as in a group committed to the ideals of scientific research)." Janis speculates that Johnson's staff members were prone to entrapment because they were highly cohesive *and* had developed the norm of requiring members to continue supporting the group's past escalation decisions.

It should be emphasized that Janis' groupthink analysis of escalation in Vietnam is highly speculative. Two important tasks confront future researchers. First, it would seem important for historians and political scientists to provide independent evidence that Janis' analysis of the dynamics of Johnon's policy-making group is accurate (i.e., that the group was cohesive and had developed norms favoring continued commitment). Second, experimental social psychologists would be well advised to perform empirical tests of Janis' theoretical rationale. Controlled experiments need to be performed evaluating the joint effect of group cohesiveness and group norms on entrapment behavior. For exmaple, a 2×2 factorial design should be conducted in which the following variables are manipulated (Group Cohesiveness: high or low, and Group Norms: favoring persistence or not). According to Janis' reasoning, entrapment should be most pronounced in the Highly Cohesive–Persistent Norm condition relative to the other three conditions.

To this point we have discussed entrapment as a type of groupthink, that is, highly cohesive groups can make poor decisions through the self-justification process underlying entrapment. There are other mechanisms, however, by which cohesive groups can become victims of groupthink. In short, in this analysis entrapment has been subsumed by the groupthink concept. We hasten to add, however, that in other ways, the entrapment process is much more general than is groupthink. For one, groupthink refers to a *group* decision-making process. Although highly cohesive groups may be prime candidates for entrapment (depending upon the nature of the group norms) it is probably not necessary for the group to be cohesive in order for entrapment to occur. For example is the Bazerman, Giuliano, and Appleman (in press) study, group members who were personally responsible for the earlier decision escalated their commitment to a greater extent than those who were not responsible. However, there is no reason to believe that groups were highly cohesive in that study. If anything, just the opposite might have been the case. Subjects were strangers who had been brought together to discuss a hypothetical financial decision for approximately 20 minutes. Thus, there is little reason to suspect that the group members in any way valued their membership within their respective groups.

In addition to the possibility that group cohesiveness is not a necessary antecedent of entrapment, it is clear that groups are not even necessary for entrapment to occur. In fact, many of the everyday-life situations that inspired research on entrapment, as well as almost all of the experiments, entailed individual rather than group decision making. In sum, it would be appropriate to say that entrapment describes just one of the many processes by which cohesive groups can become victims of groupthink, and that group cohesiveness may be just one of the many antecedent conditions of entrapment.

Summary and Conclusions

This chapter has attempted to integrate the empirical research on interpersonal determinants of entrapment. It should be clear by now that a variety of "social entities" may affect decision makers' tendencies to escalate commitment to a failing course of action. These "social entities" include the opponent, a model, and a co-decision maker. Several general observations can be offered regarding the effects of the social entities on entrapment.

First, the effects depend upon a host of situational/dispositional factors. For example, individuals are more likely to get entrapped when competing against a

Social (rather than a Nonsocial) opponent; however, this effect appears to be dependent upon the decision makers' sex and Interpersonal Orientation (Swap & Rubin, 1983). Similarly, the presence of an entrapped model elicits greater entrapment—but only when the model is an appropriate target for social comparison.

Future research on each of these social antecedents of entrapment should probably continue to adopt the "contingency" approach. For example, we suspect that sometimes groups will be more prone to entrapment than individuals, whereas in other instances just the opposite will be true. Work is needed to delineate the relevant situational and/or dispositional moderator variables.

Second, in delineating the antecedents of entrapment, future researchers may find it useful to seek out social-psychological information on such topics as sex-role orientation, interpersonal attraction, aggression, modeling, and group decision making. By working from existing theory and research, future investigators have much to gain, including (a) a further understanding of the interpersonal causes of entrapment, and (b) a further contribution of knowledge to already existing literature. For example, research on the Social versus Nonsocial nature of the opponent has served to deepen our knowledge of the interactive effects of individual difference variables (i.e., Sex and Interpersonal Orientation) and a situational factor (i.e, nature of opponent) on entrapment. In addition, such results have served to sharpen our understanding of several notions in the sex-role literature (e.g., the conceptual nature of the Interpersonal Orientation scale recently developed by Swap & Rubin [1983]).

Third, it may prove useful to examine the joint and possibly interactive effects of the various sources of social influence on entrapment. To this point the research on the interpersonal antecedents of entrapment has been fractionated into various component parts. However, a truly comprehensive understanding of the social causes of entrapment will necessitate the simultaneous investigation of the effects on entrapment of the various sources of social influence. For example, Teger (1980) observed that groups responded differently than individuals in the Dollar Auction (i.e., female groups became more entrapped whereas male groups became less entrapped). In the Dollar Auction, decision makers compete against a Social opponent. Would similar group effects emerge if the "opponent" were Nonsocial?

Finally, in discussing the effects on entrapment of the various cast of characters, we have deliberately neglected to mention another potentially influential source: the effect caused by the presence of an observing audience. The role of an audience is considered in the next chapter, in which we analyze the effects of self-presentational motives on entrapment. As will soon become apparent, the need to save face is an important entrapment determinant. Thus, the presence or absence of an observing audience may be more usefully construed as one of a number of variables that affect decision makers' face-saving concerns.

Chapter 6
The Role of Self-Presentation in Entrapment

A variety of social-psychological factors may influence people's tendency to escalate commitment to a failing course of action. Three such factors were discussed in the preceding chapter: the nature of the opponent, the presence of models, and the effect of group decision making. This chapter is concerned with yet another fundamental social determinant of entrapment—the need to save face.

According to sociologists (e.g., Goffman, 1959) and social psychologists (e.g., Snyder, 1981), social behavior is in large part motivated by the desire to "look good," preserve self-esteem, or to present oneself favorably in the eyes of significant others. The basis of our need to save face in social situations is a matter of some controversy. (William James [1890/1952] even went so far as to suggest that the need to save face is instinctually rooted!) Whatever the reason(s) for our need to save face however, there is hardly a social behavior that has not been shown to be mediated at least in part by self-presentational concerns (Baumeister, 1982; Schlenker, 1980). To cite just one of many examples, Brown (1968) discovered that bargainers may accept personal financial loss in order to retaliate against an opponent who has previously made them appear foolish in the presence of an observing audience. Presumably, the act of retaliation enables bargainers to regain some of their lost face.

While face saving in general is an important mediator of social behavior, there are reasons to believe that this self-presentational motive is a significant factor underlying entrapment in particular. As mentioned throughout this book, the tendency to escalate commitment to an entrapping course of action is due to an effort-justification process. In essence, decision makers are reluctant to admit that they were mistaken in previously committing themselves to the chosen course of action. The prospect that their prior behavior was inappropriate could be quite threatening to their self-image in several ways. At a strictly *private* level, most decision makers should experience discomfort or dissonance about allocating resources and receiving negative feedback about the outcome of that resource allocation.

Furthermore, most individuals should be concerned with their self-presentation in the *eyes of others*. Other entrapment researchers (e.g., Teger, 1980) have also called attention to the distinction between private (internal) versus public (external) sources of justification. As Staw (1979) has noted:

> When justification is a largely internal process, individuals attend to events and reconstruct them to protect their own self images and identities. However, justification may also be directed externally. When faced with an external threat or evaluation, individuals may resort to retrospective forms of rationality or justification. Like Richard Nixon in the case of Watergate, . . . individuals may go to extreme lengths to prove that they were not wrong in earlier decisions. This type of justification is externally directed, since it is designed to prove to others rather than oneself that he or she is competent.

To appreciate the potential impact of face-saving motives on entrapment, it may be useful to think of several examples. Consider, for instance, the plight of labor leaders whose constituency has been involved in a prolonged strike. In this entrapping dispute, in which both labor and management continue to lose heavily with each passing day, union negotiators may find it particularly difficult to reach an agreement with management. Having been on strike for so long, and having lost so much money, the union chiefs are probably under considerable pressure from their constituency to win an even more favorable settlement—or at least retain previously extracted concessions. Similarly, one of the reasons the United States may have found it extremely difficult to withdraw from the highly entrapping conflict in Vietnam is that our nation's leaders were concerned with the appearance of the U.S. government and military in the eyes of the American public and the world at large.

The present chapter is divided into two major sections. In the first section we shall review the empirical research which has shown the impact of face-saving or self-presentational motives on entrapment. Several themes—pertaining to both methodology and results—highlight this presentation. First, face-saving (independent) variables were operationalized in different ways in the various studies. For example, in one study, some subjects were led to believe that they were observed by an audience whereas the others were not; presumably, face-saving concerns are aroused to a greater extent in the former than latter condition. Thus, audience members can now be added to the "cast of characters" mentioned in the preceding chapter (i.e., the opponent, model, and groups) in which the social antecedents of entrapment were discussed.

Second, while face saving may influence entrapment, it is not being suggested that its effects inevitably will be to heighten entrapment. Rather, we are suggesting that the decision-makers' need to behave in a socially desirable fashion will be more salient to the extent that face-saving concerns are aroused. Under such circumstances they are apt to be attentive to environmental cues that indicate whether persistence or withdrawal is the more socially appropriate course of action.

Suppose, for example, that the presence of an evaluative audience has stimulated the decision makers' face-saving concerns. If so, the decision makers are likely to "size up" their audience, and draw inferences about the type of behavior deemed appropriate by the audience. If the audience values risk taking and/or persistence, then the decision makers may become more entrapped in its presence than its absence. Alternatively, if the onlookers are perceived to view caution and/or flexibility as desirable modes of behavior, then the decision makers may be more likely not to become entrapped in the audience's presence than absence.

The second section of this chapter discusses the impact on entrapment of a variable closely related to face saving: self-diagnosticity. Self-diagnosticity describes the extent to which behavioral outcomes, such as the negative feedback associated with prior resource allocations, are seen as self-revealing. A more complete discussion of the nature of this factor, including its relationship to face saving, will be deferred until we come to that portion of the chapter. Let us now turn to the empirical research.

Face Saving and Entrapment

Brockner, Rubin, and Lang (1981)

The two experiments in this report were designed to demonstrate that an individual's investment decisions in a potentially entrapping conflict are attributable to both nonsocial (or expectancy value) and social (or face-saving) forces. In previous research (Rubin & Brockner, 1975) it had been shown that decision makers became less entrapped when information about the costs associated with persisting was made more rather than less salient. How can this effect be explained? From a purely perceptual/economic perspective, those made more aware of the costs may have realized that it was not prudent to escalate their commitment. As a result, they were more likely to quit than those not made so aware. Or, this effect at least partially could have been mediated by face-saving concerns. Subjects may have wanted not only to avoid making a poor economic decision, but also may have been concerned with how it *would appear in the eyes of a significant other* (i.e., the experimenter) to have made a poor economic decision. In this sense, the entrapment-reducing effect of the cost salience manipulation may be better construed as due to self-presentation concerns.

If decision makers are less likely to persist when they are made more attentive to the *costs* associated with persisting then it stands to reason that those more focused on the associated *rewards* would be more likely to persist. Furthermore, if these hypotheses were to receive support, it would be important to evaluate the extent to which self presentation plays a mediating role. In two studies subjects received information that made more (or less) salient the costs and rewards associated with continued commitment. In general, it was expected that entrapment would be enhanced when cost salience was low (rather than high) and/or when reward salience was high (rather than low). Additional variables (described below) were included in the two studies to determine whether face-saving needs influenced the participants' entrapment behavior.

Experiment 1. In this study, the perceived salience of costs and rewards associated with continued investments was manipulated through instructions given to subjects before they entered the potentially entrapping conflict. Half of them were urged by the experimenter to focus on the rewards and ignore the costs associated with continued investments (Risky condition), whereas the remaining half were advised to attend to the costs and ignore the rewards (Cautious condition). If degree of entrapment is mediated by the desire to look good in the eyes of others, then the effect of the manipulation should be stronger when (1) other persons, including the experimenter, can observe the decision makers' behavior, and (2) the decision makers' face-saving concerns are high rather than low.

It was expected that entrapment would be greater in the Risky than in the Cautious condition. This prediction was partly based on the fact that the experimenter remained present and watched the subjects after giving them recommendations concerning appropriate behavior in all conditions. Many studies (e.g., Orne, 1962) have shown that the experimenter's opinion of them is of considerable psychological significance to subjects in laboratory experiments. Thus, subjects should reason that they will be more apt to win favor in the eyes of the experimenter by following rather than ignoring recommendations for appropriate behavior.

To test the mediating role of face saving more directly, however, additional independent variables were included in the design. Presumably, subjects' face-saving concerns should be heightened by an increase in the size of the audience. Thus, half of the decision makers performed the experiment in full view of two observers in addition to the experimenter (Large Audience condition), whereas half participated in the presence of the experimenter only (Small Audience condition). It was expected that the experimenter's instructions would have a more powerful effect on subjects in the Large Audience than in the Small Audience condition.

Furthermore, there are bound to be individual differences in the extent to which social behavior is motivated by the desire to make a favorable self-presentation. If so, it would seem worthwhile to classify subjects along such a dimension and then determine if this individual difference variable relates to entrapment. One appropriate individual difference measure is the Social Anxiety Scale, which measures "discomfort in the presence of others" (Fenigstein, Scheier, & Buss, 1975). This 6-item scale requires individuals to indicate the extent to which several statements are self-descriptive (e.g., "I have trouble working when someone is watching me," and "I get embarrassed very easily"). In one study, unrelated to entrapment, Turner (1977) found that this variable is directly related to concern with self-presentation. Just as the presence of a Large rather than a Small Audience was expected to sensitize participants differentially to the experimenter's recommendation, it was predicted that highly socially anxious individuals would be more affected by the experimenter's recommendations than would those low on this dimension.

In summary, the following results were predicted: (1) a main effect for Experimenter's Recommendation, with subjects becoming more entrapped in the Risky than in the Cautious condition, (2) an Audience × Recommendation interaction, such that subjects will be most entrapped in the Large Audience–Risky condition and least entrapped in the Large Audience–Cautious condition, and (3) a Social Anxiety × Recommendation interaction, such that decision makers will become most entrapped in the High Social Anxiety–Risky condition and least entrapped in the High Social Anxiety–Cautious condition. In addition, based on a face-saving analysis, subjects were expected to be most responsive to the Recommendation variable in the High Social Anxiety–Large Audience condition, and least influenced in the Low Social Anxiety–Small Audience condition.

Method. Ninety-two (56 female, 36 male) introductory psychology students at SUNY College at Brockport received extra course credit for participating in the Counter Game paradigm. Upon entering the laboratory subjects were encountered by a female experimenter and told that this study of "decision making" would consist of several parts. In the "first part" participants were asked to complete the Social Anxiety Scale developed by Fenigstein et al. (1975). A median split was employed to classify subjects as high or low on this trait. As in previous research, subjects were then given an initial stake of $5.00 in cash, and were told that by taking part they would have the opportunity to win a $3.00 jackpot. They were not able to calculate the exact probability of winning the jackpot, but rather, were told: "While you do have a good chance of winning the jackpot if you remain in the experiment long enough, you will not be told exactly what your chances are. There is a possibility that the winning number will be greater than 500, in which case no jackpot would be awarded and you would be forced to forfeit your entire initial stake."

In the Large Audience condition the experimenter then casually mentioned that several students who were working for psychology professors were interested in watching the procedures, because they might be using them in a future experiment. At this point two confederates were led into the room. They remained present for the duration of the experiment, during which they silently observed the subject. No such confederates were introduced in the Small Audience condition.

The experimenter administered the Risk versus Caution Recommendation manipulation in a seemingly impromptu fashion. After the rules of the Counter procedure had been explained, but before subjects were asked if they wished to try for the jackpot the experimenter said (in the Risky condition):

> Before we begin, let me offer you some advice. People often wonder what is
> the best thing to do in this situation. Probably the smartest thing to do is to

invest a good portion of your initial stake to win the jackpot. There are probably
a few reasons why investing is the intelligent thing to do. First, by so doing you
may end up winning the $3.00 jackpot. Second, it really doesn't cost you too
much to invest—only a penny for each number that the counter ticks off. In
fact, one question that people often ask us before they begin is "What do other
people do in this situation?" Obviously, not everyone does the same thing, but
most people who have done this experiment have been willing to spend a
considerable portion of their $5.00. Of course, what you do is entirely up to
you.

In the Cautious condition the first two sentences were identical to those in the
Risky condition. The experimenter then said:

Probably the smartest thing to do is to not invest too much of your initial stake
to win the jackpot. There are probably a few reasons why not investing too
much is the intelligent thing to do. First, even if you invest there is no guarantee
that you will win the $3.00 jackpot. Second, if you invest it will cost you
money, regardless of whether you win the jackpot. In fact, one question that
people often ask us before they begin is: "What do other people do in this
situation?" Obviously, not everyone does the same thing, but most people who
have done this experiment have not been willing to spend much of their $5.00.
Of course what you do is entirely up to you.

One conceptual and one methodological aspect of the Risk–Caution
independent variable should be mentioned. First, the operationalization of the
factor is multifaceted. The Risk condition is designed to make people attend to
the potential reward ("By investing, you may end up winning the $3.00
jackpot") and ignore the actual costs ("it doesn't really cost you too much")
associated with investing. By contrast, the Cautious condition downplayed the
potential reward ("there is no guarantee that you'll win the jackpot") and
highlighted the actual costs ("it will cost you money, regardless of whether you
win the jackpot"). Furthermore, different social comparison information was
provided to participants in the two conditions. Those in the Risk condition were
told that "most people have been willing to spend a considerable portion of their
initial stake," whereas those in the Caution condition were told just the
opposite. Second, because we were interested in determining the extent to which
subjects' adherence to the experimenter's recommendation was mediated by
face-saving needs, the extra observers were present in the Large Audience
condition when the experimenter offered her "advice." Thus, participants knew
that the observers were aware of the recommended "smart" behavior in both the
Risk and Caution conditions.

After allowing subjects 30 seconds to ponder her recommendation, the
experimenter asked them if they wished to go for the jackpot. The primary
dependent variable was the amount of money subjects expended in their
(fruitless) attempt to win the jackpot. Participants subsequently completed a
postexperimental questionnaire, and were then debriefed.

Results. Although men invested more money than did women ($p < .025$), Sex
of subject did not interact with any of the three independent variables.

Table 6-1. Mean Amount Invested as a Function of Risk–Caution Advice, Audience Size, and Social Anxiety (Source: Brockner, Rubin, & Lang [1981], Experiment 1)

		Advice	
Social Anxiety	Audience Size	Risk	Caution
High	Large	$3.06	$0.84
	Small	$2.84	$0.95
Low	Large	$2.61	$1.35
	Small	$2.94	$2.34

Note: Scores could range from $0.00 to $5.00, with higher scores reflecting greater entrapment.

Moreover, there was no sex difference on the social anxiety measure. The data were therefore collapsed across the Sex of Subject dimension in subsequent analyses. A three-factor unweighted-means analyses revealed (1) a main effect for the Risk–Caution manipulation, $F(1,84) = 27.46$, $p < .001$, with subjects becoming considerably more entrapped in the Risky ($M = \$2.83$) than in the Cautious condition ($M = \$1.21$); and (2) a Social Anxiety $\times$ Risk–Caution interaction, $F(1,84) = 4.19$, $p < .05$. As predicted, highly socially anxious participants were more influenced by the Risk–Caution manipulation (investing $2.93 and $0.90, respectively) than were those low in social anxiety (who spent $2.76 and $1.84, respectively). Stated differently, highly socially anxious subjects were less entrapped than low-social-anxiety participants in the Cautious condition ($F(1,84) = 5.56$, $p < .025$), and slightly but not significantly more entrapped than the latter group in the Risky condition ($F < 1$).

Contrary to prediction, the Audience variable yielded no significant effects in the analysis of variance. Several other comparisons, however, suggested that the effect of this variable was not entirely trivial. As indicated in Table 6-1, the effect of the Risk–Caution manipulation was greatest in the High Social Anxiety–Large Audience condition and least in the Low Social Anxiety–Small Audience condition, which is precisely what the face-saving analysis had prescribed. In fact, the Risk–Caution effects were significantly different from one another in these two conditions ($F(1,84) = 4.04$, $p < .05$). Furthermore, individual comparisons showed a significant (p values $< .05$ or better) Risk–Caution effect in all conditions except the Low Social Anxiety–Small Audience cell, $F(1,84) = 1.11$, $p > .25$. Put another way, as long as there was a situationally or dispositionally produced source of concern for evaluation, the Risk–Caution variable significantly influenced the degree of entrapment.

Although both the Social Anxiety and Audience variables were expected to interact with the Risk–Caution manipulation, only the former did so to a significant extent. Several factors may explain why the Audience proved to be the weaker variable. First, it may have been that the experimenter constituted the "audience" of primary psychological significance to participants. After all, she (rather than the observers) had offered the subjects advice on appropriate investment behavior. Thus, the decision makers were well aware of the behavior that the experimenter deemed to be desirable, but had no inkling of the other observers' values. Moreover, the vast literature on methodological processes such as experimenter effects and demand characteristics (e.g., Carlsmith, Ellsworth, & Aronson, 1976) suggest that the experimenter's desires, intentions, and so forth are psychologically salient to subjects. Given that the experimenter remained present throughout the experiment in both the Large Audience and Small Audience conditions, it becomes more understandable that the Audience variable produced a relatively weak effect, weaker than that produced by the Social Anxiety factor.

Second, the observers in the Large Audience condition were not explicitly presented to subjects as evaluative of the latter's behavior. Presumably, the observers simply wished to "watch the procedures because they might be using them in a future experiment." This information inadvertently may have led subjects to believe that the observers were more interested in the task itself, rather than with the subjects' behavior at the task. Had subjects been informed that the observers in the Large Audience condition would be evaluating their decision-making abilities or their ability to follow advice offered by an important other person, then subjects may have become more responsive to the observers' presence or absence.

This is not to say that the Audience manipulation was completely unsuccessful. Several of the reported analyses suggested that it had some effect on subjects' behavior. Moreover, the questionnaire data below imply that, as predicted, the Audience and Social Anxiety independent variables produced parallel effects on subjects' internal reactions to the experimental situation. All subjects responded to two items designed to assess their *discomfort* with being observed. Based on Turner (1977), who observed that socially anxious individuals showed a greater tendency to engage in face-saving behavior than those low in social anxiety, it was hypothesized that those more concerned with saving face would report feeling more anxious in the presence of others. Perhaps it is a discomforting experience to be preoccupied with winning favor in the eyes of others. The measures were "How much did the experimenter's presence bother you?" and "How much did the feeling of being observed bother you?" The endpoints in both instances were labeled "Not at all" (1) and "Very much" (41). Subjects' responses to these two measures were highly correlated ($r(89) = .71, p < .01$), and thus summed to provide a single index. The analysis of this index revealed only main effects for the Social Anxiety and Audience variables. Subjects were more bothered by being observed if they were high ($M = 24.82$) rather than low ($M = 13.98$) in social anxiety ($F(1,84) = 6.41$, $p < .025$), and more anxious if the audience was large ($M = 25.64$) than if it was small ($M = 14.35, F(1,84) = 5.93, p < .025$).

The results on this "observation anxiety" index were thus consistent with a face-saving analysis. Subjects were most anxious about being observed in the High Social Anxiety–Large Audience condition, and least bothered in the Low Social Anxiety–Small Audience condition. If face saving mediated subjects' adherence to the experimenter's recommendation concerning appropriate investment behavior, then (1) the effect of the Risk–Caution manipulation on degree of entrapment should have been most pronounced in the High Social Anxiety–Large Audience condition, and (2) the effect of the Risk–Caution manipulation should have been smallest in the Low Social Anxiety–Small Audience condition. As Table 6-1 (and the accompanying statistical analysis of the behavioral measures) revealed, both of these predictions were supported.

Experiment 2. The second experiment reported by Brockner, Rubin, and Lang (1981) also yielded data consistent with a face-saving analysis. Unlike the just-reported experiment, Cost Salience (High vs. Low) and Reward Salience (High vs. Low) were manipulated orthogonally in a 2×2 design. All subjects participated in the Counter Game procedure used in the previous experiment. The Cost Salience manipulation was very similar to the one used by Rubin and Brockner (1975). In the High Cost Salience condition a chart had been affixed to the cubicle wall adjacent to the subject. Subjects were told, "Before we begin, please take a look at the chart. It shows you what your earnings could be at each point. For example, you can see that if you spent 50 cents ($.50, first column) and the jackpot were awarded at this point ($3.00, second column) your actual earnings would be $3.00 − .50, or $2.50 (third column). You can keep track of your possible earnings by consulting this chart." No such chart existed in the Low Cost Salience condition.

In the High Reward Salience condition subjects were provided with a sheet of paper labeled "Progress Toward Jackpot." A thermometer-shaped figure had been drawn on the paper, with calibrations marked in multiples of 25 (running from 0 at its base to 500 at the top). The instructions given to subjects were as follows: "Please keep track of your progress toward the jackpot. In order to do this, take a moment during each decision point to fill out the diagram. During each decision point simply ink in the space corresponding to the decision point you are at. This way you can continually follow your progress toward the jackpot goal." No such sheet was provided to subjects in the Low Reward Salience condition.

Results yielded only a main effect for the Cost Salience manipulation ($p < .05$). Consistent with the results of Rubin and Brockner (1975), subjects were more entrapped in the Low than in the High Cost Salience condition. A postexperimental questionnaire, on which subjects were asked to explain their behavior, yielded results more germane to the present face-saving analysis. One item was, "I thought that it would look good if I kept going." Mirroring the behavioral data, Low Cost Salience subjects rated this as a more important reason for their behavior than did those in the High Cost Salience condition ($p < .05$). In essence, Low Cost Salience subjects were saying that they invested more of their resources in order to make a desirable self-presentation. Based on our experience with thousands of subjects, we find that they are reluctant to admit that they are motivated by face-saving concerns (perhaps because they think that they would look foolish by admitting such concerns!). Thus, it is particularly noteworthy that a Cost Salience effect (consistent with the behavioral results) appeared on the face-saving questionnaire item. Given participants' general tendency not to say that they are concerned with looking good, these self-report data may grossly underestimate the extent to which this factor influenced their behavior.

Four other experiments, not performed in our laboratory, also suggest that decision makers' concern with their social image can sharply affect their degree of entrapment. All of these studies have used the role-playing methodology discussed in Chapter 2. Several have shown that the conditions under which face-saving concerns are aroused engender the greatest entrapment. However, as in the first experiment reported above, there is support for the more general proposition that self-presentational motives in interaction with other variables can produce greater *or* lesser entrapment.

Fox and Staw (1979)

By couching the study of escalated commitment in a more specific context, Fox and Staw have extended the range of phenomena to which the entrapment analysis may apply. In particular, Fox and Staw note that the entrapment process might run counter to Campbell's (1969, 1977) call for an "experimenting society." According to Campbell, administrators should use evaluation research data to improve their policies. If a particular plan of action seems to be working (according to some objective standard) then the policy planners would be well advised to persist with that plan. Alternatively, if the evaluation data suggests that the chosen course of action has not proved fruitful, then it should be altered if not abandoned.

Psychological entrapment, however, may make it more difficult to implement Campbell's call for experimentation. If decision makers receive negative feedback about the already chosen course of action, they may become even more resistant to change. After all, to change (or even worse, to abandon) a social policy upon which decision makers have worked long and hard would imply that the policy was lacking in some important way. Rather than admit to this and alter the social program—something that would be potentially threatening to their self-esteem—the policy planners may become even more intransigent. They might reason, for example, that the benefits to be produced by the policy will only manifest themselves in the long haul, rather than in the short run. Thus, they may conclude, a greater commitment of resources is necessary. Note that this type of decision-making "logic" sounds perilously close to what we have been calling entrapment.

Fox and Staw (1979) have suggested that the more administrators have to lose politically, when the efficacy of their policies are refuted by scientific data, the more likely they are to escalate their degree of commitment to a failing course of action. Their reasoning is very similar to the face-saving analysis that was proposed earlier. The worse individuals perceive their appearance to be in the eyes of important others, the more they will become motivated to present themselves subsequently in a socially desirable light. What are the behavioral implications of this prospect for entrapped policy makers? Most likely, they will reason that they must persist in order to look good. By persisting, they can avoid being labeled as "inconsistent" or "indecisive," both of which have negative connotations (Staw and Ross, 1980).

Viewed from this perspective, many variables can influence the extent to which decision makers experience a loss of face when the evaluation of their plan of action produces unflattering results. For example, the more negative the appraisal, the greater the loss of face. In addition, the greater the dependency of the decision maker on the audience (or even vice versa), the greater the loss of face. In either case, the decision maker should become more, rather than less, committed to the chosen course of action.

Fox and Staw (1979) investigated the effects of two other variables pertinent to loss of face on subsequent degree of commitment. First, they reasoned that decision makers would be more motivated to prove that their prior course of action was correct if they felt insecure rather than secure in their ability to retain decision-making power within the organization. Second, it was hypothesized that decision makers who had experienced prior resistance (rather than approval) from their constituency, when embarking on the chosen plan of action, would suffer a greater loss of face upon receiving negative feedback about the chosen plan. Both of these factors (high job insecurity and high prior resistance) were expected to produce greater subsequent commitments to the failing course of action than their respective counterparts (low job insecurity and low prior resistance).

Method. Subjecs were 160 undergraduate business majors at the University of Illinois. All participants were given materials for the "Adams and Smith" case described earlier in Chapter 2. In addition, all participants were run in what amounted to the High Responsibility–Negative Feedback condition of the Staw (1976) experiment (see Chapter 3); that is, all participants made initial funding decisions (of $10 million to one of the two divisions of the company), defended these decisions in written form, and were then given feedback on the results of their decisions. In all cases the feedback suggested that their prior expenditures had produced no noticeably positive effect on subsequent sales.

Job insecurity manipulation. All participants had been told at the outset to assume the role of vice president of finance for Adams and Smith. This role represented a significant promotion from their previous one within the company. Thus, they were motivated to maintain this position. In the High Insecurity condition they were further told:

> Unfortunately, you have only been temporarily assigned to the position (your official title is Acting Vice President). A complete evaluation of the re-organization which resulted in your promotion will occur in the future and your job will become permanent or you will be demoted, depending upon your performance. In the interim, you have to deal with other executives who are well-qualified and envious of your position. Indeed, they were unhappy that you were chosen over them to fill the temporary position. Thus, you cannot expect support and assistance from your peers, especially if you do not perform well immediately.

In the Low Insecurity condition subjects were informed:

> You have been permanently assigned to fill the position (your official title is Financial Vice President). A complete evaluation of the re-organization which resulted in your promotion will occur in the future, but you will only be asked what changes in your job you would like to have. In the interim, other executives feel you are well qualified for the job. Indeed, they were happy that you were chosen to fill the position. Thus you can expect support and assistance from your peers, especially if you do not perform well immediately.

Resistance manipulation. In the High Resistance condition subjects received a negative evaluation from the Board of Directors about their initial funding decision ("The Board members were very dissatisfied and critical of your recommendation . . . and were firmly convinced that you had recommended the wrong course of action. The Board reluctantly deferred to your judgment.") In the Low Resistance condition subjects were informed that the Board of Directors had responded very favorably to their initial funding decision ("The Board members were highly supportive of your recommendation . . . and were firmly convinced you had recommended the correct course of action.").

In spite of the fact that their earlier funding decision had met with little success, all subjects were informed that there was still a need for greater expenditures on research and development. As Financial Vice President subjects were required to make another funding recommendation. Subjects could allocate anywhere from $0 to $20 million to their previously chosen division. (Any remaining funds, they were told, would be retained for other uses.)

Results. A 2×2 analysis revealed main effects for both independent variables. As predicted, subjects made larger allocations in the High Insecurity ($M = \$14.54$ million) than in the Low Insecurity condition ($M = \$12.56$ million; $F(1,76) = 5.86, p < .02$). Also as expected, decision makers escalated their commitment more in the High Resistance ($M = \$14.58$ million) than in the Low Resistance condition ($M = \$12.51$ million; $F(1,76) = 6.40, p < .02$). The interaction effect did not approach significance.

Subsidiary analyses indicated that both high insecurity and high resistance produced not only greater subsequent commitments, but also increased rigidity on the part of participants. Specifically, subjects also had to make maximum and minimum funding recommendations. Interestingly, the ranges of the recommendations (computed by subtracting the minimum from the maximum score) were somewhat smaller in the High Insecurity than in the Low Insecurity condition ($p < .08$) and in the High Resistance than in the Low Resistance condition ($p < .06$). Thus, subjects in the High Insecurity and High Resistance conditions manifested greater inflexibility in their tendency to become more entrapped than their counterparts in the Low Insecurity and Resistance conditions, respectively.

The Fox and Staw (1979) findings have considerable theoretical as well as practical implications. First, in a manner very different from Brockner, Rubin, and Lang (1981), the authors have provided highly suggestive evidence for the mediating role of face saving in entrapping dilemmas. When the situation had been structured so that decision makers likely perceived a greater need to justify their prior actions in the eyes of others (i.e., high insecurity and/or high resistance) they subsequently allocated a significantly larger amount of resources to the already chosen plan. Second, the Fox and Staw analysis identifies one of many social-psychological obstacles to change within organizations, an issue to which we will return in Chapter 10.

Third, the findings have a pessimistic and paradoxical implication concerning the uses to which evaluation research data can be put. One purpose of evaluation research is to provide administrators with feedback on the efficacy of their policies. When the evaluation suggests that the program has not proved successful, decision makers often (though not always) would do well to alter the policy in some way, rather than to become even more committed to it. Under certain conditions (e.g., when decision maker's need to save face is high), however, negative feedback will lead to heightened commitment. The paradox, then, is this: whereas evaluation research data *could* be used to enhance the quality of decision making, it may well produce defensive posturing that is detrimental, rather than beneficial, to the long-term goals of administrators and organizations.

This is not to say that administrators whose policies yield negative outcomes inevitably will become even more committed to those policies. Whether this happens may well depend upon the bases on which administrators think they will be evaluated. Too often, Fox and Staw (1979) suggest, decision makers are led to believe that their occupational well-being within the larger organization depends on the *outcomes* of their decisions (i.e., the so-called "bottom line").

Fox and Staw have written:

> One fundamental cause of the trapped administrator problem seems to be due to the status of the administrator being tied to program performance. A program that fails is frequently treated as an administrative *failure* and is cause for demotion or dismissal. In contrast, a program *success* often leads to increased funding, power, and promotion in the organization (emphasis added).

Is it possible for negative feedback concerning outcomes not to elicit defensive escalation of commitment? Perhaps. If administrators were led to believe that they were evaluated for the prudence of their decision-making *process*, as well as *outcome*, then they may respond less defensively (and more adaptively) to negative *outcome* feedback. Suppose administrators believed that both process and outcome (as oppposed to merely outcome) measures were being collected to assess the quality of their decision making. Suppose further that the outcome results of their chosen policy suggested that the policy was ineffective, but that the decision makers responsible for planning and implementing the policy did the best job possible at the time of the original formulation of the policy (it is entirely possible for a policy to be well thought out—yet meet with negative results—due to some factor that was reasonably unforeseen at the earlier point in time). We suspect that administrators would feel much less trapped if evaluations of their performance took into account the *process* by which decisions were made. As long as policy makers knew that they did the best job possible under the given circumstances, they should respond with greater openness to negative *outcome* feedback. Indeed, they should, as Campbell had originally hoped, use the feedback to alter their subsequent actions for the longer-term betterment of the organization.

Two points stemming from the above remarks are worthy of mention. First, readers familiar with Janis' (1982; see also 1st ed., 1972) conception of groupthink will recognize a similar emphasis on *process* in the evaluation of decision making. Janis hypothesized that highly cohesive groups sometimes engage in decision making processes that lead to fiascos. The focus of Janis' theoretical analysis, however, was on the link between the antecedent causes (e.g., group cohesiveness) and processes of groupthink. According to Janis, it is possible for a cohesive group to show all of the manifestations of groupthink even in the absence of a negative outcome (if, for example, the opposing group engaged even more in a groupthink decision-making process).

Second, if evaluations of decision makers do become more focused on the *processes* of planning and implementation, in addition to outcome, it becomes incumbent upon evaluation researchers to develop techniques of assessing process efficacy (independent of outcomes). At the very least, process evaluations should be conducted in the absence of knowledge about outcome. Otherwise, evaluators might fall prey to a "hindsight" (Fischhoff, 1975) type of logic; that is, if the policy produces unfavorable *outcome* results it may inadvertently be viewed as due to faulty administrative decision-making *processes* (rather than some other, perhaps more appropriate, factor independent of the decision-making process).

Levi (1982)

Fox and Staw (1979) demonstrated that two face-saving manipulations influenced decision makers' levels of escalation following a negative setback: When prior resistance and/or job insecurity were high, subjects perceived that they could make a more favorable self-presentation by committing more of their resources to the failing course of action. A study performed by Levi (1982) adds considerable generality to the proposition that decision makers will show a greater tendency to escalate when face-saving needs are high rather than low. Levi used a role-playing methodology that was entirely different from those employed by Staw and his associates. Male and female introductory psychology students acted as decision makers in a hypothetical military conflict between two countries (Blue and Red). Subjects, acting on behalf of the United Nations, had to decide on the amount of military aid Blue should receive. According to prior information provided to participants, Blue controlled an economically valuable border territory. A crisis occurred when Red placed its forces along the border and invaded the territory. Blue appealed to the United Nations, calling for the withdrawal of Red's troops, but Red, the militarily stronger of the two countries, ignored Blue's pleas. As events unfolded the military trend of the war became increasingly unfavorable for Blue, the U.N.-aided country. Subjects had to decide upon the amount of aid to allocate to Blue, measured in terms of troops. After Decision Points 1, 2, and 3 subjects learned that the troop allocations to Blue were not sufficient to hold off Red's forces. By Decision Point 4 (the last one in the scenario) the situation had become desperate for Blue. At this point subjects had to decide (1) whether to escalate their troop commitment further or withdraw by suing for peace, and (2) how many additional troops to allocate, if the former option were chosen.

Levi's operationalization of Public Accountability represented a very different way of manipulating face-saving concerns, relative to the procedure used by Fox and Staw (1979). Before the initial decision points those in the High Accountability condition were told that they had the final say on the magnitude of the commitment of the U.N. force on behalf of Blue. Moreover, the subject had to give a brief "speech" (to the U.N. Security Council) explaining why the chosen course of action had been taken. In the Low Accountability condition the subjects' role was that of an advisory group member who made recommendations but was not accountable for the final decision. In addition, subjects in this condition did not have to make a public speech justifying their decisions.

Of greatest current relevance is the effect of the Accountability manipulation on subjects' actions at Decision Point 4. Of the 120 participants, approximately 59% chose to escalate their commitment further at this point, when the military situation had become quite grim for Blue. Contrary to prediction, there was no effect of the Accountability variable on the binary choice measure of whether to escalate. However, for the subset of subjects who did choose to escalate rather than opt for peace, those in the High Accountability condition made larger commitments (77.8% of the maximum) than did those in the Low Accountability condition (55.5%; $F(1,63) = 4.38$, $p < .04$). Thus, given that subjects had chosen to escalate, the more that they had to justify their action to others, the larger their commitments tended to be. Of course, the external validity of the Accountability effect is limited by the fact that nearly 40% of the participants (i.e., those who had chosen peace rather than escalation) did not complete this dependent measure. Nevertheless, the results are highly suggestive, especially when taken in conjunction with Fox and Staw's (1979) finding that conditions necessitating greater public justification for one's actions elicited greater entrapment.

Conlon and Wolf (1980)

The basic thesis of our face-saving analysis is that self-presentational concerns, such as those produced by the presence of an audience, mediate (and therefore can further increase or decrease) entrapment. The tendency for Fox and Staw's

(1979) and Levi's (1982) subjects to become more entrapped in the high than in the low "need to save face" conditions should be interpreted as part of a more general tendency for entrapped decision makers to want to behave in a socially desirable manner. Viewed from this perspective, a number of factors can affect an individual's perception of what constitutes socially desirable behavior. For example, the decision makers may try to "get inside the head" of onlookers in order to learn their values. Upon learning observers' values, decision makers may try to act in a manner consistent with them in order to enhance their social image. Brockner, Rubin, and Lang (1981) observed that individuals more concerned with their social image (highly socially anxious subjects) became more or less entrapped in response to the experimenter's recommendations for appropriate investment behavior than did those less concerned (low-social-anxiety participants). In this study, subjects presumably inferred the experimenter's valued behavior based on her advice, and acted more in accordance with the valued behavior when face-saving needs were high rather than low.

Other environmental cues (besides the observers' stated preference) also can suggest to decision makers whether persistence or withdrawal in an entrapping dilemma is the more desirable course of action. If face saving mediates entrapment, then individuals' level of commitment should be more affected by these cues when face-saving concerns are high rather than low. One relevant cue is information pertaining to the cause of the failure of the prior resource allocation. In a role-playing experiment by Staw and Ross (1978, discussed in the attribution section of Chapter 4), participants were more likely to escalate their commitment if the prior setback was due to unstable rather than stable causes; subjects probably reasoned that an unstable deterrent was less likely to persist over time. Therefore, they should have been more optimistic that increased commitment would facilitate goal attainment.

A follow-up study by Conlon and Wolf (1980) strongly suggested that subjects' rational use of this kind of attribution information may be mediated by face-saving concerns. In this experiment 96 students from an introductory business course were told to imagine that they held the job of allocation officer with the World Bank. All participants had made an earlier allocation of $80 million to an economic project in Africa. Their 1-year feedback report informed them that the project had not proceeded as smoothly as was hoped: "To date $70 million of the original allocation of $80 million has been spent for the project. However, the industrial complex is only one-half completed." As in the Staw and Ross (1978) study, half were led to believe that the failure was due to an unstable cause ("an unusual amount of rainfall") whereas half thought that it was due to a stable cause ("basic indifference of the labor force"). Extending Staw and Ross' (1978) procedure, Conlon and Wolf (1980) included a manipulation similar to Levi's (1982) accountability variable. In their so-called "High Visibility" condition subjects had been told at the outset of the experiment that "Your supervisor requires bimonthly review sessions in which all of the allocation officers meet and review each other's allocation decisions. At this meeting you are required to present the details of each allocation and the logic used to make the decision. The other officers will then critique your decision. Today, you should be prepared to verbally present the details of your decisions, as well as their results to the other allocation officers." In the Low Visibility condition subjects were informed: "You have total autonomy over allocations to African nations. No one else needs to know about the decisions you make or reasons for those decisions." Thus, at the very outset of the experiment (i.e., even before subjects made their initial $80 million funding allocation) they were operating in the mindset of either having to defend themselves publicly (High Visibility condition) or not (Low Visibility condition). The primary dependent variable was the amount of money subjects allocated (out of $80 million of additional funds) to their previously chosen alternative on the second decision point.

The results of this study revealed an Attribution $\times$ Visibility interaction. Replicating Staw and Ross (1978), subjects overall allocated more subsequent resources in the Unstable than in the Stable attribution condition. However, this effect actually was obtained to a far greater extent in the High Visibility ($Ms = \$44.21$ vs. $\$23.6$ million, $p < .001$) than in the Low Visibility ($Ms = \$38.0$ vs. 35.0 million, n.s.) condition.

Three additional aspects of the Conlon and Wolf (1980) experiment, all germane to face saving, are worthy of further discussion. First, it seems reasonable that the Attribution $\times$ Visibility interaction reflected a tendency for the more ego-involved (i.e., High Visibility) participants to be increasingly vigilant to, and therefore influenced by, relevant cues for appropriate investment behavior. The implication is that a face-saving manipulation is but one example of the more general category of "ego-involvement" variables. In theory, nonsocial modes of manipulating ego-involvement should produce the same effect as the Visibility variable. Conlon and Wolf did, in fact, include an additional manipulation which appeared to capture the essence of ego-involvement, but in a much less social fashion than the Visibility variable. That is, their "Involvement" variable seemed to be related to the psychological (rather than social) significance that decision makers should have attached to performing their roles well.

In the High Involvement condition subjects were informed at the outset:

> There is a high demand (for the role of allocation officer) from individuals who are particularly devoted to the betterment of developing nations. Most allocation officers believe that the development of these nations is both morally beneficial and essential to world political stability. The job is very meaningful and important to you. You take pride in your job and in the fact that you are involved in aiding developing nations. You would be content to remain in your position until retirement.

In the Low Involvement condition subjects were told:

> There is a high demand (for the role of allocation officer) from individuals who want to move up quickly in the banking industry. Most allocation officers care very little about the progress of developing nations. They have taken the job because of its history as a "stepping stone" to vice presidential positions in the

international banking departments of more conventional banks. Your sole purpose for taking this job is to move up quickly to a vice presidential position and you are always on the lookout for such a job. The success of the projects you fund mean little to you except as a contribution to your upward mobility.

In short, those in the High Involvement condition were told to imagine that they were intrinsically motivated to do the best possible job, whereas those in the Low Involvement condition were instructed to act as if they had little intrinsic motivation.

The results of this psychological manipulation of ego-involvement were quite similar to those produced by the social operationalization of the same underlying process. Within the High Involvement condition subjects allocated more in the Unstable ($M = \$51.7$ million) than in the Stable condition ($M = \$27.0$ million, $p < .003$). The attribution effect did not even approach significance, however, in the Low Involvement condition ($M = \$34.8$ vs. $\$30.4$ million, respectively).

Second, an important difference in the results obtained by Conlon and Wolf (1980) from those found by Staw and Ross (1978) should be made explicit. Staw and Ross observed that subjects became more entrapped in the Unstable than in the Stable condition. Conlon and Wolf observed this tendency only when subjects' level of ego involvement was high rather than low (i.e., in the High Visibility and Involvement conditions, but not in the Low Visibility and Involvement conditions). How can this apparent discrepancy be explained? It may be that Conlon and Wolf extended Staw and Ross' findings; that is, when the data were collapsed across the ego-involvement manipulations in the Conlon and Wolf study, the results were identical to those of Staw and Ross: greater entrapment was found in the Unstable than in the Stable condition.

Importantly, Conlon and Wolf (1980) have demonstrated further that the effect of the attribution variable is mediated by degree of ego-involvement. The fact that Staw and Ross (1978) did not manipulate ego-involvement but still obtained the attribution effect implies that their subjects overall tended to be high in ego-involvement. This conjecture also seems reasonable. Unlike Conlon and Wolf, Staw and Ross required subjects to make a financial allocation decision for a different project prior to making recommendatons for the African project employed by both sets of authors. Subjects randomly received either success or failure feedback concerning the initial decision. From a face-saving or ego-involvement perspective, *all* participants in the Staw and Ross study received an *evaluation* of their prior decision. By virtue of having been evaluated, their level of ego-involvement in the subsequent phase of the study may have been heightened. If their level of ego-involvement was heightened then their subsequent decisions *should have* been influenced by the attribution variable in the manner shown, much like the ego-involved participants in the Conlon and Wolf (1980) study.

Third, unlike Staw and Ross (1978) Conlon and Wolf (1980) classified subjects into two groups based on the type of decision-making strategy they reported using for the final allocation. Conlon and Wolf reasoned that some subjects would approach the decision-making task more "scientifically" than would others; that is, when deciding upon the amount of money to allocate on the second decision, "calculators" would base their recommendation on "initial budget figures, information about the amount of money spent at that point, information about the state of completion of the project, and an assumption about the likelihood that the cause of the setback would persist." By contrast, their so-called "noncalculators" would not use such strict mathematical rules for making their decisions. Conlon and Wolf hypothesized that this individual difference variable would interact with the attribution manipulation, such that Calculators were expected to make greater allocations in the Stable than in the Unstable condition, whereas Noncalculators (like Staw and Ross' participants) were expected to show just the opposite pattern.

Conlon and Wolf's (1980) reasoning that the Calculators would reverse the Staw and Ross (1978) findings was as follows: by taking all of the relevant information into account, Calculators should come to realize that a larger allocation was needed to complete the project in the Stable than in the Unstable condition. Recall that all subjects were told that $70 million of the original $80 million was already spent, but that the project was only half completed. If the cause of the setback was perceived as likely to persist then Calculators should have determined that another $70 million would be necessary to complete the remaining half of the project. Alternatively, if the cause of the setback was perceived as unlikely to persist then Calculating subjects should have deduced that an amount considerably less than $70 million would be needed to complete the project. For example, Calculators in the Unstable condition might have reasonably assumed that one-half of the original allocation ($40 million) would be needed if the cause of the original setback was not expected to remain present for the second half of the project.

Before describing the methodology Conlon and Wolf (1980) used to classify subjects as Calculators or Noncalculators, and before discussing the effects produced by this variable, we should mention that *all of our previous discussion of the Conlon and Wolf data applied to the Noncalculators only.* As Conlon and Wolf had suspected, the Calculators did respond very differently.

After making their allocation decision subjects were asked to describe as completely as possible how the decisions were made. Three judges independently scored these open-ended responses, and majority rule was employed to determine each participant's category. Overall, the ratio of Calculators to Noncalculators was 3:2. An example of a calculating strategy in the Unstable condition was as follows: "Allocate $40 million: If the weather is the only problem and the weather is generally good, I say go ahead and finish it. I figure if it took $70 million to finish half, $40 million should finish the rest, assuming no more rain." Contrast this to the reasoning provided by a subject in the Unstable condition who was classified as a Noncalculator: "I decided to allocate $20 million. I didn't want to altogether drop the project because of the cost already incurred while at the same time realizing that weather conditions were not stable. I felt it best not to risk the entire amount, because I want to move up in the organization. I don't want it to appear as if the project was a complete failure." Notice that the noncalculator based his or her decisions on less easily quantifiable factors.

In accordance with Conlon and Wolf's (1980) predictions, there was a Calculator × Attribution interaction effect. As already mentioned, Noncalculators made larger allocations in the Unstable than in the Stable condition. However, Calculators were more entrapped in the Stable ($M = \$47.7$ million) than in the Unstable condition ($M = \$40.6$ million, $p < .03$). Although Calculators and Noncalculators responded very differently to the Attribution manipulation, it is crucial to emphasize that for both groups the effect of the Attribution variable was mediated by face-saving concerns. Earlier it was reported that the effect of the Attribution variable (on the Noncalculators' allocations) was significant in the High but not in the Low Visibility condition. A similar statement can be applied to the Calculators. Interestingly, Calculators in the High Visibility condition made much larger allocations in the Stable ($M = \$52.0$ million) than in the Unstable condition ($M = \$36.0$ million, $p < .01$). However, in the Low Visibility condition the Calculators' allocations were virtually identical in the Stable and Unstable conditions (Ms = $\$44.4$ vs. $\$44.2$ million, respectively).

Given the previous suggestion that Visibility and Involvement were different modes of operationalizing the more general variable of "ego involvement," one might have expected the Involvement variable also to mediate the effect of Attribution for the Calculators. Just as the *magnitude* of the Attribution effect was greater in the High than Low Involvement condition for Noncalculators, it was expected that the same would hold true for Calculators (although of course, the *direction* of the Attribution effect should be directly opposite to that of the Noncalculators). Unfortunately, this was not found to be true. For reasons that are not entirely clear, the Attribution effect for Calculators was somewhat, though not significantly, greater in the Low (Ms = $\$49.8$ vs. $\$37.2$ million) than in the High Involvement condition (Ms = $\$45.5$ vs. 43.6 million in the Stable and Unstable conditions, respectively).

The different results obtained for Calculators and Noncalculators suggest more generally that individual-difference variables may affect how decision makers come to define socially desirable behavior in an entrapping dilemma. Calculators and noncalculators utilized the Attribution information very differently from one another when trying to decide upon appropriate allocation behavior. Nevertheless, although Calculators and Noncalculators arrived at directly opposite conclusions, both groups' behavior appeared to be markedly influenced by face-saving concerns. For both groups, the magnitude of the Attribution effect was considerably larger in the High than in the Low Visibility condition. It is precisely under the former condition that subjects should have been more concerned about their social image.

A final comment on the Conlon and Wolf (1980) study is in order. We find their conceptual distinction between Calculators and Noncalculators to be in need of further refinement. Conlon and Wolf predicted that Calculators would become more entrapped in the Stable than in the Unstable condition, because they would "calculate" that larger allocations would be necessary to complete the project when the reason for the earlier setback was stable rather than unstable. However, this prediction only holds true if decision makers assumed that the subsequent allocation would have unequivocally enabled them to complete the project. It seems to us that in the Stable condition Calculators could have also "calculated" that the likelihood of being able to complete the project was uncertain or even low. Under such circumstances, it seems more reasonable to have expected decision makers to allocate *less* of their resources in the Stable than in the Unstable condition. The important question, then, is this: What information are calculators using (and what assumptions are they making) upon arriving at their decisions? Presumably, Calculating subjects in the Conlon and Wolf study were generally optimistic that the subsequent allocation would enable them to complete the project. If, however, they had been operating under the opposite assumption, then an entirely different data pattern (in fact, one similar to that shown by the Noncalculators) may have emerged.

Caldwell and O'Reilly (1982)

In all of the studies discussed to this point the primary dependent measure of entrapment has been resource allocation (i.e., the amount of time, money and/or effort that decision makers commit to the failing course of action). If resource allocation is mediated at least partially by self-presentation needs, then other dependent measures should be sensitive to the individual's desire to save face following a setback. Moreover, the experimental conditions that produce greater escalated commitment should produce parallel effects on other measures of face-saving behavior, provided that escalated commitment was motivated by face-saving concerns.

In fact, a recent study by Caldwell and O'Reilly (1982) utilized alternative dependent measures. In this experiment subjects (72 undergraduate business students of both sexes) were assigned the role of administrative manager of a small, growing technical company. They had either chosen an individual to serve as the contract officer in their company (Choice condition) or were told that the individual had been hired by the president (No Choice condition). Later, all subjects learned that their company had lost a major government contract due to the poor performance of the new contract officer. Half of the participants (High Responsibility condition) were led to believe that their Board of Directors and President held them personally responsible for the outcome, "since you were both the Contract Officer's manager and in charge of personnel relations." This factor was supposedly going to be reflected in their performance evaluations. Subjects in the Low Responsibility condition, by contrast, were told that they were not being held responsible by their superiors for the contract officer's failure.

A typical dependent measure of entrapment would tap some form of commitment to the employee (e.g., how much subjects were willing to let the contract officer retain his or her job). Caldwell and O'Reilly (1982), however, measured face-saving motivation differently. Specifically, subjects had been provided with a packet containing 34 items of information supposedly collected from company files relevant to the hiring and performance of the contract officer. Subjects had to select those items that they wanted to appear in a report documenting the hiring decision and subsequent performance of the contract officer. This report was to be forwarded to higher-level management for review. Some of the items, if revealed, were classified as Favorable to the subject's self-image (e.g., "You saw an outline of the proposal which the Contract Officer prepared and were quite satisfied. It conformed to the format used in other government proposals which had been funded."). The items designated as Unfavorable would have reflected poorly on subjects (e.g., "Your secretary had indicated that several requests for information from the Contract Officer had gone unanswered."). Still other items were classified as Open or Defensive (tapping the extent to which subjects made self-, rather than external, attributions for the contract officer's failure). Presumably, if subjects wished to produce a favorable image in the eyes of their boss, they would present more Favorable and Defensive (i.e., external blaming) items and/or fewer Unfavorable and Open (i.e., self-blaming) items.

Caldwell and O'Reilly (1982) employed orthogonal manipulations of Choice and Responsibility because these two factors typically have been confounded in previous research (e.g., Staw, 1976). They predicted that subjects who felt more accountable for (1) having chosen the contract officer, and/or (2) the contract officer's failure would be more likely to show commitment behavior (motivated by the need to save face) than those deemed less accountable by their superiors in the organization. Why? As Salancik (1977) has discussed, a variety of factors affect individuals' degree of commitment to their chosen behaviors. Salancik suggests that individuals feel more committed to the extent that they make self-attributions for their behavioral choices and/or for the outcomes of those choices (i.e., as in High Choice and Responsibility conditions used in this experiment).

The typical dependent measure of escalating commitment is resource allocation behavior. In this experiment subjects were not given the opportunity to express their commitment through escalating allocations. The results that did emerge, however, strongly suggested that felt commitment was mediated by face-saving concerns; that is, the conditions that should have fostered escalated commitment (if that were the dependent variable) produced greater face-saving behavior. Specifically, subjects in the High Responsibility condition presented more favorable items than did those in the Low Responsibility condition ($p < .05$). High Choice participants presented fewer unfavorable ($p < .05$) and more defensive ($p < .10$) items than did those in the Low Choice condition. Thus, under conditions that have been shown previously to engender greater escalation of commitment (High Choice and Responsibility; Bazerman et al., in press; Staw, 1976) there is evidence that subjects presented themselves in fashions designed to bolster their public image. In addition to the main effects produced by the Choice and Responsibility variables, interaction effects emerged. In the condition in which their degree of personal commitment was lowest (i.e., the Low Choice–Low Responsibility condition), subjects presented the fewest number of Favorable ($p < .05$) and Defensive items ($p < .10$) relative to the other three conditions.

In short, by employing a dependent variable different from allocation, Caldwell and O'Reilly (1982) have shown that factors producing escalated commitment also engender greater face-saving behavior. When subjects felt more accountable for the behavior producing negative consequences, they were more likely to present themselves to their evaluators (i.e., the organizational superiors) in a self-enhancing or self-preservative fashion. Such results strongly suggest that the heightened commitment to a failing course of action shown by subjects in related studies is a behavioral manifestation of their desire to save or restore face.

Face-Saving and Entrapment: Summary and Implications

The results of the studies described in the preceding section provide consistent evidence for the mediating effects of self-presentation motives on entrapment. What makes the self-presentational analysis so compelling is the fact that despite different entrapment methodologies as well as different modes of operationalizing face saving needs, the following common findings emerge:

1. When decision makers feel personally responsible for an earlier setback— that is, the condition which Staw (1976) initially demonstrated as necessary to produce the escalation effect—they will allocate more of their resources to the failing course of action when the need to justify their behavior to significant others is high rather than low (Fox & Staw, 1979; Levi, 1982).

2. More generally, self-presentational concerns can produce increased or decreased entrapment. Presumably, when placed in an entrapping dilemma, individuals try to identify whether persistence or withdrawal is more appropriate. A variety of factors can influence this decision, such as the advice offered by a significant audience member (Brockner, Rubin, & Lang, 1981), the perceived stability of the cause of the original setback (Staw & Ross, 1978), or individual-difference variables related to how the situation is cognitively structured (e.g., Conlon & Wolf, 1980). These types of factors should give rise to the *direction* that the decision makers's future behavior will take. The presence or absence of the need to look good should influence, however, the *magnitude* of their escalation or deescalation behavior.

3. Throughout this section (indeed, throughout the book) we have attempted to explain the experimental results at increasingly higher levels of abstraction. Accordingly, the Cue × Face-Saving interaction analysis proposed above (i.e., that cues will have a greater effect when face-saving concerns are high) may be

part of a more general tendency for people to be more responsive to cues for appropriate (entrapment) behavior when their ego involvement in the task at hand is high rather than low. In our estimation Conlon and Wolf (1980) employed two orthogonal manipulations of ego-involvement, one social (Visibility) and the other psychological (Involvement). These factors produced parallel effects on the allocation behavior of Noncalculators: heightened responsivity to the attribution manipulation when level of involvement was greater. Thus, regardless of whether individuals' level of ego involvement was heightened publicly or privately, their degree of entrapment may be more affected by cues for appropriate investment behavior. Clearly, further research is needed to evaluate this more general proposition, as the results exhibited by Conlon and Wolf's (1980) Calculator subjects are less consistent with it.

What are the implications of the fact that decision makers' need to save face can markedly affect their degree of commitment to a failing course of action? First, the face-saving analysis may make it more possible to identify a priori those decision makers who are prime candidates for entrapment. When individuals have to justify their decision to embark upon a chosen course of action that subsequently fails to produce its intended effect(s), they may be more likely to become entrapped. Consider, for example, the public debate surrounding the United States Government's decision to provide military aid to El Salvador in the early 1980s. Many Americans, both politicians and private citizens alike, voiced concern that the political/military situation in El Salvador would become "another Vietnam." Their (entrapment-based) logic was that as in Vietnam, it would become increasingly difficult for the U.S. to withdraw as it escalated its level of military aid. As of this writing, those opposed to U.S. aid in El Salvador have initiated considerable political activity designed to minimize the U.S.' involvement. Whether they are successful or not remains to be seen. The face-saving analysis, however, suggests a possibly paradoxical effect of this opposition activity: If members of the Reagan Administration do escalate U.S. aid to El Salvador *in the face of* considerable opposing public sentiment (both at home and abroad), then it may be even more difficult for them to withdraw at a later point in time. In the presence of many doubters the administration may feel even more compelled to demonstrate the soundness of its policies if favorable results are not produced immediately. Like the subjects in the High Resistance condition of the Fox and Staw (1979) experiment, they may do so by making increasingly larger future allocations.

Fox and Staw's (1979) finding that high-insecurity decision makers allocated more of their resources implies that new employees within organizations also may be likely victims of entrapment. Industrial/organizational psychologists (e.g., Louis, 1980; Wanous, 1980) have noted that incoming workers experience considerable stress in the initial stages of their job tenure. The entry process is one in which new employees are apt to feel a good deal of insecurity about themselves, their jobs, and their role in the larger organization. If so, then the potential for entrapment is even greater for new employees as they carry out their organizational duties.

Second, the fact that face-saving mediates escalation decisions suggests that it may be possible for decision makers to become less prone to entrapment, to the extent that they believe that they can look good by withdrawing (rather than escalating). In several studies (Fox & Staw, 1979; Levi, 1982) individuals became more entrapped when face-saving needs were high rather than low. Presumably, subjects believed that increased rather than decreased commitment was socially desirable in those situations. However, there are undoubtedly circumstances in which just the opposite is true. In several experiments (Brockner, Rubin, & Lang, 1981; Conlon & Wolf, 1980) decision makers became less entrapped under certain conditions when their need to save face was high rather than low. The issue of how to reduce entrapment will be considered further in Chapter 9.

Third, the results of the face-saving experiments raise concerns of theoretical (as well as practical) significance. Rubin and Brockner (1975), Staw (1976), and Teger (1980) originally conceptualized entrapment phenomena as examples of a more general self-justification or dissonance process (Festinger, 1957). Over the past 25 years dissonance has been subjected to a great deal of theoretical scrutiny. Bem (1972), for example, proposed that many experimental results previously interpreted within a dissonance framework can be more reasonably explained with his nonmotivational theory of self-perception. The focus of both dissonance and self-perception theories, however, is on intrapsychic change processes that occur when individuals make postbehavioral inferences about their attitudes.

In contrast, Tedeschi, Schlenker, & Bonoma's (1971) self-presentation analysis of "dissonance" phenomena highlights the public or interpersonal underpinnings of individuals' descriptions of their attitudes. According to Tedeschi et al., individuals placed in a dissonance-arousing situation do not alter their attitudes or behaviors in order to reduce the intrapsychic discomfort associated with dissonance. In fact, Tedeschi et al. have suggested that people in the forced-compliance situation—the classic experimental paradigm for producing dissonance—do not privately change their attitude at all. Rather, they alter their public *description* of their attitude in order to foster a desirable self-presentation. If people perform counterattitudinal behavior under no external pressure, they can at least appear consistent and thus save face (Staw and Ross, 1980) by changing their description (if not actual perception) of their attitude, so that it is consonant with their behavior. Several recent studies have suggested that attitude "change" following forced compliance is, in fact, nothing more than "insincere verbal statements intended to mend a spoiled identity" (Gaes, Kalle, & Tedeschi, 1978). In essence, the self-presentation theorists are suggesting that phenomena previously thought to be mediated by dissonance (e.g., the self-justification process underlying entrapment) will not occur (or will occur to a far lesser extent) if the individual's self-presentational concerns are low.

The results of the experiments described in the preceding section suggest that a significant portion of the self-justification process mediating entrapment can be heightened by self-presentational motives. Time and again it was reported that decision makers became more (or less) entrapped when their need to save face was high. This seems to support the self-presentational analysis of the nature of dissonance arousal. *However, we do not believe that the justification process underlying entrapment is entirely the result of interpersonal rather than intrapersonal processes.* Stated differently, a decision makers's face-saving motivation (defined as a concern with one's appearance *in the eyes of others*) need not be high in order for entrapment to occur. It is possible to think of numerous situations in everyday life in which decision makers exhibit entrapment, even though they are not in the actual presence of others. For example, the individual who is waiting alone at the bus stop cannot be entrapped for self-presentational reasons. Similarly, individuals who have had to take their automobile from one repairman to another in order to have different car parts mended (the transmission, body, etc.) are probably not entrapped out of a desire to save face. In short, entrapment often occurs in totally private situations. However, whether individuals persist in or withdraw from potentially entrapping situations can be greatly influenced by their desire to win favor in the eyes of others.

Self-Diagnosticity and Entrapment

Another variable conceptually related to face saving, which could affect the extent to which decision makers escalate their commitment to a failing course of action, is the "self-diagnosticity" of their prior resource allocations. Self-diagnosticity refers to the extent to which behavioral outcomes are seen by the self and/or others as self-revealing. There are at least two important components to self-diagnosticity:

(1) *Breadth*. The more an outcome is perceived to be revealing of a *wide variety* of self-aspects, the greater is its breadth. For example, individuals who perform well on an exam, may (at least temporarily) infer that they are also desirable romantic partners, good athletes, and fine cooks.

(2) *Depth*. The more an outcome is perceived to be reflective of *important or fundamental* aspects of the person's self-concept, the greater is its depth. For example, workaholics may attach considerable self-diagnosticity to their work-performance appraisal, in that it provides them with feedback about a central aspect of their self-concept.

Prior theory and research suggest that the self-diagnosticity variable may be an especially influential antecedent of entrapment. We have defined entrapment as the escalation of commitment to a failing course of action, executed in the service of justifying prior resource allocations. Many factors can affect decision makers' justification needs (and thus their propensity toward entrapment) including the self-diagnosticity of hitherto unfruitful resource allocations. If this negative feedback is seen as self-diagnostic, then individuals should feel greater pressure to justify the appropriateness of those prior investments. Entrapment may be especially apt to occur under such conditions. Alternatively, if the negative feedback is not viewed as self-diagnostic, then it may be easier for decision makers to "cut their losses" and not become entrapped.

Wortman and Brehm's (1975) theoretical analysis of the effects of failure on subsequent persistence is also germane. This view suggests that individuals' initial response to failure is reactance (i.e., a redoubling of effort intended to increase the likelihood of success). Furthermore, Wortman and Brehm posited that reactance arousal in response to failure is directly proportional to the psychological importance or significance attached to the failure. It seems reasonably straightforward that decision makers will assign greater significance to those failures which are seen as self-diagnostic, rather than non-self-diagnostic.

Both theoretical perspectives seem to predict that entrapment will be heightened when decision makers perceive the (negative) feedback associated with past expenditures to be self-diagnostic. The study by Staw (1976), discussed in considerable detail in Chapter 3, provides some empirical backing to this assertion. In that study subjects were more apt to become entrapped when they, rather than their "predecessor in the organization," were responsible for making the prior resource allocation that had met with failure. One interpretation of this finding (but by no means the only one) is that decision makers perceived the failure feedback to be more self-diagnostic when they, rather than their predecessors, were personally responsible for the earlier investment decision. In order to "prove" that their prior investment was not reflective of their incompetence, subjects who were personally responsible for the decision may have escalated their commitment to that course of action.

While theory and research are consistent with the notion that self-diagnosticity leads to heightened entrapment, this hypothesis has never been tested directly. Accordingly, we performed three experiments (Brockner, Houser, Lloyd, Nathanson, Deitcher, Birnbaum, & Rubin, 1985), each of which explored the effect of self-diagnosticity on entrapment. Before turning to the specific studies we should mention two organizing principles of the following presentation. First, the self-diagnosticity construct can be operationalized in several ways. In order to provide converging validity for the thesis that self-diagnosticity affects escalation decisions a variety of operationalizations were employed in the three experiments. Second, while self-diagnosticity may sometimes lead to heightened entrapment, it may also be the case that the reverse is sometimes true. An important purpose of the second (and to some extent the third) experiment is to specify some of the conditions under which self-diagnosticity leads to increased *or* decreased entrapment.

Experiment 1

The first experiment tested the hypothesis that the perceived self-diagnosticity of the negative outcomes associated with earlier investments would be causally related to degree of subsequent commitment. All subjects took part in an entrapment decision-making task, in which they incurred irretrievable costs while attempting to achieve the goal. Half of the subjects were informed that their task performance was reflective of important self-aspects (Self-Diagnostic condition), whereas half were informed that their task performance was not especially self-revealing (Non-Self-Diagnostic condition). It was expected that entrapment would be significantly greater in the former than in the latter condition.

Method. Fifty-two undergraduate students at Tufts University took part in the Carnival Game procedure described in Chapter 2. To summarize that procedure, subjects were given an initial stake of money ($3.50) and told that they could earn a substantially larger amount ($10.00) by successfully taking part in the experimental task. Subjects were shown a series of white cards that had black geometric patterns inscribed on them; their task was to estimate the percentage of cards that had been blackened by the pattern. The number of points they earned on each trial was directly proportional to the accuracy of their estimates ("in relation to judgments made by the other research participants"). Subjects had to pay for each trial that they completed, regardless of whether they won the jackpot. They were informed of the amount of each trial immediately beforehand, in accordance with the schedule presented in Table 6-2. In addition, subjects were free to quit at any point.

Prior to being asked whether they wished to take part, the self-diagnosticity manipulation was introduced. In the Self-Diagnostic Condition subjects were told:

> Before we begin, you may find it useful to learn what we know about this task. It has been given to more than 100,000 people from all walks of life, and has been used to make important judgments about people. Although it seems reasonably straightforward, it actually measures a number of significant traits. For one, it measures perceptual abilities and mathematical reasoning. In addition, and interestingly enough, how well peole do on this type of perception task seems to be correlated with their performance on *social* perception tasks, that is, how well they can "figure out" what other people are really like. For instance, many employment agencies and businesses use tests very simlar to this one when making hiring decisions. In short, high scores on this test are positively correlated with intelligence, personal happiness, and job satisfaction.

In the Non-Self-Diagnostic Condition subjects were informed:

> Before we begin, you may find it useful to learn what we know about this task. It has only recently been developed and tested on approximately 30 people. Needless to say, its usefulness in making judgments about people is very much in doubt at this point. It does not appear that this task measures any intellectual traits. It was developed by a graduate student who thought that this test might

be related to performance on *social* perception tasks, that is, measures of how well an individual can "figure out" what other people are really like. Even that idea seems a bit farfetched at this point. In short, neither intelligence, nor personal happiness, nor job satisfaction are related to what this measures.

The experimenter provided subjects with record sheets enabling them to keep track of their costs and number of points earned over time. Table 6-2 reveals the following facts about the financial cost of taking part: (1) it cost subjects no money to complete the first two trials; (2) the costs associated with each trial increased from the third trial onward; and (3) subjects had spent all of their $3.50 initial stake by the end of trial No. 21. Those who persisted beyond that point were willing to invest money other than that which had been given to them at the outset of the experiment.

After subjects completed each trial the experimenter provided them with feedback about their performance for that trial. Unbeknownst to the partici-

Table 6-2. Cost Function (Experiments 1-3)

Trial Number	Cost Per Trial (cents)	Cumulative Cost (dollars)
1	0	0.00
2	0	0.00
3	1	0.01
4	2	0.03
5	3	0.06
6	4	0.10
7	5	0.15
8	6	0.21
9	8	0.29
10	15	0.44
11	18	0.62
12	19	0.81
13	23	1.04
14	24	1.28
15	26	1.54
16	27	1.81
17	28	2.09
18	29	2.38
19	30	2.68
20	32	3.00
21	50	3.50
22	71	4.21
23	104	5.25
24	137	6.62
25	182	8.44
26	207	10.51
27	289	13.40
28	338	16.78
29	426	21.04
30	560	26.64

pants, this feedback had been preprogrammed to foster the impression that they were doing rather poorly at the task. The experimenter went to some length, however, to lead subjects to think that the feedback was dependent upon their performance. After subjects made their estimates the experimenter appeared to enter their responses into a (hidden) small computer, which would then indicate the number of points that subjects should receive for that trial. From Table 6-3 it can be seen that the number of points allocated ranged from 3 to 24. Given that their scores could range from 1 to 200 points per trial, this feedback was quite negative. Consequently, subjects never even came close to amassing the 1,000 points needed to win the jackpot. For example, after the 21st trial subjects had been awarded a cumulative total of 204 points.

Thus, in no case did subjects ever win the jackpot. The behavioral measure of entrapment was the number of trials that subjects completed (in the face of

Table 6-3. Number of Points Received (Experiment 1)

Trial Number	Number of Points Received	Cumulative Points
1	5	5
2	10	15
3	3	18
4	7	25
5	15	40
6	5	45
7	12	57
8	23	70
9	5	75
10	10	85
11	4	89
12	11	100
13	4	104
14	6	110
15	13	123
16	7	130
17	15	145
18	20	165
19	6	171
20	9	180
21	24	204
22	11	215
23	5	220
24	15	235
25	4	239
26	6	245
27	10	255
28	4	259
29	5	264
30	6	270

Note: Subjects had been told that the amount of points they could earn per trial ranged from 1 to 200, with higher point allocations representing better performance. To achieve the goal, they needed to earn a total of 1000 points.

mounting costs and negative feedback). Before the experiment began we had decided to stop the proceedings after the 30th trial, if subjects had not quit by that point. It was never necessary to do so in this experiment, although it was in several instances in the subsequent experiments. Afterwards subjects completed a brief questionnaire which included items assessing the importance of various motives underlying their behavior.

Results. As predicted, subjects escalated their commitment to a greater extent in the Self-Diagnostic than in the Non-Self-Diagnostic condition, attempting 18.68 trials in the former and 16.19 trials in the latter condition, $t(50) = 2.26$, $p < .03$. Moreover, this effect held true for subjects of both sexes. Thus, the basic prediction—that high self-diagnosticity leads to greater entrapment—received firm support.

Experiment 2

In this study we wished to explore the effect of self-diagnosticity on entrapment under conditions of more variable feedback. In the previous study subjects received consistently negative feedback about their task performance (see Table 6-3). However, in many entrapment situations the feedback that decision makers receive about their prior allocations may be much more variable. Suppose that a failing course of action seems to be showing some improvement in its return on investment. For example, an entrapping career may start to feel less dissatisfying; the entrapping romantic relationship may (at least temporarily) take a turn for the better; the decline in the value of the stock to which the investor feels wedded may slow for the time being. In all of these entrapment situations the overall feedback is negative (i.e., the career is still dissatisfying in an absolute sense, the relationship is still unrewarding overall, and persisting with the stock is still a losing proposition). However, unlike in Experiment 1, the decision makers' fortunes have changed for the better.

For several reasons it can be predicted that self-diagnosticity will further heighten entrapment under such conditions of "Increasing Fortunes." First, as mentioned in the introduction to the previous experiment, self-diagnosticity associated with an initially poor performance should elicit greater commitment. Furthermore, if the performance shows signs of improvement, then decision makers may infer that they have acquired the "knack" needed for goal attainment (e.g., how to find happiness in careers, relationships, etc.). If the knack is perceived to be self-diagnostic then the individual stands to gain all of the benefits associated with persisting with an initially dismal, but subsequently improving, course of action.

In other entrapment situations performance feedback may change for the worse, rather than the better. In the real-world example which inspired the Carnival Game procedure (see Chapter 2), individuals perform very well at a carnival task, at little expense. As they get closer to their goal, however, their performance takes a turn for the worse (while it costs more and more to continue playing). To cite another example of "Declining Fortune" feedback, many organizations may cling steadfastly to outdated policies or technologies, which initially yielded high returns but have long since outlived their usefulness.

The predicted effect of self-diagnosticity on persistence under such conditions is more tentative than in the case of Increasing Fortune feedback. On the one hand, it could be that self-diagnosticity will cause the decision maker to become even more rigid or perseverant (e.g., Staw, Sandelands, & Dutton, 1981). On the other hand, the prospect of being self-diagnostically linked to a "sinking ship" could be quite aversive, and thus cause decision makers to terminate their commitment.

In Experiment 2 all subjects took part in the Carnival Game procedure, and received highly variable performance feedback. For half of these participants the performance was initially quite poor, but then became more positive over time (Increasing Fortune condition). For the remaining half their performance was initially quite favorable but then gradually declined over time (Declining Fortune condition). In the overall sense, however, all subjects' performance was poor.

The self-diagnosticity manipulation differed from that used in the previous experiment. Subjects in the "self-diagnostic" condition were told that performance at the task was due to skill, whereas those in the "non-self-diagnostic" condition were told that it was due to luck. In short, this study consisted of a 2×2 factorial design, in which the independent variables were Performance Feedback (Increasing Fortune vs. Declining Fortune) and Self-Diagnosticity (Skill vs. Luck). An interaction effect was predicted: within the Increasing Fortune condition entrapment was expected to be greater in the Skill than in the Luck condition. Within the Decreasing Fortune condition this difference was expected to be significantly reduced, or even reversed.

Method. Forty-five introductory psychology students at Tufts University completed the experiment. The procedure was very similar to that employed in the previous experiment. There were, however, two modifications which dealt with the implementation of the independent variables.

(1) *Skill–Luck manipulation.* Subjects in the Skill (i.e., self-diagnostic) condition were told beforehand: "Although this task seems reasonably straightforward, it actually involves a number of basic skills, such as perceptual abilities, mathematical reasoning, and other intellectual skills. *Thus, how well you do is largely a matter of your own skill.*" Those in the Luck (i.e., non-self-diagnostic) condition were informed: "The task does not seem to be a measure of any known perceptual or intellectual skills. *Thus, how well you do is largely a matter of luck.*"

(2) *Performance feedback manipulation.* The number of points that subjects earned on each trial (as well as the cumulative total) is shown in Table 6-4. Note that in the Declining Fortune condition the number of points earned was very high (given the maximum of 200 points) on the first five trials, but then

began to taper off rapidly such that by the 10th trial subjects never received positive performance feedback again. In the Increasing Fortune condition subjects received very negative feedback for the first 12 trials, but then received much more positive feedback for the next 8 trials before their performance waned again. In both conditions the feedback was identical on trials 21–30 (see Table 6-4), and subjects never attained the 1,000 points necessary for goal attainment. What differed between the two conditions was the pattern of feedback on the first 20 trials.

It was decided a priori to include subjects' data only if they had persisted until at least the 13th trial. From Table 6-4 it can be seen that those who quit prior to this point were not fully exposed to the change in feedback, especially in the Increasing Fortune condition. The data of six additional participants were

Table 6-4. Number of Points Received (Experiment 2)

Trial Number	Declining Fortune		Increasing Fortune	
	Points Received	Cumulative Points	Points Received	Cumulative Points
1	185	185	1	1
2	163	348	2	3
3	141	489	1	4
4	178	667	1	5
5	132	799	3	8
6	28	827	1	9
7	71	898	2	11
8	11	909	5	16
9	40	949	1	17
10	3	952	2	19
11	1	953	4	23
12	3	956	11	34
13	4	960	132	166
14	1	961	44	210
15	1	962	185	395
16	1	963	178	573
17	2	965	163	736
18	1	966	151	887
19	2	968	28	915
20	1	969	54	969
21	5	974	5	974
22	2	976	2	976
23	1	977	1	977
24	3	980	3	980
25	1	981	1	981
26	1	982	1	982
27	2	984	2	984
28	1	985	1	985
29	1	986	1	986
30	1	987	1	987

Table 6-5. Task Persistence as a Function of Skill–Luck and Performance Feedback (Experiment 2)

	Performance Feedback	
	Increasing Fortune	Decreasing Fortune
Skill	$N = 11$ $M = 22.46$ $SD = 3.33$	$N = 12$ $M = 18.75$ $SD = 4.03$
Luck	$N = 9$ $M = 18.22$ $SD = 3.87$	$N = 13$ $M = 21.08$ $SD = 4.29$

Note: Scores could range from 13 to 30. Higher scores reflect greater escalation of commitment to the failing course of action.

discarded for this reason. These six subjects were (nearly) equally distributed among the four experimental conditions. The external validity of the results thus pertain only to those individuals who persisted long enough to experience the full Performance Feedback manipulation (i.e., 45/51 or 88% of all participants).

The cost per trial was identical in both conditions, and was based upon the schedule used in Experiment 1 (see Table 6-2). After completing the task subjects responded to a postexperimental questionnaire which included several items tapping the importance of various motives for their behavior.

Results. The only significant finding to emerge from a two-factor analysis of variance of the persistence data was the interaction effect ($p < .01$). As predicted, and as can be seen in Table 6-5, subjects in the Increasing Fortune condition were more entrapped in the Skill than in the Luck condition ($p < .025$, according to a simple effect analysis). The means were in the opposite direction in the Declining Fortune condition, though not significantly different from one another (according to a simple effect analysis). These results suggest that Performance Feedback moderates the effect of self-diagnosticity on entrapment; said differently, it is overly simplistic to assume that heightened self-diagnosticity inevitably increases entrapment.

Experiment 3

Experiment 3 was designed to be a partial replication and extension of the previous study. All subjects took part in the Increasing Fortune condition. Two operationalizations of self-diagnosticity were employed: the self-diagnosticity manipulation used in Experiment 1, and trait self-esteem.

The latter was intended to be a dispositional (rather than a situational) determinant of self-diagnosticity. Much evidence has shown that low-self-esteem individuals (low SEs) are very tuned in to the extent to which their behavior will be seen (by the self and/or others) as self-diagnostic (e.g., Brockner, 1983). By contrast, their high-self-esteem counterparts (high SEs) are much less likely to view their performance in evaluative situations as tests of their mettle. This is *not* to suggest that low SEs are more concerned than are high SEs with performing well in evaluative situations. Rather, self-diagnosticity refers to the extent to which individuals will go "beyond the information given" by their behavioral outcomes. Current conceptualizations of self-esteem suggest that the tendency to do so will be much stronger for low than high SEs. Therefore, it was predicted that the effect of self-esteem would parallel the one produced by the experimental manipulation of self-diagnosticity. Just as subjects were expected to become more entrapped in the Self-Diagnostic than in the Non-Self-Diagnostic condition (i.e., the finding obtained in the Increasing Fortune in Experiment 2), so were low SEs expected to exhibit greater entrapment than high SEs.

Method. Forty-six Tufts University introductory psychology students took part in the study. The procedure was identical to the one employed in Experiment 1, with several exceptions. The Performance Feedback which all subjects received was taken from the Increasing Fortune condition in Experiment 2 (see Table 6-4), rather than that which was used in Experiment 1 (see Table 6-3). The Self-Diagnosticity manipulation was the one employed in Experiment 1, rather than Experiment 2.

The postexperimental questionnaire included (1) The Rosenberg (1965) Self-Esteem Scale. To increase the likelihood that the scale measured trait (rather than state) self-esteem subjects were carefully instructed to complete the scale "with regard to how you feel in general, not necessarily how you are feeling this minute." A median split was utilized to classify subjects as high or low in self-esteem. (2) Two measures of psychological involvement with the perception task. (3) Four measures of underlying motives for behavior used in each of the previous experiments. (4) A measure of perceived confidence while performing the task.

Results. In order to experience the changing Performance Feedback subjects had to persist until at least the 13th trial (see Table 6-4). As in Experiment 2, the data of all participants who quit prior to the 13th trial were not included in the analysis of the entrapment results. Unexpectedly, given the low dropout rate in Experiment 2, a relatively high proportion of subjects (15/46 or 32.6%) quit prior to the 13th trial. This dropout rate did not differ significantly as a function of the four conditions created by this 2×2 (Self Diagnosticity $\times$ Self-Esteem) factorial design ($\chi^2(3) = 3.42$, $p < .30$). A two-factor unweighted means analysis of variance of the remaining 31 subjects' persistence data yielded no significant effects (all $Fs < 1$).

However, post hoc inspection of the data of *all* participants (including the 15 persons who quit prior to the 13th trial) revealed several interesting, though unexpected, patterns. Specifically, in the Self-Diagnostic condition subjects who quit prior to the 13th trial ("Quitters"; $N = 9$) tended to quit sooner ($M = 8.33$ trials) than those who quit prior to the 13th trial in the Non-Self-

Diagnostic condition ($N = 6$; $M = 10.17$). In addition, within the Self-Diagnostic condition those who remained beyond the 13th trial ("Stayers"; $N = 17$) persisted slightly longer ($M = 22.94$ trials) than did those who persisted beyond the 13th trial in the Non-Self-Diagnostic condition ($N = 14$; $M = 21.86$ trials). Stated differently, the Self-Diagnostic condition appeared to produce greater within-condition *variability* in behavior, in that decision makers who quit did so relatively early, whereas those who persisted remained for a relatively longer period. To test this notion more formally, we computed for all subjects absolute difference scores between their degree of persistence and the mean degree of persistence within that condition. The mean degree of persistence in the Self-Diagnostic and Non-Self-Diagnostic condition was 17.88 and 18.35 trials, respectively. The difference scores were, in fact, significantly larger in the former than in the latter condition ($Ms = 6.91$ vs. 4.91, respectively; $t(44) = 2.13, p < .05$).

It was predicted that the self-esteem variable would yield an effect similar to that produced by the experimental manipulation of self-diagnosticity. As mentioned above, the experimental manipulation affected variability (but not mean degree) of entrapment. Did self-esteem produce a similar (though unexpected) effect on within-condition variability in behavior? Yes. Across self-diagnosticity conditions, low SEs who quit prior to the 13th trial ($N = 9$) did so slightly earlier ($M = 8.78$ trials) than did the high SEs ($N = 6$) who quit early ($M = 9.56$ trials). The low SEs who persisted beyond the 13th trial ($N = 11$) persisted somewhat longer ($M = 23.64$ trials) than did the high SEs ($N = 20$) who invested beyond the 13th trial ($M = 21.80$ trials). Low SEs showed greater variability around their group mean (16.96 trials) than did high SEs around their group mean ($M = 18.96$ trials); the comparison of absolute difference scores around the group mean revealed a significant difference between the low and high SEs ($Ms = 7.36$ vs. 4.74, respectively; $t(44) = 2.74, p < .01$).

As expected, then, the experimental manipulation of self-diagnosticity and trait self-esteem yielded similar effects on behavior in Experiment 3. The nature of these effects, however, was contrary to prior expectations. Decision makers did not become *systematically* more or less entrapped as a function of the Self-Diagnosticity and/or Self-Esteem variables. Rather, those who should have attached greater self-diagnosticity to their performance feedback—those in the Self-Diagnostic condition and/or low SEs—showed greater within-group variability in behavior than did those who were less apt to view their task performance as self-diagnostic (i.e., Non-Self-Diagnostic condition subjects and/or high SEs).

Internal analyses. Why did the experimental manipulation of self-diagnosticity (and trait self-esteem) cause greater variability in degree of persistence? The results of several internal analyses may provide at least a partial answer. Subjects indicated on the postexperimental questionnaire how confident they felt while working on the task. Responses could range from "not at all confident" (1) to "very confident" (41). The effects of two independent variables were tested in an unweighted-means analysis of variance: (1) Self-Diagnosticity, and (2) whether subjects quit prior to the 13th trial (Quitters) or at or beyond the 13th trial (Stayers). The only significant finding to emerge from the analysis of variance was the interaction effect, $F(1,42) = 10.01, p < .01$. In the Non-Self-Diagnostic condition, Stayers reported feeling much more confident than Quitters ($M = 26.4$ and 11.8, respectively). However, in the Self-Diagnostic condition there was a slight, though nonsignificant tendency for Stayers to report feeling less confident than Quitters ($M = 20.4$ and 25.4, respectively).

Subjects also responded to two questions measuring their psychological involvement with the perception task ("How important was it for you to do well at the task?" and "How involved did you feel while you were working on the task?"). Responses to each measure could range from "not at all" (1) to "very much" (41). Responses to these two measures were significantly correlated ($r = .56$, $p < .001$), and summed into an index. A two-factor (Self-Diagnosticity × Quit–Stay) internal analysis of variance yielded a significant Quit–Stay main effect, $F(1,42) = 4.34$, $p < .05$, such that Stayers reported feeling more involved than the Quitters. The interaction effect was also marginally significant ($p < .10$). Simple effect analyses revealed that within the Self-Diagnostic condition Stayers reported feeling much more psychological involvement than the Quitters ($Ms = 51.06$ and 33.00, respectively; $p < .02$). This difference was trivial, however, in the Non-Self-Diagnostic condition ($Ms = 48.14$ vs. 46.33, respectively).

The results of these internal analyses may shed some light on the previously reported finding that degree of persistence was more variable in the Self-Diagnostic than in the Non-Self-Diagnostic condition. In the Self-Diagnostic condition subjects felt either very involved or very uninvolved with how well they were performing, psychological states that directly correlated with their decisions of whether to persist longer or quit earlier. (Recall that Stayers felt much more involved than Leavers, but only in the Self-Diagnostic condition.) Interestingly, the positive correlation between involvement and persistence in the Self-Diagnostic condition did not appear to be mediated by confidence in performing well at the task (in that the Stayers reported feeling somewhat less confident than the Leavers in the Self-Diagnostic condition).

The basis of subjects' persistence in the Non-Self-Diagnostic condition seemed much more "logical." That is, if they reported feeling confident, then they persisted; if they reported feeling unconfident, then they quit. (Recall that Stayers felt much more confident than Leavers, but only in the Non-Self-Diagnostic condition.) In short, we are suggesting that the predominant factor affecting persistence was very different in the Self-Diagnostic and Non-Self-Diagnostic conditions. In the former, high self-diagnosticity either increased or decreased psychological involvement, which, in turn, caused subjects to persist longer or to quit earlier. In the latter, subjects' concerns about the self-diagnosticity of their performance were not aroused. Consequently, their degree of persistence could be influenced by more (intrapsychically) logical factors (e.g., felt confidence).

If experimentally manipulated heightened self-diagnosticity caused subjects either to become very involved and persist *or* very uninvolved and withdraw, then similar results should be produced by low self-esteem—a dispositional determinant of heightened self-diagnosticity. Accordingly, we performed an additional two-factor (Self-Esteem × Quit–Stay) internal analysis of the psychological involvement data. The Quit–Stay main effect was, of course, still significant ($p < .05$), with subjects who stayed reporting greater involvement than those who quit. The interaction, while not significant ($p < .15$), took the same conceptual form as the previously reported Self-Diagnosticity × Quit–Stay interaction. Low SEs (for whom self-diagnosticity concerns presumably are salient) reported feeling much more involved if they had Stayed rather than Quit ($Ms = 53.82$ and 35.11, respectively; simple effect $p < .02$). High SEs, like those in the Non-Self-Diagnostic condition in the earlier internal analysis, reported feeling equally involved, regardless of their decision to Stay or Quit ($Ms = 47.50$ and 43.17, respectively; simple effect $F < 1$). Thus, for those subjects whose self-diagnosticity concerns were salient (through situational or dispositional determinants) there was a strong relationship between their self-reported psychological involvement and degree of persistence at the task. No such correlation emerged, however, for those decision makers whose self-diagnosticity concerns were not aroused.

Did persistence reflect entrapment? The Carnival Game procedure used in all three studies was specifically designed to capture the necessary ingredients of an entrapment situation. Here is how: (1) decision makers were required to make continued resource allocations if they wished to attain the goal; (2) there were financial costs associated with each resource allocation (beyond the first two trials); (3) subjects received negative feedback about their task performance; and (4) in all instances subjects had free choice about whether to invest their money or to quit.

Did subjects experience the entrapping dilemma which we had intended to create? To answer this question subjects in all three experiments were asked to indicate the extent to which various factors influenced their decisions to persist for as long (or as short) as they did. Two of these questionnaire measures were designed to tap felt entrapment ("I had already been in for so long that it seemed foolish not to continue," and "Once I had stayed as long as I did I decided to keep going. Otherwise all of the previous effort would have been a waste of time and money.") Subjects' responses to these two items correlated in the .55 range ($p < .001$) in all three studies, and were thus summed into an index. The other items were designed to measure financial motivation ("I wanted to make more money") and the desire to be a "helpful" subject ("I wanted to help the experimenter with the research").

If, in fact, subjects felt increasingly entrapped by persisting at the task, then there should have been a positive correlation (across all conditions) between

Table 6-6. Correlations Between Task Persistence and Self-Reported Motives

| | Motive | | |
	Feeling Entrapped	To Help the Experimenter	To Make Money
Experiment 1	.25 ($p < .10$)	.14	−.17
Experiment 2	.49 ($p < .01$)	−.30 ($p < .10$)	−.04
Experiment 3	.34 ($p < .02$)	.01	.24 ($p < .10$)

their degree of persistence and the extent to which they endorsed the entrapment items as self-descriptive. As can be seen in Table 6-6, the relationship was statistically significant in Experiments 2 and 3, and marginally significant in Experiment 1. Table 6-6 also reveals that there was no consistently significant correlation between task persistence and the other two (highly plausible) reasons why individuals might have persisted for as long or as short as they did.

Because subjects were only given four measures of motivation, it could be argued that the entrapment items were simply the best of a small, bad lot. In rebuttal, we should mention that subjects in Experiments 1 and 3 were also instructed to "write down, in your own words, any other reasons why you persisted for so long (or as short) as you did." About 30% of the subjects wrote nothing at all. No single motive was mentioned with great regularity; the most frequent ones, however, included the desire to improve their performance (indicated typically by those who persisted to a considerable extent), the desire not to spend more than their initial stake of money (indicated generally by those who quit at or before the 21st trial), and the desire to escape from a task at which they were performing poorly (indicated typically by those who quit relatively early). Thus, the results in Table 6-6—that the entrapment measures correlated with behavior whereas the others did not—were probably not due to the possibility that the entrapment measures were simply the best of a bad lot. Rather, the significant correlations between the entrapment items and persistence (and the nonsignificant correlations between the nonentrapment items and behavior) emerged in the context of subjects also having "free rein" to explain why they behaved as they did.

General Discussion

The results of Experiments 1–3 suggest that the perceived self-diagnosticity of performance feedback can have a marked effect on entrapment. Moreover, the effect of self-diagnosticity, like the effect of face-saving variables, is not unidirectional (i.e., self-diagnosticity can increase *or* decrease persistence). Experiment 1 showed that in the face of constantly negative feedback decision makers were more apt to escalate their commitment under self-diagnostic than non-self-diagnostic conditions. Experiment 2 showed that in the context of negative, but improving, task performance a self-diagnostic cause of behavior (skill) engendered greater entrapment than a non-self-diagnostic cause (luck). However, this skill–luck difference was significantly reduced when performance feedback deteriorated over time. The results of Experiment 3 were more complex than anticipated but still suggested that self-diagnosticity had an important impact on investment decisions. Subjects whose self-diagnosticity concerns were salient showed greater *variability* in their degree of entrapment relative to those who were less concerned with the self-evaluative implications of their performance.

The data raise two issues—one specific and the other more general—that warrant further explanation. Specifically, the results of Experiment 3 are apparently inconsistent with those of the previous two experiments. In Experiment 1 and in the Increasing Fortune condition of Experiment 2 high self-diagnosticity lead to heightened entrapment. The procedure used in the third experiment drew upon several aspects of Experiments 1 and 2. In particular, the self-diagnosticity manipulation was taken directly from the first study, and the performance feedback was identical to that which subjects had received in the Increasing Fortune condition of Experiment 2. Contrary to the prediction that high self-diagnosticity would systematically increase entrapment, it was found that high self-diagnosticity increased within-condition variability, in that subjects' degree of entrapment was either relatively small or large.

Why were the results of Experiment 3 contrary to expectation? To speculate, there were two important procedural differences between Experiment 3 and the previous studies that may have accounted for the unexpected results. First, the negative performance feedback which subjects received on the early trials (Trials 1–12) in Experiment 3 was even more negative than the unfavorable feedback which subjects received on comparable trials in Experiment 1 (compare Tables 6-3 and 6-4). Consequently, subjects in the last experiment should have been sensitized to the fact that their initial performance was *very* poor. This extremely poor performance may have been more psychologically aversive in the Self-Diagnostic (or Low-Self-Esteem) condition than in the Non-Self-Diagnostic (or High-Self-Esteem) condition, causing the "Quitters" to leave earlier in the former than in the latter conditions. If, however, subjects were able to withstand the initial negative feedback (true for the "Stayers") then the expected results emerged: Self-Diagnostic condition subjects (or low SEs) became somewhat more entrapped than did those in the Non-Self-Diagnostic condition (or high SEs).

A second possibly influential procedural difference is that the manipulation of self-diagnosticity in Experiment 3 may have been more psychologically impactful than the one employed in Experiment 2. In Experiment 2 subjects were told that their task performance was a matter of skill (Self-Diagnostic condition) or luck (Non-Self-Diagnostic condition). In Experiment 3 subjects in the Self-Diagnostic condition were told that their task performance was revealing of many important self-aspects (perceptual abilities, mathematical reasoning, social perceptivity, intelligence, and happiness), whereas those in the

Non-Self-Diagnostic condition were not. It is possible that self-diagnosticity concerns were greater in the Self-Diagnostic condition in Experiment 3 than in the corresponding condition in Experiment 2. This possibility, coupled with their extremely negative performance on the early trials, may have produced greater discomfort for at least some of the subjects in the Self-Diagnosticity, Increasing Fortune condition in Experiment 3 (the Quitters). This discomfort may have been lessened in the corresponding condition in Experiment 2 (Skill, Increasing Fortune); thus, there were virtually no Quitters in this condition, and the few who did quit did not do so any earlier than the Quitters in the Luck, Increasing Fortune condition.

This analysis of Quitters' tendency to leave earlier in the Self-Diagnostic than Non-Self-Diagnostic condition in Experiment 3 highlights the importance of two (related) variables: the magnitude of the negative feedback, and the degree of self-diagnosticity of that feedback. We are suggesting that the effects of these two factors on persistence following failure may be curvilinear and possibly interactive; i.e., if the magnitude of the failure feedback is low, and if the self-diagnosticity of that feedback is low, there will be little to recoup. Accordingly, persistence should be low. If the magnitude of the failure feedback is high, and if self-diagnosticity is high, then at least for certain individuals, there could be a good deal of resulting psychological discomfort; as a result, these individuals may also withdraw from the situation. Persistence may be high, however, if the magnitude of the failure is moderate while its self-diagnosticity is moderate to high, or if the magnitude of the failure is high and self-diagnosticity is moderate.

This reasoning, while clearly post hoc, may explain the discrepant results obtained in Experiment 3 and its predecessors. In Experiment 1 subjects may have experienced their failure feedback as moderately intense. In that study a relatively strong self-diagnosticity induction produced escalated commitment. In the Increasing Fortune condition of Experiment 2 the initial failure feedback was quite intense, but the potency of the self-diagnosticity manipulation may have been more moderate. As a result, virtually all subjects were able to withstand the initially negative feedback, and persisted long enough to experience their "positive" change in performance. In Experiment 3, however, both the intensity of the initial failure feedback and its associated self-diagnosticity seemed relatively high. Consequently, some of the subjects were driven to an early withdrawal (i.e., prior to the 13th trial), whereas those who persisted beyond the 13th trial became somewhat more entrapped in the Self-Diagnostic than Non-Self-Diagnostic condition, as predicted.

Clearly, the validity of this reasoning needs to be evaluated by further research. However, it is consistent with recent theory and research in the "learned helplessness" literature, which deals with the effect of failure on subsequent task persistence. Wortman and Brehm (1975) have argued that moderately impactful failure leads to increased striving (reactance), whereas highly impactful failure leads to withdrawal (learned helplessness). Let us assume that in Experiment 3, the combination of extremely negative performance feedback and the high self-diagnosticity of that feedback produced a failure of high impact. If so, then (at least some of the) subjects should have quit relatively early on, which is exactly what was observed.

This logic still does not explain, however, why most or all participants in the Self-Diagnostic condition in Experiment 3 did *not* quit relatively early. Recent research by Brockner, Gardner, Bierman, Mahan, Thomas, Weiss, Winters, and Mitchell (1983) has shown that all individuals do not respond the same way to highly impactful failure. Specifically, this type of negative feedback is most apt to produce withdrawal behavior (i.e., lack of persistence) in low, rather than high, self-esteem persons. Accordingly, in Experiment 3 most of the participants who quit relatively early in the Self-Diagnostic condition should have been low in self-esteem. Did this occur? Yes, to some extent. Seven out of the 14 low SEs (50%) in the Self-Diagnostic condition quit prior to the 13th trial; the corresponding proportion for the high SEs was 17% (2 out of 12). An arcsin transformation was applied to these proportions (Winer, 1971) and an analysis of variance of these transformed data was then conducted. The two proportions were shown to be marginally different from one another ($F(1,\infty) = 3.45$, $p < .07$).

Clearly, further research is warranted to clarify the specific results obtained in Experiment 3. In addition, there is a more general and probably more important future research concern embedded in the results of all three experiments. These studies have suggested that performance feedback self-diagnosticity has a significant effect on decision making in an entrapment context. However, the findings seem "contradictory," in that heightened self-diagnosticity led to increased entrapment under some conditions and decreased entrapment under others. The important global issue is to understand better the factors affecting whether self-diagnosticity will lead to greater or lesser entrapment.

The preceding analysis suggests that at least three variables are of importance in this matter: negativity of feedback, self-diagnosticity of feedback, and self-esteem. However, there are undoubtedly many other variables that could be influential. For instance, is the effect of self-diagnosticity affected by the *publicity* of the individuals' decisions? In the present experiments subjects received feedback about their decisions in the immediate presence of a significant other—the experimenter. Would similar results occur under more private conditions? Queried differently, is the effect of self-diagnosticity mediated by decision-makers' concerns about their self-identities in their own and/or others' eyes? Given our earlier discussion in this chapter on the effect of face saving on entrapment, it may well be that the significance level of the results in the self-diagnosticity experiments were at least partly due to the publicity of the decision-making task. That is, the publicity may well have *magnified* the extent to which self-diagnosticity lead to increased or decreased entrapment. However, it may not have affected the *directionality* of entrapment.

Regardless of the factors that future researchers may choose to study, we strongly advocate that the choice process be theory-driven. There currently exists in the literature numerous theories to explain the effects of failure on subsequent persistence, including dissonance (Festinger, 1957), reactance/ learned helplessness (Wortman & Brehm, 1975), and the cybernetic theory of self-focused attention (Carver, 1979). Theory-guided research will simultaneously enable investigators to evaluate the appropriateness of the theory as well as to better understand the mechanism(s) by which independent variables affect decision makers' level of entrapment.

Self-Diagnosticity and Entrapment: Some Closing Comments

Numerous other possibilities exist for further empirical and conceptual work on the link between self-diagnosticity and entrapment. For example, if further research continues to demonstrate that self-diagnosticity affects escalation of commitment decisions, it may become useful to delineate the antecedents of self-diagnosticity. What are the personal, interpersonal, and organizational factors that cause individuals to make further self-inferences from their behavioral outcomes?

Finally, and at a more conceptual level of analysis, it is important to distinguish between self-diagnosticity and a range of other closely related (but not identical) processes. For instance, attributing one's behavior to internal (rather than external) causes is similar to, but not isomorphic with, perceiving one's behavior as self-diagnostic. The former is concerned with the perceived *cause* of behavior, whereas the latter is concerned with the perceived *meaning* of behavior. If, for example, individuals attribute their poor task performance to lack of effort, or even to lack of ability, it does not automatically follow that they will view their poor task performance as diagnostic of other significant self-aspects. They may or may not.

In addition, self-diagnosticity is not exactly the same as face saving. Both constructs imply that motivations which "preserve" the self-concept are important factors mediating entrapment behavior. However, the two concepts, while highly related, differ (subtly) in the self-aspect that is being preserved. Face saving refers to the need to restore, maintain, or boost self-esteem. Self-diagnosticity refers to the need to maintain a coherent, stable sense of self-identity. In a sense, self-diagnosticity is the psychologically deeper, more encompassing motive of the two. According to a face-saving analysis, the decision about whether to escalate commitment to a failing course of action is made in the service of "looking good." According to a self-diagnosticity analysis, the decision about whether to escalate commitment is made in the service of maintaining one's self-identity. Consider the following, more extreme impact of self-diagnosticity on escalation decisions: a decision maker who does *not* escalate commitment in the face of self-diagnostic negative feedback may initiate an "identity crisis" of sorts. That is, if the individual's self-identity is inextricably bound to pursuing a particular course of action, and if that course of action is no longer functional, then the (necessary) cessation of that behavior may cause the individual to ask, "If I am not the person who persists with this particular course of action, then who am I?"

It is also worth noting that this reasoning could be applied at the organizational as well as individual level of analysis. That is, the organizational graveyard is replete with instances in which firms persisted with policies or strategies that had long since outlived their usefulness. A comprehensive treatment of factors mediating organizations' resistance to change is beyond the scope of this chapter. However, the present analysis highlights one possible mediator of resistance to change: the organization may perceive that its identity will be shaken or lost, *unless* it persists with its previously chosen, though now failing, courses of action.

Chapter 7
The Psychological Process of Entrapment

The preceding chapters have described the results and implications of studies exploring the social and nonsocial antecedents of entrapment. In virtually all of this research, the independent variables were manipulated or measured prior to the subjects' initial decisions about whether to allocate their resources. While this experimental technique has enabled us to delineate a number of factors that bear upon the *causes* of entrapment, it is less informative about the *process* of entrapment itself.

We might add that the methodological procedure used to identify the causes of entrapment is generally quite similar to that used in many social-psychological studies of conflict. As Teger (1980) has pointed out, much conflict research has adopted a static perspective; that is, conflict has often been studied at one point in time, most typically at its beginning or ending stages. Thus, researchers have explored factors that cause covert, underlying hostilities between antagonists to materialize into overt conflict. In addition, there has been much research activity on how conflicts may be resolved (Deutsch, 1973), including the establishment of several multidisciplinary professional journals (e.g., *Journal of Conflict Resolution, Negotiation Journal*) focused on this theme.

Much less research, however, has dealt with the psychological dynamics of conflict that are bound to accompany, if not mediate, the behavioral processes of escalation and deescalation. This relative underemphasis on process is most unfortunate, because some of the most important and interesting ideas about conflict may well stem from the study of its underlying dynamics.

The *psychological process* of entrapment is the subject matter of this chapter, which has been divided into two major sections. In Chapter 1 it was suggested that the psychological states of decision makers change as they become more committed to a previously chosen course of action. In the first part of this chapter we consider more precisely the nature of these psychological changes. For example, our conceptualization of entrapment suggests that there should be certain shifts over time and commitment in decision makers' perceptions of their motives for investing. Empirical evidence pertinent to these and other cognitive consequences is considered in the first part of the chapter.

While the first part of the chapter focuses on the cognitive changes that presumably accompany entrapment, the second section explores some behavioral implications of these cognitive changes. In particular, it will be shown that identical factors (i.e., independent variables) may have quite a different effect on degree of entrapment, depending on the point in time at which the factor's effect is assessed. For example, it has been demonstrated repeatedly that heightened cost salience reduces entrapment (Brockner et al., 1981; Rubin & Brockner, 1975). In these studies cost salience has been experimentally manipulated *prior to* the beginning of the decision-making task. Would the cost salience factor produce a similar result were it to be introduced *after* the decision maker had invested a substantial amount of resources? These and related questions are considered in the latter part of the chapter.

Before discussing the relevant research, we should mention one caveat. The data to be presented here are in some instances less clear-cut than those presented in previous chapters. Alternative explanations for at least some of the findings are quite possible; wherever appropriate these alternative accounts will be considered. Nevertheless, taken together the findings provide at least suggestive evidence about the psychological process—that is, the dynamics—of entrapment.

Some Psychological Consequences of Entrapment

Perceived Motivation

Anecdotal evidence suggests that decision makers are motivated at least in part by rational, economic considerations when they first embark upon a course of action that later proves entrapping. For example, classroom demonstrations of the Dollar Auction typically stimulate a flurry of low bids from numerous people, each of whom is hoping to make some money. (This is not to say that economic factors are the *only* motives decision makers have for getting started. Some get involved in the Dollar Auction game in order to "have fun." Moreover, many subjects in our laboratory studies report that they feel it is "only fair" to invest some of their resources.)

As their commitment deepens, decision makers in classroom demonstrations of the Dollar Auction game report a change in their motivation. The two bidders who become entrapped in trying to outbid one another are likely to say things like, "I knew I was going down, but I wanted to make sure that I brought the other person down with me," or "I wanted to show the auctioneer (typically the professor) and everyone else that was watching that I would not back down," or "I had already gone so far that I had too much invested to quit." To be sure, *some* of the motivation at this later stage of the entrapping task remains economic in nature; as opposed to maximizing monetary gain, however, decision makers now wish to minimize losses. (For example, an MBA student at the Massachusetts Institute of Technology wrote some rather elaborate mathematical calculations in his notebook when the bids between him and his opponent reached $1.35 and $1.40, respectively. When questioned later, he reported that he was trying to calculate the bid that would enable both his opponent and himself to lose an equal amount, in the hopes of ending the auction. Indeed, his next bid was $2.40, whereupon the other person did proceed to quit.) On the whole, however, the later motivations in the classroom demonstrations have a distinctly more rationalizing, rather than rational quality: decision makers are concerned with "looking good," both in their own eyes and those of salient others (e.g., their opponent, the auctioneer, the onlooking audience).

In addition to anecdotal evidence there has been some empirical research pertinent to this issue. Two research strategies have been utilized to study the self-reported psychological changes accompanying the entrapment process. In one approach the post hoc motivation of decision makers who became entrapped are compared to those who did not. In essence, this procedure represents a cross-sectional methdology. This procedure assesses the psychological changes accompanying entrapment to the extent that two assumptions are met: (1) decision makers report their most recent motivations, and (2) decision makers exhibiting entrapment were motivated at an earlier point in time by the same factors described by those who did not become entrapped.

The other research strategy adopts more of a longitudinal approach. More specifically, subjects take part in some entrapping decision-making task, but are interrupted at various points in time. During these interruptions participants are asked to describe the factors motivating their behavior at that particular moment. This technique enables one to track the changes (if any) that the *same* individuals experience as they become increasingly entrapped (in contrast to the cross-sectional approach, which compares different individuals at different points in time).

"Cross-sectional" research. Brockner (1977) had pairs of subjects take part in a Dollar Auction. Although they were under the impression that they were competing against one another, in reality the "opponent's" bids were experimentally programmed. In all instances the experimental program increased the bidding level above the subjects' previous bid. Thus, subjects either quit before investing their entire initial stake of money, or were required to stop when they had exhausted all of their money. Most subjects (71%) invested all or almost all of their initial stake of $2.05. The remainder of the participants quit at a point which enabled them to retain a substantial portion of their initial sake (i.e., at or before $1.50).

After the auction all subjects were asked to rate the importance of various reasons for their behavior (along 41-point dotted continua). Several of these factors tapped economic motives (i.e., "I wanted to add as much money as possible to my initial stake," and "I wanted to lose as little money as possible from my initial stake"). Other possible motives pertained to the need to rationalize or justify previous expenditures, both in one's own eyes (i.e., "I had already invested so much, it seemed foolish not to continue") as well as in the eyes of others (i.e., "I wanted to show the other person that I would not give in," and "I wanted to show the experimenter that I would not give in to the other person").

The responses of those who had spent all (or nearly all) of their money were compared to those who had quit the bidding relatively early. The two groups reported being equally motivated by the desire to add money to their initial stake. However, those who quit early reported being motivated by the need to minimize losses from their initial stake to a far greater extent than those who quit late ($Ms = 27.6$ vs. 16.5, respectively; $t(105) = 4.77$, $p < .001$). Those who quit late reported being more motivated by the desire to justify previous commitments in their own and in their opponents' eyes than those who quit early ($Ms = 23.7$ vs. 9.5; $t(105) = 5.06$, $p < .001$; $Ms = 19.8$ vs. 7.4; $t(105) = 4.78$, $p < .001$). There was also a slight, though nonsignificant, tendency for late quitters to be more concerned than early quitters about showing the experimenter that they would not give in to their opponent (Ms 7.26 vs. 4.97, $t(105) = 1.49$, $p < .15$). In short, the results of this study suggest that economic concerns (i.e., the desire to minimize losses) motivated the behavior of those who did not become entrapped, whereas self- (and other-) justification factors mediated the decisions of those who did become entrapped.

Of course, the above data are merely suggestive of the possibility that decision makers' motives change as they become more committed to an entrapping course of action. Several alternative explanations are possible. First, subjects' self-reported motivations, measured after the behavior occurred, may simply reflect their post hoc rationalizations (rather than true motivations) for acting in the manner that they did. This possibility exists, of course, whenever self-reported motivation is measured after the behavior has already occurred. Second, the individuals who became entrapped (i.e., those who invested all, or nearly all, of their money) may not have been motivated at the earlier stages by the same factors influencing the behavior of those who did not become entrapped (i.e., those who quit at a much earlier point in the process). This is an example of the more general problem associated with assessing change by the use of a cross-sectional methodology.

The latter problem can be minimized by studying changes in self-reported motivations of the same individuals at different points in the process. We turn now to the results of this "longitudinal" research.

Longitudinal research. Several of the experimental paradigms mentioned in Chapter 2 have been used to study self-reported change in motivation. For example, Teger (1980) assessed subjects' motives at various stages of the Dollar Auction game. Subjects who had become entrapped (i.e., those who had spent at least $1.50 of their initial stake) were asked (when the bidding had reached $.50, $1.00, and $1.50) to rate the importance of the following factors in guiding their behavior: (1) the desire to make money, (2) concern about the possibility of losing more money, and (3) the need to show that they were better at this task than their opponent. As their investments mounted, subjects reported becoming less motivated by the fear of losing more money, and more driven by the desire to "outperform" their opponent. (There was no reported change in the strength of their desire to make money.)

In our own research laboratory we have utilized the jigsaw puzzle and carnival games (both described in Chapter 2) to study self-reported changes in the motivations of entrapped decision makers. In the jigsaw puzzle procedure subjects were interrupted after they had requested 20, 40, 60, and 80 pieces of the 80-piece puzzle. Stated differently, subjects were queried after having spent $1.00, $2.00, $3.00, and (all) $4.00 of their initial stake. In the carnival game subjects completed questionnaires near the beginning, in the middle, and near the end of their involvement at the task. More specifically, participants in the carnival game procedure were interrupted after the 3rd, 12th, and 21st cards had been shown (i.e., after having invested $0.01, $0.81, or [all] $3.50 of their initital stake).

In addition to assessing motivational shifts, we were interested in studying other psychological changes that might accompany the entrapment process. For instance, subjects were asked to report their degree of involvment in the task, and their confidence in attaining the goal as they invested more of their resources.

Jigsaw puzzle study. Subjects indicated along 51-point continuum scales the extent to which the following factors were motivating their behavior: (1) "I am interested in the challenge of the puzzle, not just the making of more money," (2) "I have too much invested to quit in the solution of this puzzle to quit working on it," and (3) "I feel that the experimenter wants me to work on the puzzle." In addition, subjects were asked other questions not having to do with perceived motivation. These included (4) "How confident are you about completing the jigsaw puzzle?" and (5) "To what extent has this questionnaire interrupted your concentration on the jigsaw puzzle?"

Subjects did report systematic changes in their motivations and perceptions upon being questioned after requesting 20, 40, 60, and 80 pieces. Specifically, they felt increasingly motivated by the challenge of, rather than the money associated with, completing the puzzle ($Ms = 27.1$, 29.9, 29.9, and 31.5 respectively; $F(3,36) = 3.87$, $p < .02$). In addition, they were more apt to report having "too much invested to quit" at the later than the earlier stages of their involvement ($Ms = 18.8$, 19.7, 25.2, and 24.4 respectively; $F(3,36) = 3.18$, $p < .05$). Subjects also reported that their motivation to continue working on the puzzle in order to please the experimenter lessened after the initial stage of the task ($Ms = 28.5$, 24.9, 26.1, and 25.0; $F(3,36) = 3.64$, $p < .03$).

Other significant findings ($p < .05$) included the tendencies for subjects to become less confident over time that they would be able to complete the puzzle, and to feel increasingly that the questionnaire interrupted their concentration on the puzzle.

Carnival game study. Several significant results similar to those observed in the jigsaw puzzle experiment were obtained in this study as well. For example, subjects heightened the perceived importance of having too much invested to quit over time ($Ms = 3.22$, 17.28, and 22.94, $p < .001$). In addition, they reported becoming significantly less confident ($p < .03$) and more pessimistic ($p < .03$) about their chances of success. They also felt more "distracted by having to fill out this questionnaire" ($p < .06$) as their degree of investment deepened. The consistencies across the two studies are striking in that the entrapping tasks are obviously quite different from one another.

Several other measures were included in this, but not in the preceding, experiment. Thus, subjects reported feeling more involved ($p < .01$), yet more frustrated ($p < .03$), over time. In addition, subjects were more apt to say that they were "fully concentrating on the task to the exclusion of any other thoughts" in the later stages of the entrapping task.

Taken together, the results of our and Teger's (1980) longitudinal studies suggest several themes. First, the (self-reported) motivations of entrapped decision makers do undergo systematic changes as the investers become more committed to their failing course of action. At the outset they are concerned with making money, or at least with not losing much money. In the later stages they report being motivated by more rationalizing (than rational) forces, such as the perception of having too much invested to quit (in the jigsaw puzzle and carnival game), or the need to outbid their opponent (and thus not lose face) in the Dollar Auction game. In an important sense, these data reinforce a point raised by the studies in Chapters 4–6 on the antecedents of entrapment; namely, that entrapment behavior is motivated by a variety of factors, some economic/rational and others more psychological or social-psychological in nature. The present results go one step further, however. More specifically, the extent to which these different categories of variables affect decision making may interact with the stage of the entrapping dilemma. "Economic" variables (i.e., those derived from expectancy/value models of human choice behavior) may be more potent determinants of behavior in the earlier stages, whereas psychological and/or social-psychological needs may prevail in the later phases.

Second, heightened investments in the jigsaw and carnival game experimental situations do seem to be reflective of entrapment. Subjects increasingly reported having "too much invested to quit" as they invested more of their resources. We might add that they did *not* increasingly endorse other plausible, though non-entrapment-related, causes for their behavior over time (e.g., "I wanted to make more money" or, "I enjoy solving jigsaw puzzles"). These findings suggest that the jigsaw puzzle and carnival game provide plausible procedures for the study of entrapment.

Third, other psychological processes (besides perceived motivation) appear to change as degree of entrapment heightens. For example, subjects in both the jigsaw puzzle and carnival game procedures reported feeling *less* (rather than more) confident about being able to attain their goals as their investments mounted.

"Tunnel vision" and entrapment. Finally, subjects reported feeling more psychologically challenged (in the jigsaw puzzle study) or involved (in the carnival game experiment) as they became more entrapped. We speculate that the nature of this increased psychological involvement is a sort of heightened "tunnel vision"; that is, a tendency to focus on one's involvement at the task to the exclusion of any other (relevant or irrelevant) external stimuli. In fact, several findings were consistent with this proposed tunnel vision effect that accompanies entrapment. For example, subjects in the carnival study reported that they were more focused on the task to the exclusion of any other thoughts in the later stages of the decision task. Furthermore, this finding may explain several others. Recall that subjects in both the jigsaw and carnival studies experienced the later questionnaires as more "distracting" and more of an "interruption" than the earlier ones. Perhaps the later questionnaires were more distracting because they required decision makers to shift their attentional focus from the entrapping task at hand to the questionnaires. In addition, subjects in the jigsaw puzzle study reported being less motivated over time by the experimenter's (real or imagined) desire for them to work on the puzzle. Again, this finding may have reflected subjects' reported tendency to increase their attention to the task at hand, relative to other cues; that is, as subjects became more involved with their commitment to the task they were less apt to be concerned with the wishes of the experimenter.

Much more needs to be learned about the cognitive consequences of entrapment; clearly, the data presented thus far are quite speculative. Even so, the possibilities that entrapped decision makers may become less confident about achieving their goals, and/or more prone to exhibiting tunnel vision, have interesting implications. For one, such psychological effects may help us understand the difficulty decision makers have in disengaging from an entrapping, failing course of action. At first blush, it seems only logical that individuals will withdraw from a course of action that seems doomed to fail; however, the justification process underlying entrapment may make individuals feel even more committed to the failing course of action. After all, if individuals have invested a lot, and prospects for success look gloomy, they may feel intense pressure to justify the correctness of their actions. In the truest sense, then, it may not be that entrapped decision makers persist *in spite of* their pessimistic chances for goal attainment. Rather, they may persist *because of* such negative expectations. This line of reasoning, is hardly novel, having been advanced more than 25 years ago in Festinger, Riecken, & Schachter's (1956) classic study of The Seekers.

Moreover, the presence of tunnel vision may make decision makers less attentive to important external stimuli. When faced with the uncertainty that most entrapping tasks pose, we suspect that decision makers initially scan their environment for cues to aid them in choosing the most prudent course of action. If tunnel vision emerges, however, then individuals will be less vigilant about attending to such cues. The picture that emerges is one of the entrapped decision maker saying, in essence, "Don't bother me with facts (because I can't attend to them anyway); my mind is already made up!"

Alternative explanations. There may be other ways to explain the findings that different stages of entrapment are associated with a host of psychological changes. Perhaps most compelling of these alternative explanations is the possibility that the self-reported changes in motivation/cognition were not related to degree of entrapment, but rather were caused by the fact that subjects had to answer the same questions repeatedly. It is possible that the act of completing questionnaire items repeatedly, quite independent of the stage of the entrapping conflict during which the measurement process occurred, produced systematic changes in self-reporting.

It has been shown that the act of completing questionnaires can produce reactive effects on behavior (e.g., Dweck & Gilliard, 1975). In one study Teger (1980) doled out initial stakes of $2.00 or $5.00 to subjects with which to bid in the Dollar Auction. In addition, half of these subjects completed questionnaires measuring their motivation(s) during the actual course of the auction, whereas the other half were not interrupted during the bidding in order to complete questionnaires. An interaction between the independent variables emerged: those completing the questionnaires midstream became more entrapped in the $2.00 condition, and less entrapped in the $5.00 condition, relative to those who were not queried about their motivations during the course of the bidding. Not only are such findings interesting in their own right—Teger suggests that the process of answering questions midstream is not unlike that which occurs when entrapped disputants in an international, or labor–management conflict hold press conferences during which they must field questions from the media— but also they are germane to the issue at hand: that the process of completing questionnaires can influence subsequent behavior.

Other findings from the jigsaw puzzle study, however, fail to support this reactivity explanation. In that experiment three groups of subjects were studied, in addition to the already described group who was interrupted after requesting 20, 40, 60, and 80 pieces. One group was interrupted and questioned after requesting 40, 60, and 80 pieces (i.e., the 40-60-80 group), a second group was questioned after requesting 60 and 80 pieces (i.e., the 60–80 group), whereas a third group was only queried after requesitng all 80 pieces (i.e., the 80 group). If the differences in self-reporting are somehow attributable to the number of times that the subjects were interrupted and questioned, and not related to the stage of the entrapment process, then one should find differences in the *final* ratings of subjects in the four groups. For example, subjects in the 80 group, who have only been questioned once, should make different ratings than the last set of ratings completed by subjects in the 20-40-60-80 group, who completed the questionnaire for the fourth time. Similarly, if reactivity is the cause of self-report differences, then the ratings made after 60 pieces were requested should differ in the 20-40-60-80, 40-60-80, and 60-80 groups. In addition, ratings made at the 40-piece interval should differ in the 20-40-60-80 and 40-60-80 groups.

If, however, the previously reported differences were related to the stage of the decision process, then there should be no differences in the above-mentioned comparisons. Out of the 30 one-way analyses that were performed, only one effect proved significant. (When questioned after requesting 60 pieces, subjects in the 20-40-60-80 group gave higher ratings to the perceived entrapment item "I have too much invested to quit" than did those in the 40-60-80 and 60-80 groups; $p < .05$). Overall, then, there is little support for an alternative explanation based on reactivity due to the repeated administration of the questionnaire.

Before we speculate about possibilities for future research, an additional point should be discussed. All of the "longitudinal" data reported to this point were drawn only from those participants who exhibited entrapment at the behavioral level (i.e., all of these subjects had invested their entire initial stake). The underlying logic is that in order to delineate the sequential cognitive consequences of entrapment it is necessary to study the reactions of decision makers who ultimately became entrapped. Of course, not all subjects in the Dollar Auction, Jigsaw Puzzle, or Carnival Game procedures invested their entire initial stake. In fact, more than 50% of the participants in each study failed to do so.

What can be said about the decision makers who did not become entrapped? How did their psychological states change over time? Were the changes similar to those shown by those who did become entrapped? To state the preceding question differently, is it possible to predict decision makers' ultimate level of entrapment, based upon the self-reports that they offer during the earlier stages of the process?

The Carnival Game data revealed some similarities, but also some intriguing differences in the self-reports offered by subjects who ultimately did ($N = 9$) or did not ($N = 12$) become entrapped. The latter group consisted of those participants who persisted long enough to complete the second questionnaire (i.e., after the 12th card), but who quit before their entire initial stake had been invested (i.e., before the 21st card). Both groups endorsed the perceived entrapment item ("I had too much invested to quit") to the same extent on the first and second questioning, showing a marked increase over time.

In addition, like the entrapped group, the nonentrapped subjects reported an increase in "pessimism" and "frustration" and a decrease in "confidence" from the time of the first to the second questionnaire. However, the *absolute* level of pessimism, frustration, and lack of confidence was always greater for the group of participants who quit, rather than persisted. The level of "effort into judging the cards" was also consistently lower for the former group. Furthermore, unlike the entrapped group, the nonentrapped participants reported feeling *less* involved, and that they were concentrating on the task to a *lesser* rather than greater extent over time.

To explore further the self-report differences between the entrapped and nonentrapped participants, we computed a series of correlations between their questionnaire responses and ultimate degree of entrapment at each of the interruption periods. Interestingly, several of the responses given by decision makers to the initial questionnaire, when they had only completed three trials, were predictive of future behavior. Subjects were apt to become significantly more entrapped if they reported (1) feeling confident about being able to win the jackpot, and (2) expending greater effort to judge the cards accurately, and (3) feeling satisfied rather than frustrated.

Self-reports offered at the time of the second interruption (after 12 trials had been completed) were also significantly correlated with degree of entrapment. To wit, subjects' degree of entrapment was greater to the extent that they reported that they: (1) were concentrating on the task to the exclusion of any other thoughts, (2) were confident about winning the jackpot, (3) were putting effort into the task, and (4) felt "involved" and 'interested" in the task.

It is theoretically as well as practically important that the decision makers' ultimate degree of commitment was predictable from their earlier self-reports. At the theoretical level, several of the findings are consistent with the tunnel vision explanation of escalated commitment. Not only did the entrapped subsample report becoming increasingly focused on the task at hand (perhaps at the expense of attention to peripheral cues), but also the nonentrapped subgroup reported no such tendency. At the practical level, the results suggest that it may be possible to identify, a priori decision makers who are "at risk" to become entrapped (e.g., individuals who report that they are focused on the task to the exclusion of any other stimuli). Given the disastrous psychological consequences that may befall entrapped decision makers, it is important to identify likely candidates for entrapment. Once these individuals are identified it may be possible to intervene in ways that reduce their propensities toward escalating commitment to a failing course of action.

Further research. In summary, the results of the "cross-sectional" and "longitudinal' studies suggest that decision makers experience a variety of *sequential* cognitive changes as they become increasingly entrapped. In particular, perceived motivation seems to shift from the rational to the rationalizing. Furthermore, there is suggestive evidence that the "vigilance" (Janis & Mann, 1977) with which decisions are made decreases as level of entrapment escalates.

Future research on the cognitive consequences of entrapment may find useful leads in other social-psychological literatures. If entrapment can be construed as a form of commitment, then the cognitive consequences of entrapment may be similar to the cognitive consequences of commitment. Kiesler (1971), for example, reports a study exploring the effects of commitment on memory. More specifically, subjects were asked to make a proattitudinal speech, and then take part in a memory task in which they had to recall word pairs that were consistent, inconsistent, or irrelevant to the position advocated in the speech. Committed subjects were led to believe that the audience could identify them; uncommitted participants were led to believe that they could not be identified. As predicted, Committed subjects recalled more consistent word pairs, and fewer inconsistent and irrelevant word pairs, than did Uncommitted subjects. By way of explanation, Kiesler suggested that "commitment affects either the *salience* of cognitions (thoughts, previous behaviors, etc.) consistent with the behavior performed or the organization of these cognitions into a consistent whole."

It would be interesting to determine whether the process of entrapment also makes salient cognitions that are consistent with the underlying behavior. For example, subjects could be asked to perform a memory task composed of words that were consistent or inconsistent with their escalatory behavior. Would entrapped individuals be more likely to remember words such as "persistent," "tenacious," "risky," and "committed," and less apt to recall words such as "withdrawing," "cautious," and "uncommitted," relative to those who have not become entrapped in an escalating conflict? If the process of escalating commitment does make salient the cognitions associated with that process, then the self-perpetuating quality of entrapment may be more easily understood. That is, the behavior generates cognitions consistent with the behavior, which may in turn promote future behavior (i.e., escalation of commitment) congruent with the cognitions.

Another potentially rich source of ideas for future research is the work of Janis and Mann (1977) who have written extensively about the cognitive consequences of commitment. The following quotations from Janis and Mann (1977) make clear the relevance of their work to entrapment:

1. "The higher the degree of commitment, the lower the probability that the challenged decision makers will lightly dismiss the risks associated with changing to another alternative" (p. 285). In the context of an entrapment situation, the above quote implies that the tendency to withdraw from the entrapping dilemma may actually be perceived as more risky than the tendency to persist. Several investigators (Bazerman, 1983; Levi, 1982; Teger, 1980) have postulated that escalation, rather than withdrawal, is the riskier course of action in an entrapping dilemma. Thus, it would be interesting to determine if entrapped decision makers—i.e., those directly involved in the dilemma— perceive that withdrawal is actually more risky than is escalation.

2. "The higher the degree of commitment to a prior choice, the higher the probability that when alternatives (to the chosen course of action) are being considered, the challenged decision makers will be pessimistic about finding a course of action better than the current one" (p. 285). In the process of becoming entrapped, decision makers undoubtedly entertain the possibility of

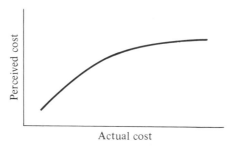

Figure 7-1. Hypothesized relationship between actual and perceived cost.

changing their behavior. According to Janis and Mann (1977) they may make two types of cognitive judgments which could prove to be (disastrously) erroneous: First, they may prematurely abandon their search for alternative responses to the situation, thinking that none will be effective. Second, even if alternatives were generated, they may not be adopted because of the decision maker's belief that they will not be more effective than the chosen course of action. Future research should explore if subjects' perception of the relative efficacy of various responses, including the already chosen one, change during the process of the entrapping dilemma.

3. "The higher the degree of commitment, the less the likelihood that any given setback or loss entailed by the decision will constitute an effective challenge [to change policies]. High commitment makes for an initially high threshold of regret, which is manifested as a tendency to dismiss attacks on the current policy as relatively trivial and unimportant" (p. 286). In the domain of entrapment, this means that the costs incurred by decision makers are not apt to be perceived as costly as they "should." It would indeed be interesting to measure changes over time in perceived costs. Janis and Mann's hypothesis predicts that the cost value function would be concave, as indicated in Figure 7-1; note that the psychological impact of the costs (i.e., the perceived cost) is not related to actual cost in a direct linear fashion.

Interestingly, this notion has been suggested, though in a very different context by Kahneman and Tversky (1979). Their prospect theory has suggested, for example, that the difference in subjective value between losses of $110 and $120 is not as great as the difference in subjective value between losses of $10 and $20. If actual costs incurred by entrapped decision makers are, in fact, perceived as relatively less costly over time, then yet another explanation for the self-perpetuating quality of entrapment may be proffered. Simply stated, the increasing costs associated with escalated commitment are not sufficiently psychologically aversive to motivate withdrawal.

The vast psychological literature on decision making under conditions of stress, arousal, anxiety, or uncertainty may also stimulate light-shedding research on the cognitive consequences of entrapment. Much research has shown that psychological stress produces systematic changes in the ways individuals process information. Janis and Mann (1977) have proposed that stress can lead to a variety of defective or "nonvigilant" decision-making processs. One example of such nonvigilance particularly relevant to entrapment is the failure of the decision maker to "correctly assimilate and take account of any new information or expert judgment to which he is exposed, *even when the information or judgment does not support the course of action he initially prefers*" (our emphasis added). Experimental psychologists (e.g., Easterbrook, 1959) have shown that the effect of arousal, stress, or anxiety upon perception/cognition is to narrow the range of cue utilization by focusing the individual's attention on central cues to the exclusion of peripheral cues. If effective decision making depends upon the extent to which the individuals attend to perhipheral cues, then arousal or stress is bound to interfere with the quality of their judgments. For example, entrapped decision makers may fail to heed peripheral cues suggesting that withdrawal, rather than persistence, is the more prudent course of action. Note that the evidence presented earlier in this chapter, which suggested that tunnel vision accompanies escalated commitment, is wholly consistent with Easterbrook's hypothesis.

Of course, in order to apply previous theory and research from the stress/anxiety literature to the entrapment setting, we need to know that decision making in entrapping conflicts causes stress or anxiety. Several conceptual and empirical points can be offered to suggest that the entrapping dilemma is indeed stressful and/or anxiety provoking for decision makers. In their conflict theory of decision making, Janis and Mann (1977) repeatedly imply that decisions made in entrapment situations are fraught with stress. They state,

> When a person encounters new threats or opportunities that motivate him to consider a new source of action, the degree of decisional stress is a function of the degree to which he is committed to adhere to his present course of action. (p. 50)

The Janis and Mann quote suggests that the basic ingredients needed to produce stress are very much present for the entrapped decision maker. In the context of entrapment, "new threats or opportunities that motivate him to consider a new source of action" are the ever-increasing costs associated with remaining entrapped, and the feedback suggesting that goals have not been attained. The greater the commitment (e.g., the greater the amount of costs incurred) the more stressful it will be for the decision maker to contemplate withdrawal.

Empirical evidence is also consistent with the proposition that decision makers experience greater stress as they become more entrapped. For example, in the Carnival study discussed earlier in this chapter, subjects reported feeling increasingly "unconfident," "pessimistic," and "frustrated" in the later stages of their decision making. Moreover, a study by Teger (1980) found that subjects' skin temperature gradually decreased (suggestive of increased fear or arousal) as their level of commitment approached and then passed the $1.00 point in the Dollar Auction. In another study pairs of decision makers were tape-recorded as they pondered the next bid that they should make against the opposing side. The tapes were then rated for indications of anxiety such as nervous laughter and expressions of worry (e.g., "this is getting dangerous"). As in the previous study, anxiety increased as the bidding approached and then surpassed the $1.00 mark (Teger, 1980).

We have suggested that entrapping conflicts are stressful for decision makers, and that psychological stress produces a variety of effects on decision making and information processing. Future entrapment research needs to (1) provide additional evidence that entrapping dilemmas pose stress, and (2) explore the consequences of this stress for entrapment behavior. To state the latter point differently, it would be important to extend research findings on the cognitive effects of stress in general to the specific domain of entrapment.

Finally, on a procedural note it may be useful to consider the utility of different research methodologies. In particular, the use of a verbal protocol technique may provide a more complete analysis of the psychological dynamics of entrapment. In this procedure research participants essentially are asked to "think out loud," that is, to describe the thoughts and feelings they are experiencing as the decision-making process unfolds. The great advantage of this procedure is that subjects are allowed to express freely their salient thoughts and feelings along a wide variety of dimensions, not simply those that the researcher deems important.

The Psychological Process of Entrapment: Implications for Behavior

The first part of this chapter provided suggestive evidence concerning the psychological process of entrapment; the focus was on the sequential cognitive consequences of heightening one's commitment to a failing course of action in order to justify the allocation of previous resources. It may be useful at this point to consider some behavioral implications of these cognitive consequences. By so doing we will be serving at least two important purposes: First, a richer, more complete understanding of the process of entrapment should emerge. Whereas the preceding discussion focused on what was in the decision makers' heads as they became more entrapped, the present material highlights some behavioral consequences of their changing cognitions. Second, the data presented in the first part of the chapter were open to several alternative interpretations. Consequently, they less definitively shed light on the nature of the entrapment process. The research presented in this section is also designed to elucidate the entrapment *process*, but in a manner very different from the previously presented studies. To the extent that the findings fit the conceptual analysis that has unfolded to this point, we gain increased confidence in that conceptual analysis; simultaneously, alternative explanations become less parsimonious.

Timing and Entrapment

One intriguing implication of the psychological changes that appear to accompany entrapment is that the same independent variable can have very different effects on entrapment behavior, depending upon the point in time at which the effect of that variable is assessed. Let us suppose that decision makers are, in fact, more vigilant at the earlier, rather than later, stages of their involvement in the entrapping dilemma. If so, then their behavior should be influenced to a greater extent by cues for appropriate commitment behavior in the earlier than in the later stages. Stated differently, decision makers may be "level headed" at the outset of a potential entrapment situation. If reliable external cues suggest that persistence is the more prudent course of action, then their level of commitment should increase. If trustworthy external cues imply that withdrawal is wiser, then their level of commitment should decrease.

At the later stages, entrapped decision makers may manifest tunnel vision, reduced vigilance, or other related processes that interfere with their ability to think coolly and rationally. At this point their behavior may not be susceptible to influence by external cues for appropriate commitment decisions.

Three experiments conducted in our laboratory have been designed to test the effects of various independent variables on entrapment at different stages of the entrapping conflict. The experimental procedure is conceptually analogous in all three experiments, although the exact methodology differs between studies. All subjects are required to take part in some decision-making task that later proves entrapping. For half of the subjects, the independent variable is manipulated prior to their initial decision to invest resources to attain the goal. For the other half of the participants, the same independent variable is introduced after they have made a considerable resource investment. If our analysis of the dynamic, ever-changing nature of the psychology of entrapment is correct, then the same variable can have markedly different effects on commitment decisions at these two points in time. (More precise predictions can be found in the introduction to each experiment.)

Experiment 1. Expectancy value theory posits that decision makers will be more likely to become entrapped if they think that the likelihood of goal attainment is high rather than low. For example, Rubin and Brockner (1975) discovered that subjects persisted to a greater extent when they thought that they were close to, rather than far from, attaining the resource needed to solve the experimental task. Suppose that decision makers received reliable information suggesting that goal attainment was either likely or unlikely, and furthermore, that this information was received either prior to or after they have invested some of their resources. The "waning vigilance" hypothesis—that vigilance dissipates over time—suggests that decision makers would be more likely to allocate their resources when they were informed *beforehand* that goal attainment was likely rather than unlikely; however, *after* having made a substantial investment, they may be less vigilant and thus less affected by the very same information that influenced earlier commitment decisions. At the later stage decision makers may be no more likely to persist when the perceived likelihood of goal attainment is high rather than low.

Method. Forty-one Tufts University undergraduates took part in the study as part of a course requirement. The experimental methodology used was the Waiting Game (see Chapter 2 for greater detail). Briefly, subjects entered the research cubicle for a "Mood Experiment," and were seated at a desk in front of a clock. Once there they were told that the experiment would "consist of a number of parts." In the "first part" they completed the Revised Janis-Field Self-Esteem Scale (Eagly, 1967).

After collecting the completed personality measure the experimenter then said, "OK, the first part of the experiment is now over. Now you will do the second part. Unfortunately, the second experimenter has not yet arrived."

The experimenter then hurriedly looked at her watch and said (on a seemingly impromptu basis), "Look, why don't we do the following. Please wait here for the other experimenter. If you want to leave at any point before the experimenter gets here, you can. Obviously, you will receive *some* experimental credit for having done the first part of the experiment. However, if you do leave, you will not receive as much credit for participating as you would if you waited for the experimenter. So, I'll leave it entirely up to you as to what you want to do."

Before deciding whether to wait, some subjects were then given information about the likelihood of the second experimenter's arrival. In the Likely condition the experimenter said, "In fact, I spoke with your experimenter earlier today, and he seemed certain that he would be here on time. So he should be here shortly." In the Unlikely condition subjects were told: "In fact, I spoke with your experimenter earlier today, and he said that it was not likely that he would be here on time; so, I don't know if and when he'll be here." In the Control condition subjects were told nothing at all about the likelihood of the second experimenter's arrival. The experimenter then exited the room in all three conditions.

A second group of subjects were not told about the likelihood of the second experimenter's arrival until after they had made a time investment. More specifically, after telling subjects that it was "entirely up to you as to what you want to do," the experimenter exited the room. She then returned 10 minutes later (at which point 80% of the participants were still waiting) and administered the same manipulation that had been given to the aforementioned participants. (Only Likely and Unlikely conditions were studied at this point; that is, no Control condition was run.)

In reality, no second experimenter existed. The primary dependent variable was the amount of time subjects spent waiting. Subjects were not allowed to bring any books or reading materials with them into the experimental room. Pilot testing revealed that some subjects chose to bring some reading activity into the waiting room, perhaps to reduce boredom, or perhaps to reduce the conflict associated with whether they should wait or leave. If allowed to read, work, or perform some other distracting activity, then subjects would have little chance to experience the entrapping conflict. Thus, subjects literally had nothing to do but wait for the second experimenter, while staring at the clock in front of them.

No participant was forced to wait for more than 25 minutes. Subjects either exited the cubicle before 25 minutes had elapsed, or were told by the first experimenter after 25 minutes that the second experimenter would "not be showing up." All subjects completed a short questionnaire after their waiting period, assessing their perceptions of the purpose of the study, as well as the extent to which they felt entrapped. (For the latter question subjects were asked to indicate the extent to which the following statement applied to their waiting behavior: "Once I decided to wait, I figured that I might as well wait until the other experimenter came. Otherwise, all of that waiting would have been a waste.")

Results. The data of seven additional subjects were discarded, because they did not need any additional experimental credit in order to fulfill the course requirement. These subjects should have lacked incentive to wait for the "second experimenter" and in fact the average length of wait of these participants was much shorter than that of those who needed additional credit ($t(46) = 3.03$, $p < .003$). (The seven subjects not needing additional credit were nearly equally distributed among the five experimental conditions.)

The waiting times of subjects who were given information about the likelihood of the second experimenter's arrival *before* starting to wait were analyzed separately from those who were exposed to the manipulation *after* having waited. It seemed inappropriate to perform a single analysis, because the range of the dependent variable differed between the two groups. The range of waiting times for subjects exposed to the manipulation beforehand was 0–25 minutes, whereas the range for the group who received the manipulation after having waited for 10 minutes was 10–25 minutes. Three subjects in this latter group quit at the very outset. Consequently, they did not experience the manipulation that would have occurred 10 minutes later had they decided to wait. Of course, this fact presents possible subject mortality problems to the interpretation of the data, a hypothesis to which we will return later.

For subjects exposed to the manipulation prior to deciding to wait, there was a marked difference in waiting times. One-way analysis of variance yielded a highly significant effect, $F(2,23) = 7.45$, $p < .005$, such that subjects waited longest in the Likely condition ($M = 24.82$ minutes), least in the Unlikely condition ($M = 12.74$ minutes), and for an intermediate amount of time in the Control condition ($M = 20.07$ minutes).

For those subjects exposed to the manipulation after having waited for 10 minutes, the means were in the same direction, but did not even approach significance. Participants in the Likely condition waited for an average of 22.49 minutes, whereas those in the Unlikely condition waited 16.06 minutes on average ($t(10) = 1.69$, $p > .10$).

Several other findings from this study are worthy of mention. First, subjects reported feeling more entrapped as they continued to wait. The correlation (across all conditions) between waiting time and self-reported entrapment was significant, $r(36) = .41$, $p < .01$. (Subjects also endorsed other plausible explanations for their waiting behavior to a greater extent as they continued to wait. However, the correlations between waiting time and these self-reports were less statistically significant. Specifically, subjects who waited longer for the second experimenter were also more apt to say that they did so "in order to get more experimental credit," $r(36) = .35$, $p < .05$, and to "help the experimenters out with their research," $r(36) = .30, p < .10$. These self-report data suggest that subjects' waiting time was motivated by a variety of factors, one of which was felt entrapment.)

Second, there was suggestive evidence that the personality trait of self-esteem had different effects for subjects who received the manipulation before versus after waiting. These findings should be interpreted with extreme caution because of the very small sample size, but they are intriguing nonetheless. Median splits were used to classify subjects as high or low in self-esteem. Two-factor (Self-esteem $\times$ Likelihood Manipulation) analyses of variance of waiting time were then performed. Self-esteem had no effect (either main or interaction) for those subjects exposed to the manipulation prior to waiting. However, there was a marginally significant SE $\times$ Likelihood interaction for those participants who experienced the manipulation after having waited 10 minutes ($F(1,8) = 3.82$, $p < .10$). High-self-esteem subjects waited longer when the second experimenter was Likely rather than Unlikely to arrive ($Ms = 25.00$ vs. 10.08 minutes, respectively), whereas low-self-esteem participants did not show differences in waiting as a function of the likelihood of the second experimenter's arrival ($Ms = 19.98$ vs. 19.05 minutes, respectively).

In sum, the results of this study provide initial evidence that decision makers may become less vigilant to external cues as degree of entrapment heightens. Based on the information provided to them about the likelihood of the second experimenter's arrival, subjects *should* have become more entrapped in the Likely than the Unlikely condition. However, this effect was only significant when the manipulation occurred prior to, rather than after, their decision to wait. The effect of self-esteem differed between subjects who experienced the manipulation before (Before condition) vs. after (After condition) waiting.

An alternative explanation is that the difference in subjects' reaction to the experimental manipulation in the Before and After conditions was not due to declining vigilance over time, but rather to sampling differences. Recall that some subjects in the After condition quit prior to experiencing the manipulation. It may have been that the participants who persisted long enough to experience the manipulation were somehow different from subjects in the Before condition, and that such differences caused the different results between conditions. For example, the subjects in the After condition may simply be the types of individuals who are insensitive to a variety of external cues, independent of stage of entrapment.

This alternative explanation cannot be completely eliminated, but several factors render it less plausible. First, the absolute number of subjects who quit waiting prior to experiencing the manipulation in the After condition was not great (only 3 out of 15 did so). Therefore, the subjects who did persist long enough to experience the manipulation were at least somewhat representative of all participants who had been assigned to that condition. Second, the available evidence indicated no systematic individual-difference variation between subjects in the Before and After condition; the mean level of self-esteem was practically identical in the two conditions ($t < 1$).

We conclude by reiterating that the data are merely consistent with the notion that decision makers in entrapping dilemmas become less vigilant over time. The data are suggestive at best, given the small sample sizes and the fact that alternative explanations cannot be completely eliminated. The next two experiments (Brockner, Rubin, Fine, Hamilton, Thomas, & Turetsky, 1982) were also designed to assess the effect of various independent variables on decision making at different stages of the entrapping process.

Experiment 2. In an earlier discussion (Rubin & Brockner, 1975; see Chapter 3), we suggested that decision makers initially allocate resources to courses of action that later prove entrapping because of their failure to be vigilant to the associated costs. For example, upon first deciding to wait for a bus to transport us to a destination to which we could have just as easily walked, we rarely ask ourselves the question, "How costly is this wait going to be?" Or, when we make that initial repair on the old jalopy, we typically do not consider the long-term costs that await us if the car begins to malfunction repeatedly.

One implication of the above remarks is that decision makers may be less prone to entrapment if they are made to attend *beforehand* to the long-term costs associated with persisting in a failing course of action. In fact, both Brockner, Rubin, and Lang (1981), and Rubin and Brockner (1975) have produced results supportive of this notion. In these experiments some subjects were given a payoff chart *prior* to deciding whether, and for how long, they should allocate their resources, whereas other subjects were not given a payoff chart. (The chart simply made more salient information of which subjects were already aware: the costs associated with continued allocations.) Although the experimental procedures used were quite different, the results were quite consistent: subjects who received the payoff chart invested significantly less of their resources (i.e., became much less entrapped) than did those who were not provided with this information.

It is important to emphasize that in both studies this "Cost Salience" manipulation occurred *prior to* the decision makers' initial investment decisions. What would happen, one wonders, if the same manipulation was invoked *after* the participants had already invested some of their resources? According to the "waning vigilance" hypothesis, the impact of cost-salience information should be greatly reduced at this later stage. Why? As we saw in Experiment 1, when decision makers are psychologically occupied with the process of entrapment, they may be less responsive to information concerning appropriate investment behavior.

This experiment was designed to replicate and extend previous research exploring the effect of cost salience on entrapment. All subjects took part in the Counter Game methodology. As in previous research (Brockner, Rubin, & Lang, 1981; Rubin & Brockner, 1975) half of the subjects received a payoff chart detailing the costs associated with persisting *prior to* making their initial commitment decision, whereas half did not (Before conditions). A second group of participants experienced the very same manipulation, but only after they had invested a considerable portion of their initial stake (After conditions). In the Before conditions subjects were expected to exhibit less entrapment if they received, rather than did not receive the payoff chart. (If confirmed, this finding would replicate the results of previous studies.) In the After conditions, however, we expected the effect of this manipulation to be greatly reduced and perhaps even nonsignificant.

Method. The original sample consisted of 54 Boston area residents who were recruited through newspaper ads inviting participation in a study of decision making. The data of 11 subjects in the After condition had to be discarded because they did not persist long enough to experience the Cost Salience manipulation. Thus, the final sample consisted of 43 subjects (19 male, 24 female) who ranged in age from approximately 18 to 30. All had completed at least 1 year of college.

Subjects took part in a modified version of the Counter Game procedure. They were provided an initial stake of $5.00, and were told that the counter, once set in motion, would run continuously until either (1) the "randomly chosen winning number" had been reached, or (2) they decided to quit. As in previous studies in which the Counter Game procedure was employed, subjects were required to pay 1 cent for each unit that had expired on the counter, and that the "jackpot," if reached, would yield them an additional $3.00.

Independent variables. Subjects in the high-cost-salience condition received a chart consisting of two columns. The first was labeled, "When the counter reaches." Below this label were the numbers 1, 50, 100, 150, 200, and so on. The second column was labeled, "You must pay the following amount." Below this label were the corresponding amounts of $0.01, $0.50, $1.00, $1.50, $2.00 etc. Upon receiving the payoff chart subjects were told: "A number of people who have done this experiment said that they found it useful to have a chart, which allowed them to keep track of their costs at various points in the study. Take a look at the chart on your desk. You can keep track of your potential costs by consulting your chart at any time. Please take a few moments to study it now." Subjects in the Control condition did not receive the payoff chart.

It is noteworthy that the payoff chart did not present subjects with any new information. If they truly understood the instructions for the experiment, then they should have been familiar with the information contained in the payoff chart. The chart was merely designed to heighten the decision makers' attention to costs, rather than to provide additional information.

In the Before condition, the manipulation of cost salience occurred prior to subjects' initial decisions about whether to wait. In the After condition, the very same manipulation was invoked after subjects had invested a considerable portion of their initial stake. Specifically, the counter stopped upon reaching 179; in the high-cost-salience condition the experimenter (who was situated in an adjoining room) called subjects' attention to the payoff chart, which had been hitherto lying face down on an adjacent chair. At this point subjects received the same information as did those in the Before–High Salience condition. In the After–Control condition, the counter was also stopped upon reaching 179, in order to control for the effect of merely interrupting the proceedings. The experimenter announced: "OK, the counter has stopped working momentarily. This has been happening a lot recently. It should be a minute or so before I'll get it going again. I'll let you know when it is ready." The experimenter allowed 45 seconds to pass (i.e., an amount of time comparable to that taken to inform subjects of the presence of the chart in the High Salience condition), before restarting the counter.

(The reader may be wondering why 179 was chosen as the point at which the counter was stopped. There were several reasons. First, we wanted to choose a number that seemed random, in order to reduce the likelihood of arousing subjects' suspicions. It might have seemed particularly peculiar to participants if the counter were halted at a round number such as 150 or 200. Second, we wanted to stop the counter at a point that was neither too early nor too late. If the counter was stopped too soon (e.g., at 50) the subjects might not have felt committed enough to persist. If it were stopped too late (i.e., after most of their initial stake had been spent) then we were inviting the possibility of little variability in subsequent behavior. As Teger (1980) has shown, once decision makers invest a certain amount of their money in the Dollar Auction game, they are quite likely to invest all of it. After considerable pilot testing, the 179 point was chosen as satisfying all of the above criteria.)

After the decision-making phase, subjects completed a brief questionnaire and were then thoroughly debriefed.

Results. Separate analyses of variance of time spent waiting were conducted in the Before and After conditions. (As in the preceding experiment, the possible range of waiting time differed in the two conditions, i.e., it was $0.00–$5.00 in the Before condition and $1.79–$5.00 in the After condition). Consequently, the mean amount invested is much greater in the After than in the Before condition. The results in the Before condition replicated previous findings: those who received the payoff chart were significantly less entrapped than those who did not ($Ms = $1.86 vs. $3.31; $t(19) = 1.88$, $p < .04$, one-tailed). In the After condition, however, the effect of the cost salience manipulation was trivial ($Ms = $3.88 vs. $4.28, respectively; $t(20) < 1$).

Why did the payoff chart only affect the behavior of subjects in the Early condition? It could have been that the effect of the payoff chart was to heighten cost salience in the Before, but not in the After condition. To test for this possibility, participants were asked on the posttask questionnaire, "While you were waiting, how much did you find yourself thinking about how much it was costing you to continue waiting?" Responses could range from "not at all" (1) to "very much" (8). Interestingly, subjects reported being more cost conscious in the High Salience than in the Control condition, regardless of whether the manipulation occurred before or after their decision to wait. Therefore, the differential impact of the cost-salience manipulation on amount invested in the Before and After conditions cannot be attributed to differences in subjects' attention to cost factors caused by the payoff chart's presence or absence.

How can the behavioral results be explained? On the postexperimental questionnaire subjects were also asked to indicate the extent to which they were attentive to the possible reward associated with continued waiting. ("While you were waiting, how much did you find yourself thinking about reaching the jackpot number?") In the Before condition, subjects reported being less reward-focused in the High Salience than in the Control condition. In the After condition, however, just the opposite was true.

The results reported in Table 7-1 highlight these results. In the Before condition, subjects receiving the payoff chart were more attentive to costs and less focused on the reward associated with continued waiting. A 2×2 analysis of variance (Cost Salience $\times$ Scale Item) with repeated measures on the last factor yielded a marginally significant interaction effect, $F(1,16) = 3.86$, $p < .07$. Simple effect analyses revealed that high-cost-salience participants were much more attentive to costs than rewards ($F(1,16) = 10.20$, $p < .01$), whereas Control condition subjects were not ($F(1,16) < 1$). In the After condition, the two-factor analysis of variance yielded only a main effect for the cost salience variable, $F(1,20) = 8.40$, $p < .01$, such that subjects were much more attentive to both costs *and* rewards in the High Cost Salience than in the Control condition.

It has been shown that cost salience decreases entrapment, whereas reward salience increases entrapment (Brockner, Rubin, & Lang, 1981; Rubin & Brockner, 1975). These facts may help explain the behavioral results of the

Table 7-1. Perceived Cost and Reward Salience (Experiment 2)

	Payoff Chart	Cost Salience[a]	Reward Salience[b]
Before	Present	6.22	3.67
	Absent	5.00	4.67
After	Present	5.18	5.59
	Absent	3.18	3.73

Note: Scores could range from 1 to 8, with higher scores reflecting greater perceived salience.
[a]"While you were waiting, how much did you find yourself thinking about how much it was costing you to continue waiting?"
[b]"While you were waiting, how much did you find yourself thinking about reaching your destination?"

present study. In the Before condition, subjects were made to feel both more attentive to costs and less attentive to rewards by the payoff chart. Thus, entrapment should have been lower when they received the chart compared to when they did not. Those in the After condition reported that the payoff chart simultaneously made them more attentive to entrapment-reducing and entrapment-enhancing stimuli (i.e., costs and rewards). The net effect of attending to both stimuli may have been to cancel their impact on behavior. Accordingly, subjects were no more (or less) entrapped when they received the chart than when they did not in the After condition.

Of course, this analysis of the questionnaire data, while consistent with the behavioral results, does not explain why subjects in the After condition would report attending to both costs *and* rewards in the High Cost Salience than in the Control condition. To speculate, it could have been that the administration of the payoff chart initially heightened the decision makers' attention to the costs. However, unlike in the Before condition, when no investment had been made, subjects may have felt pressure to justify the correctness of their chosen path, given that (1) a substantial portion of their initial stake had been invested, and (2) they were now being confronted with cost information. Perhaps they justified their prior behavior by becoming more focused on the possible reward to be gained.

"Low-Balling" and Entrapment. In brief, cost-salience cues decreased entrapment when introduced prior to, but not after, the point at which the decision makers had invested some of their resources. Interestingly, such findings are consistent with recent research in the compliance literature. Cialdini, Cacioppo, Bassett, and Miller (1978) have described a compliance-inducing technique known as "low-balling," which is apparently popular among new car dealers. As Cialdini et al. report,

> the critical component of the (low-balling) procedure is for the salesperson to induce the customer to make an active decision to buy one of the dealership's cars by offering an extremely good price. *Once the customer has made the decision for a specific car*, the salesperson removes the price advantage in one of a variety of ways. For example, the customer may be told that the originally cited price did not include an expensive option that the customer had assumed was part of the offer (emphasis added).

After describing various ways in which the initial price advantage is removed, Cialdini et al. (1978) comment, "In each instance the result is the same. The reason that the customer made a favorable purchase decision is removed and the performance of the target behavior (i.e., buying that particular car) is rendered more costly. The essence of the low-ball procedure, then, is for a requester to induce another to make a behavioral decision concerning a target action. It is assumed that the decision will persist even after the circumstances have changed to make performance of the target action more costly."

In a clever series of experiments, Cialdini et al. (1978) have demonstrated the efficacy of the low-ball technique in gaining compliance. In their first study Cialdini et al. telephoned subjects and asked them if they wished to take part in a psychology experiment. In the low-ball condition, subjects were informed of the cost associated with performing the experiment only *after* they verbally agreed to take part. (Specifically, these subjects were told that the experiment was being run at 7:00 AM on weekday mornings, a time well before undergraduates typically arise.) The experimenter then asked subjects if he could assign them to a specific date. In the control condition participants were informed about the 7:00 AM starting time *before* being asked if they wished to commit themselves to a specific date. The rates of verbal *and* behavioral compliance were greater in the low-ball than in the control condition; that is, subjects were more likely to commit themselves verbally to a specific time (and were actually more likely to participate) in the former than in the latter condition.

In a second experiment participants were asked if they were willing to display United Way posters on their dorm room doors and windows. In the low-ball condition the associated cost (i.e., going downstairs to the dorm desk within the next hour in order to procure the posters) was introduced only after subjects had agreed to perform the target behavior. In the control condition this cost was made salient at the outset (i.e., before they had decided to comply). Unlike in the preceding experiment the rate of verbal compliance did not differ between these two conditions. However, the levels of behavioral compliance (i.e., the proportion of subjects who actually went downstairs to procure the posters) was significantly greater in the low-ball than in the control condition.

How are the procedures and results of the low-ball experiments similar to those of Experiment 2? The procedural similarity is that in both contexts the timing of the introduction of costs is varied. With regard to results, in both instances cost information deterred commitment to a course of action when introduced *prior to* the decision to embark upon that course of action. However, when the very same cost information was made salient *after* a partial commitment had been made to a course of action, it was less apt to reduce heightened commitment.

Note that the logic presented here is consistent with the material presented in the first half of this chapter: the process of becoming entrapped (or more generally, committed) appears to have cognitive consequences. That is, the same information (e.g., that pertaining to costs) may be processed very differently at different stages of commitment. Cialdini et al.'s (1978) explanation for the low-ball effect also seems quite applicable to Experiment 2: "To the extent that one is committed to a decision, for instance, the decision will be less changeable; the decision itself and the cognitions representing it will be 'frozen,' to use Lewin's (1947) terminology."

There is at least one important difference between the procedure in the After condition in Experiment 2 and those utilized in the low ball conditions of the Cialdini et al. (1978) studies. In the latter, the decision makers' *actual* costs were increased after the individual was psychologically committed, whereas in the former it was only *perceived* costs that were made more salient by the payoff chart; the actual costs incurred by decision makers in Experiment 2 remained the same.

There are alternative explanations for the chief findings that cost salience decreased entrapment in the Before, but not in the After, condition in Experiment 2. For example, differences in subject mortality remains problematic. (We will return to this issue in the discussion of the next experiment.) Furthermore, it could have been that cost salience reduced entrapment in the Before condition by introducing demand characteristics; that is, the payoff chart may have served as a cue to participants that withdrawal, rather than persistence, was experimentally "appropriate" behavior. In rebuttal, there was nothing in the subjects' written or verbal accounts of the purpose of the experiment that would support a demand-characteristics interpretation. Moreover, if the payoff chart reduced entrapment in the Before condition as a result of demand characteristics, then it should have produced the same effect in the After condition.

Experiment 3. The results of Experiments 1 and 2 suggest that cues pertinent to the prudence of investing influenced entrapment when introduced before, rather than after, some commitment was made. When informed beforehand that the likelihood of goal attainment was low (Experiment 1), or when led to focus on the costs associated with commitment (Experiment 2), decision makers were significantly less likely to become entrapped. When these same cues were introduced at a later stage of the conflict, they had no discernible effect on degree of commitment.

What *does* affect entrapment decisions in the later stages of the conflict? One theme expressed throughout this chapter is that decision makers' motives switch from the rational to the rationalizing as their degree of entrapment increases. Entrapped decision makers reputedly become more concerned about justifying the correctness of their chosen course of action, particularly in the eyes of others (see Chapter 6).

The social/evaluative nature of the experimental setting was not varied in either of the previous two experiments. If, however, such self-presentational variables are important determinants of entrapment in the later stages of the conflict, then it would seem worthwhile to investigate the effects of these face-saving factors. This was the general purpose of Experiment 3. All participants took part in the same experimental task used in Experiment 2. The effects on entrapment of several independent variables thought to be related to face-saving concerns were studied both before and after decision makers had committed themselves to attempting to win the jackpot. More specifically, in order to operationalize face saving, we informed most of the participants that they were being observed by an audience as they completed the Counter Game procedure.

Of course, the decision to persist in an entrapping dilemma can be socially desirable or undesirable, depending upon the decision maker's perceptions of the audience's values. In a study reported in the previous chapter (Brockner, Rubin, & Lang, 1981, Experiment 1), for example, subjects were either told by the experimenter that it would be smart to invest their resources (Risky condition) or refrain from investing (Cautious condition). Entrapment was significantly greater in the Risky than the Cautious condition, perhaps because subjects thought they could make the best self-presentation by following the experimenter's advice. Consistent with this face-saving explanation, Brockner et al. found that the experimenter's advice had a stronger effect on highly socially anxious participants who are in greater need of social approval (Turner, 1977).

The description of the audience varied in Experiment 3, in order to manipulate subjects' perceptions of the nature of socially desirable behavior. Some of the subjects were told that they were being observed by "experts in decision making, who would be carefully evaluating the prudence of their decisions to invest or withdraw" (Evaluative condition). Other participants were told that the audience consisted of individuals who wished to "use the experimental apparatus in a future experiment; they simply want to see how the task works, and they will not be evaluating you in any way" (Nonevaluative condition). We hypothesized that subjects would feel foolish if they persisted in the presence of the evaluative audience. Presumably, one would not want to invest more money than the value of the jackpot in the presence of an expert in decision making. On the other hand, subjects may have perceived that the nonevaluative audience valued persistence. After all, the nonevaluative audience "wished to see how the task operated," and subjects may have perceived that they could be most helpful by investing more of their resources, thereby providing the audience with more opportunity to learn about the experimental task.

The above remarks lead us to predict that entrapment would be greater in the nonevaluative than in the evaluative condition. However, two moderating variables need to be taken into account. First, the effect of the audience should be more pronounced on those individuals who show greater concern for their social image. To tap such individual differences we administered the Fenigstein, Scheier, and Buss (1975) public self-consciousness and social-anxiety scales. Previous research has shown that highly publicly self-conscious and socially anxious individuals are more likely to engage in social approval-seeking behaviors than are their counterparts lower on these dimensions (Brockner et al., 1981; Buss, 1980; Turner, 1977). Thus, we expected the tendency for there to be greater entrapment in the nonevaluative than evaluative condition to be exhibited to a greater extent by high public self-consciousness/social-anxiety participants than those low on these trait dimensions.

Second, the point at which the face-saving factors became salient was also experimentally manipulated. For some subjects this occurred prior to their initial investment decision (as in the Before condition of Experiment 2), whereas for others this happened after they had committed a substantial portion of their resources (as in the After condition of Experiment 2). Face-saving variables presumably increase in importance in the later stages of entrapment situations. Accordingly, the hypothesized interaction between the audience and individual difference variables should be more apt to arise in the After than in the Before condition.

Method. Subjects were drawn from the same population as those who participated in Experiment 2. (The two studies were conducted concurrently; subjects were randomly assigned to experiments.) The original sample consisted of 64 participants. However, eight subjects in the After condition quit before the audience manipulation was operationalized. The final sample thus included 56 participants (30 male, 26 female).

Apart from the operationalizations of the independent variables, the procedure was virtually identical to the one employed in Experiment 1. Upon arriving at the laboratory each subject was seated at a table in a private cubicle facing a two-way mirror that was covered by a shade. (Subjects assigned to the control condition, described below, did not face the shade, so as not to draw their attention to it.) Three treatments were studied in the Before condition. In the evaluative audience treatment subjects were told,

> At some point in the study you will be asked to raise the shade which is now covering the mirror in front of you. After, but not before you lift the shade, a group of three people will begin to observe you. They are Tufts professors who are experts in the study of decision making. They will be studying your behavior carefully, to watch what you do and how you do it—and to evaluate your effectiveness as a decision maker.

In the nonevaluative condition subjects were told,

> At some point in the study you will be asked to raise the shade which is now covering the mirror in front of you. After, but not before you lift the shade, a group of three people will begin to observe you. These individuals are planning some related research and have asked permission to observe you. They will not be here to judge or evaluate you. Rather, they are simply interested in finding out more about this sort of research, and how it is conducted.

Just before being asked if they wished to try for the jackpot, subjects in these two conditions were told that the observers had arrived, and that they were to raise the shade so that the audience could observe them. The experimenter allowed 30 seconds to pass (to increase the impact of the audience) before asking subjects if they wished to try for the jackpot. In the control condition no mention was made of the presence of an audience. Subjects were simply asked if they wished to try for the jackpot.

In the After condition the experimenter announced that the observers had not yet arrived, but that it was still necessary to begin the decision-making task. Subjects were further informed that they would be notified when the audience had arrived. As in Experiment 2, the counter was stopped upon reaching 179. At this point subjects were told that the audience had arrived, and that it was therefore necessary for them to lift the shade before them for the duration of the Counter Game. All subjects in the After condition participated in the presence of an audience. Some had been told (as in the Before condition) that the audience was evaluative, whereas others were informed that it was non-evaluative. In short, most subjects in the Before and all participants in the After condition were observed as they completed the decision-making task. The key differences between the Before and After conditions was the point in time at which the audience's presence was made salient. In the Before condition this occurred prior to subjects' initial investment decisions, whereas in the After condition this was achieved after subjects had invested $1.79 from their initial stake.

After the decision-making task was completed, all subjects responded to a postexperimental questionnaire. The questionnaire included the Fenigstein et al. (1975) Self-Consciousness Scale, consisting of subscales of private self-consciousness, public self-consciousness, and social anxiety. In order to obtain a trait rather than a state measure of these dimensions, we asked subjects to describe themselves "as you are in general, not simply how you feel right now." Median splits were used to classify subjects as high or low on each of the three traits. In addition, the questionnaire tapped subjects' evaluation apprehension while taking part in the decision-making task. ("How much did you feel like observers were evaluating you in some way?"; "How much did you feel like you were being observed?"; "How much did the feeling of being observed bother you?"; "How much did you feel self-conscious?"; "How much did you feel like you were 'on the spot'?"). Responses could range from "very much" (1) to "not at all" (8). After completing the questionnaire subjects were debriefed, paid, and thanked for their participation.

Results. The predicted interaction between the audience variable and public self-consciousness/social anxiety did emerge in the After condition ($F(1,19) = 10.26$, $p < .005$). As can be seen in Table 7-2, high publicly self-conscious subjects were more entrapped in the nonevaluative than in the evaluative condition, whereas low publicly self-conscious participants were somewhat, though not significantly (according to simple effect analyses), less entrapped in the nonevaluative than evaluative condition. The Audience $\times$ Social Anxiety interaction was also significant, $F(1,19) = 5.92$, $p < .05$, and took the same form. No other effects were significant in the After condition.

The pattern of results was quite different in the Before condition. Public self-consciousness and social anxiety produced no significant effects. There was a significant, though unexpected, main effect for the audience variable ($F(2,29) =$

Table 7-2. Mean Amount of Money Invested in After Condition of Experiment 3

Public Self-Consciousness	Evaluative[a]	Nonevaluative[a]
High	$3.03 (5)	$4.61 (5)
Low	$3.93 (6)	$2.88 (7)

Note: Scores could range from $1.79 to $5.00, with higher scores reflecting greater entrapment. The pattern of means is quite similar when social anxiety is substituted for public self-consciousness in the experimental design.
[a]Cell *N*s are in parentheses.

4.90, $p < .025$) such that subjects were most entrapped in the evaluative condition ($M = \$3.67$), least entrapped in the nonevaluative condition ($M = \$1.29$), and moderately entrapped in the control condition ($M = \$3.08$). A Newman-Keuls multiple comparison test on these three means revealed that subjects in the nonevaluative condition differed from the other two groups ($p < .05$); however, the evaluative and control conditions did not differ significantly.

The only other significant finding in the Before condition was a main effect for private self-consciousness, $F(1,23) = 5.36$, $p < .05$, indicating that highly private self-conscious subjects became more entrapped than their slightly private self-conscious counterparts ($Ms = \$3.53$ vs. $\$2.03$, respectively); there was no trace of a private self-consciousness main effect in the After condition ($F < 1$).

General Discussion

Taken together, the results of the three experiments suggest that the effects of certain situational and dispositional variables on entrapment may well interact with the point in the time at which the conflict process is being studied. Interestingly, none of the seven independent variables that were shown to affect entrapment across the three studies produced similar effects in the Before and After conditions. In Experiment 1 the perceived likelihood of the second experimenter's arrival significantly influenced degree of entrapment in the Before, but not in the After condition. The marginally significant Self-Esteem $\times$ Likelihood interaction that emerged in the After condition was not even close to significance in the Before condition. In Experiment 2 the cost-salience variable was significantly related to entrapment in the Before condition (replicating previous research), but it had no effect in the After condition. In Experiment 3 there were main effects for the audience and private self-consciousness variables in the Before, but not in the After condition. Finally, Experiment 3 revealed that the public self-consciousness $\times$ audience and social anxiety $\times$ audience interactions were significant in the After, but not in the Before, condition.

This array of timing effects is indeed impressive. However, an important question still remains; namely, is there any coherence to the seemingly disparate findings? We believe that there is, with one exception to be noted below. At the outset of a decision-making task that only later proves to be entrapping, individuals appear to be thinking in a cool-headed, unemotional fashion. They are behaviorally responsive to external cues that suggest whether persistence or withdrawal is the more prudent course of action. Three of the significant results in the Before conditions are consistent with this interpretation. Specifically, in Experiment 1 subjects were much less likely to wait (and become entrapped) when their expectation of the second experimenter's imminent arrival was low rather than high. In Experiment 2, decision makers were much less likely to invest their financial resources (and become entrapped) when they were led to attend to the costs associated with so doing. These two findings are consistent with expectancy-value models of choice behavior. While such results are hardly surprising, it is interesting that expectancy-value theory was not supported in the After conditions, in that neither of the above-mentioned effects was significant.

A third finding—that highly private self-conscious subjects became more entrapped than those low on this dimension in the Early condition of Experiment 3—is also consistent with the thesis that decision makers are more responsive to external cues concerning appropriate decision making in the initial stages of an entrapping conflict. How? In order to fit this finding within the broader theoretical framework, we need to assume that at the outset, the standard for appropriate behavior was to invest resources. This assumption seems reasonable. Just before being asked if they wished to invest, subjects were informed by the experimenter that it would be advisable for them to spend at least some of their money. For example, they were told, "It doesn't really cost too much—only a penny for each unit on the counter." In addition, demand characteristics to start investing are probably present in experimental studies of entrapment (cf. Chapter 4).

Why must it be assumed that investing constitutes the standard of "correct" behavior? The self-awareness literature has shown that heightened self-focused attention makes individuals more behaviorally responsive to standards for appropriate behavior. For example, it has been shown that high private self-attention causes subjects to behave more in accordance with their underlying attitudes (Carver, 1974, 1975; Gibbons, 1978; Scheier, Buss, & Buss, 1978). The self-awareness theory explanation for these findings (i.e., Wicklund & Frey, 1980) is that the subjects' attitudes constitute their personal standards for correct behavior, and that self-focus enhances adherence to standards.

The fact that private self-consciousness produced no effect in the After condition of Experiment 3 is also consistent with self-awareness theory. More recent theorizing (e.g., Scheier & Carver, 1977) suggests that self-focus enhances adherence to standards, provided that such standards are the self-aspects that are the most salient at that time. The standard to invest resources may have become increasingly less salient over time in Experiment 3. Why? The time at which this standard was invoked (i.e., right before subjects made their initial investment decisions) was much more remote in the After than in the Before condition. Moreover, as was suggested previously in this chapter, in the later stages of the entrapping conflict subjects may have been more emotionally aroused. It has been shown that emotionality is a much more attention-getting aspect of the self than are standards for correct behavior (Scheier, 1976). In the process of becoming entrapped, subjects' need to justify themselves may be much more salient than the earlier, experimentally imposed standard for correct behavior. This possibility may account for the failure of private self-consciousness to affect entrapment in the After condition in Experiment 3.

In the later stages of entrapment situations, the decision makers' may act more in the service of self- or other-justification. At this point their behavior should be less influenced by external (i.e., expectancy value) cues for appropriate behavior. Three of the significant (or marginally significant) results in the After conditions are consistent with this interpretation, although more research is clearly warranted, given the extremely small sample sizes. First, it is intriguing that in the After condition of Experiment 1, high-self-esteem subjects (high SEs) were still responsive to external cues for appropriate behavior, whereas the low-self-esteem participants (low SEs) were not. Even when they were first informed about the likelihood of the second experimenter's arrival after waiting 10 minutes, high SEs were more apt to wait in the Likely than Unlikely condition (as expectancy-value theory would predict). The waiting times of low SEs, by contrast, were unaffected by this information.

This self-esteem effect may reflect individual differences in the ability to remain responsive over time to relevant external information. Although we know of no empirical evidence suggesting that high SEs are more responsive to appropriate cues than low SEs in entrapping decision-making tasks, there are theoretical speculations that this is in fact true. For example, Janis (1982) relied heavily on a self-esteem-based mechanism in trying to account for cohesive groups' proneness to Groupthink. Janis writes:

> Even when (group) members are not particularly concerned about risks of material losses ... they may be subjected to *internal* sources of stress. This source of stress involves a temporary lowering of self-esteem as a result of situational provocations. The most frequent provocations are: (1) recent failures, such as an unanticipated poor outcome resulting from a prior decision for which the members of the policy-making group feel responsible; (2) a current complicated and perplexing choice requiring the members of the policy-making group to carry out extremely difficult decision-making tasks that they perceive as being beyond their level of competence, and (3) a moral dilemma posed by the necessity to make a vital decision when the members of the policy-making group perceive a lack of any feasible alternative except ones that violate their ethical standards of conduct ... No one is likely to be exempt from undergoing a temporary lowering of self-esteem occasionally as a result of being exposed to any one of the three types of situational provocations.

In essence, Janis suggests that low self-esteem may interfere with the group members' abilities to be rational, critical decision makers. This speculation is consistent with the self-esteem effect obtained in Experiment 1, in which only high SEs behaved in accordance with the expectancy value model of decision making.

To return to the significant effects observed in the After condition: Second, the face-saving hypothesis in Experiment 3 posited that entrapment would be greater in the presence of a nonevaluative than an evaluative audience, especially for subjects who were concerned with their social image (e.g., those high in public self-consciousness). In fact, high publicly self-conscious subjects were significantly more entrapped in the nonevaluative than evaluative condition, whereas low publicly self-conscious participants showed a non-significant reversal of that finding. Third, the same effect was obtained when another individual-difference factor related to concern with saving face (i.e., social anxiety) was employed as the predictor variable.

The only significant effect that does not fall neatly into the overall package was the audience main effect in the Before condition of Experiment 3. In particular, we need to explain why the level of entrapment was so much lower in the nonevaluative than in the evaluative and control conditions. To speculate, nonevaluative subjects reported feeling much more evaluation apprehension than did the other two groups. (The five questionnaire measures of evaluation apprehension were moderately correlated with one another [average $r = .46$, $p < .01$, with 9 of the 10 correlations significant at least at the .05 level]). For each subject the measures were summed into a single index. The one-way analysis was significant ($F(2,22) = 4.90$, $p < .025$). Newman-Keuls analysis revealed that, as with the behavioral data, the nonevaluative condition ($M = 19.20$) differed from the control ($M = 30.87$, $p < .05$) and the evaluative conditions ($M = 26.17$, $p < .10$). The latter two conditions did not significantly differ. Perhaps the resulting discomfort was sufficient to motivate the non-evaluative participants to quit the experiment.

Of course, even if this reasoning is correct the finding that subjects felt most uncomfortable in the nonevaluative condition still warrants explanation. To speculate even further, perhaps this was because the identity of the audience members was not clearly stated (i.e., "individuals planning related research"). The uncertainty surrounding the nature of the audience may have caused discomfort for subjects in the nonevaluative condition. By contrast, subjects in the evaluative condition were well aware of the identity of the audience (i.e., "Tufts professors who are experts in decision-making"). Further research is needed, both to replicate the audience main effect in the Before condition, as well as to explain this curious finding.

Alternative Explanations

Perhaps the biggest problem plaguing our interpretation of the results of these three experiments is the fact that subject attrition rates differed in the Before and After conditions. As mentioned in the discussion of Experiment 1, it could have been that the participants who were retained in the analyses of the After conditions (i.e, those who persisted long enough to experience the manipulation) were systematically different from subjects in the Before conditions. Perhaps these subject variations were responsible for the different effects of the independent variables on entrapment in the Before and After conditions, instead of psychological differences associated with the different stages of entrapment.

The rate of subject loss for this reason was somewhat greater in Experiment 2 (11 out of 33, or 33%) and Experiment 3 (8 out of 32, or 25%) than in Experiment 1 (3 out of 15, or 20%). Thus, subject attrition may present even greater ambiguity in our interpretation of the results of the last two experiments. We cannot discount an alternative explanation based upon differential subject attrition. However, several facts suggest that this may be less of a problem than first appears. For example, the available evidence suggests that subjects who were retained in the analyses in the After condition were not different from those in the Before condition. In Experiment 1, as previously reported, the two groups did not differ in self-esteem. In Experiment 3, the two groups were equivalent along the dimensions of public self-consciousness and social anxiety, and there was only a marginally significant difference between groups in private self-consciousness ($t(50) = 1.87, p < .10$) with the Before condition subjects reporting greater self-attention than those in the After condition. Stated differently, there was no evidence in Experiment 3 that subjects' personalities were significantly different in the Before and After conditions, even though their personality variables produced different effects on entrapment behavior in the two conditions.

The pattern of the frequency distributions of quitting points in Experiments 2 and 3 provides further evidence of the similarity of subjects in the Before and After conditions. In both experiments subjects tended to quit at or before the $3.00 point (i.e., the value of the jackpot), *or* invest all of their initial stake once having spent beyond the $3.00 point. Moreover, this was true for subjects in both the Before and After conditions in both studies. These findings are reminiscent of Teger's (1980) bimodal distribution of quitting points in the Dollar Auction game.

Even better evidence that the Before versus After behavioral variations are due to psychological differences associated with the stage of the conflict, rather than differential subject attrition would be offered by a longitudinal study. With this methodology, the effect of independent variables on the entrapment behavior of the *same* individuals could be tested at different points in time. Suppose that: (1) the effects of certain factors on entrapment do interact with the point in time at which the factors are studied (as suggested by the results of Experiments 1–3), and (2) there is no subject attrition, that is, participants are studied at each point in time. If so, then the effects of the factors on entrapment cannot be due to differential subject attrition, and may be related to psychological differences associated with the various stages of the entrapping dilemma.

In fact, one study (Levi, 1982) did employ this type of longitudinal methodology. In this experiment (described in greater detail in Chapter 6), subjects completed a role-playing military exercise, in which they had to decide on the amount of U.N. military aid one of two warring countries should receive. In the scenario the aggressor nation (Red) had massed its forces along the border of the other nation (Blue). Subjects had to make repeated troop allocations to Blue, in face of evidence that the previous troop commitments had not met with success (i.e., that Red's forces continued to advance).

One of the independent variables was the extent to which subjects were accountable for their decisions. In the High Accountability condition it was emphasized that the subjects' role was that of "a decision maker who has the final say on commitment" of the U.N. troops to Blue, the defending nation.

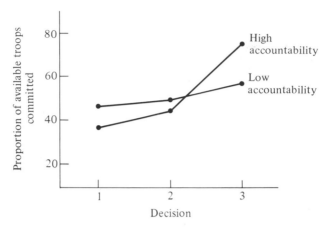

Figure 7-2. Proportion of available troops committed by subjects on decisions 1, 2, and 3 as a function of accountability. (*Note*: Higher troop allocations reflect greater entrapment.)

Moreover, these subjects had to give a short, tape-recorded speech to the U.N. Security Council justifying the troop allocation decision. In the Low Accountability condition subjects' role was that of an advisory group member who made recommendations, but was in no way accountable for the troop allocation decision. In addition, these subjects did not have to make a speech defending their decisions. As Levi points out, the accountability manipulation had two components: responsibility for the decision outcome and necessity of justifying the decision. In any event, it seems reasonable to say that the accountability variable affected subjects' face-saving needs, such that they were greater in the High than in the Low Accountability condition.

To summarize the procedure: subjects made three sequential decisions in which they had to allocate troops to defend Blue. After each of the first two decisions they were told that the military picture had deteriorated for Blue. The final decision was thus made with the knowledge that the scene had grown desperate for Blue. The dependent variable was the percentage of available troops committed to Blue's (losing) cause.

As can be seen in Figure 7-2, there was an interaction effect between accountability and decision stage ($p < .05$). For the first two decisions, high-accountability subjects allocated slightly fewer troops than did low-accountability participants. In the last stage of the decision-making task (i.e., when things had turned desperate for Blue) high-accountability subjects assigned a much greater proportion of troops than did their low-accountability counterparts.

Such results are wholly consistent with those from the previous three experiments. The face-saving variable (Accountability) had a significant effect on allocation decisions at the later stage of the entrapping conflict, but had no effect during the earlier stages. When subjects were in a position in which they had to defend their actions (in their own and/or in others' eyes), they escalated their commitment to the failing course of action to a far greater extent, but only after their prior degree of investment was substantial. In the absence of this prior investment (i.e, during the earlier decisions), the accountability variable had little effect. Moreover, these results suggest that face-saving variables are influential determinants of entrapment in the later (but not earlier) stages of the process, in a manner that eliminates differential subject mortality as a rival interpretation.

Summary and Conclusions

In our estimation, the dynamic quality of decision makers' psychological involvement in entrapment situations is one of the most intriguing aspects of these sorts of conflicts. This chapter was intended to describe the (1) nature and (2) behavioral implications of the psychological changes that accompany entrapment. The results of a number of studies using self-report methodologies suggest that decision makers do experience a variety of psychological changes as they become entrapped in an escalating conflict. Perceived motivation appears to change from the rational to the rationalizing. Whereas decision makers are initially motivated by the desire to have fun, win money, or minimize loss of money, they later report that they want to outlast their opponent, or more generally that they have "too much invested to quit." Information processing also appears to become increasingly focused on their commitment to the entrapping task (and all of the justificatory trappings therein), to the exclusion of other, perhaps more relevant, stimuli for their decision making. This so-called "tunnel vision" effect is more generally consistent with much research exploring decision making under stress.

The second section of the chapter explored the behavioral implications of the psychological changes accompanying entrapment. In particular, the same independent variables were shown to have different effects on the degree of entrapment, depending upon the stage of conflict at which the effects of these variables were studied. Such findings serve two important theoretical functions. First, they provide evidence about some behavioral implications of the entrapment process. Whereas the first half of the chapter delineated some of the cognitive consequences of entrapment, the studies described in the second half illustrate the implications of those cognitive changes for subsequent resource allocation decisions. Second, the studies in which the timing of the independent variables' introduction was also varied supported the central thesis of the chapter: that certain psychological changes accompany heightened commitment to a failing course of action. If this thesis is correct, then the effects of various factors on entrapment *should* interact with the decision stage. In general, this is exactly what was found in three of our own studies and one performed by Levi (1982).

Many of the results discussed in this chapter are open to alternative explanations. Consequently, the conclusions that we have drawn are somewhat tentative, awaiting the validation of additional research. It should be noted, however, that different kinds of alternative interpretations must be invoked for the results of the different studies. For example, reactivity may be a viable alternative to the results of the studies in which subjects were repeatedly questioned about their motivational and cognitive states. Subject mortality is a threat to the internal validity of the experiments in which the effects of various factors were explored both before and after decision makers had invested their resources. The available evidence does not support such alternative accounts of the data. Nevertheless, they cannot be eliminated entirely. In short, the theoretical stance that we have taken has the advantage of parsimony. It can explain virtually all of the results that have been described in this chapter, whereas the various alternative interpretations can only account for smaller portions of the data.

Chapter 8
Individual Differences

We have taken the "classic social-psychological approach" (Asch, 1951; Darley & Latane, 1968; Milgram, 1974; Zimbardo, 1972) in our discussion thus far of the antecedents of entrapment. This position generally espouses the importance of environmental, and particularly interpersonal, factors as determinants of social behavior. However, in keeping with Lewin's (1947) famous dictum that social behavior is a function of both Person and Environment variables, a more complete analysis of the antecedents of entrapment should also take individual difference variables into account. While situational variables have been shown to affect the degree of entrapment to a significant extent, even in these instances much of the variance in behavior was left unexplained. It is quite possible that individual-difference factors can account for substantial portions of the unexplained variance, either in isolation or in interaction with relevant situational factors.

The role of individual-difference variables has been discussed, at least in passing, in previous sections of the book. For example, in Chapter 5, considerable attention was devoted to sex differences in entrapment behavior. The effect of personality determinants of face-saving behavior (social anxiety, public self-consciousness) was discussed in Chapters 6 and 7. However, individual differences were not the main topic of these discussions. The purpose of this chapter, then, is to make individual-difference research on the entrapment phenomenon the primary focus. In particular, we will discuss the various ways in which the role of individual differences has been or could be explored empirically. First we will describe the results of the search for the "entrapment-prone" individual; several investigators have speculated that certain personality variables should be systematically related to the extent to which decision makers escalate their commitment to a failing course of action. Second, we will consider studies that have explored the interactive effects of personality and situational variables on entrapment behavior; these studies are consistent with the prevailing view in personality and social psychology (cf. Sarason, Diener, & Smith, 1975) which posits that person–situation interaction effects account for greater variance in social behavior than does either category of factors alone. Finally, we will examine the relationship between individual differences in decision makers' psychological states during the course of an escalating conflict and their ultimate degree of entrapment.

The Search for the Entrapment-Prone Personality, or Individual Differences as "Main Effects"

Intuitively one might think that certain individuals would be more likely to become entrapped than others. Accordingly, several researchers have included personality variables in their experimental designs on the grounds that such factors should theoretically correlate with entrapment. Unfortunately, this research strategy has been singularly unsuccessful in distinguishing between those who are versus those who are not susceptible to entrapment. Teger (1980) investigated the effects of four personality variables on escalating commitment in the Dollar Auction: risk taking, locus of control, tolerance for ambiguity, and machiavellianism. None of these factors yielded a significant relationship with entrapment. (Interestingly, several of these individual differences were correlated with physiological indices of relaxation during the course of the auction. High risk takers, those high in tolerance for ambiguity, and those high in machiavellianism were more relaxed, especially in the later stages of the auction, than their counterparts lower on the respective dimensions.)

Staw and Ross (1978) investigated the effects of dogmatism, tolerance for ambiguity, and self-esteem, while Levi (1982) included measures of locus of control, mania, and depression in their role-playing simulations. In both studies none of the personality variables was related to the degree of entrapment. In short, across three different studies, none of the 10 attempts to correlate personality factors with entrapment has yielded significant results. Before discussing possible explanations for these findings, we should mention that the findings themselves are consistent more generally with the results of many studies which have unsuccessfully attempted to correlate personality with behavior. In fact, it was results similar to those found in the present entrapment experiments that produced several scathing indictments of personality research (e.g., Mischel, 1968).

Why are personality variables so consistently unrelated to entrapment in the Levi (1982), Staw and Ross (1978), and Teger (1980) studies? The problem probably is not one of measurement, in that the researchers typically used well-validated personality scales (e.g., the Rotter [1966] Locus of Control Scale, the Rosenberg [1965] Self-Esteem Scale, or the Beck [1967] Depression Inventory). Furthermore, at the more conceptual level, at least several of the personality variables *could* have been related to the degree of entrapment. For example, the tendency to escalate (rather than withdraw) has been conceptualized as risk-taking behavior. If so, then those with risk-taking propensities should have been more likely candidates for entrapment. Instead,

Teger found no effect for the risk-taking variable. Similarly, the tendency to escalate commitment to a failing course of action can be viewed as rigidity in the face of a threatening event (Staw, Sandelands, & Dutton, 1981). If so, then those with low tolerance for ambiguity (i.e., greater rigidity) should have become more entrapped than their more ambiguity-tolerant counterparts. However, both Staw and Ross (1978) and Teger (1980) observed no effect for this personality variable.

The nonsignificant personality results may have been attributable to another, more general conceptual failing in the aforementioned studies. In two of the studies (Levi, 1982; Staw & Ross, 1978), the researchers included several situational manipulations in their experimental designs. Consequently, these manipulated variables may have minimized the role of individual-difference factors by causing participants to interpret the experimental situation similarly (regardless of their personality differences). This argument is similar to one advanced by Mischel (1973), who suggested that individual differences variables are not likely to influence behavior to the extent that the situation is *well-structured*; that is, the more that external cues lead people to arrive at similar definitions of the situation, the less likely it is that individual differences will affect behavior. In the third study (Teger, 1980), no independent variables were tested. Nevertheless, subjects may have also felt constrained by the experimental situation. All participants took part in the Dollar Auction against an unrelenting confederate, while simultaneously being connected to various devices to measure their physiological states. It is perhaps little wonder that subject-personality variables had little impact on behavior under such conditions.

One implication of this "Mischelian" analysis is that personality variables may, in fact, influence entrapment behavior to the extent that the situation is not well structured. What factors affect the "structuredness" of entrapment situations? The clarity of the feedback about one's prior investments may be one relevant variable. In all of the entrapment situations discussed to this point, decision makers' prior investments have met with immediate, negative feedback. However, it is possible to imagine some entrapment contexts in which the feedback that decision makers receive as they escalate their commitment is much more ambiguous. Some projects requiring prolonged commitment may only provide individuals with feedback at the end of their involvement. Negative feedback *along the way*, which is typically inherent to most entrapment situations, is lacking in these instances. For example, in some courses students only receive feedback about their performance at the very end of the semester (e.g., law school courses). It may be possible for students to become entrapped in this type of course if, midway through the term and against their better judgment, they decide to continue with the course in order not to "waste" the time already devoted to it.

Another factor affecting the "structuredness" of the entrapment situation is present when the decision maker is competing against a social rather than nonsocial opponent (see Chapter 5 for a further discussion of the social/

nonsocial distinction). In many instances decision makers have lots of information about the opposing party: the amount of resources available to be invested, his or her preferences about various outcomes, and so on. However, at other times the information about the other party is much less clear. Person A may be unaware of much important information about Person B, which, if known, would readily cue in Person A to appropriate competitive behavior with Person B. In fact, this information may be ambiguous because of B's deliberate attempt to render it so, and thereby avoid giving the competitive advantage to Person A.

It is precisely under such circumstances of ambiguity (e.g., unclear feedback, an undefined opponent) that personality variables may relate to entrapment behavior. In fact, one of our students (Bob Houser) recently performed an experiment exploring the effect of personality in a less-structured entrapment situation (Houser, 1982). The "carnival game" was chosen as the experimental task. The basic procedure was very similar to the one used in the experiments exploring the effect of self-diagnosticity on entrapment (see Chapter 6). Over a series of trials, subjects had to indicate the extent to which white cards had been blackened by geometric figures. By making accurate guesses, subjects were told that they might be able to amass the necessary number of points to win a cash jackpot. Furthermore, subjects had to spend money to complete each trial, and these monetary amounts increased with each trial.

In previous research (Brockner, Houser, Lloyd, Nathanson, Deitcher, Birnbaum, & Rubin, 1985, Experiment 2) half of the subjects were led to believe that their task performance was due to skill, whereas the other half was told that it was due to luck; this skill–luck manipulation was retained in the Houser study. Unlike the previous research, subjects were given no feedback about the quality of their task performance. Instead, they were told,

> One of the purposes of this experiment is to study perception under conditions of uncertainty. Thus, you will not be told how many points you have earned on each trial. Only the experimenter will know. If and when you accumulate the points needed to win the jackpot, the experimenter will let you know.

Under no conditions did subjects ever win the jackpot. The dependent variable was degree of persistence at this costly, failing task.

The uncertainty (due to the lack of clear performance feedback) should have increased the likelihood that conceptually relevant personality variables would affect degree of persistence. For example, in the absence of concrete feedback, personality variables could influence subjects' inferences about how well they are performing. Subjects who see themselves as generally successful in their endeavors may infer that they are closer to the goal, and therefore may be more likely to persist (Rubin & Brockner, 1975). In fact, subjects scoring high on a self-competence measure were more likely to persist with the failing course of action ($p < .05$). To operationalize self-competence, Houser factor-analyzed subjects' responses to the Revised Janis-Field Self-Esteem Scale. Six items loaded on a factor labeled self-competence, including "In general, how often do you feel confident about your abilities," and "How often do you feel that you are a successful person."

In addition, Houser observed that locus of control (Rotter, 1966) was significantly related ($p < .05$) to persistence behavior. Entrapment was exhibited to a greater extent by individuals who were Internal rather than External in locus of control. Note that a similar result was predicted but not obtained, in the experiments performed by Levi (1982) and Teger (1980). However, in the previous studies subjects' behavior could have been "constrained" by a number of situational cues, thereby minimizing the potential impact of individual-difference variables. The Houser methodology, in which performance feedback was undefined, may have enabled subjects to project their personalities onto their decision-making behavior.

Finally, it should be noted that subjects in the Houser study reported feeling more entrapped as they persisted at the task. All participants rated the importance of 11 motives for their decisions to persist for as long or as short as they did. The responses to each of these questions were then correlated across conditions with the behavioral measure of persistence. Only two items were significantly related to game behavior, one of which was the self-report measure of entrapment ("I had already been in so long that it seemed foolish not to continue," $r(56) = .30, p < .025$).

The other self-report item that was significantly correlated with persistence was the perceived control measure ("I felt that I had control over the number of points I had accumulated," $r(56) = .36, p < .01$). This finding, when coupled with the previously described effect of trait Locus of Control, suggests that perceived control may be maladaptive under certain conditions. This notion has been raised elsewhere in this book and by other authors (Janoff-Bulman & Brickman, 1980; McFarlin et al., 1984), and thus will not be discussed at great length here. The basic point is that, contrary to the value underlying most "learned helplessness" research (Seligman, 1975)—that persistence at a task is adaptive, whereas withdrawal is maladaptive—it may be that persistence due to perceived control may be dysfunctional (e.g., it could lead to entrapment) to the extent that the decision maker's perception of control is overinflated.

Personality × Situation Interactionism

The results of the Houser (1982) study are consistent with a more general theme in personality and social psychology: that traits and states jointly affect behavior, and typically do so in an interactive fashion. Mischel's (1973) version of this statement is very general; namely, that when situations are unconstraining, ambiguous, or ill-structured, personality variables will affect behavior; when situations are constraining, clear, and well structured, personality variables are less apt to be influential.

It is possible, however, to conceive of personality $\times$ situation interaction effects on entrapment behavior with greater specificity. For example, are certain individuals more prone than others to entrapment across a wide variety of situations? This question is related to, but not identical with, the issue addressed in the previous section of this chapter, which dealt with personality variables as "main effect" determinants of entrapment behavior. Rather than asking whether different people will vary in their degree of entrapment within the same situation, we are now wondering whether the same individual will manifest consistent levels of entrapment across different situations. An affirmative response to the latter question would be consistent with the notion that an entrapment trait exists; it may not be embedded within already existing personality measures (e.g., tolerance for ambiguity, locus of control), but it may well exist. Alternatively, a negative response to this question would be more consistent with the interactionist perspective; that is, just because individuals may be susceptible to entrapment in one situation does not mean that they are similarly vulnerable in other contexts.

Preliminary evidence suggests that there may be little transsituational consistency in proneness toward entrapment. Two of our doctoral students at Tufts University, Susan Harrison and Sinaia Nathanson, developed a questionnaire designed to measure the existence of an entrapment trait. Their scale included items assessing risk-taking (e.g., "I enjoy gambling"), tolerance for ambiguity (e.g., "I try to avoid situations which are unclear or uncertain"), patience (e.g., "I find the process of waiting for something I want very aggravating"), meticulousness (e.g, "There is no excuse for carelessness"), commitment (e.g., "If you believe in something, it is important to do whatever is necessary in the service of this belief"), and decisiveness ("I tend to admire people who stick to their guns"). In addition, there were several situation-specific measures of entrapment (e.g., "I try to finish every book I start, even if I don't enjoy it very much").

A total of 52 Tufts University undergraduates completed the questionnaire, in which they were instructed to indicate the extent to which each statement was self-descriptive. The authors performed intercorrelations between the first 15 items of this 77-item scale. (Unfortunately, the intercorrelations of the remaining items were lost, due to a computer error.) Nevertheless, it is interesting to note the pattern of intercorrelations. First, out of the 105 pairings only 12 attained significance at the .05 level. This "hit rate" is not much more than what would be expected by chance. Second, the items assessing situation-specific proneness to entrapment were not significantly intercorrelated (e.g., the correlation between "I am the kind of person who would never leave a play in the middle, even if I found it boring" and "I try to finish every book I start, even if I don't enjoy it very much" was nonsignificant and *negative*). Situation-specific items such as the two just mentioned did not even correlate with more general measures of persistence such as, "Once I start doing something, I usually stick with it until I am done."

Clearly, there is not ample evidence from this preliminary study to determine whether there is consistency in subjects' self-reports about their proneness to entrapment. The generally nonsignificant findings could be due to a host of factors besides the possibility that the trait for entrapment-proneness does not exist. It may be that the meaning of many of the scale items was very unclear, paving the way toward nonsignificant intercorrelations. Or possibly the conceptual content of the scale items (risk-taking, tolerance for ambiguity, patience) is simply not at the heart of what makes people prone to entrapment. Perhaps some measures of effort justification and/or face saving needs should have been included. Still another possibility is that a host of factors could significantly influence entrapment (risk-taking, tolerance for ambiguity), but these factors are not significantly correlated with one another. Practically speaking, then, few firm conclusions can be drawn from the Harrison and Nathanson data. No evidence of a trait for entrapment-proneness was suggested by their data; on the other hand, much more research needs to be done before this null hypothesis is accepted. Still, the work is valuable in that it suggests how one might go about constructing an individual-difference measure of susceptibility to entrapment.

Personality as Moderators

Another approach to interactionism is to treat personality factors as moderator variables. According to this logic, situational factors govern escalation decisions, but they do so more for certain individuals than for others. The notion that personality variables moderate the effect of situational factors has received support in several studies. For example, in Chapter 5 it was shown that decision makers became more entrapped when competing against another person rather than a nonsocial entity (e.g., chance). Further analyses demonstrated that two individual-difference variables moderated these findings: (1) sex of subject—the effect was true for males, but not for females; and (2) Interpersonal Orientation (Swap & Rubin, 1983)—the effect was found for those men who were low rather than high in Interpersonal Orientation.

In Chapter 6 we reported that entrapment was heightened by instructions that advocated the intelligence of risky rather than cautious investment behavior; as predicted, entrapment was much greater in the Risky than in the Cautious condition. However, individuals high in social anxiety, who are presumably more concerned with their social image, were much more influenced by the Risk–Caution variable than were those low on this dimension. Other examples of the moderating influence of personality variables is provided in studies performed by Conlon and Wolf (1980; see Chapter 6) and Brockner et al. (1982; see Chapter 7).

To summarize what has been said to this point about person × situation determinants of entrapment:

1. Research has yet to uncover the "entrappable personality." Seemingly relevant psychological constructs (tolerance for ambiguity, risk-taking) have shown no overall effect, and one attempt to develop an individual-difference measure (Harrison & Nathanson, 1982) revealed little evidence that a more specific entrapment trait even exists.

2. Similarly, to the extent that personality variables affect entrapment behavior, they will do so primarily in interaction with situational factors. At a general level of analysis, this means that personality variables are most apt to affect behavior in unstructured situations which allow individuals to make different interpretations of the same context (Houser, 1982; Mischel, 1973). At the more specific level this implies that personality will rarely be related to entrapment in an overall or "main effect" sense. The studies by Levi (1982), Staw and Ross (1978), and Teger (1980), all of which yielded nonsignificant relationships between personality and entrapment, might have met with more success had the researchers statistically tested for personality–situation interaction effects, rather than simply for personality main effects.

3. Finally, personality variables may moderate the effects of situational determinants of escalated commitment (e.g., Brockner, Rubin, & Lang, 1981; Conlon & Wolf, 1980).

Individual Differences as Mediating Variables

The effects of individual differences on entrapment has hitherto been discussed in the context of research in which personality factors were incorporated as independent variables in the experimental design. There is at least one other way, however, in which individual difference factors could be studied: as mediating variables. One of the pitfalls of experimental research on entrapment is that the nature of the entrapment process invites rather large within-condition variability. For theoretical as well as empirical reasons it would be valuable to understand better the high degree of within-condition variability. One way in which this may be achieved is by measuring those factors that are believed to *mediate* the effects of the indepndent variables on level of entrapment.

This strategy was employed in a study by Bazerman, Schoorman, and Goodman (1980), which was a partial replication and extension of Staw's (1976) seminal study. All subjects completed the "Adams and Smith" decision-making task, in which they learned that a prior allocation of company research and development funds had met with negative feedback (see the description of the Failure condition of the Staw [1976] experiment in Chapter 3). Half of the subjects were responsible for the prior decision (Personal Responsibility condition), whereas half were not (Control condition). Replicating Staw (1976), Bazerman et al. found that subjects were much more likely to escalate their commitment to the previously chosen though failing, course of action in the Personal Responsibility than in the Control condition ($p < .01$).

In addition to this successful replication of the Staw (1976) study, the authors obtained large within-condition variability. To account for this variability, they reasoned that several cognitive reactions to the initial setback information could be germane: (1) perceived disappointment, and (2) perceived importance. After making the second allocation decision, subjects indicated how disappointed they were with the initial setback, and how important they believed the initial decision to be.

Across the Personal Responsibility and Control conditions, it was found that both of these individual difference factors were correlated with subsequent investment decisions. As predicted, subjects were more likely to escalate their commitment to the extent that perceived disappointment ($p < .05$) and perceived importance ($p < .01$) were high. (It is also worth mentioning that these results were obtained from two very different samples of participants: college students and upper- and middle-level executives.)

Bazerman, Giuliano, and Appleman (in press) hypothesized that individual variation in other psychological processes besides disappointment and perceived importance could mediate subsequent escalation. All participants took part in the "Adams and Smith" decision-making task, either individually or in groups of four. Once again, half of the participants were personally responsible for the initial decision that had produced negative results, whereas half were not. As reported in Chapter 5, both groups and individuals in the High Personal Responsibility condition showed greater escalation than their counterparts in the Low Responsibility condition.

Bazerman et al. predicted that, across-conditions, escalation would be greater when subjects (1) viewed the later decision as *related* to the previous one, (2) were *confident* about their ability to make the optimal choice on the second decision, and (3) felt that additional funds would *reverse* or "turn the situation around." In fact, each of the relatedness, confidence, and reversibility factors was significantly related (at the .05 level) to level of commitment on the second decision task.

It is important for future research on individual differences as mediator variables to specify the factors that influence the mediator processes. Methodologies similar to that used by Bazerman et al. (1980) (in which mediating variables are measured) may be useful in accounting for a significant portion of unexplained variance in entrapment behavior. However, such studies account for the unexplained variance in a somewhat limited fashion. More specifically, Bazerman and his colleagues have demonstrated that entrapment will be heightened by perceived disappointment and/or perceived importance. But this research has not identified the factors that affect perceived disappointment or importance.

To further our understanding of the antecedents of entrapment, future investigators should include measures of the processes that presumably mediate the predicted findings. This research strategy will serve at least two purposes: First, it will enable researchers to evaluate the correctness of their hypotheses about the mechanisms by which the independent variables affect entrapment;

this can be achieved by statistically analyzing the relationship between the independent variable(s) and the mediating variable(s). Second, as in Bazerman et al. (1984) it may allow investigators to account for a significant portion of the variance left unexplained by the independent variables; this may be accomplished by statistically analyzing the relationship(s) between the presumed mediators and the dependent variable—degree of entrapment.

Several other experiments performed in our laboratory suggest that individual differences in cognition and/or affect may be predictive of subsequent entrapment. Briefly, subjects took part in a potentially entrapping task and were interrupted at various points along the way. During these interruption periods, participants responded to a series of questions about their cognitive and motivational states. The results of these studies are mentioned in Chapter 7; thus, they will not be repeated in detail here. The point is that the decision makers' ultimate degree of entrapment was correlated with their earlier self-reports (e.g., subjects who indicated relatively early on that they were "concentrating on the task to the exclusion of any other thoughts" were more likely to become entrapped). As in the Bazerman et al. (1980, in press) studies, however, this individual difference analysis is incomplete in that it did not delineate, in turn, the variables that influenced the cognitive predictors of entrapment. For example, it would be useful to identify the factors that led subjects to "concentrate on the task to the exclusion of any other thoughts" to a greater or lesser extent. In short, this experiment has many of the same benefits and shortcomings as those performed by Bazerman and his colleagues. On the plus side, it enables us to identify likely and unlikely candidates for entrapment. On the minus side, it does not identify the factors that influence the processes which are in turn highly correlated with subsequent behavior. Once again, the latter problem poses a challenging prospect for future research.

Summary and Conclusions

When all is said and done, it is clear that we and others have only scratched the surface in our quest to identify relevant individual-difference antecedents of entrapment behavior. It seems obvious that simple-minded attempts to correlate personality with entrapment behavior will not shed much light (i.e., Levi, 1982; Staw & Ross, 1978; Teger, 1980). Person–situation interactionist approaches have proved more successful, but even here our knowledge is somewhat limited. Needed is firm evidence on whether the obtained interaction effects are themselves situation-specific. For example, utilizing the Counter Game procedure, Brockner et al. (1981) found that subjects' social anxiety interacted with experimentally provided instructions to act in a risky or cautious manner. Would a similar effect have emerged had a different entrapment paradigm been employed? Similarly, Conlon and Wolf (1980) obtained personality–situation interaction effects in the context of a role-playing paradigm. It is unclear, however, whether such findings are generalizable to other entrapment scenarios.

Future research should also attempt to discover whether there is such a thing as "the entrapment-prone personality." The evidence suggests that numerous psychological constructs (e.g., tolerance for ambiguity, risk-taking) are not related to escalation of commitment in a main-effect sense. However, it is possible that the entrapment-prone personality consists of a hybrid of several traits. It may be useful to correlate individual items from a variety of seemingly relevant scales. For example, in the Houser study (1982), in addition to locus of control and self-esteem, subjects' private self-consciousness, public self-consciousness, and social anxiety were assessed. Individual item analyses from all of these scales could be conducted to discover which set of measures are most powerfully related to entrapment, even if such items are drawn from different scales.

In a similar vein, it would also be important to determine whether cross-situational consistency exists in individuals' tendencies towards entrapment. An initial attempt to demonstrate cross-situational consistency did not prove successful (Harrison & Nathanson, 1982), but these results were based solely on subjects' *self-reports* of their past behavior across different entrapment situations. Far more conclusive evidence would be gleaned from research that studies the same decision makers' *actual behavior* across a variety of entrapment situations.

Finally, it should be noted that some important information may be overlooked by studies which simply explore *mean* differences between individuals in entrapment behavior. For example, it is possible to envision certain types of individuals who are very reluctant to get involved in potentially entrapping situations; such individuals may either avoid entering the situation entirely, or withdraw shortly after entry. However, these very same individuals may be prime candidates for prolonged entrapment, once they have persisted beyond a certain critical point. Other people may be more moderate (less variable) in their proneness to entrapment. *On the average*, these two groups of decision makers will not differ in their degree of entrapment. The former group will be comprised of individuals whose level of entrapment was *either* very high or very low. The latter group will be comprised of individuals whose level of entrapment was moderate. By focusing on mean differences, however, researchers may overlook a potentially important difference between the two groups: the tendency for the former group to show much greater *variability* in behavior than the latter. For example, in a recent study, Brockner et al. (1985, Experiment 3) found that an experimental manipulation of high self-diagnosticity caused subjects either to quit very early *or* become quite entrapped, relative to those in the non-self-diagnostic condition. In that same study trait self-esteem exerted a similar effect. Subjects low in self-esteem (who are chronically more concerned with the self-diagnosticity of their behavioral outcomes) showed greater variability in behavior than their high-self-esteem counterparts (who are less concerned with self-diagnosticity issues).

We encourage future researchers on individual-difference variables to be wary of such differences in variability of behavior, in addition to differences in the average behavior. Of course, even if it were shown that two groups differed in the variability, rather than the average, of their behavior, the conceptual/empirical task should not stop at that point. Rather (and here is where the person–situation interactionism concept may once again become relevant) it is necessary to discover why, within the more variable group, some individuals exhibited one behavioral extreme while others exhibited the opposite extreme.

Chapter 9

Toward the Reduction of Entrapment

The following stories recently appeared in the Business Section of *The New York Times*.* The first, dated December 7, 1981, read as follows:

Lockheed to Halt Output of Tristar (13-Year Loss Near $2.5 Billion)— "Lack of Orders" Blamed
    The Lockheed Corporation announced today that it had decided to halt production of its L-1011 Tristar jumbo jetliner and write off losses of $400 million. The company said it had lost $2.5 billion on the L-1011 program since it began 13 years ago in a trans-Atlantic partnership with Rolls-Royce. With the Tristar, Lockheed was hoping to recapture the commerical airliner business that it had abandoned . . . By taking a $400 million write-off in phasing out the L-1011, Lockheed has plenty of company. In 1979 the United States Steel Corporation wrote off 14 steelmaking and fabricating facilities at a total charge of $809 million. In the same year International Telephone and Telegraph Corporation, as a result of closing its Rayonier pulp mill in Quebec, wrote off $320 million . . . The Chairman (of Lockheed) said, "Despite an intensive marketing effort the existing backlog of orders is not enough to sustain continued production at an economically justifiable level."

The other story, appearing May 4, 1982, read:

Exxon Abandons Shale Oil Project
    The Exxon Corporation, the world's largest energy company, announced yesterday that it had withdrawn from the Colony shale oil project in Colorado, America's most ambitious attempt to produce synthetic fuels commercially . . . "While construction has been progressing satisfactorily, the estimated probable cost of the project has continued to increase," said Randall Meyer, president of the Exxon Company. Exxon believes "the final cost would be more than twice as much as we thought it would be when we entered the project . . ." Exxon spent $300 million to purchase its 60% share of the Colony project in 1980. Since then, it and Tosco (Exxon's partner in the venture) have spent $400 million on the project . . . Under the operating agreement between Exxon and Tosco, Exxon must buy Tosco's share of Colony, if Tosco asks that it do so.

Tosco said yesterday it was exercising the option and that it would therefore
receive about $380 million from Exxon.

The preceding accounts appear to have much in common. Both describe
business ventures in which the investing organizations allocated huge sums of
money to failing courses of action over a prolonged period of time. Said
differently, both Lockheed and Exxon appear to have been entrapped in an
escalating conflict. Of course, it is difficult to know whether the corporate
decision makers' long-term persistence reflected underlying entrapment. Nevertheless, the real possibility exists that entrapment was at work in these, and
countless other, examples of corporate failures.

It is also worth mentioning that in both examples, the organizational decision
makers ultimately were able to extricate themselves from these failing ventures
(although they might have wished, in retrospect, that they had done so sooner).
In Chapter 1, indeed throughout the book, we stressed the fact that entrapping
conflicts have a self-perpetuating quality. However, it is equally important to
mention that self-perpetuation continues, but only up to a certain point. Clearly,
people terminate failing interpersonal relationships (witness the high divorce
rate in this country), stop waiting on hold for the operator to return with the
needed information, stop spending money on the repair of their old cars, and, as
in the preceding examples, withdraw from failing business ventures.

Whereas the style of this chapter is similar to that of its predecessors—that is,
that heavy emphasis is placed on empirical research—the focus is somewhat
different. More specifically, the issue of greatest practical concern in the
growing body of entrapment research is whether it is possible for decision
makers to lessen their tendencies towards entrapment. Said differently, what are
the conditions that enable individuals to avoid or reduce entrapment, preferably
before they have incurred the great costs described in our opening examples.
The preceding chapters presented material that was mainly theoretical, devoted
to delineating the factors that increase *or* decrease the likelihood of entrapment.
The present chapter has both theoretical *and* practical concerns: it deals with
the circumstances under which entrapment is less apt to occur, relative to a
baseline control condition.

The underlying goal of this chapter, then, is to provide information that
ultimately may help decision makers avoid becoming entrapped. The ensuing
research will suggest two general possibilities in this regard: First, it will identify
some cognitive strategies which may be profitably utilized to reduce entrapment
proneness; that is, by performing certain mental operations, decision makers
will be better able to avoid becoming entrapped. Second, the research will
specify a host of situational factors that lessen individuals' entrapment
propensities. Said differently, the research presented in this chapter implies that
decision makers may rely upon two different tactics to reduce the likelihood of
entrapment: (1) at least under certain conditions, they may be able to implement
the cognitive strategies that have proven successful in experimental research,
and/or (2) they may be able to exert influence over their environment, such that

they can create the very conditions that have been proven to deter entrapment.

Before turning to the relevant research, we should mention two other concepts related to the material presented in this chapter. First, some factors reduce entrapment by causing decision makers not to enter the situation initially (as in the case of the person who decides at the outset not to wait for the bus). Others reduce entrapment by enabling decision makers to withdraw from dilemmas in which they have already allocated some of their resources (as in the example of the individual who waits several minutes for the bus, but then decides to walk). The distinction between factors that prevent entry and those that promote withdrawal is not trivial. As discussed in a preceding chapter, the psychological process of entrapment is quite dynamic: decision makers' perceptions (of their motivation for investing, among other things) change dramatically as the entrapping dilemma develops. One implication of this fact is that the factors which prevent entry will not necessarily promote withdrawal. This is not to say that factors preventing entry cannot also promote withdrawal. They may or may not. We are simply suggesting that factors preventing entry should not automatically be assumed to promote withdrawal, and that factors promoting withdrawal should not automatically be assumed to prevent entry.

Second, there is an important value underlying the scope of this chapter— namely, that it is normative for entrapment to be reduced. In general, we do believe that it is prudent for decision makers to withdraw from entrapping courses of action. Nevertheless, there may be circumstances in which it is functional or rational for decision makers to escalate their commitment to a failing course of action, even if such heightened commitment stems from their need to justify previous resource allocations (e.g., Christensen-Szalanski & Northcraft, 1984; Northcraft & Wolf, 1984). This possibility will be discussed further later in this chapter, as well as in Chapter 11.

Factors Decreasing Entrapment: An Overview

Researchers have tested the effects of a variety of factors that may reduce entrapment. In organizing the following host of deterrents to entrapment, we have relied upon a well-known, if somewhat blurred distinction in psychology: that between cognitive and motivational determinants of behavior. The cognitive viewpoint is captured by Teger's (1980) suggestion that, "we can best remove ourselves from a too much invested to quit situation by gaining perspective on it." The preceding statement seems to imply that decision makers' susceptibility toward entrapment may be lessened by leading them to focus on certain information that heretofore has been ignored. More specifically, what if they attended to the costs associated with continued commitment? What if they considered the longer-term implications of not achieving their goals in the shorter haul? Such empirical questions are based on a predominantly cognitive view of human nature. The logic is that if people are provided with certain information it is bound to affect their behavior. Thus, if decision makers are led to attend to certain cues, it could lessen their proneness to entrapment.

An alternative or complementary viewpoint is that decision makers can be *motivated* to avoid or withdraw from potential entrapment situations. In fact, in a handful of studies to be described, it seems that entrapment was reduced because persistence was associated with psychological discomfort for decision makers.

Cognitive Deterrents of Entrapment

One of the major causes of entrapment is individuals' lack of awareness of what they are getting themselves into by making their initial resource allocations. The decision to wait for a bus, for example, is often made without much conscious attention or forethought. More likely, we arrive at the bus stop, and "mindlessly" decide to wait. That is, upon making the initial decision to wait we do not say to ourselves, "Gee, I better think about whether to wait. What if I wait 10 minutes and the bus has not yet arrived? I'm likely to continue waiting in order to justify the previous time spent waiting. To avoid that entrapping state of affairs, I better start walking now." Indeed, as we listen to our friends' and colleagues' personal "war stories" of entrapment, we are struck by the frequency with which they report that they did not begin to contemplate what they were getting into at the outset. Then, almost suddenly, the impact of their previous commitment comes crashing down around them, as they realize how far they have been sucked into an unrewarding course of action.

In the terminology of Janis and Mann (1977), the decision to enter what ultimately proves to be an entrapping situation is made with a lack of "vigilance." The focus of decision makers at the outset (to the extent that a clear focus even exists) is the short-term reward(s) to be reaped. They are less attentive to costs, especially those that would accompany a prolonged commitment. (Indeed, it is possible that decision makers do not even entertain the possibility, at the outset, that they are setting themselves up for a long-term commitment. After all, if such a prospect were to be considered, then they may be less apt even to embark upon that course of action.) In short, we suspect that decision makers, at the outset, fail to attend to the longer-term implications of not realizing their goals in the shorter term. Said differently, their time perspective is locked into the present, or near future; they do not view their impending commitment as a potentially long-term process with a past that will have to be justified, a present, and a future.

To make decision makers more vigilant, it may be necessary, as Teger (1980) puts it, to broaden their (time) perspective. For example, it would seem important to encourage them to think about (1) the possibility that their goals may not be achieved (at least not quickly), (2) the costs associated with a long-term commitment, and (3) whether they wish to embark upon the chosen course of action, given that short-term payoffs may not be imminent. Note that decision makers still may wish to invest their resources even after contemplating such prospects. Fine. If so, the decision will have been made with much greater vigilance, thereby reducing the possibility that the decision makers will "wake up" one day only to discover that they have too much invested to quit.

More likely, upon being made vigilant, decision makers may opt to avoid entering the potentially entrapping situation, or will withdraw shortly after embarking upon the potentially entrapping course of action. For example, in several studies, we found that subjects were much less apt to become entrapped if the costs associated with investing were made salient prior to subjects' initial investment decisions (Brockner et al., 1981; Brockner et al., 1982; Rubin & Brockner, 1975). In theory, a variety of factors (besides cost salience) may stimulate the vigilant mindset needed for efficient decision making in would-be entrapment situations. Let us now consider some of these possibilities.

Setting Limits

One technique that may deter entrapment is limit-setting. A psychological analysis of the act of limit-setting may explain why this is so. Setting limits causes individuals to anticipate future outcomes, something that the soon-to-be-entrapped decision maker often fails to do. In essence, those who set limits on the amount that they wish to invest *before* embarking upon a particular course of action are contemplating the possibility that the goal(s) may not be attained in the short run. Given that prospect, decision makers, in setting limits, are specifying the degree of cost that they are willing to incur.

Limit-setting makes the decision to enter a potential entrapment situation much more mindful than that which typically occurs. Moreover, limits may serve as much needed anchors that can rescue the decision maker from the entrapping dilemma. In a sense, in setting a limit the decision maker is making a commitment to avoid overcommitment. Once individuals have invested the amount specified in their limit without having attained the goal, they may more easily withdraw on the grounds that by doing so they are living up to a previous commitment (not to invest more than the limit).

Four studies have investigated the effect of prior limit-setting on degree of entrapment. Three of these experiments were performed by Teger (1980). Subjects were asked before the bidding began in the Dollar Auction, "How much of the money given to you do you think you would be willing to bid in the auction?" In two studies Teger observed significant but modest correlations ($r = .40$ and $.32$) between the magnitude of the limit set and the amount actually bid. In a third study subjects made decisions in teams of two. In the course of their deliberations some of the dyads spontaneously set limits early on, whereas other pairs never set limits at all. For the former group there was a highly significant correlation beween the size of limit and the amount actually invested

($r = .83$). The latter dyads were very likely to become entrapped, relative to those who had spontaneously set limits.

At least two questions are generated by the results of the Teger (1980) limit-setting studies. First, did the process of setting limits actually *cause* subjects to become less entrapped? Teger's methodology does not allow for a definitive answer to this question, since subjects were not randomly assigned to different limit-setting conditions. An alternative possibility is that the relationship between limit-setting and entrapment was correlational in the aforementioned studies; subjects who set low limits and did not get entrapped may simply have been cautious individuals. Their inherent cautiousness may have been causally responsible for their tendencies both to set low limits and to not become entrapped.

Second, it is interesting that the correlation between limit set and amount invested was considerably larger in the study in which subjects invested in teams ($r = .83$) rather than as individuals ($rs = .32$ and .40). It could be that the limit set in the presence of another (i.e., one's teammate) induced greater commitment to that limit. Kiesler (1971), Salancik (1977), and others have remarked that the process of making one's intentions public induces greater commitment to act in a manner consistent with those intentions. Teger's own speculation was consistent with this reasoning:

> Possibly the limit is observed more vigorously when it is made by a team—for then when the pressure to continue bidding to regain losses begins, the limit may be brought up as a rationale to permit the members to quit. This will not happen as easily with an individual, for he knows that he can simply change or abolish the limit in his own mind, and need not justify or explain it to anyone else. (Teger, 1980, p. 40)

A study performed in our own laboratory (Brockner, Shaw, & Rubin, 1979) addressed these two issues. In order to evaluate whether limit-setting causally reduces entrapment, subjects were randomly assigned to different experimental conditions. Before embarking upon the potentially entrapping decision-making task, some individuals were encouraged to set limits (i.e., to think about the amount that they wished to invest in order to achieve the goal), whereas other subjects (those in the Control condition) were not provided with explicit instructions to set limits. In order to test the hypothesis that the publicity of the limit will affect commmitment to act consistently with the limit, subjects who set limits were further divided into two groups. Half were required to make their limits known to the experimenter (Public condition) whereas half were not (Private condition). If limit-setting causally reduces entrapment, and if publicly set limits induce greater commitment, then subjects should become most entrapped in the Control condition, least entrapped in the Public condition, and moderately entrapped in the Private condition.

Method. The method and procedure of the Counter Game procedure used in this study have been described previously (see Chapter 4, pp. 43–44). To reiterate briefly, subjects had been given an initial stake of $4.00, and were told that the jackpot was worth $2.00. Before being asked if they wished to attempt to win the jackpot, the limit-setting manipulation was introduced. In the Public condition subjects were given a slip of paper with the following instructions:

> Before we begin, please take a few moments to set a limit on the amount of your $4.00 initial stake that you think you would be willing to invest in order to win the jackpot. *This decision is not binding.* You are allowed to change your mind at any point during the experiment. Write this amount in the space below. The experimenter will collect this paper from you immediately afterwards.

The experimenter then collected the paper from the subjects. In the Private condition the instructions were identical except that the last sentence was deleted and subjects' paper slips with their limits written on them were not collected. In the Control condition subjects were not provided with an opportunity to set a limit (at least on paper). They might have done so in their own minds, of course.

Results. As predicted, subjects invested the least money in the Public condition ($M = \$1.46$), the most in the Control condition ($M = \$2.11$), and an intermediate amount in the Private condition ($M = \$1.80$). The one-way analysis of variance did not yield a significant effect, $F(2,75) = 1.75, p < .20$. Several additional analyses did suggest, however, that the limit-setting variable had an important impact on subjects' degree of entrapment. A planned comparison (in which the overall error term was employed) demonstrated that subjects were somewhat less entrapped in the Public than in the Control condition ($t(75) = 1.87, p < .07$, two-tailed).

Furthermore, although the degree of entrapment did not significantly differ in the Public and Private conditions, there was some evidence that participants were more *committed* to their limits in the former than in the latter condition. The mean limit set was virtually identical in the two conditions ($t < 1$). Using a difference score analysis (amount invested minus limit set), we discovered a nonsignificant tendency for Private condition subjects to invest farther past their limits than did those in the Public condition ($t(50) = 1.60, p < .11$). This effect would have been even more pronounced were it not for the fact that several of the subjects in the Private condition (but none in the Public condition) actually spent *less* than the amount specified in their limits. A subsequent *absolute* difference score analysis revealed that Private condition subjects deviated from their limits more than did those in the Public condition ($t(50) = 2.47, p < .02$). Stated differently, the correlation between limit set and amount actually invested, while high overall, was significantly higher in the Public ($r = .95$) than in the Private condition ($r = .82; z = 2.33, p < .02$).

In sum, several findings of interest were obtained in the present study. First the fact that (only) Public condition subjects became somewhat less entrapped than did those in the Control condition suggests that (a) limit-setting may be causally related to reduced entrapment, and (b) the binding effect of the limit is greater to the extent that its publicity is enhanced. Why was the difference in entrapment between the Public and Control conditions not even more pronounced? We had anticipated that subjects would not set limits, unless they were experimentally prompted to do so. However, when later asked whether they had spontaneously set a limit in their own minds before starting to invest (and if so, to indicate the size of the limit), the vast majority (85%) of those in the Control condition responded that they had in fact set limits; moreover, the size of their limits was similar, on the average, to those observed in the Private and Public conditions. It is perhaps interesting in its own right that most of the Control subjects (reported that they) set limits; nevertheless, the effect of this unanticipated outcome was to weaken the limit-setting manipulation. In other words, the "Control" condition may not have been a true Control condition in which there should have been little or no spontaneous limit-setting. Indeed, the limit-setting variable may have been given an extremely conservative test in this experiment. In future research Public limits may cause an even greater reduction in entrapment relative to that found in a Control condition, provided that the Control condition was one in which little or no spontaneous limit-setting occurred.

Second, the significant limit-deviation differences between the Public and Private conditions were most intriguing. It could be argued that *any* Public versus Private comparison represented a conservative test, given the apparent procedural similarities between the two conditions. In particular, the Private condition was reasonably "public" too. Private condition subjects knew that the experimenter was unaware of their limits *during* the experiment. Nevertheless, they probably suspected that the experimenter would learn of their limits *after* the investment stage had been completed. The fact that publicly set limits induced greater commitment (though not necessarily less entrapment) than did privately set limits suggests that the conceptual variable which distinguished these two conditions (i.e., limit publicity) may be an extremely influential determinant of behavior in entrapping conflicts.

Third, given that Public and Private condition subjects differed on the absolute, but not the directional, difference score analysis, it may be appropriate to modify the prediction that publicly set limits will lead to less entrapment than privately set limits. The data instead suggest that public limits induce greater commitment to act consistently with the limit. If the limit is set at a relatively high level, then the publicly set limit may cause greater entrapment than the privately set one. During the debriefing in the Brockner, Shaw, and Rubin (1979) experiment several subjects in the Public condition who had set relatively high limits (and spent those amounts) reported that they had thought of quitting earlier. However, they persisted until they had spent the amount specified in their limit because they reported feeling committed to invest that amount. In addition, the few subjects who invested less than the amount specified in their limits were in the Private condition. Thus, *because they are more committing*, publicly set limits may lead to reduced entrapment, *provided that the limits are set at a relatively low level*. (Most, but not all, of the subject in the aforementioned study set fairly low limits.) However, and somewhat paradoxically, publicly set limits may also lead to greater entrapment if the limits are set at a relatively high level.

To test this hypothesis in future research, two independent variables should be orthogonally manipulated in a 2×2 factorial design. As in the previous study, half of the participants should set their limits privately, whereas the other half should do so publicly. In addition, half of the subjects should be led (somehow) to set low limits, whereas the other half should be induced to set relatively high limits. If our previous reasoning is correct, then an interaction effect should emerge: subjects should become less entrapped after setting low limits in the Public than in the Private condition. However, they should become more entrapped after setting high limits in the Public than in the Private condition.

The effects of limit-setting: Summing up. In summary, the results of both correlational and experimental research suggest that limits can deter entrapment. How does this occur? Limits may serve as "psychological contracts" that bind decision makers to behave in a manner consistent with their limits. The fact that limits have such a committing quality may make them especially useful as a deterrent to entrapment. The image of the entrapped decision maker is one of an individual who, through a process of "psychological inertia,' persists in a previously chosen, though failing, course of action. In order to reduce the likelihood of entrapment, some force is needed to counteract the self-perpetuating dynamic underlying entrapment. The process of limit-setting may provide one such force.

One implication of the limit-setting research is that limits may most effectively deter entrapment if (1) the limits are set at a realistic (i.e., not excessively high) level, and (2) decision makers are committed to act consistently with their expressed limits. Future research should evaluate these speculations by testing for the effects of a host of variables that directly influence either (or both) of these two underlying mechanisms. What factors affect the extent to which decision makers set reasonable limits? Degree of direct prior experience with the decision making task may be one relevant variable. The amount of indirect, or vicarious, experience may be another. What variables influence decision makers' degree of commitment to their limit? The public–private distinction is one possible factor. The work of Kiesler (1971) suggests that other variables are germane. For example, perceived volition surrounding the decision-making act may be important. To test this hypothesis some subjects could be led to believe that the process of limit-setting was self-, rather than externally, generated. Another group could be led to perceive that the impetus to set the limit was external. We would predict that commitment to the limit would be greater in the former than in the latter condition.

One other possible side benefit of setting limits beforehand should be mentioned. The decision-making process in entrapping dilemmas often is cognitively and/or affectively unpleasant. As entrapment deepens, decision makers experience greater degrees of decisional conflict, probably in response to the uncertainties posed by the entrapping dilemma. Commitment-producing limits may provide the additional advantage of reducing the aversive psycho-logical experience of entrapment. Brockner, Shaw, and Rubin (1979) observed that subjects in the Public condition reported *feeling* (on a posttask survey) much less entrapped than did those in the Private condition. That is, the Public condition participants were much less likely to explain their continued investments as arising out of their need to justify previous investments. In other words, by being committed to invest the amount specified in their limit, Public condition subjects did not have to agonize about whether to persist or withdraw at each decision point. Their commitment-producing limit may have reduced their decisional conflict, by "directing" them to invest the amount of their limit and then to quit, given that the goal had not been attained.

The view that limits serve as psychological contracts suggests another useful route by which entrapment may be reduced. To this point we have discussed the effect of setting limits *on the amount to be invested*. It may also be important for decision makers, prior to embarking upon a potentially entrapping course of action, to make another psychological contract with themselves—namely, to specify the *goal(s)* which they hope to attain through their resource allocations. That is, there may be some entrapment situations in which decision makers' investments were faring well before they began to do poorly. Consider, for example, the case of stock-market investors who are "wedded" to their failing stocks. Suppose further that these stocks had risen in value before taking their current nosedive. If the investors had set a specific, verifiable goal on the amount which they hoped to earn, then they might have sold their stock after its rise (assuming that the goal had been reached) but before its fall. In this way the entire process of entrapment could have been avoided. There are undoubtedly other situations in which entrapment could have been avoided if the decision maker had "gone while the going was good." By setting specific, plausible achievement goals investors are better able to know when, in their own minds, the going is good. Consequently, they can exit the situation before their fortunes take a turn for the worse and thereby sow the seeds of entrapment.

Finally, there is an alternative way to conceptualize limit-setting as a deterrent of entrapment. We have argued that limits should be most apt to prevent entrapment if they are set *prior to* the initial allocation of resources. However, this recommendation does not take into account the possibility that the subjective expected utility of goal attainment may change in the period between the times at which the limit is set and the amount of resources specified in the limit is allocated. For example, suppose you have set a limit of 15 minutes to wait for a bus to take you someplace to which you could have just as easily walked. Suppose further that the bus has not arrived after 15 minutes, but at that point you receive highly reliable information that it will appear within the next three minutes. Should you stick to your limit and start to walk? Or, should you invest beyond the amount specified in the limit? It seems clear that in this example you should persist further than the limit.

The disadvantage of limit-setting—at least within the context in which it has been discussed thus far—is that it does not consider the possibility that under certain conditions it may be more prudent for the decision maker to allocate resources beyond those specified by the limit. This would be especially true if the subjective expected utility of goal attainment changed dramatically during the initial resource allocation period. In short, we are suggesting that it is desirable for decision makers to be committed to their limits, provided that doing so enables them to avoid entrapment, rather than to interfere with optimal decision making.

Given a highly uncertain decision environment (i.e., one in which the subjective expected utility of goal attainment may change drastically), perhaps limit setting can be profitably employed in a somewhat different way. Rather than to quit automatically upon investing the amount specified by their limits, decision makers should use their limit point as a time to *reassess* whether persistence or withdrawal is wiser, *independent of the fact that prior investments have been made.* That is, if individuals decide to invest beyond their earlier set limit, this must be the result of a prospective, future (rather than past-oriented) cost-benefit analysis.

In essence, this conceptualization of the role of limit setting—that decision makers use the limit point to reassess their behavior—is related to the "Active-Passive" decision structure variable discussed in detail in Chapter 4. We are suggesting that limit-setting, when used as an inpetus toward "reassessment," could make the decision about whether to continue more "active" than "passive." Not trivially, entrapment was found to be less apt to occur in the former than in the latter circumstances.

Additional Routes to Mindful Decision Making

It was hypothesized above that prior limit-setting makes individuals more mindful of their behavior in entrapping conflicts. The act of setting limits requires decision makers to anticipate the future, something that they might not ordinarily do before entering would-be entrapment situations. Limit-setting may force decision makers to consider the possibility that their goals may not be attained. Given that prospect, they must consider the amount that they wish to invest in their quest for goal achievement. In short, we suspect that prior limit-setting produces greater *intentionality* in behavior, which may prevent decision makers from being swept away by the justificatory processes underlying entrapment.

How else might this increase in intentionality be induced? It may be achieved by factors that cause decision makers to be more *aware* of the process of entrapment, *at the time that they are about to invest their resources in what may ultimately prove to be an entrapping situation.* It is not being suggested that individuals are unaware of the concept or principle of entrapment. Rather, decision makers may not be focused on, or attentive to, the process of entrapment at the point in time in which it may be most crucial to be attentive— when initially embarking upon a course of action that could later prove to be entrapping.

It is our contention that decision makers for whom the process of entrapment is psychologically salient will be less likely to start and/or continue investing in entrapping courses of action. Two kinds of factors—informational and experiential—may make the process of entrapment more salient. These factors will be discussed in turn.

Informational factors. Informational factors inform, or perhaps more accurately, forewarn decision makers that they are about to embark upon a course of action that could prove entrapping. For example, consider the possible impact of models, discussed in detail in Chapter 5. In one study, subjects observed a model who became very entrapped (and also very regretful about his entrapment) prior to the point at which subjects made investment decisions. What information is conveyed by the model's behavior and attitude? Among other things, subjects may be led to consider that they too could become (regretfully) entrapped if they invested their resources. In fact, subjects' overall level of entrapment was quite low in this condition.

What if decision makers, before entering the situation, were required to read some material about entrapment and its perils? Presumably, this would make (the irrationality of) entrapment more cognitively salient. Questioned differently, if individuals are made more aware of their potential for decisional bias, does this make them less likely to fall prey to the bias? This question was addressed in a recent experiment (Nathanson et al., 1982).

Method. A field methodology unlike that used in previous research was employed. Subjects were 793 men and women whose names had been drawn at random from phone books of the Boston metropolitan area. All subjects were mailed a cover letter in which we introduced ourselves as "researchers from Tufts University interested in how a wide range of people solve problems." Subjects were told that by taking part in this study they had an opportunity to win a $75 cash prize. The instructions then continued:

> During the next several weeks you will be asked to solve a series of puzzles. All you need to do is to correctly solve them and mail them back to us. If your answer is correct, we will mail you the next problem in the series. If not, you are out of the running for the $75. After all of the problems have been mailed back to us we will pool the names of all people who have correctly solved all of the puzzles. There will be six winners, chosen randomly, and each will receive a check for $75 at the conclusion of the contest.

Subjects were told that they were under no obligation to start or to continue taking part in the study. If they did withdraw, however, they would forfeit their chance for the $75 prize.

The Informational independent variable was then manipulated. In the condition in which we wished to heighten subjects' awareness of entrapment (Informed condition) the cover letter continued:

> Before you decide whether you want to start doing the puzzles, let us tell you about some of the research that we have been doing. As mentioned we are interested in how people solve problems. Also, we are interested in how people

behave in situations in which they have made some effort to achieve a goal, but still have not achieved that goal. Will people continue making an effort to achieve the goal, or will they withdraw from the situation? For example, think about a situation in which a person waits for a bus to transport him someplace to which he could have just as easily walked. Once this person starts to wait for the bus, it probably will become more difficult to start walking to his destination. Why? It could be any number of reasons, including that the person would continue waiting in order to "make up" for the time already spent waiting. This example, and many everyday life situations, seem to share an important "entrapping" quality. Even though people no longer wish to continue in these situations, they also feel that they cannot leave. They feel that they must continue expending effort in order to justify their previous effort in that situation. In any event, we are hopeful that this information will give you some idea about our research interests.

This material was deleted from the cover letter mailed to the other half of the subjects (Control condition).

The puzzles were designed to become increasingly more difficult to solve. Specifically, in order subjects were asked to (1) form 20 four-letter words out of the letters appearing in the word "Massachusetts," (2) determine four U.S. state capital cities named after American presidents, (3) solve a 3×3 "Magic Square," (4) form 20 five-letter words out of the letters appearing in the word "experimental," (5) solve a 5×5 Magic Square, (6) solve 60% of the words appearing in a crossword puzzle taken from a 1970 edition of the newspaper, *The Boston Globe*, and (7) solve a 7×7 Magic Square. (To solve a 3×3 Magic Square one must place one digit from the integers 1–9 in each box of a 3×3 grid, such that the sums of all rows, columns, and diagonals are identical. A 5×5 [and 7×7] Magic Square is based on the same principle, but is lengthier and much more difficult to solve. For the 5×5 Magic Square the grid has 25 rather than 9 spaces, requiring the usage of integers 1–25; for the 7×7 Magic Square there are 49 spaces on the grid, in which the integers 1–49 must be used.)

After completing each puzzle those subjects who had chosen to take part mailed their solutions to us. They were allowed 2 weeks to solve each puzzle. If it was completed correctly then they were mailed the next puzzle in the series shortly after the 2-week period for the previous puzzle had expired. Thus, for those participants who took the time to solve all seven puzzles the study spanned a period of nearly 4 months.

Several aspects of this situation should have engendered entrapment. First, subjects had to make a time investment in order to solve the problems and mail them back to us. Second, the time needed to solve each puzzle undoubtedly increased during the course of the experiment, because each puzzle deliberately had been made more difficult than the previous one. (In fact, subjects reported expending considerably more "effort" in solving the later than the earlier puzzles.) Third, to increase the likelihood of initial compliance with our request to participate, subjects were provided with a stamped, self-addressed envelope in which they could return their responses to the first puzzle. However, for each subsequent puzzle they had to furnish their own postage and stationery. Finally, the rule that they had to solve all seven problems in order to be eligible for the $75 prize was intended to make them feel in the later stages of the study that they had to continue in order to justify their previous effort. In fact, one subject enclosed the following message with one of the later puzzles in the series: "I enjoyed doing the first few puzzles to help you guys out with your research. But now I'm finding that you and your puzzles are getting to be a real pain in the neck!" Note, of course, that this subject was continuing to work on the puzzles in spite of the fact that they had lost their intrinsic appeal. It is tempting to suggest that this subject (as well as the other persistent ones) experienced the intended entrapping conflict.

Results. The primary dependent variable was whether subjects returned the (correctly solved) puzzle. Overall, 175 (22.1% of the entire sample) responded to the initial puzzle. As predicted, however, a significantly smaller proportion of these respondents were in the Informed than in the Control Condition (18.6% vs. 25.6%, respectively; $\chi^2(1) = 5.21, p < .025$).

Subjects did not receive the next puzzle if they failed to return and complete the previous one accurately. Thus, the return rates on Puzzles 2–7 were determined by dividing the number of people who attempted to solve the puzzle by the number of people who had received the puzzle. The return rates on Puzzles 2–4 were high overall (78%, 92%, and 94%, respectively) and did not differ as a function of experimental condition. The overall return rate on Puzzle 5 was much lower (44%), probably because this puzzle was (rated as) much more effortful than the previous ones. The return rates on Puzzles 6 and 7 were 74% and 93%, respectively, with no condition differences (see Table 9-1 for summary data).

In brief, providing subjects with information about entrapment made them less likely to make an initial commitment to take part in the task. It did not affect subsequent decisions about whether to persist. The fact that this manipulation only affected initial investment decisions is noteworthy in its own right. As mentioned at the outset of this chapter, entrapment can be avoided if individuals decide not to make even an initial investment.

Why did the independent variable not influence subsequent persistence decisions? At least two explanations can be offered. First, the manipulation occurred in the initial cover letter sent to participants, and at no other point. Thus, by the time subjects had to respond to the second puzzle a whole month had elapsed since the initial cover letter had been sent. As a result, the information about entrapment may have no longer been salient. Second, a subject selection factor may have been at work. Subjects who participated in Puzzles 2–7 only consisted of those who had responded to the initial puzzle, regardless of condition. Thus, subjects who returned the initial puzzle in the Informed condition may simply have been the kinds of individuals who were not easily deterred by forewarnings of entrapment. Or, it could have been that their decision to return the initial puzzle served to strengthen further their commitment to the task. That is, if subjects in the Informed condition returned the puzzle *in spite of* the fact that they were forewarned about entrapment, they

Table 9-1. Percentage of Subjects Returning Puzzles (Source: After Nathanson et al., Experiment 2 [1982])

Condition	Puzzle Number						
	1	2	3	4	5	6	7
Informed	18.6%	80%	93%	96%	49%	80%	100%
	$\frac{74}{398}$	$\frac{59}{74}$	$\frac{55}{59}$	$\frac{52}{54}$	$\frac{25}{51}$	$\frac{16}{20}$	$\frac{16}{16}$
Control	25.6%	77%	91%	93%	39%	68%	85%
	$\frac{101}{395}$	$\frac{78}{101}$	$\frac{71}{78}$	$\frac{66}{71}$	$\frac{26}{66}$	$\frac{13}{19}$	$\frac{11}{13}$

Note: The numbers below the percentages are the ratios of those who returned the puzzles to those who received them. Subjects were only mailed the next puzzle in the sequence if they successfully solved the preceding puzzle (e.g., in the Informed condition one of the 55 subjects who returned Puzzle #3 did not solve the puzzle correctly; consequently, only 54 subjects were mailed Puzzle #4 in this condition).

would be under even greater pressure to justify the appropriateness of their behavior. It is precisely such justification pressures that may elicit continued commitment to the previously chosen course of action.

Several possible interpretations exist for the key finding that subjects were less likely to make an initial commitment to take part in the study in the Informed than in the Control condition. The one which we most prefer is that the information about the process of entrapment induced more mindful decision making; that is, subjects in the Informed condition may have considered the possibility that by making an initial commitment to take part they would in effect be planting the seeds for their own subsequent entrapment. Rather than risk becoming entrapped they avoided the situation entirely. Those in the Control condition may have been less apt to engage in this reasoning, and therefore were more likely to return the initial puzzle. In other words, Informed condition subjects may have been more thoughtful about whether they wished to take part, in that they were led to consider the possibility that they might be setting themselves up for a much longer-term commitment to take part in the study.

This line of reasoning fits nicely with the results of several studies exploring the effect of commitment forewarning on vigilant decision making (Mann, 1971; Mann & Taylor, 1970). In these experiments subjects were asked to choose between two alternatives of various types of objects (e.g., paintings, toys) that were relatively equal in attractiveness. Half of the subjects were informed predecisionally that their choice was irrevocable ("Be sure to think about your choice very carefully, because once you choose you will not be able to change your mind"), whereas the other half were told that their choice was not binding ("Be sure to think about your choice very carefully. Choose one, but if you want to change your mind later and decide that you would like to take the other one, you can bring it back"). In both experiments subjects who had been forewarned about the committing nature of their choice took significantly more time to make their decisions than did those not so forewarned. In addition, in the Mann and Taylor (1970) study experiment the former group showed less of a tendency than the latter group to engage in the faulty information search process known as bolstering. In bolstering—a predecisional process—individuals spread the difference in their ratings of the chosen versus the unchosen alternative. Janis and Mann (1977) have demonstrated that this process is much more likely to occur under conditions that foster faulty, rather than vigilant, decision making. In summary, the results of the Mann experiments suggest that the commitment forewarning caused subjects to be more mindful in their decision making.

Note the similarities (in both method and results) between the Mann studies and the one performed by Nathanson et al. (1982). In both instances the independent variable was whether subjects received information suggesting that they will be (or could become) committed to some upcoming course of action. The commitment was externally imposed in the Mann experiments, in that subjects were told that they would not be allowed to revoke their decision. The commitment in the Nathanson et al. (1982) experiment was described to be the result of an inexorable psychological process (entrapment); in theory, subjects were "free" to revoke their earlier commitment at any point by not continuing to participate in the study. In practice, however, it was suggested that it may be difficult for them to not remain committed to the previously chosen, though failing, course of action. Regardless of the nature by which perceived irrevocability was induced in the Mann and Nathanson et al. studies, those given such forewarnings manifested evidence of more conscious, mindful, or intentional decision making.

This is not to say that decision makers will *always* be less likely to fall prey to (the perils of) entrapment if they are made more aware of the nature of this process. It may be that heightened awareness is most effective in preventing individuals from making the initial resource investment. However, once the initial commitment is made it seems possible for individuals to be aware of the general concept of entrapment, indeed even aware of the very fact that they are entrapped, but still escalate their commitment to the failing course of action. Furthermore, it is possible that commitment or entrapment forewarnings will produce heightened *variability* in resource allocation behavior. Individuals may be less likely to embark upon a potentially entrapping course of action if they are forewarned of its committing nature. However, given that they have invested their resources in the face of such forewarnings, they may show even greater resolve to persist with the chosen course of action. More generally, the effect of making people more aware of their faulty decision-making processes on the quality of subsequent decisions is an interesting research area worthy of much further pursuit (e.g., Fischhoff, 1982).

Experiential factors preventing entrapment. Perhaps the most effective means of increasing the salience of entrapment is by having decision makers experience the process directly. Numerous studies have shown that the meanings of one's attitudes and behaviors are more psychologically salient when the attitudes and behaviors are experienced directly rather than indirectly (Janis & King, 1954; Regan & Fazio, 1977). Suppose a decision maker had just become entrapped in an escalating conflict. Would this experience make him or her less likely to get entrapped in subsequent situations?

The only data relevant to this question come from a study performed by Teger (1980). Subjects (undergraduates at the University of Pennsylvania) competed against a confederate in the Dollar Auction. Only after the auction had taken place were subjects told that it was "for practice," and that the "real" auction would now take place. The effect of the outcome of the "practice" auction on subsequent behavior was studied. All subjects competed against an opponent who never quit. Thus, in no case did subjects ever win the "practice" auction. Rather, they either spent all of their money, or quit before that had occurred. However, in some instances the bidding exceeded the value of the goal ($1), in which case both the subject and the confederate stood to lose money, whereas in other auctions subjects quit before the bidding had reached the $1 level. Presumably, those for whom the bidding exceeded $1 had a more powerful experience of entrapment than those who quit prior to the $1 point.

The dependent variable was whether the bidding level (i.e., degree of entrapment) in the second ("real") auction was less than, greater than, or equal to that in the first ("practice") auction. If subjects truly learned about the dangers associated with taking part in an entrapping task, then the amount invested should have been lower in the second than in the first auction, especially when the first auction was more costly to subjects. Out of the 50 sets of auctions, 31 showed reduced escalation in the second relative to the first auction. Moreover, when the first auction equalled or exceeded the $1 mark, 82% (18 out of 22) quit earlier during the second auction. However, when the first auction ended before the $1 bidding level had been reached, only 46% (13 out of 28) quit earlier in the second than in the first auction. These two proportions differed significantly ($\chi^2(1) = 5.13, p < .02$).

These results suggest that decision makers may have the capacity to learn from their previous negative experiences of entrapment. However, the results of this study are limited in a number of important respects. First, the independent variable—outcome of initial auction—was not experimentally manipulated. In order to know that prior negative experience with entrapment situations deters subsequent entrapment, it is of course necessary to create different experimental conditions and then randomly assign participants to them. Subsequent research needs to manipulate subjects' degree of entrapment as an independent variable, in order to evaluate whether heightened entrapment reduces the future likelihood of its occurrence.

Second, it is important to specify the conditions under which such "learning from experience" is most apt to occur. Just because decision makers have the potential to learn from their previous experience does not insure that such learning will take place. If anything, the methodology employed in the aforementioned study may have maximized the likelihood that learning or transfer would occur. After all, subjects took part in an entrapping task that was identical to the one which had provided them with the prior experience, namely the Dollar Auction. In addition, the experimental environment (e.g., the experimenter, the opponent, and the research room) was identical to that in the original situation. Such factors may have cued subjects to base their subsequent behavior on that which had transpired previously in that situation. Moreover, there was very little time lapse between the learning experience and the subsequent task, minimizing the possibility that forgetting would take place. Given such conditions, it is hardly surprising that decision makers who became entrapped initially were less likely to become entrapped the second time around.

Would learning take place, however, if the prior experience were more dissimilar to the actual test task? Said differently, if individuals experience entrapment in one domain of their life, will such experience influence the likelihood of becoming entrapped in another, seemingly unrelated, area? In order for individuals to profit from their previous experience in entrapment situations some type of learning or transfer must occur. Teger's (1980) preliminary study, as well as the vast learning theory research (e.g., Skinner, 1953) suggest that such learning *can* take place. However, there is at least anecdotal evidence that decision makers fail to learn their lessons from experience in previous entrapment situations. Future research should delineate the conditions under which the previous experience of entrapment is an effective deterrent to entrapment in subsequent situations.

Other cognitively based factors reducing entrapment. Before concluding this discussion of the cognitive deterrents to entrapment, we should mention that some of the material presented in earlier chapters is germane. For example, in Chapter 5 the effects of models on entrapment was considered. Under certain conditions subjects were less likely to become entrapped due to their exposure to the model. The effects of models can be viewed as complementary to the just-cited material on the effects of personal experience. That is, just as one may be less likely to become entrapped by virtue of just having experienced entrapment directly, it also appears that one can become less entrapped as a result of *indirect* experience (i.e., by witnessing the behavior exhibited by others in similar circumstances). We repeat our plea, originally made in the discussion of modeling effects in Chapter 5, for research aimed at exploring the conditions under which models may serve as useful deterrents to entrapment.

In addition, in Chapter 4 research was reviewed suggesting that individuals were less prone to entrapment to the extent that they were led to attend to the costs (and/or not to focus on the rewards) associated with heightened commitment. Subjects who were shown payoff charts before starting to invest became less entrapped than those who were not (e.g., Rubin & Brockner, 1975). Furthermore, in Chapter 4, we speculated that entrapment was less likely to occur in situations in which investments were made on an Active, rather than Passive, basis because perceived costs were rendered more salient by Active decision making. More generally, a wide variety of factors could affect decision makers' degree of attention to costs. In addition to the situational determinants already discussed, individuals may show chronic tendencies to attend predominantly to either the rewards or costs associated with various behaviors. In theory, cost-oriented individuals may be less likely candidates for entrapment than are those who are reward oriented.

In summary, entrapment may be reduced by making decision makers more mindful of their behavior. Instead of being inexorably "swept away" by the self-justification mechanism(s) underlying entrapment, individuals need to be vigilant about what it means to commit their resources to a course of action that could prove entrapping. "Being vigilant" refers to a host of psychological processes, including (1) the anticipation of possible negative outcomes, in particular the prospect that goal attainment may be excessively costly and/or uncertain; (2) awareness of the psychological or emotional implications of having committed resources to a hitherto failing course of action, in particular, that the need to justify those commitments is apt to be felt; and (3) constant attention to the costs (both short- and long-term) associated with persistence. Numerous experiments have been conducted in which the independent variables were designed to influence some aspect of degree of vigilance. These factors have included limit-setting, forewarning about entrapment, direct experience with entrapment, exposure to models, and salient information about the costs associated with persistence. Taken together, the results imply that entrapment can, in fact, be reduced to the extent that decision makers adopt a more mindful or vigilant state. We turn next to the motivational deterrents to entrapment.

Motivational Deterrents to Entrapment

Entrapment is a motivational phenomenon; as a result of decision makers' *need* to justify previous resource allocations, they may escalate their commitment to a failing course of action. In the previous section we described the entrapment-reducing effects of a variety of factors that were presumably cognitively mediated. In this section we explore additional factors that may make entrapment less apt to occur. However, the underlying logic in this section is somewhat different from that of the preceding section. More specifically, it may be that just as decision makers are driven to persist in entrapping conflicts, so too can they be driven to withdraw. If the motivational forces are strong enough to overcome the justification needs that underlie escalated commitment, then withdrawal rather than persistence should be more apt to occur.

Learning theorists distinguish beween negative and positive motivation, a distinction that may prove useful in our discussion of motivational deterrents to entrapment. The former refers to behavior driven by the desire to avoid some undesirable outcome (e.g., physical pain, social disapproval). The latter refers to action taken in order to attain some desirable outcome (e.g., money, food, social recognition). In the following pages we shall discuss how entrapment can be decreased, first through negative motivation and then through positive motivation.

Negative Motivation: The Case of Anxiety

In Chapter 7 it was suggested that decision makers experience increasing levels of stress, conflict, and/or anxiety as they become more entrapped in an escalating conflict. If decision makers are already in an anxiety-laden, conflictual state, it may be possible to nudge them "over the hump" to withdraw from the situation, if their anxiety level can be heightened to an even greater degree. In theory, a variety of factors may heighten entrapped decision makers' level of anxiety. It is our contention that, in general, significant increases in anxiety (i.e., heightened worries beyond those which are inherently produced by the nature of the decision-making dilemma) will lead to reduced entrapment.

Why? There is ample evidence that a high level of anxiety is aversive. Indeed, many escape or avoidance behaviors (in nonentrapment situations) are motivated by the individual's desire to reduce or eliminate anxiety. It thus seems reasonable that the same logic will apply to entrapment situations. The act of withdrawing from, or not entering, an entrapment situation may be construed as an escape or avoidance behavior performed in the service of alleviating actual or anticipated anxiety. If this reasoning is correct, then the task for experimentation is to delineate important, nonobvious factors that might affect decision makers' level of anxiety in entrapping situations.

Recent theorizing in the self-awareness literature suggests that self-focused attention is one such variable. According to Wicklund and Frey (1980), self-attention causes individuals to evaluate themselves against some standard of correctness. To the extent that they perceive themselves to fall short of the standard (which self-awareness theorists have suggested, is often the case), they will experience anxiety. To reduce the unpleasant anxiety the person either can (1) take action to reduce the negative discrepancy between self and standard, or (2) attempt to avoid or escape from the self-focusing stimulus altogether.

Theoretical controversy exists in the self-awareness literature concerning the relative prepotence of these two responses to self-focus (and its resultant anxiety) (Carver, 1979; Wicklund, 1975). In spite of their dissimilarities, the conceptualizations of both Carver (1979) and Wicklund (1975) imply that self-focus will be anxiety provoking, and thus motivate escape or avoidance behavior to the extent that it is impossible to reduce the discrepancy between self and standard. How is this notion relevant to the reduction of entrapment? If attention is self-directed while subjects are faced with an entrapping dilemma, and if no means of discrepancy reduction are available, then they should experience relatively high levels of anxiety and, as a result, withdraw from the situation.

This logic was tested in a recent experiment by Nathanson et al. (1982). The experimental procedure consisted of the "Waiting Game" (described in Chapter 2) in which subjects had to wait in order to achieve their goal. It was expected that self-attention would induce awareness of the negative discrepancy betewen self (i.e., waiting behavior) and standard (i.e., goal attainment). Furthermore, the experimental situation had been structured such that it was not possible for participants to take any discrepancy-reducing action. It is precisely under such circumstances that self-focus should be anxiety provoking and thus motivate escape behavior. To test this hypothesis, half of the participants waited in the presence of a mirror (Mirror condition) whereas half did not (No Mirror condition). Entrapment was expected to be lower in the former than in the latter condition.

Method. Thirty-four introductory psychology students at SUNY College at Brockport participated. Upon arrival, subjects were led to a research cubicle in which they were informed that the experiment "would consist of a number of parts." It was explained that when the "first part" (which consisted of completing a short survey) was completed, another experimenter would conduct the "second part." The short survey was the Revised Janis-Field Self-Esteem Scale (Eagly, 1967). After completing the first part subjects were escorted to another cubicle which contained a large wall clock. Before subjects entered the cubicle the experimenter mentioned that the "second experimenter" had not yet arrived and that it was thus necessary for the subject to wait for him. Subjects were left to wait by themselves. They had been told that they were free to leave at any point but that if they did leave they would not receive as much credit for participating as they would if they waited for the second experimenter. The opportunity to receive additional credit for waiting thus served as the reward, which is a necessary element in all entrapment situations.

Self-awareness manipulation. A large mirror had been placed directly in front of subjects as they waited. To reduce their suspicions about the mirror's presence a sign had been affixed indicating that the mirror should not be moved because it was "being used for another experiment." In the Mirror condition the reflective side of the mirror faced the subjects, whereas in the No Mirror condition the nonreflective side faced the subjects. In both conditions the experimenter recorded the amount of time that subjects waited before deciding to leave. Subjects who left were intercepted by the experimenter and ushered back to the original cubicle. If they had not left before 25 minutes had elapsed, the experimenter reentered the room and led them back to the original cubicle. Once they were back in the original cubicle, all participants completed a brief questionnaire. The questionnaire included a self-awareness manipulation check ("While you were waiting, how self-conscious did you feel?"), as well as several questions pertaining to the reasons for their waiting behavior. Some of these reasons were related to entrapment (e.g., "Once I decided to wait, I figured that

I might as well wait until the experimenter came. Otherwise, all of that waiting would have been a waste"), whereas others were not (e.g., "I waited as long as I did in order to help the experimenters out with their research").

Results. As predicted, subjects waited for a significantly shorter period (i.e., they were less entrapped) in the Mirror than in the No Mirror condition ($Ms = 17.19$ vs. 21.61 minutes, respectively; $t(32) = 2.27$, $p < .03$). Questionnaire data suggested that (1) the mirror produced heightened anxiety, (2) heightened anxiety motivated withdrawal from the entrapping conflict, and (3) a longer time spent waiting was, indeed, reflective of underlying entrapment.

First, subjects in the Mirror condition reported feeling significantly more "self-conscious" than those in the No Mirror condition ($t(32) = 2.96$, $p < .01$). The term "self-conscious" may have had a variety of meanings to subjects in this experiment. It could have referred to the *process* of self-focused attention; that is, Mirror condition participants may have directed attention to themselves to a greater extent than did those in the No Mirror condition. In addition, "self-consciousness," as used in everyday parlance by subjects, probably also refers to a *reaction to* the process of self-focused attention (i.e., discomfort or anxiety as a result of inwardly directed focus). In describing themselves as feeling more self-conscious than those in the No Mirror condition, Mirror subjects, we suspect, were also reporting that they felt more anxious.

Second, although the data reported to this point clearly show that the Mirror decreased entrapment and increased self-consciousness, they do not demonstrate that the reduction of entrapment was motivated by the anxiety-provoking aspect of self-consciousness. Some indirect evidence can be offered to support this notion. Previous research, not performed in entrapment situations, has shown that low self-esteem causes individuals to avoid or escape from situations that engender self-focused attention (Brockner & Wallnau, 1981; Duval & Wicklund, 1972; Gibbons & Wicklund, 1976). By contrast, high self-esteem does not motivate such avoidance or escape behaviors. Why? When attention is self-directed, low-self-esteem individuals are apt to focus on negative, or in other words, anxiety-provoking self-aspects. The process of self-attention should not be nearly as anxiety laden for high-self-esteem individuals (Brockner & Hulton, 1978).

Let us relate these findings to the present experiment. If the mirror induced self-consciousness, then such self-consciousness should have aroused greater anxiety, and consequently produced greater withdrawal behavior for individuals who were low, rather than high, in self-esteem. Several analyses were conducted to test this reasoning. Subjects were classified as high or low in self-esteem on the basis of a median split on their scores on the self-esteem inventory administered at the beginning of the experiment. A 2×2 (Self-Esteem $\times$ Mirror Presence) analysis revealed no main or interaction effects involving the self-esteem variable. However, inspection of the raw data showed that within the Low Self-Esteem, Mirror condition (i.e., the one thought to engender the greatest anxiety), seven out of the eight participants (88%) withdrew before the maximum waiting period (25 minutes) had expired. By contrast, the exit rate of low-self-esteem participants in the No Mirror condition, and of all high-self-esteem subjects, was 46% overall (12 out of 26), with no differences between subgroups. A Fisher exact probability test revealed that these two proportions differed significantly ($p = .046$).

The results of another internal analysis also suggested that low-self-esteem individuals showed greater withdrawal behavior in response to self-focused attention than did the high-self-esteem persons. Specifically, the correlation across conditions between self-reported self-consciousness and length of wait was calculated for each self-esteem group. Low-self-esteem subjects showed a strong negative correlation ($r = -.57, p < .02$). The fact that this group waited less as they felt more self-conscious suggests that their self-consciousness was anxiety-laden. High-self-esteem participants exhibited no relationship between self-consciousness and waiting length ($r = -.10$). The differential reaction of the two self-esteem groups to self-directed attention is thus consistent with the thesis that subjects' withdrawal behavior was motivated by their desire to escape an anxiety-provoking situation.

Third, there was some evidence that the tendency to continue waiting for the second experimenter was reflective of underlying entrapment. On the post-experimental questionnaire subjects were required to indicate the extent to which a variety of reasons for waiting were self-descriptive. Interestingly, there was a significant correlation (across conditions) between length of wait and perceived entrapment (e.g., "I had already waited so long it seemed foolish not to continue," $r = .45$). However, subjects' ratings on several other possible reasons for waiting (e.g., "I wanted to get more extra credit," and "I wanted to help the experimenters with their research") were not related to length of wait ($r = .18$ and $.27$, respectively). Thus, longer waiting times were associated with increased feelings of entrapment, but not with other, highly plausible explanations for subjects' behavior.

Other results from our laboratory (Brockner et al., 1982, Experiment 2) suggested that heightened anxiety can lead to reduced entrapment. In this study, unlike the one just reported, the experimental manipulation was not specifically intended to operationalize anxiety. Nevertheless, the condition associated with heightened anxiety produced decreased entrapment. This experiment has already been reported in considerable detail in Chapter 7; thus, it will be described only briefly here. Subjects took part in the Counter Game, and three experimental conditions were studied. In two conditions subjects were led to believe that they were being observed by an audience as they made their investment decisions. Some were told that the audience consisted of "professors who were expert in decision-making, who would be carefully monitoring and evaluating their behavior" (Evaluative condition). A second group had been informed that the audience consisted of individuals "who wanted to use this task in future research, and who would not be evaluating their behavior in any way" (Nonevaluative condition). A third group was not observed as they took part in the task (Control condition). Unexpectedly, the level of entrapment was much lower in the Nonevaluative condition ($M = \$1.29$) than in the Evaluative ($M = \$3.67$) and Control conditions ($M = \$3.08$). In large part this was due to the fact that 5 of the 10 subjects in the Nonevaluative condition invested none of their initial stake. Rather, after being exposed to the description of the audience they decided to retain their entire $5.00 and quit the experiment. By contrast, none of the 12 subjects in the Evaluative condition, and 2 of the 10 in the Control condition, refused to invest any of their resources.

Those subjects who did invest some of their resources also completed a postexperimental questionnaire. This questionnaire asked them to indicate their degree of apprehension while taking part in the task (e.g., "How much did you feel like you were being observed?," "How much did the feeling of being observed bother you?," and "How much did you feel like you were 'on the spot'?"). Once again unexpectedly, though consistent with the behavioral data, subjects reported feeling most apprehensive in the Nonevaluative condition relative to those in the other two ($p < .05$). Unfortunately, we have no way of knowing whether those subjects who quit without investing any of their initial stake in the Nonevaluative condition also felt a high degree of apprehension; data were only collected from those participants who did make an investment. However, it is quite possible that the noninvestors in the Nonevaluative condition, like the investors, felt a high degre of discomfort. In fact, it is entirely possible that such discomfort motivated their early escape. Of course, *why* subjects' level of discomfort would be highest in the Nonevaluative condition is not at all clear. In any case, if the Nonevaluative condition did engender anxiety, and if such anxiety motivated earlier withdrawal than that observed in the other two conditions, then the findings are conceptually analogous to the previous experiment suggesting that aversive arousal or anxiety may elicit a reduction in entrapment.

Positive Motivation

To this point we have suggested that decision makers may be driven from an entrapping situation in order to avoid some unpleasant stimulus (e.g., anxiety). It is also possible for such motivated behavior to stem from their desire to attain positive outcomes. In Chapter 6 it was mentioned that the decision to escalate commitment to a failing course of action may be mediated by face-saving concerns. Thus, the "positive outcome" that sometimes follows from escalated commitment is successful impression management. By continuing to invest, the decision makers may believe that they have presented themselves to significant others in the desired fashion(s) (e.g., to be seen as smart, competent, strong, or consistent). However, there may be some conditions under which successful impression management can be achieved by withdrawing from, rather than by persisting in, an entrapment situation. For example, Brockner, Rubin, and Lang (1981) told subjects before they took part in the Counter Game procedure that in order to "look smart" they should invest little of their resources. Not surprisingly, these subjects became less entrapped than those who had been advised that they could look smart by investing much of their resources. Moreover, and consistent with a face-saving analysis, it was those individuals who were most concerned with their social image (i.e., those scoring on the high end of a measure of dispositional social anxiety) who became least entrapped when advised that they could look good by so doing. Similarly, Brockner et al. (1982) discovered that high-social-anxiety/public self-consciousness subjects became less entrapped than those less concerned with face-saving needs (i.e., those scoring on the low ends of the aforementioned dimensions) when situational cues suggested that withdrawal, rather than escalation, was the more appropriate course of action.

The implications of such results for the reduction of entrapment are reasonably straightforward. All too often successful self-presentation depends (or so decision makers think) upon their ability to act in a fashion that ultimately will serve to foster entrapment. For example, socialization often preaches the benefits of persistence (e.g., "If at first you don't succeed . . . "). Indeed, the underlying cultural value in many psychological theories of motivation (Seligman, 1975) is that passive or withdrawal behaviors are maladpative for individuals, groups, and organizations. However, as Janoff-Bulman and Brickman (1980) have pointed out, there may be instances in which withdrawal, rather than persistence, is more personally as well as socially desirable (e.g., McFarlin, Baumeister, & Blascovich, in press). In short, it may be worthwhile for decision makers in entrapping situations to entertain the possibility that (at least under certain conditions) their public esteem will be heightened, rather than reduced, by withdrawal.

Skillful third parties may be useful in this regard. For example, in an entrapping bargaining impasse, it may be difficult for individuals who are in direct negotiation with one another to resolve their dispute, in part because concessionary behavior may be viewed as a sign of weakness and thus produce face loss. To the extent that a third party (e.g., a mediator) is attentive to the adversaries' face-saving concerns—for instance, the third party can point out that concessionary behavior is socially appropriate—then a successful resolution of the entrapping conflict should be more apt to occur (Pruitt & Johnson, 1970; Rubin & Brown, 1975).

One problem with this analysis is that it may be difficult to convince entrapped decision makers that their public image will be heightened by withdrawal. Our culture values not only persistence, but also consistency. For example, it was suggested that President Carter lost much of this nation's esteem during his tenure in office because his policies were perceived as inconsistent (Gallup, 1978). Consistent with this conjecture, experimental research has shown that consistent (rather than inconsistent) behavior is perceived as more socially desirable. More specifically, Staw and Ross (1980) described the behavior of entrapped decision makers to a group of subjects. All subjects were given a brief sketch of an administrator who was faced with the dilemma of how to alleviate poor housing conditions. Subjects were informed of the administrator's actions over a period of several years in response to the crisis; in all instances the housing situation remained bleak, regardless of the administrator's decisions. However, half of the subjects were told that the administrator was consistent in his actions (Consistency condition), whereas the other half were told that the administrator continually changed his policies in response to the negative feedback concerning the previous decision (Experimenting condition). Note that the depiction of the administrator in the Consistency condition is highly similar to that of the entrapped decision maker. This individual persisted with his original policy, in spite of continued negative feedback. The experimenting administrator was not entrapped by his original policy choice. Rather, he saw fit to alter his behavior in the hope that one of his policies would yield success.

Subjects were then asked to appraise the administrator's performance. The consistent administrator was rated much more favorably (e.g., he was seen as more deserving of a pay raise and promotion) than was the experimenting one ($p < .001$). Note that this finding is compatible with a self-presentational view of entrapment behavior. Decision makers may perceive that they can present themselves most positively in entrapment situations by being persistent. Again, the difficult task is to delineate the conditions under which decision makers can be led to believe that withdrawal, rather than persistence, will win them favor in the eyes of significant others.

Additional data reported by Staw and Ross (1980) suggest how difficult it may be to achieve this goal, at least within the context of business organizations. Staw and Ross employed three different groups of subjects in their experiment: undergraduate psychology students, undergraduate business students, and practicing managers enrolled part-time in an MBA program. The effect of the Consistency versus Experimenting manipulation was assessed for these groups. The psychology students rated the administrator equally in the two conditions. By contrast, those who were most likely entertaining a career in business (undergraduate busines students) and, to an even greater extent, those already employed by business organizations (the manager/MBA students) showed significant tendencies to rate the consistent administrator more favorably than the experimenting one.

Concluding Comments

This chapter was based on the thesis that entrapment often produces costly outcomes for individuals, groups, and organizations; therefore, it is important to understand how this dangerous form of escalated commitment can be prevented or reduced. Future research should address the following questions:

1. How can the theory and research presented in this chapter be put to practical use? In the first half of the chapter, we stressed that it is crucial for decision makers to remain vigilant. Practically speaking, there are at least two

general strategies that decision makers can rely upon in order to increase vigilance and thus decrease their likelihood of becoming entrapped.

First, they may find it useful to implement certain cognitive mechanisms. For example, the limit-setting studies imply that prior to entering a potentially entrapping situation, individuals typically do not spontaneously set limits to which they feel highly committed. If, however, they make it a regular practice to contemplate beforehand the amount that they wish to invest, then they may be less prone to entrapment. Another cognitive strategy is suggested by the effect of framing (Kahneman & Tversky, 1979) originally discussed in Chapter 4. If decision makers can perceive their commitment through a positive, rather than a negative, frame, then risk-seeking behavior (i.e., entrapment) should be less apt to occur.

The second ploy which decision makers may utilize is related to, but not identical with, their reliance on cognitive strategies. Many of the studies—in both the cognitive and motivational domains—reveal that entrapment can be significantly lessened under appropriate environmental conditions (e.g., when cost salience at the outset is high, when situational cues forewarn about entrapment, and when models who are appropriate targets for social comparison do not become entrapped). This implies that entrapment may be reduced to the extent that decision makers are able to enact or create environments that deter entrapment.

Consider, for example, the practice of "zero-based budgeting," in which it is intended that the amount of resources previously allocated to a particular course of action not affect subsequent resource allocation decisions. By adopting a zero-based budgeting rule, decision makers are changing what could be a "passive" investment situation into an "active" one. That is, there is no assumption that resources will continually be allocated to previously chosen courses of action on an "automatic" or "mindless" basis. Rather, with true zero-based budgeting, the decision to continue is the result of a more active or vigilant process; as we saw in Chapter 4, it is precisely the active (rather than passive) decision rule that deters entrapment.

In the motivational domain it was shown that face-saving concerns are an important determinant of resource allocation decisions. If so, then it may be possible for decision makers to shape their environment such that they can "look good" by withdrawing from the potential entrapment situation. Given that social norms in our culture often advocate persistence and consistency, this may be no easy task. Nevertheless, it may be one that is well worth undertaking.

In short, the logic underlying the research presented in this chapter was that certain factors could reduce entrapment. In these studies the various factors were the independent variables, and degree of entrapment was the dependent variable. In future research it would be useful to delineate the variables that affect decision makers' tendencies to enact environments that either increase or decrease the likelihood of entrapment. In this proposal for future research, what were previously the independent variables—the presence or absence of certain situational factors—would become the dependent variables.

2. Is escalated commitment to a course of action *always* reflective of underlying entrapment? There are undoubtedly some situations in which decision makers escalate their commitment to a previously chosen course of action, but are not simultaneously entrapped. For example, suppose that a student has completed 2 years of medical school, an experience that was found to be worthwhile. Suppose further that this person wishes to pursue a career in medicine. Would we view this person's decision to attend medical school the following year (i.e., heightened commitment to the previous course of action) to be a manifestation of entrapment? No. In Chapter 1 we discussed the defining elements of entrapment, several of which are lacking in this example. In general, the more individuals' decision to persist is based upon the justification of past investments (rather than on an accurate appraisal of future-oriented costs and benefits), the more likely it is that their persistence is a sign of entrapment.

Future theoretical work should include the development of a taxonomy of decision-making situations that elicit escalating commitment, in which the escalating commitment either is reflective of entrapment or not. To improve decision-making quality in these situations, it may be necessary to go beyond the scope of this chapter. That is, it may not be adequate simply to equip decision makers with strategies to reduce continued commitment to a course of action (e.g., limit-setting). It may also be necessary for decision makers to be aware of whether their escalation to a previously chosen course of action is reflective of underlying entrapment. Armed with such discriminatory abilities, they may be better able to "know when to hold them, and know when to fold them."

3. If it can be established that escalated commitment is a manifestation of entrapment, does this mean that the decision makers should *always* terminate their involvement? At first glance, it seems that a negative response to this question runs counter to the focus of this chapter. After all, we have been discussing how entrapment may be avoided or reduced. Does this not imply that, whenever possible, entrapment *should* be avoided or reduced? Perhaps not. As Northcraft and Wolf (1984) have recently pointed out, it may be logical under certain conditions to heighten one's commitment to a hitherto failing course of action. Like accountants, Northcraft and Wolf prescribe that sunk costs should not enter future-based resource allocation decisions; rather, such decisions should be made on the basis of cost–benefit analyses of the upcoming decision, *regardless of past investments*.

For example, let us suppose that an organization has invested $1000 in some project for each of 3 months, with the expectation that at the end of 4 months they will net a total revenue of $4000. At the end of 3 months, however, the organization receives the following negative feedback: (a) no revenue has been accrued to this point, and the organization will not be able to collect any revenue until the end of the fourth month, when the project is to be completed; (b) the project will require another $1000 investment in order for it to be completed, and (c) contrary to earlier projections, the completed project will only net the organization $1500, rather than $4000. This situation has many of the earmarks of entrapment. Perhaps the organization should "cut its losses" at this point, and not throw good money after bad. In fact, many managers or policy makers may advocate persistence (i.e., make the additional $1000 allocation) precisely *because* they feel entrapped. However, in this particular instance it would be perfectly rational, Northcraft and Wolf argue, for the organization to allocate the additional $1000. Why? To reiterate, the $3000 that has already been committed should not affect the decision to persist. That is a sunk cost, which *should* be ignored. (This does not mean, of course, that actual decision makers in this example *will* ignore this sunk cost.) What *should* influence subsequent decision making are the economic considerations; that is, by investing $1000 the organization stands to gain $1500.

This example demonstrates that it may not be enough for decision makers to "scarch their souls" in order to identify whether the desire to escalate commitment is reflective of entrapment. Decision makers may *feel* entrapped (i.e., they may wish to persist in order to justify past commitments), and they may even *act* entrapped (i.e., by allocating additional resources). However, under certain conditions it may be perfectly appropriate to allocate additional resources, *in spite of* the fact that the additional resource allocation was motivated by justification needs. Thus, in addition to, or perhaps instead of, trying to assess whether escalated commitment is reflective of underlying entrapment, decision makers should consider whether it is rational to persist, *independent of the fact that prior resources have been allocated.*

Northcraft and Wolf's (1984) "life-cycle" model of resource allocation decisions identifies three variables which decision makers should consider when attempting to determine whether it is rational to persist in entrapment situations: (a) The pattern of increments of the costs needed to complete the project. The magnitude of incremental costs can decrease, increase, or remain the same. In some entrapment situations the size of additional costs decreases over time. This would occur, for instance, if the costs of repairing an old automobile were $400, $300, $100, and $50. In other instances the magnitude of increments can increase or remain the same. (b) The pattern of revenues to be realized. Here again, the magnitude of revenues can decrease, increase, or remain the same over time. (c) The stage of project completion. In order to assess whether costs and/or revenues can be expected to increase, decrease, or remain the same (given accurate forecasting), decision makers need to be aware of the stage of project completion at which they find themselves. This third variable is important because it enables decision makers to make appraisals about the magnitude of additional costs and revenues. For example, if a project having decreasing costs is in a later stage of completion, then the decision makers' subsequent resource allocation will be smaller than if the same project is in an earlier stage of completion.

In general, Northcraft and Wolf (1984) suggest that it is economically defensible to persist in entrapping situations when (1) more of the total costs have been incurred early on in the process, and/or (2) rewards can be expected to increase continually over time, and/or (3) a very large reward can be realized only upon project completion, with little or no reward being garnered along the way (a prospect that is true in many, if not most, entrapment situations).

Evaluation of Northcraft and Wolf (1984)

We find the Northcraft and Wolf (1984) reasoning to be quite useful, at both the theoretical and normative levels. Theoretically, it serves as an interesting counterpoint to the thesis of this chapter in suggesting that under certain conditions it may be perfectly appropriate for entrapped decision makers to escalate their commitment to a failing course of action. Normatively, it is quite specific in delineating the factors that dictate whether persistence or withdrawal is the more prudent course of action.

However, the "life-cycle" analysis is lacking on both descriptive and practical grounds. We quite agree with the assertion that resources *should* be allocated on the basis of the three variables specified in the life-cycle model and not on the basis of justifying past commitments. The important point, however, is that decision makers simply do not act that way. The whole purpose of this chapter was to identify ways in which decision makers may come to behave more normatively. The life-cycle analysis is worthwhile in describing in some detail what a normative model might look like. But it does little in the way of specifying how decision makers can, in fact, be led to be more responsive to the rules of the life-cycle model, rather than to their needs to justify past commitments.

Finally, the utility of the life-cycle model may be limited in a practical sense. To be used effectively, decision makers must be able to quantify the costs that are apt to be incurred, and the revenues to be gained, by persisting with a chosen course of action. Clearly, this will be very difficult to do in some entrapment situations (e.g., how does one assess the costs and rewards associated with trying to resolve an entrapping romantic relationship?). In addition, their model dictates that decision makers must be able to make accurate predictions about the pattern of incurred costs and (to be) accrued rewards over time. In many, if not most, entrapment situations it may be difficult (if not impossible) to make such forecasts accurately. Even worse, we can envision some conditions under which a trapped administrator may deliberately try to mislead his or her superior into thinking that "the worst (in terms of costs) is over," or that the pot of gold (empty to this point) is sure to be attained with just another, small resource allocation. And yet, it is precisely under such conditions (i.e., when additional costs actually are low, and/or the increase in revenue is high) that Northcraft and Wolf (1984) suggest that it is wise to persist with the previously chosen course of action.

Chapter 10
Applications

To a great extent, our interest in entrapment was stimulated by its high degree of "real-world" relevance. It is only fitting, therefore, that this, the book's penultimate chapter, should return to the real world and the realm of applicability. Two general questions are raised within the context of this chapter. First, how may the theory and research discussed thus far help us to understand better the actions that "real-life" decision makers take when they believe that they have too much invested to quit? Second, to what extent does the analysis of entrapment within applied contexts help us to understand further the nature of entrapment itself? These two questions capture the reciprocal conceptual gains to be made from studying entrapment in applied settings. That is, entrapment may help shed light on "real-world" decision making; in addition, working from an applied-setting base may further elucidate the very nature of the phenomenon itself.

The relevance of entrapment to three applied settings is discussed in this chapter. First, we will look at the domain of organizational behavior. Entrapment in the work world can occur when individuals make decisions that are primarily of personal importance, or when they make decisions within the context of their organizational roles. The implications of the entrapment process for a host of topics of organizational relevance (e.g., turnover, performance appraisal, organizational change) will be woven into the presentation. Second, processes of entrapment in interpersonal relationships will be covered. In our everyday dealings with other people we can fall prey to a variety of destructive forms of entrapment. Several such relationship traps are analyzed, and ways of avoiding these traps are considered. Third, entrapment within the context of political decision making is discussed. The perpetuation of the United States military presence in Vietnam in the 1960s and 1970s has been viewed by some to be the result of entrapped decision making. We entertain the possibility that entrapment may also account for the United States' deepening military and economic commitment to the civil war in El Salvador.

The three applied domains discussed in this chapter hardly constitute an exhaustive list of the practical situations that readily lend themselves to an entrapment analysis; other applied settings could have also been selected (see Rubin, 1985). We have chosen these three particular domains for several reasons. First and foremost, these settings reflect the *diversity* of the applied settings to which entrapment analyses may be fruitfully applied. From these three examples, it should become clear that decision making in entrapment situations is potentially of great significance to individuals, organizations, and even nations.

Second, and particularly within the organizational behavior domain, there exists empirical research on topics related to entrapment. This will enable us to relate entrapment to other bodies of theory and research, an approach that is consistent with the style of this book. It should be mentioned, however, that the tone of this chapter is somewhat different from its predecessors. There will be less of an emphasis on empirical results (although wherever appropriate relevant research will be discussed), and more in the way of deduction and speculation.

Entrapment in Work Organizations

Organizational settings provide fertile ground for the "growth" of entrapment. Many of the factors that give rise to entrapment (e.g., repeated rather than one-shot decision-making, the need to save face) are firmly embedded within the organizational context. Indeed, there are several indications that entrapment is a ubiquitous process within organizations. First, it is relatively easy to generate a large number of examples of entrapment within business organizations (cf. Staw, 1976, 1979). Second, the vast majority of "entrapment reseachers" were trained in the field of organizational behavior, and are currently employed as faculty members in business schools.

It may be useful at this point to categorize the different types of entrapment situations that could arise in work organizations. Several variables seem particularly relevant in this taxonomic effort.

First, we need to consider the nature of the decision-making entity. Entrapment may be the result of an individual, intragroup, intergroup, or even organizational process. A second dimension, related to the first, is the party upon whose behalf the decision makers are acting. In some instances entrapment can occur when individuals make decisions that affect their own personal welfare (e.g., upon deciding whether to persist with an unsatisfying job or career); this shall be labeled "personal" entrapment. In other circumstances, entrapment arises when the individuals' decisions are made within the context of their organizational roles (e.g., upon deciding whether the company should continue using outdated machinery which was purchased at considerable expense). We shall refer to this as "role-related" entrapment.

In discussing entrapment within work organizations we will rely upon both dimensions for categorical purposes. Note, however, that the two dimensions do not lend themselves to a completely crossed "factorial design"; that is, individual entrapment can be either personal or role related. However, intragroup, intergroup, or organizational entrapment are always role related.

Individual/Personal Entrapment

Rubin (1985) has identified a number of ways in which individuals become entrapped in organizations when making decisions of personal relevance. Perhaps most typical is the category of "dissatisfaction traps," in which individuals remain in an increasingly dissatisfying career or organization in order to justify prior resource commitments to those entities. For example, after having invested years of schooling and training in a particular career path, newly hired MBA graduates may perceive that they have "too much invested to quit" now that the new career seems much less rewarding than had been anticipated. Or, after having spent many years climbing their corporation's ladder, middle-aged executives who find their work more unrewarding with each passing day may feel compelled to "stick it out" with their present organization, in order to feel that their previous years of commitment to the organization were not spent in vain.

The results of several recent studies (Farrell & Rusbult, 1981; Rusbult & Farrell, 1983) are consistent with the notion that individuals' previous investment in the work organization binds them to that organization. In one study, both accountants and nurses were asked to complete measures of investment size and organizational commitment at 4-month intervals during a 1-year period. Investment items included, "All things considered, to what extent are there activities/events/persons/objects associated with your job that you would lose if you were to leave?," and "In general, how much have you invested in this job?" Commitment measures included, "How attached are you to staying at your current job?," and "How long would you like to stay at this job?" The relationship between investment size and degree of commitment was not significant during the initial months of the subjects' job tenure, a finding that is not surprising in that most participants' job investments were small during that time period. However, in the later administrations of the questionnaire (8 and 12 months after they had accepted the position) the correlations between investment size and commitment were highly significant.

In the other study a very different subject population was employed to study the relationship between investment size and commitment—blue-collar industrial workers. No data were presented on the length of the employees' tenure in their work organization. However, the overall relationship between investment size and commitment was statistically significant ($p < .01$). Based upon the results of the previous study, it may be surmised that the reported correlation would be even stronger for those workers who had been employed by their organization for longer periods of time.

Clearly, there are a number of explanations for the positive association between investment size and commitment to the organization. For example, it could have been that the individuals with a growing sense of commitment were more likely to make investments in the organization. Note that the entrapment analysis makes the opposite causal prediction—that investment leads to commitment. In fact, the causal influence of investment size on commitment was investigated in an experimental study performed by Farrell and Rusbult (1981). The methodology consisted of a laboratory analogue of a work setting, in which undergraduate business students were required to perform a clerical task. Those who had invested a greater amount of time preparing for the task, as predicted, reported feeling significantly more committed to their "job" than those who had not invested much in the way of job preparation. Furthermore, subjects in the former group reported a lower likelihood of leaving their job for an alternative one than did those in the latter group. Thus, it is possible that in the field studies just reported, investment size did causally influence level of commitment.

A clearer interpretation of the results of the Farrell and Rusbult field studies necessitates the use of a methodology (e.g., cross-lagged panel design) that allows the causal relationship(s) between correlated variables to be teased apart. In addition, at the more conceptual level of analysis, the positive correlation beween investment size and level of commitment is pertinent to the entrapment process *only to the extent that workers are dissatisfied, rather than satisfied, with their jobs.* Entrapped employees are those who increase their commitment to the organization *in the face of* job dissatisfaction. If, instead, the workers are highly job satisfied, and as a result increase their investment and level of commitment, then any positive correlation between investment and commitment is not reflective of underlying entrapment. To know whether the positive association between investment and commitment was due to entrapment will either require further data collection, or additional analyses of the Rusbult and Farrell (1983) data. The authors did, in fact, include a measure of job satisfaction. For those who were relatively dissatisfied, there should be a positive correlation between investment and commitment, in order for the entrapment analysis to be relevant. If, instead, the previously reported positive investment–commitment relationship was mainly attributable to the job-satisfied participants, then entrapment becomes a less useful explanatory mechanism.

If the positive relationship between investment and organizational commitment is mediated by entrapment, then the entrapment process has relevance for a widely researched organizational behavior: turnover. Several theories of organizational behavior (e.g., Vroom, 1964) suggested that job dissatisfaction was the primary determinant of turnover. However, more recent theory and research (Farrell & Rusbult, 1981; Porter, Crampon, & Smith, 1976) have posited that job commitment is a far better predictor of turnover than is job satisfaction/dissatisfaction. To the extent that job commitment is influenced, in turn, by the process of entrapment that accompanies increased investments, then entrapment becomes an important mediator of turnover decisions—a central "dependent variable" in the organizational behavior literature.

The concept of entrapment may also help us to understand better the distinction between job satisfaction and job (or organizational) commitment. In spite of the statistically significant positive correlation between these two constructs, it is possible for workers to be satisfied but not committed, or committed but not satisfied. In the former, workers may enjoy their job, but leave it if a better offer were to come along; in the latter (in which entrapment is germane), workers may escalate their commitment to a dissatisfying job or organization in order to justify all of their prior investments in that job or organization.

Entrapment and the investment model: A comparison. Rusbult and Farrell (1983) also have developed a more general model to predict organizational commitment, and it may be worthwhile to compare their conceptualization with that of entrapment. In their so-called "investment model," individuals' commitment to the organization is a function of three sets of variables: (1) the amount of prior investments, (2) the rewards and costs associated with becoming (and remaining) committed, and (3) the number of alternatives to the chosen course of action. In several laboratory and field studies they have shown that commitment is enhanced when prior investments are high, rewards are high, costs are low, and alternatives are few. The common strand between the Farrell and Rusbult thesis and the entrapment analysis is that both emphasize the significance of prior investments in the commitment process.

In other ways, however, entrapment differs substantially from the investment model. For example, the entrapment process *requires* the decision maker to have some degree of choice about whether to become and/or remain committed. By definition, entrapment cannot occur if the individual has no choice but to remain committed to the chosen course of action. The investment model, by contrast, posits that commitment is inversely related to the number of alternatives, suggesting that decision makers will be most committed when they lack choice (i.e., when they have no other alternative but to persist with their previously chosen course of action).

In addition, commitment through the process of entrapment is less dependent on reward–cost considerations than is commitment through the processes inherent in the investment model. This is not to say that reward and cost considerations do not influence decision making in entrapment situations. As discussed in Chapter 4, entrapment is heightened when the value of the reward is high and/or when cost salience is low. Such findings are perfectly compatible with the investment model. The difference is one of emphasis: reward and cost concerns are not given a central role in our analysis of the antecedents of entrapment. In fact, what makes decision making in entrapment situations interesting is that individuals may not act in a manner predicted by a simple reward–cost analysis. In sum, the investment model places heavy emphasis on "rational" or prospective determinants of commitment (e.g., high rewards, few alternatives) while still allowing for some role played by degree of prior investments. The entrapment analysis places far greater weight on the "rationalizing" or retrospective causes of commitment (i.e., the justification of prior investments) than does the investment model.

Professional advancement entrapment. Another individual/personal type of dissatisfaction trap which people may experience in their professional lives stems less from what they do, and more from what they do not do. More specifically, suppose that you are displeased with your current employment status, and are contemplating a job or career change. Obviously, you will be highly motivated to ensure that the new occupation or profession is considerably more rewarding than your present one. Imagine further that you have rejected other job or career opportunities that were likely to be more satisfying than your present status, but not so much more satisfying that it was deemed worthy of the transition costs.

In passing up alternative after alternative, you may become more entrapped in your current job. How? The continuous rejection of other options may increase your commitment to an (unreasonable) quest for the "perfect" job. That is, if you had the opportunity to, but did not accept, other, more attractive positions, then you may reason that it will require a much more appealing job (i.e., the "perfect" job) to budge you from your current (dissatisfying) position. Obviously, the perfect job is not easy to come by. This example of a "procrastination trap" makes clear that job entrapment may result from the actions that decision makers do not take, rather than (or perhaps in addition to) those that they do take. The "past investments" in this and other examples of entrapment-by-procrastination is the repeated rejection of alternatives to the status quo. We know of no empirical research on this form of career entrapment; consequently, this could be an interesting area of future research.

Individual/Role Entrapment

It should be emphasized that individual/personal entrapment has consequences not only for the individual, but perhaps also for the organization. We would speculate, for example, that employees who persist with their jobs because of entrapment are not likely to be highly productive or creative in their work. Rather, they may be "marking time" on the job, waiting for something better to present itself.

It is even clearer that entrapment can produce significant organizational consequences when individuals are making decisions within the context of their organizational roles. Role-related entrapment refers to those instances in which members of the organization, in performing their job duties, escalate their commitment to a failing policy, product, or person, in order to justify prior commitments made to that policy, product, or person.

Entrapment in appraising performance. Most organizations provide their employees with periodic feedback about the manner in which they have been conducting their organizational roles and tasks. Ideally, such performance appraisals, by evaluating as well as counseling employees, enhance the quantity and/or quality of their future work. Evelutions serve as the basis for organizational rewards (e.g., promotions, pay raises) which, if doled out contingently upon the employee's performance, can increase productivity. The counseling element of performance appraisals enables workers to discover the improprieties of their organizational behaviors, and may thereby serve as an impetus to improved performance.

A basic proposition in the performance appraisal literature is that for the process to be effective, evaluators must transmit accurate feedback to employees about the latter's performance. Indeed, much empirical research has attempted to delineate the factors that produce evaluator bias in performance appraisals (e.g., Latham, Wexley, & Pursell, 1975). Recent evidence suggests that the entrapment process may be one such source of bias. Imagine that you have developed a prior commitment to an individual whose performance you will now have to appraise. This commitment may have developed through formal organizational channels (e.g., you were responsible for the decision to hire or promote the individual), or through more informal mechanisms (e.g., you eat lunch with this person regularly). Now imagine that evidence comes before you suggesting that this employee's performance for the appraisal period in question is negative. Will your evaluation of the (poorly performing) employee be overly positive because of your prior commitment to this individual?

Several studies have looked at this question, one in the laboratory and one in a field setting. In the laboratory study (Bazerman, Beekum, & Schoorman, 1982) undergraduate business majors were asked to assume the role of vice president of a corporation. In this position their job was to appraise the performance of their subordinate, the regional director in the organization. The regional director had been promoted 2 years ago from the position of merchandise manager. In the High Responsibility condition subjects were personally responsible for making that promotion decision, whereas in the Low Responsibility condition the promotion decision had been made by the preceding vice president. All subjects were informed that the regional director's performance during the first 2 years in office was rather negative. The dependent variables in this study were various measures of performance appraisal (rewards, appropriateness of promotion or demotion, and forecasted future performance). As expected, subjects in the High Responsibility condition, who had probably developed some form of psychological commitment to the poorly performing subordinate, appraised the regional director's performance much more favorably than did those in the Low Responsibility condition on all dependent measures.

In the field study (Schoorman, 1984) supervisors of clerical employees of a large public service organization had made appraisals of the employees' performance. In this archival study, three groups of supervisors were identified: (1) those who had taken part in, and agreed with, the organization's decision to hire the employee (Agree condition), (2) those who had taken part in, but disagreed with, the organization's decision to hire the employee (Disagree condition), and (3) those who had not taken part in the initial hiring decision (Control condition). The hypothesis that decision makers escalate their commitment to a previously chosen course of action suggests that the supervisors in the Agree condition will yield more *positive* evaluations than supervisors in the Control condition, and that supervisors in the Disagree condition will render more *negative* evaluations than supervisors in the Control condition. This is precisely what was found.

One conceptual concern about the field study is whether the situation allowed for the study of entrapment. More specifically, entrapment refers to the escalation of commitment to a previously chosen, *though failing*, course of action. In the laboratory study (Bazerman, Beekum, & Schoorman, 1982) it was made clear to subjects that the object of their appraisal had performed quite poorly during the period in question. However, in the field study there was no evidence that the clerks' performance during the appraisal period was negative; in fact, there was even some evidence to suggest that just the opposite was true. The clerks' performance was evaluated along 5-point scales, with higher scores reflecting more favorable performance. The mean performance appraisals in the Agree, Disagree, and Control conditions were 4.26, 3.47, and 4.08, respectively. The clerks' level of performance thus appears to be quite positive in the Control condition, in which their supervisor presumably had little prior commitment to their evaluations. True, these evaluations became either more or less favorable, depending upon whether those who had participated in the hiring decision agreed or disagreed (respectively) with that decision. However, such results merely demonstrate that those who appraise others' performance will escalate their commitments to their previously chosen alternative. (Clearly, these findings are worthy of attention in their own right, for they illustrate a systematic bias in the performance appraisal process.) Such findings do not, however, demonstrate the relevance of entrapment. For entrapment to be relevant to the performance appraisal process there must be evidence that the evaluatee's performance during the period in question was negative in some way.

In spite of this possible shortcoming in the Schorman (1984) study, we view such findings as significant. When taken together with the results of the laboratory study (Bazerman, Beekum, & Schoorman, 1982) they suggest that the escalation-of-commitment effect may be generalizable to a wide range of organizational decisions. Provided that the decision is part of an ongoing sequence of decisions in which prior investments have been made and therefore psychological commitments have presumably developed, the possibility exists that entrapment may occur. Virtually all of the laboratory research performed by organizational behaviorists has explored the conditions under which decision makers escalate their commitment to a failing *financial* course of action. As the performance appraisal studies suggest, the consequences of entrapment may extend beyond financial decision-making in organizations.

A similar point was raised in the study by Caldwell and O'Reilly (1982), considered in greater detail in Chapter 6. Caldwell and O'Reilly suggested that being personally responsible for a poorly performing resource allocation has a host of implications for organizational behavior, only one of which is that the responsible parties may escalate their commitment to the prior course of action. Caldwell and O'Reilly demonstrated that organizational decision makers may also selectively transmit information to their superiors, as a function of being personally responsible for a previously chosen, though failing course of action.

Competency traps. As Rubin (1985) has suggested, in performing our work we often need to believe that we are doing so in a competent fashion. Being competent in our professional lives is apt to produce both extrinsic rewards (e.g., pay raises, promotions, and the admiration of coworkers) as well as intrinsic rewards (e.g., a sense of accomplishment). There is nothing necessarily wrong with, or maladaptive about, our need for felt competence, unless it steers us into an entrapping course of action. For example, suppose that you have worked in the personnel office of a large corporation for a number of years, and have developed a highly favorable reputation for your creative methods of personnel selection; you are very proud of the work that you have done to this point. Suppose further that recent advances in the selection process suggest that methods developed by others would be more cost-efficient than the one that you have used. How quick would you be to adopt the new selection method? On purely technical (i.e., cost-efficient) grounds, it seems clear that the new methodology should be employed. However, your sense of self-worth in the organization has come to be associated with the selection procedures that you have developed. To switch to this more cost-efficient procedure could engender a reduced sense of felt competence.

There are undoubtedly many situations within organizations in which decision makers heighten their commitment to a failing course of action in order to preserve their pride. In general, the more that decision makers' self-concepts are associated with seeing the prior course of action through to a successful conclusion, the more difficult it should be for them to avoid the bite of entrapment.

How might previous research help us to understand better the nature of such competency traps? The self-diagnosticity construct mentioned in Chapter 6 seems especially relevant. Self-diagnosticity refers to the extent to which behavioral outcomes are seen as reflecting or revealing of the self. Experimental evidence suggests that, at least under certain conditions, self-diagnosticity can lead to heightened commitment to a failing course of action. Decision makers may be particularly reluctant to admit that their hitherto unfulfilled resource allocations went for naught, for to do so would shake their sense of self-identity.

Group/Role-Related Entrapment

Entrapment in organizations can also arise when groups (rather than individuals), acting in the context of their organizational roles, escalate their commitment to a failing course of action. For example performance appraisals sometimes are performed by groups of decision makers, rather than individuals. It is entirely possible that the "entrapment effect" in performance appraisal, which has been demonstrated for individual decision makers (Bazerman et al., 1982), may also generalize to instances in which the appraisals are made by groups (Bazerman et al., in press).

In Chapter 6 we discussed one possible group basis of entrapment: groupthink. Based on the findings of small-group research, Janis (1982) has theorized that highly cohesive groups strive toward unanimity in the service of maintaining their sense of cohesiveness. This concurrence-seeking tendency of cohesive groups may impair each group member's ability to think and act in a rational, level-headed fashion. As previously mentioned, the group's tendency to escalate commitment to a failing course of action may be one of the specific mechanisms by which their groupthink is enacted. Of course, members of highly cohesive groups may become victims of groupthink in ways having little to do with entrapment. Still, there is ample theoretical overlap between the groupthink and entrapment constructs.

In Chapter 6 it was mentioned that research is sorely needed which investigates the relationship between groupthink and entrapment. In this chapter this sentiment is repeated, but with one important extension—namely, that it may be particularly appropriate to study the groupthink-entrapment link *within business organizations*. All of Janis' case studies explored the effects of group cohesiveness on decisions made by small political groups (i.e., presidential cabinets). However, the groupthink hypothesis is presented as theoretically generalizable to a wide range of cohesive decision-making groups. Either laboratory or field research could be performed. In the laboratory it would be possible to simulate situations in which groups of varying levels of cohesiveness decide whether to escalate their commitment to, or withdraw from, a prior allocation of resources that has hitherto met with negative results. In the field it may be possible to conduct archival research in a manner similar to Janis; the main difference is that decision-making groups in business organizations rather than political circles would be the unit of analysis. Quite conceivably, some of the classic cases of organizations' throwing good money after bad were the result of groupthink processes. Obviously, this speculation can only be addressed through empirical research.

to "pass the buck" as an entrapment phenomenon. Consider the following organizations, it is most likely the result of a *within-group* process. However, group-based entrapment in organizations can also be the result of a *between-group* process; that is, it may be possible to construe groups' notorious tendency to "pass the buck" as an entrapment phenomenon. Consider the following example, described in a book entitled *In the Name of Profit*, written by Kermit Vandivier (1972), an engineer then working for the B. F. Goodrich company. B. F. Goodrich was awarded a potentially quite lucrative contract by the government to develop a brake assembly for a new Air Force fighter plane.

Engineer John Warren was given the task of developing the initial brake design. A subordinate of Warren, one Searle Lawson, was assigned to modify Warren's design for production readiness, at which point the constructed prototype would be subjected to demanding qualifying tests. The test results were to be sent to the Air Force, who would give final approval for overall production.

Warren's design was a disaster, a finding confirmed in repeated tests by Lawson. Warren rejected Lawson's analysis, prompting Lawson to tell the project manager, Robert Sirk, about the problem. Sirk similarly rejected Lawson's findings (perhaps because of the fact that Sirk had already notified those above him in the corporate hierarchy that the plans were proceeding nicely!). This lack of support from his superiors led Lawson to continue testing the original design, in the hope that his previous negative findings were unreliable. They were not.

Meanwhile, Lawson's unflattering results about the brake were fed to Kermit Vandivier, the engineer encharged with issuing the formal qualification report. Vandivier, in turn, notified his supervisor, Ralph Gretzinger, who then went to his boss, Russell Line, to tell him of the problem. Line rejected the pleas of Gretzinger to scrap the project; eventually, Line threatened to fire Vandivier and Lawson (the initial "troublemaker") unless they wrote a fraudulent report. The ensuing travesty from this buck-passing trap is described in further detail in Vandivier's book.

The case of B. F. Goodrich exemplifies buck-passing entrapment. In all entrapment situations, resources are allocated to what proves to be a failing course of action. These repeated decisions are made by the *same individual* (Staw, 1976). Presumably, the psychological "inertia" that leads decision makers to throw good money after bad is based in their (need to justify) prior investments. In buck-passing entrapment the "inertia" stems from the collective commitment of *different individuals*, at different points in time.

The decision maker(s) at the end of a buck-passing chain (much as the person in Russell Line's role in the example above) have "too much invested to quit." However, the irrepressible investment is not their own prior commitments, but rather, the fact that *other* decision makers in the organization could have called a halt to the proceedings, but chose not to.

Buck-passing entrapment in organizations is worthy of empirical scrutiny.

Three social-psychological principles seem to underly each decision-making entity's willingness to permit a failing course of action to continue:

1. Conformity pressure (e.g., Asch, 1951). In the typical scenario decision makers who act after the juggernaut has already started are subjected to potentially intense conformity pressure. After all, these individuals or groups must act with the knowledge that previous parties in the chain were willing to approve the chosen, though flawed, course of action.

2. Diffusion of responsibility (e.g., Darley & Latané, 1968). In the typical buck-passing situation individuals make decisions with the knowledge that other people have acted before them and others will decide after them. Thus, each decision-making entity may feel little personal responsibility to "blow the whistle" on the faulty plan or policy.

3. The reluctance to transmit bad news (e.g., Tesser & Rosen, 1975). In buck-passing entrapment situations the individuals or groups in the chain or hierarchy are receiving negative feedback. Much social psychological research attests to the generality of the "MUM effect" (i.e., individuals' general unwillingness to be the bearers of bad news). This reluctance can only be heightened by the conformity and diffusion of responsibility factors noted above.

This analysis of buck-passing entrapment in organizations has two theoretically intriguing and empirically testable implications. First, it may be the decision makers who find themselves in the middle of the decision chain or hierarchy (e.g., midlevel management) who are most apt to pass the buck. These decision makers are most likely to be subjected to the processes of conformity and diffusion of responsibility; that is, the individual or group that makes the initial decisions in a buck-passing chain are not exposed to conformity pressure, although they should experience diffusion of responsibility to the extent that they perceive that others will decide after them (and therefore be able to extricate the organization from a failing prior commitment). Alternatively, those who act later (or last) in the hierarchy may experience intense conformity pressures, but cannot diffuse responsibility onto subsequent decision makers ("The buck stops here"). Those in the middle of the chain or hierachy should experience both of these presumed antecedents of buck-passing entrapment.

Second, the buck-passing analysis seems to contradict one of the basic tenets of entrapment research: that high rather than low personal responsibility for negatively performing resource allocation makes entrapment more likely to occur. In buck-passing entrapment we suggested that it was the *diffusion* of personal responsibility that may partially contribute to entrapment. Is it possible to integrate these apparently conflicting propositions? It may be that the reconciliation of the two perspectives will depend upon the specific nature of the felt responsibility. If decision makers feel personally responsible *for the prior resource allocation* (as in the Staw [1976] study) then they may be more likely than those who do not feel responsible to escalate their commitment. If, however, as in the case of buck-passing entrapment, decision makers feel low personal responsibility for *stopping continued commitment to the failing course of action*, then the organizations' level of commitment to the failing policy will inexorably escalate.

The above reasoning suggests that the active versus passive nature of the escalating commitments may interact with the level as well as type of responsibility to affect persistence with a failing course of action. If the nature of the commitment is "passive" in the sense described in Chapter 4, then buck-passing entrapment may be apt to occur; diffusion of personal responsibility to stop the failing course of action will lead to heightened commitment. In passive-entrapment situations escalating commitment accrues continuously, often without any conscious intention on the decision maker's part to become too committed. Passive-entrapment situations, in which commitments are renewed "automatically," require decision makers to take intentional action to terminate their involvement. If no one in the decisional chain perceives that it is his or her responsibility to discontinue the failing course of action, then the organization's level of commitment to the failing policy or plan will inevitably increase.

If, however, the nature of the commitment is "active" as discussed in Chapter 4, then buck-passing entrapment is probably less likely to occur. It is one thing to "pass the buck" when doing so requires little decisional effort, as in the case of a passive-entrapment situation. It is quite another thing to pass the buck in an active context. In the active context escalated commitment can only occur if the decision maker "actively" decides to allocate additional resources. Individuals in the decisional chain or hierarchy may surmise, however, that it would be inappropriate for them to take such extreme actions on matters for which they feel low personal responsibility.

This is not to say that within active situations the level of responsibility will not affect subsequent degree of entrapment. Rather, we are simply saying that buck-passing entrapment is more apt to arise in passive than in active situations, especially if the decision makers' level of perceived responsibility for stopping the juggernaut is low. Within active situations, it has been repeatedly shown (Bazerman, Giuliano, & Appleman, in press; Staw, 1976) that high personal responsibility leads to greater entrapment. However, as discussed above, this is a different type of "personal responsibility" than that which motivates buck-passing entrapment.

Two final comments about buck-passing entrapment are in order. First, although it was labeled as a "between-groups" process, it could just as easily be thought of as an example of entrapment at the organizational level. The case of the faulty air brake design at B. F. Goodrich clearly demonstrates how the mentality of "throwing good money after bad" can pervade an entire organizational hierarchy. Said differently, in that example it makes sense to think of the organization (rather than any particular individual or group) as manifesting entrapment.

Second, at the outset of the chapter, it was mentioned that two benefits may be gained by studying entrapment in applied settings: (1) increased understanding of the way "real" decisions are made, and (2) increased understanding of the entrapment process itself. Prior to the discussion of buck passing most of the presentation served the former purpose. However, the buck-passing analysis provides a good example of the latter type of benefit—it led to further conceptualization about the nature of entrapment, the accuracy of which can be evaluated by future research.

Field Research on Entrapment in Organizations: Some Future Trends

The vast majority of entrapment research has been conducted in the laboratory, typically with undergraduate psychology majors or business students serving as subjects (see Schoorman, 1984, for a rare exception). The laboratory methodology has several virtues, but represents only one vehicle through which our understanding of entrapment can be increased. Other methodologies, higher in external validity than the laboratory paradigm, also need to be employed.

Fortunately, there is some evidence that researchers are beginning to study the escalation-of-commitment process as it unfolds in actual work settings. Initial impetus in this direction was provided in a case-study analysis by Lewicki (1980), entitled, "Bad loan psychology: Entrapment and commitment in financial lending." Lewicki considers the dilemma that can arise when a borrower who was granted an initial loan for some venture requests from the lending insitution an additional loan on that same venture. If the borrower is not a "good risk" for the additional loan, (e.g., the venture is clearly failing and is unlikely to be recovered with an additional loan), what is the responsible loan officer to do? On the one hand, by not approving the additional loan, the lending officer may be allowing the initial loan to be lost irretrievably. On the other hand, by approving the additional loan he or she may be "throwing good money after bad."

Lewicki conducted interviews with key financial officers (Vice Presidents, Executive Vice Presidents and Senior Vice Presidents) of two major banks in the Southeast. The financial officers were asked to describe their bank's procedures for (1) making initial loans, (2) evaluating bad loans (i.e., loans which begin to encounter difficulty in repayment, often prompting the borrower to request an additional loan), and (3) acting on bad loans (e.g., whether to grant an additional loan). Lewicki reports that "bankers at both institutions generally agreed on the factors and conditions which allowed loan officers to 'throw good money after bad.' " These included (a) the loan officers' emotional commitment to the loan or borrower, (b) the size of the loan, and (c) the second lender status of the bank (i.e., whether the bank is the sole, primary, or secondary partner to a large initial loan).

Although Lewicki's investigation was nonexperimental, it does suggest several hypotheses about the factors that may affect entrapment in the loan-lending process. Only empirical research can evaluate the correctness of these and other speculations. Fortunately, answers to some of the questions posed by Lewicki (1980) may be forthcoming in a study that is just beginning as of this writing. Specifically, Barry Staw is conducting a large-scale study of bank officers' responses to bad loans.

Recognizing the fact that loan officers may become overly committed to a borrower, the bank in Staw's study has separated the lending and workout functions. The lending officer's job is to make initial credit decisions; he or she tends to act as a broker, integrating the bank's interests with those of the customer. The workout officer's job is to deal specifically with nonperforming loans (i.e., loans that may not be repaid on schedule). He or she presumably maintains a more distant or "objective" view of the loan's (non)performance. To date, Staw (1984) has conducted extensive interviews with the workout officers. He reports that

> Our interviews have not shown escalation to occur in the straightforward manner demonstrated by the laboratory studies. When a case comes to the workout unit, all efforts appear to be placed on strategies to recoup bank assets. Perhaps by the time a loan reaches its workout unit the situation is so desperate that tactics to restore solvency are less salient than those to recoup bank assets. (Even in) cases in which turnaround seems possible, efforts are made to close out the lender rather than any type of escalation. If escalation appears in our bank's lending activities it probably occurs before the loan accounts reach the workout group.

Accordingly, Staw is now investigating escalation behaviors as exhibited by lending (rather than workout) officers. At the lending level, nonperforming loans are classified as "problem accounts"—accounts that are substandard but not so dire as to be sent up to the workout unit.

Extensive field research on entrapment in organizations is also currently in progress by Gerrit Wolf and Ed Conlon (1984). Unlike Staw, Wolf and Conlon are exploring the entrapment process in a wide variety of organizational settings. Managers from 30 of the largest businesses in the state of Arizona were asked to complete a lengthy questionnaire and interview procedure. The purpose of this study is threefold: (1) to identify a taxonomy of "sunk-cost" (i.e. potentially entrapping) situations that managers encounter, (2) to specify the different behavioral strategies that they have developed to deal with these dilemmas, and (3) to delineate the variables that influence manager's decisions to escalate their commitment to, or withdraw from, the failing ocurse of action. One preliminary result (contrary to that obtained in laboratory studies, e.g., Staw [1976]) is that managers who were personally responsible for the nonperforming resource allocation were no more likely to escalate their commitment than were less personally responsible managers.

Entrapment and Organizational Change: A Final Perspective

The processes by which organizations develop and change is of considerable interest to organizational scholars. The need to understand change processes is driven by both theoretical and practical concerns. At the theoretical level it is important to delineate the factors affecting change, and the mechanisms by which these factors exert their influence. At the practical level the study of change is critical, if for no other reason than the fact that the organizational "graveyard" is probably filled with cases in which the organization failed to alter its "behavior" in response to a change-demanding environment. Said differently, organizations often are resistant to change when sheer logic and external circumstances demand greater flexibility.

In a fine work, Staw (1982) has pointed out that one way to study change processes in organizations is by exploring the forces that render organizations resistant to change. It is in this sense that entrapment and, more generally, commitment processes are related to organizational change. While there are numerous manifestations of organizational commitment, many seem to include the element of "resistance to change"; that is, in most if not all instances in which an organization resists necessary change, it is because it is committed to some other course of action, however dysfunctional this other course of action might be. We are not suggesting that entrapment is *always* the mechanism by which organizations express resistance to change; rather, it is through more generic commitment processes that change is blocked. Thus, entrapment may be viewed as one of several possible types of commitment processes in organizations that serves as an obstacle to change.

Building upon the previous work of Kiesler (1971) and Salancik (1977), Staw (1982) delineates the factors that produce commitment to a chosen course of action. An important distinction is made between factors pertaining to the salience of, and responsibility for, the behavior on the one hand, and those relevant to the consequences of, and responsibility for the consequences of the behavior, on the other. Thus, organizational decision makers should be highly committed to behaviors (i.e., resistant to change) under the following conditions: (1) when the behavior is highly salient (e.g., high in publicity), (2) when they feel personally responsible for taking that action, (3) when the action elicits certain consequences (e.g., irrevocability), and (4) when they feel personally responsible for the outcome of the behavior (e.g., high accountability). The level of analysis shifts from the microlevel to the macrolevel when Staw discusses how such individual bases of commitment are translated into structural sources of inflexibility within the organization. Under extreme circumstances, for example, key actors in the organization can get so committed to a previously chosen policy or project that the policy or project becomes synonymous with the overall mission of the organization.

The commitment analysis carries with it several clear prescriptions for reducing resistance to change. For example, in order to reduce the tendency to become psychologically wedded to one's previously chosen alternative, it may be useful to consult outside experts who are able to make an informed judgment without the encumbrance of being personally responsible for the previously chosen alternative. (Interestingly, a similar remedy was proposed by Janis [1982] for offsetting groupthink tendencies.) Or, it may be worthwhile to modify the process by which managers' performance is appraised. If managers believe that their evaluation is based more on behavioral processes rather than its associated outcome, then entrapment (i.e., dysfunctional resistance to change) may be less apt to occur. Suppose managers knew that their performance appraisal was dependent upon the extent to which they made the right decision, in light of the evidence that was known (or plausibly could have been known) at the time that the decision was made. This type of evaluation process gives greater recognition to external influences on performance (those beyond the individual's control). Such process- (rather than outcome-) oriented performance appraisals may cause the evaluatee to be less concerned with justifying past decisions that produced negative outcomes, and more motivated to make the proper subsequent decision. It is precisely this latter, prospective rather than retrospective, mindset that deters entrapment.

Other remedies for reducing resistance to change, to the extent that such resistance is mediated by entrapment, may be found in Chapter 8. For example, it may be useful to provide key decision makers in organizations with training on how to recognize (and avoid the perils of) entrapment. Although some evidence (e.g., Kahneman, Slovic, & Tversky, 1982) suggests that increasing individuals' awareness of their systematic deviations from rationality is not always sufficient to enhance judgment and decision making, one study discussed in Chapter 8 yielded promising results along these lines (Nathanson et al., 1982). In any event, the management of organizational change and commitment processes should continue to be a difficult challenge with which managers must contend.

Although we have just discussed the virtues of being flexible, or at least of not allowing entrapment to interfere with appropriate organizational changes, there is also much to be said for remaining committed to a course of action. As Staw and Ross (1980) demonstrated, administrators are evaluated much more favorably when they stick with, rather than shift, their policies in the face of negative feedback—especially if their chosen policy ultimately meets with favorable results. The need to remain open to change (i.e,. not to become entrapped) and the need at least to appear committed to a course of previously chosen action seem to place conflicting demands upon managers, administrators, and policy makers. The effective management of these conflicting pressures may be one critical factor that separates the astute leader from the mediocre one.

Entrapment in Interpersonal Relationships

Another arena to which entrapment analyses may be usefully applied is the general domain of interpersonal relationships. Probably the most important dealings that we have in our everyday lives are with other people; simply put, we need and want social interaction. In those interactions, however, we can fall prey to a variety of forms of entrapment. Several of these relationship traps will be discussed in the following pages: intimacy traps, interpersonal expectation traps, and dependency traps. (For further details, see Rubin [1985].)

Intimacy Traps

One of the most painful forms of entrapment can occur in romantic relation-ships. Imagine the scenario: two people have had an exclusive relationship (e.g., courtship, marriage) with one another for a prolonged period of time. The relationship was once quite satisfying to both partners, but it has since soured and remained that way for quite some time. Undoubtedly, many couples would dissolve the romantic connection at this point. Others may seek alternatives (e.g., couples therapy) designed to improve the way things are going. Still others, we predict, will be prone to entrapment. They may consider leaving the relationship; however, the thought of having invested so much (financially, emotionally) in a relationship that is about to end may be too repugnant. To the extent that the individuals' continued commitment to the relationship is motivated by the latter belief, they have become victims of entrapment.

Unlike the previous section on entrapment in work organizations, there is scant *empirical* evidence that individuals escalate their commitment to failing intimate (or other types of) relationships. The only research that is even indirectly relevant stems from the investment model discussed previously (Farrell & Rusbult, 1981; Rusbult, 1980). In a role-playing simulation of an ongoing romantic relationship, subjects rated the extent to which they would remain committed to another person as a function of (a) the costs associated with remaining committed to that person, (b) the attractiveness of an alternative dating choice available, and (c) the degree of prior investment that subjects had made in the relationship. The investment model was firmly supported, including the most germane finding that commitment was much greater in the high- than in the low-prior-investment conditions.

Was the relationship between investment size and commitment mediated by entrapment? As mentioned in the previous discussion of the investment model, entrapment may be occurring if a positive relationship exists between investment and commitment *in the face of* attractive alternatives and/or high costs associated with remaining committed. To evaluate whether entrapment occurred in the Rusbult (1980) study, it would be necessary to study the correlation between investment size and commitment to the relationship in the High Cost–Attractive Alternative condition. Interestingly, the investment size and commitment were highly related in this condition, if anything, more so than in any other condition.

In a second study college students rated their commitment to an ongoing (or past) romantic relationship as a function of the variables specified by the investment model. Once again, the correlation between investment size and commitment in this more ecologically valid study was positive and significant. It would be interesting to know if, as in the role-playing study, this correlation was especially significant under the conditions in which an entrapment analysis is most relevant: High Cost and/or High Attractive alternatives to remaining with the same romantic partner.

In more recent research, Rusbult, Zembrodt, and Gunn (1982) once again explored the effect of investment size on commitment. The four experiments included in this report differed from previous research in two important respects. First, subjects had been explicitly instructed to rate their reactions to a once satisfying, but now dissatisfying, romantic relationship. This instructional change had the potential effect of making the entrapment process more relevant, in that entrapment in romantic relationships refers to continued commitment with a *failing* course of action. Second, the dependent variable included a variety of responses, rather than simply stay versus leave. Borrowing from the work of Hirschman (1970) on responses to decline in firms and organizations, Rusbult et al. (1982) utilized four different measures: exit, voice, loyalty, and neglect. Exit refers to ending the romantic relationship (e.g., getting a divorce, deciding to "just be friends"); voice refers to actively expressing dissatisfaction, with the hope of improving the tone of the relationship; loyalty refers to passively but optimistically waiting for things to improve (e.g., "giving things some time"); and neglect refers to passivity in the service of allowing the relationship to end.

Clearly, voice and loyalty are much more reflective of further commitment to the relationship than are exit and neglect. Is there any evidence that degree of prior investment is related to the specific behavioral response to the dissatisfying relationship? The results of four studies performed by Rusbult et al. (1982) suggest that there is. Two of the studies were of the role-playing variety, in which subjects evaluated their response to the souring relationship as a function of investment size. (Investment size was operationalized by the amount of prior self-disclosure that subjects had made to their romantic partner.) As an entrapment analysis would predict, subjects were more likely to make voice and loyalty responses (and less likely to make exit and neglect responses) when the size of their investment was large rather than small. Similar results emerged in two field studies in which subjects wrote short essays describing a time when they had become dissatisfied with their romantic relationship. Content analyses revealed that voice and loyalty responses were much more frequent (while exit and neglect responses were much less frequent) among those who indicated that they had invested more rather than less in the relationship.

The studies by Rusbult and her colleagues are the only ones of which we are aware that have related investment size to heightened commitment in a souring romantic relationship. Does any of the research presented in this book explain why failing romantic relationships provide potentially fertile ground for the development of entrapment? Perhaps. There are two factors associated with the nature of investments made in romantic relationships that could pave the way for entrapment. First, an important component of the investments is the *time* that has been committed to the relationship. Spending several years with a romantic partner, if nothing else, means that time has been taken away from other, perhaps more rewarding romantic pursuits. Situations in which time is an important currency of investment lend themselves to entrapment through a "passive" or "self-sustaining" process, as discussed in Chapter 4. Investments produced by the passage of time accrue continuously and automatically. As in any passive situation, decision makers must deliberately decide to extricate themselves from the situation. Failure to take action automatically "ups the ante" of the individual's investment, through the continued passage of time. Several experiments were discussed in Chapter 4 showing that passive situations are more apt to engender entrapment than are active ones. We are not suggesting that the mere passage of time is the sole or even primary currency of investment in romantic relationships. We become invested in or committed to our romantic partner through actions, not simply as a result of the passage of time (e.g., self-disclosure to the partner, joint purchases, having children). The point is that *in addition to* commitment-heightening behaviors, romantic partners may also take the mere passage of time into account when trying to discern how much they have invested in the relationship.

The other aspect of investment in romantic relationships that may serve to heighten the likelihood of entrapment is the "investment's" publicity. Being romantically involved with one's partner is typically common knowledge. Many of the prior investments that gave sustenance to the relationship (e.g., duration of the relationship, choice of lifestyle, number of children produced) are also known by significant others. As commitment theorists have noted (Kiesler, 1971) it is especially difficult to give up one's prior investment (even in a failing course of action) when the nature of the investments are known by significant others. In short, both the "passivity" and the publicity of prior investments in unsatisfying intimate relationships may set the stage for a painful kind of entrapment.

Several questions of practical importance stem from the prospect that unsatisfying relationships can lead to entrapment. For example, it may be useful for romantic partners in an unrewarding relationship to evaluate whether, and to what extent, their decision to remain together is mediated by entrapment. How may they go about making this inference? Entrapment refers to the tendency to persist in a failing course of action in order to justify the allocation of prior resources to that course of action. Put more simply, when we are entrapped we are "living in the past." Thus, the strained couple may find it worthwhile to examine the extent to which their relationship is based in the past. Operationally, this could mean asking themselves the following questions: (1) Are the most rewarding moments of the relationship centered around thinking about the way "things used to be?" Indeed, does most of the thinking or talking that the partners engage in focus upon the past, regardless of whether it is positive or negative? (2) Do couple-based activities include novelty (e.g., trying new restaurants or hobbies; making new friends while maintaining ties with old ones)? (3) Is the partners' relationship congruent with life's predictable developmental stages—does either partner (or possibly both) perceive that "life is passing them by" *because of the way that the relationship* has been managed?

Several other diagnostic questions could be posed. The important point is that the more the unrewarding relationship is linked to the past rather than the present or future, the more likely it is that the couple's continued commitment will be due to their felt need to justify past commitments. We are not suggesting that such a relationship should necessarily be dissolved, even if it is clear that the current inertia is driven by entrapment. Rather, the ability to determine the extent to which entrapment exists will enable the couple to make a more informed decision. Once the couple recognizes that its continued commitment is mediated by an entrapment process, the couple may be psychologically "freer" to think about ways to improve the future course of the relationship. Rather than focusing on the extent to which it has too much invested to quit, the couple may be able to devote its individual and collective energies to thinking about whether the relationship is salvageable, and if so, how. Of course, upon realizing the extent of entrapment, and upon concluding that the likelihood of future improvement is low, the couple may well choose to dissolve the relationship. Undoubtedly, such a prospect is tremendously painful, as the literature on the intra- and interpersonal consequences of divorce readily attests (Levitin, 1979). Nevertheless, in the long run, that option may be less undesirable than the choice to escalate one's commitment to the entrapping relationship.

Avoiding entrapment in relationships. Is it possible to *eliminate* entrapment in romantic relationships? Probably not. As we have argued throughout the book, a myriad of situational and dispositional variables make decision makers more or less prone to entrapment. There is no reason to think that the factors that were shown to promote entrapment in basic research are any less relevant in the realm of romance. However, there may be certain actions that couples can take to make them less apt to escalate their commitment to a failing relationship. It was suggested that romantic relationships can prove entrapping because of the "passive" rather than "active" way in which investments mount. Once the relationship is in progress, an important part of that which is invested—the individuals' time—increases on a continuous and automatic basis. The assumption is that the relationship will persist over time, until one or both parties take direct action to terminate it. Although relationships have this naturally passive element, it may be possible for partners' continuing commitment to the relationship to be the result of more active rather than passive decision making. This may be achieved by regular, periodical evaluations of the relationship, in which the partners take stock and examine how they are getting along. If the answer to this question is, "Not too well," the couple may consider what is needed to improve the quality of the relationship. They can also discuss how to go about achieving those ends.

In the process of discussing these issues several positive outcomes may result. First, the decision to continue the relationship (if such a decision is in fact reached) is apt to be the result of an active rather than passive process. Rather than allowing the inexorable passage of time to increase their degree of investment in the relationship, the couple has taken the more active position of deliberately deciding to remain committed. (One possible "danger" of transforming the decision structure to be more active than passive—suggested by the results of the "active–passive" studies in Chapter 4—is that the couple may be less likely to persist in an entrapping relationship if they have to make an active, rather than a passive, decision to do so. However, the decision to terminate a relationship fraught with entrapment may well be in the long-term interests of either or both individuals.)

Second, as a result of periodically reevaluating the relationship and deciding to continue, the couple will introduce a common, superordinate goal toward which both of the romantic partners can work. The focus is less on the dissatisfaction with the relationship, and more on working together to make things better. If the couple is earnest about its desire to remain committed and improve the future course of the relationship, then a spirit of cooperation should exist. Several areas of social-psychological research (Aronson, 1980) have convincingly demonstrated that interpersonal hostility and conflict can be substantially reduced by the introduction of a superordinate goal.

Third, to the extent that the couple has evaluated the course of the relationship, discussed its problems, considered means of improvement, and decided to continue, the channels of communication between the partners are apt to remain open. It is difficult to imagine such a reevaluation process, if conducted in mature fashion, not being accompanied by a good deal of communication. Good communication, in which each participant honestly and accurately conveys his or her opinion to the listener, is typically necessary for relationships to retain or recapture their vitality.

Coping with the loss. Suppose that a couple has decided to terminate its unsatisfying relationship, perhaps as a result of revelations that appeared during the reevaluation discussions. The prospect of separating is fraught with uncomfortable feelings, one of which may be the frustration associated with investing oneself in a relationship that ultimately dissolved. Considerable stress could be aroused by the perception that all of the time and emotion invested in the relationship was in vain. However, an important part of coping with this painful belief may be to question its veracity. Was the time spent "in vain" if the relationship ultimately dissolved? If the individual's goal was to make that particular relationship work or at least persist, then the effort expended in attempting to do so may have been for naught. However, it may be more comforting to view the time spent together in a broader temporal perspective. That is, the individual may have acquired some valuable information in the course of the relationship that remains with that individual, to be used profitably in future endeavors or relationships. We are not naive enough to suggest that such "comforting" thoughts will eliminate or even reduce the pain of separation. Rather, it may enable the individual to take solace in what has happened, and in that sense facilitate the coping process.

Entrapment in Nonromantic Relationships

It should be emphasized that romantic relationships are not the only form of social encounter that can prove entrapping. Although it is beyond the scope of the book to discuss all types of relationship traps, it may be worthwhile to mention several others briefly. (The interested reader is referred to Rubin [1985] for further discussion.)

Entrapment produced by interpersonal expectations. The social-psychological literature on stereotyping (e.g., Zanna & Pack, 1975) and expectation effects (e.g., Rosenthal & Jacobson, 1968) has repeatedly demonstrated that individuals' behavior conforms to the expectations of significant others. What would happen, however, if the behavior prescribed by these others' expectations was no longer functional, or desirable, for the individual? It may well be that this person will feel entrapped by the others' expectations. The significant others may have "too much invested to quit" their characteristic way of viewing the target person. For example, parents often find it difficult to change the manner in which they view their children, even when these views are clearly dysfunctional to both the parent and the child. This prospect presents children with a difficult dilemma: they can violate their parents' outdated expectations of their own behavior, but in so doing perhaps elicit harsh feelings from their parents. Or they can conform to their parents' expectations, but at potentially great personal expense. Even worse, the children can "buy into" the parents' expectations, and make it part of their self-identity. When this identity prescribes behavior that has outlived its usefulness, the child may wish to cease performing this behavior. However, the tremendous amount of investment (by the self and/or relevant others) that has gone into the creation of that identity may make it quite difficult for the individual to initiate the (much needed) change.

Dependency traps. In our everyday dealings we come to rely on a myriad of doctors, therapists, and repairmen to heal our aching bodies, psyches, and television sets. For a number of reasons we prefer to employ the services of these same individuals over time. Thus, our dependency relationship tends to deepen on a gradual and incremental basis. What happens, however, when this dependency relationship begins to sour (i.e., when the party on whom we depend is no longer providing help on a reliable basis)? In theory, it is usually quite possible to switch to another provider. However, individuals may show reluctance to switch from their dissatisfying dependency relationship because of all that has been invested to that point. It may be difficult, for example, for a client to terminate a long-term psychotherapy relationship, even though it feels dissatisfying or incomplete. After all, having invested so much in the pursuit of the therapeutic goal(s), the client may cling tenaciously to the therapist, even—or especially—when it has clearly outlived its usefulness to do so.

Entrapment in Political Decision Making

Individuals, groups, and organizations can fall prey to the process of entrapment when making decisions of political importance. The escalation of the United States' military involvement in Vietnam has been repeatedly considered as perhaps the most noteworthy and notorious example (Halberstam, 1969; Janis, 1982; Staw, 1976; Teger, 1980). The deepening U.S. commitment in Vietnam clearly needs to be understood in terms of factors and processes apart from entrapment; indeed, analysis of these complex factors is beyond the scope of this book. It seems equally plausible, however, that entrapment was at least partially the mechanism by which the United States prolonged its commitment in Vietnam.

Rather than discuss entrapment in Vietnam—a topic of much prior analysis—it may be more interesting to consider the possible role of entrapment in another more recent imbroglio: the civil war in El Salvador. Four years ago one of us (Brockner & Mazel, 1981) wrote a paper in which we attempted to forewarn readers about the prospect of U.S. entrapment in the military strife in El Salvador. The thesis of the paper—that the Reagan Administration was setting itself up for a prolonged (and perhaps fruitless) commitment to the existing government in El Salvador—was mainly derived from theory and research on entrapment. The paper was written for a general (rather than academic) audience; unfortunately, we were unsuccessful in our attempts to publish the piece in several popular outlets. The paper was then relegated to the "file drawer," in which it has been collecting dust for the past four years.

One of the chief virtues of the paper is that it was written *prior to* the United States' escalating military and economic commitment to El Salvador. Thus, it offers (or we should say offered) a predictive (rather than postdictive) account of the possibility that U.S. decision makers could be moved to entrapment in El Salvador. First, we will explore some of the current evidence as of this writing (February, 1984) which suggests that (1) the Reagan Administration is quite committed to defeating the leftist-backed guerrillas in El Salvador, and is likely to remain so, (2) the U.S.-backed government forces are faring poorly in their battle against the leftists, and (3) the escalated commitment of the U.S. in El Salvador is a manifestation of entrapment.

In March of 1981 Brockner and Mazel briefly described the military and economic assistance that had already been granted to El Salvador. They then went on to predict that the potential was great for the U.S. to escalate further its commitment to this failing course of action. This hypothesis was based on three factors: (a) There were clear signals, even at that earlier stage in the conflict, that a quick victory was unlikely. Consequently, the U.S. would have to allocate much more resources in order to attain its objectives. (b) The decision to provide assistance to the government-backed forces came in the face of widespread opposition, both at home and abroad. As Fox and Staw (1979) demonstrated, decision makers who implement a subsequently failing policy *in the face of opposition* are much more likely to escalate commitment to the failing policy than are those whose initial policy adoption is met with little resistance. (c) As a then-new administration, Reagan's group may have been especially eager to show its "strength," especially when U.S. interests were being threatened in a nearby country. Said differently, the fact that Reagan's administration had only begun to serve 2 months earlier may have heightened its face-saving needs, an especially important antecedent of entrapment (cf. Chapter 6).

That the United States has escalated its commitment to victory in El Salvador is abundantly clear. According to an article in *The New York Times Magazine* (July, 1983) the amount of American aid for 1983 was likely to amount to approximately $60 million on the military front and $232 million for economic ventures. Moreover, the view of top American military advisors in El Salvador suggests that a prolonged, escalating commitment may be in store for the U.S. government. More specifically, U.S. military advisors in El Salvador believe that it

> ... needs more time for training (Salvadoran) recruits and influencing the High Command—and this means a reassessment on the part of those in Washington and the American command in Panama who have been pressing for quick results. Everything they learned in Vietnam tells the advisers that in a counterinsurgency war *there are no big military victories, only slow cumulative advances*, and the economic assistance and social reform—to rally the people to the Government's side—are just as important as battlefield gains. That, the advisors feel, points to a need for an increase and improvement in the American aid program (emphasis added).

According to this view, victory in El Salvador will require a pattern of investments similar to that which promotes entrapment. In most entrapment situations decision makers make small but steady resource allocations; it is this cumulative effect that evokes the perception of having too much invested to quit. Indeed, top-level foreign policy advisors are acting as if the U.S. government has too much invested to quit in El Salvador. Consider the following quotation from an Associated Press article dated January 10, 1984:

> The Reagan Administration announced plans yesterday to nearly triple military assistance for El Salvador this year. The proposed increase of $140 million would be the largest single weapons aid request yet for the beleaguered Salvadoran army. If approved by Congress, the aid proposal would push total U.S. military aid to the Salvadoran army to more than $200 million for 1984.

In the past 3 years it is clear that the Reagan Administration has increased (or plans to increase) its commitment to achieve victory in El Salvador. But, is the administration a victim of entrapment? For entrapment to occur, there must be not only increasing commitments, but also clear evidence that (1) the course of action is failing, and (2) the increased investments are in the service of justifying past commitments. If it were clear that the U.S.'s prior investments in El Salvador were increasing its likelihood of success, then the additional commitments would be warranted on prospectively, rather than retrospectively, rational grounds.

However, the evidence suggests that the Salvadoran Army's chances for victory over the counterinsurgent guerrilla forces are moderate at best. The Army's forces lack the manpower needed to counteract the guerrilla forces. Most military experts believe that a troop advantage ratio of 10 to 1 over the guerrillas is needed to ensure victory. The ratio is currently (January, 1984) only 3–4 to 1 in the Government's favor. The quality, as well as quantity, of the Government's army is also very much in question. According to *The New York Times* (July, 1983), "most of the recruits are uneducated young men from the impoverished mass of the population. Many of them are picked up off the street and hauled off into the Army for a two-year hitch; many join up because they can't find jobs. There is hardly any re-enlistment. This means that at any given time, the army is composed 25% of new recruits. It also speaks poorly for the soldiers' motivation, even though the American advisers say that under a good commander the soldiers are eager and perform well." Other aspects of the articles, as well as a more recent news report (*The New York Times*, January 22, 1984) suggest that the Salvadoran government forces are doing poorly in their battle against the guerrillas.

Thus, the U.S. has escalated its commitment to a probably failing course of action in El Salvador. Is there any evidence that the escalated commitment is driven by the desire to justify past investments? It is relatively easy to verify that the U.S. has increased its commitments in El Salvador. It is also possible to provide evidence that the military venture thus far has not been successful. However, it is far more difficult to verify that self- or other-justification factors are the underlying motivation for the U.S.'s increased commitment to the failing course of action. We do not presume that the process of entrapment is necessarily the single best explanation of the actions taken by the Reagan administration in El Salvador. Rather, it is being suggested that the prospect of entrapment must be considered as a real possibility in this context. Certainly, there is reason to believe that justification motives may be affecting the U.S. course of action in El Salvador. As reported in July, 1983 in *The New York Times*, because another presidential campaign is imminent, "President Reagan needs some tangible evidence that El Salvador is salvageable, that his policy is working. There is pressure from . . . Congressional leaders of various political persuasions, for something to show the voters back home. There is pressure from the Southern Command Post in Panama, the headquarters for all U.S. forces in Latin America."

Clearly, further research is needed to demonstrate that the deeping commitment of the U.S. in El Salvador is reflective of entrapment. It may be possible to examine documents, memos, and other sources in order to evaluate whether, and the extent to which, entrapment was (is) occurring. Until more definitive research has been performed, we can only speculate about the possibility that a Vietnam-style entrapment is unfolding once again in El Salvador.

Summary

The purpose of this chapter has been to call attention to the role of entrapment in several applied settings, by addressing the following questions: (1) does our knowledge about the process of entrapment help us to better understand the manner in which sequential decisions are made in various applied domains, and

(2) does the analysis of entrapment from the context of an applied domain lead to further conceptualization and hypothesis generation about the process of entrapment? The answer to both of these questions, we believe, is a resounding yes.

Entrapment analyses may be fruitfully applied to a wide range of decisional contexts. Most of this applied work has related entrapment to decision making in organizational settings. Thus, individuals can get entrapped in personal, career, or occupational choices, and also when making decisions within the confines of their organizational roles. Such decisions can occur at the individual, group, and/or organizational levels of analysis. The process of entrapment, moreover, is implicated in a number of areas of organizational inquiry: career development, turnover, performance appraisal, and organizational change.

The potential for entrapment in interpersonal relationships is also evident. Some empirical evidence (Rusbult, 1980; Rusbult et al., 1982) suggests that commitments to failing romantic relationships make it much more difficult to withdraw subsequently. However, much more research needs to be done, addressed to the following questions: Is it possible to avoid feeling entrapped in romantic relationships? If so, how? Similarly, is it ever possible for an entrapped couple to stop "living in the past," to base their relationship on present and future prospects of enjoyment, rather than on all of their prior investments in the relationship? Obviously, these questions can also be evaluated in non-romantically laden entrapment relationships. Given that our interpersonal relationships are of such fundamental importance, it would seem worthwhile to discover how to improve the quality of those relationships. Eliminating, or at least reducing, the presence of entrapment in our social relationships may represent an important step in that direction.

Finally, we have examined the possibility that the United States government has embarked upon an entrapping course of action in El Salvador. It is clear that the U.S. has increasingly committed resources to the "prevailing" government in El Salvador over the past 3 years. It could be plausibly argued that the U.S.' policy in El Salvador is failing, and that the increased expenditures are based more on the need to justify past investments than on sound military thought. The discussion of entrapment in El Salvador is highly speculative, of course. More careful research is needed to document the role of entrapment in the decisions made by the Reagan Administration. More generally, it is possible to analyze the extent to which entrapment is influential in a variety of political decisions (e.g., Watergate). Doing so would be one of the many ways in which future investigators can provide sorely needed applied research on the process of entrapment.

Chapter 11
Conclusions

The writing of this book has been guided by five major objectives: first, to document the ubiquity and significance of the phenomenon we refer to as entrapment; second, to introduce the interested reader to the methods used, and results obtained, by entrapment researchers; third, to summarize and, whenever possible, integrate the results of empirical work; fourth, to nudge the study of entrapment a step or two further forward by suggesting possible avenues for future research; and finally, to help locate the study of entrapment in the broader context and rich tradition of social-psychological theory.

It is our hope and belief that each of the above objectives has been addressed—even met—throughout this book, as reflected in the organization of each of the 10 preceding chapters. The purpose of this concluding essay, therefore, is not to restate issues and themes that have already been the focus of considerable attention. Instead we wish to use these pages to move beyond existing data and theory, in an effort to conjure up the broad contours of possible future work in this general area. To put the issue most simply, and in the form of a question: Given what we already know about entrapment, what is it that we still need to learn? Where should the field of entrapment research—and more generally, the study of the psychology of escalating conflict—go next? As indicated in the following pages, we believe that the answer to these questions is fivefold.

Decisional Duality

The phenomenon of entrapment is a bit like quicksilver, and our research pursuit of this phenomenon over the last decade or so has been a bit reminiscent of hunting for the snark or Moby Dick. It is often hard to know precisely when one holds entrapment in one's hands, and the reason is simply that it refuses to stand still. Entrapment is dynamic rather than static. Indeed, even as decision makers consider the degree to which they have become entrapped, the terrain continues to change beneath their feet. Moreover, entrapment tends to look very different, depending upon where one's feet happen to be planted. Entrapment is characterized by four major instances of decisional duality, four ways in which the entrapment process, as witnessed through the "eye of the beholder,' 'is likely to be understood and responded to very differently.

First, because entrapment is largely driven along by processes of justification and rationalization, the phenomenon tends to look very different depending upon whether one is on the inside looking out, or on the outside looking in. What may seem a perfectly plausible and consistent outlook or course of behavior to an entrapped decision maker is often seen as the height of irrationality to an external observer of the identical situation. Indeed, it may well be that a relatively simple way of limiting entrapment is by shifting perspective from that of actor to that of observer, much as we described in our Chapter 9 study on the entrapment-reducing effect of self-focused attention. In short, a first decisional duality of entrapment stems from the tendency to become so enmeshed in the process that the reality of the situation looks different from within than from without.

Second, as reflected in our Chapter 7 discussion of timing considerations, the process of entrapment is likely to look very different to a decision maker, depending upon whether he or she stands early or late in the process. Standing just inside the entranceway to entrapment, decision makers are likely to be deflected from an entrapping course of action by any number of considerations which, when experienced later, either have no effect or simply further perpetuate entrapment. For example, costs that deter entrapment when introduced at the outset may become the basis for further justification when introduced after the commitment die has already been cast.

Third, degree of entrapment seems to vary in relation to decision makers' perceptions of themselves as active versus passive participants in the process. We have argued in Chapter 4 that some entrapment situations—notably those in which the currency of resource allocation is time—have the characteristics of machines which, once started, will automatically continue to operate until and unless a decision is made to switch it off; in contrast, many, perhaps most, entrapment examples have the properties of a machine whose normal state is "off," and which can only be kept in operation by keeping one's finger on the start button. If these are relatively objective states of the entrapment "world," distinguished by the degree to which an active versus passive process of resource allocation is in effect, then it is also the case that the identical objective situation may be beheld and responded to very differently simply as a function of the eye of the beholder. The decision maker who regards entrapping situations from the vantage point of an activist—someone who will continue to judge the merits and wisdom of persistent involvement, and then act accordingly—is far less likely to get enmeshed than someone who, although witnessing the identical situation, feels and acts like a passive pawn caught up in an inexorable process.

Finally, as discussed in Chapter 1, entrapped decision makers typically experience the decisional duality that arises from being able to view resource allocation either as an investment or as an expense. To the extent that decision makers, poised at a particular point along the entrapment continuum, evaluate their allocation of resources to date in relation to the goal-like objective up ahead (the return of the telephone operator after being placed on hold, the repair of an old car, victory in El Salvador) this allocation is apt to be seen as an investment that moves the decision maker ever closer to his or her coveted objective. On the other hand, when evaluated in relation to point zero—the point of entry into the entrapping tunnel, when resources were first allocated in pursuit of some goal—the status quo allotment of resources is apt to be seen as an expense. Thus, our Janus-faced, entrapped decision makers are forever swiveling in their seats, witnessing the identical history of expenditure of time, money, energy, caring, striving, and so on as the necessary cost of goal achievement (investment) and also as increasingly burdensome baggage (expense).

To summarize: Our first general observation, and recommendation for further thought and study, derives from the view that some of the most interesting decisional processes must be understood not objectively but through the subjective prism known as the eye of the beholder. Depending upon one's location in the shifting terrain of entrapment—be it on the outside looking in or the inside looking out, be it early or late in this dynamic process, be it through the eyes of a passive or an active witness to the phenomenon, be it looking behind at the expenses already incurred or forward at the approaching objective—the process is likely to be experienced in very different ways.

The Role of Choice

In a world without the possibility of choice, entrapment would not exist. For that matter, if Leon Festinger is to be believed, a world without choice would have little reason to invent the formulation of cognitive dissonance. Choice, the right and sometimes the obligation to select one alternative course of action over another, is the key to processes of rationalization and compensatory justification that leads decision makers deeper into the entrapment quagmire.

To understand the important role of choice, imagine a world without it. Not a happy or welcome place to be, to be sure, a 1984 environment in which we think and do what we are expected to do, in which all the goods and evils to befall us are beyond our personal ken, range, or competency. Like young children, we would experience outcomes in a world without choice as largely passive recipients, the beneficiaries or victims of those with the power to dictate our fate.

An entirely unwelcome, even loathsome arrangement this imagined world without choice? Not really. If we cannot make choices, then at least we are not responsible for the things that happen to us, and are therefore unlikely to suffer over the consequences of our action. While there is nothing more wonderful, perhaps, then the sense of having willingly created our own good fortunes— having exercised free will in the service of advancements, perfection, pleasure, and satisfaction—there is conversely perhaps no more painful experience than that of having been the origin of our own worst defeats. To put this point another way, the one great virtue of a world without choice is the freedom from guilt and self-recrimination at our own inability to deliver favorable situations and outcomes.

If it is the fate of the powerless to be swept along by the surging tide of the more powerful, then it is the privilege of the most powerful to bear both the privilege and the burden of choice. The right to exercise choice causes us to behave in ways that may ultimately help or hurt us. As we indicated above, the freedom to exercise choice in the service of providing ourselves or others with favorable consequences may be one of the very sweetest experiences that life has to offer. But to be able to make such choices also requires us to accept responsibility for failure and defeat and—in the instance of a phenomenon such as entrapment—to cover our tracks through renewed commitment and post hoc justification of our deeds. If the privilege of choice is being able to create our own personal world in our image, then its compensatory burden is the responsibility of living with not only victory but defeat as well.

To be sure, the existence of choice is no guarantee that entrapment will result; one of the choices that decision makers can always exercise is simply to avoid a potentially entrapping situation or to withdraw at any time. And yet it is this very possibility, the understanding that in entrapping situations we can leave if we wish to, that often leads decision makers to pursue their quixotic objective with renewed vigor.

It is our hope that research on entrapment will stimulate further study of the role and consequence of individual and social choice. Festinger (1957) opened the door with his formulation of dissonance theory, Kiesler (1971) and others kept it ajar with their subsequent explorations of the commitment process, and we would like to think of ourselves as having helped to door-stop the study of choice in an open and inviting position for some years to come.

The Virtues of Entrapment

No doubt about it, our portrait of entrapment has been a gloomy charac-terization of a costly and even pernicious process. Entrapment has been depicted as a phenomenon in which decision makers become so determined to attain some goal that they lose sight of the costs incurred along the way, and eventually come to use these very costs in order to justify additional expenditures of resources. In entrapment, we have argued, decision makers come to feel that they have too much invested to quit, and it is this reluctance to give up on investments/expenses that drives decision makers ever deeper into the entrap-ment tunnel.

But having consistently developed the position that entrapment is a costly process, is it not possible that entrapment—under certain special circumstances, at least—can be construed as a phenomenon that can serve constructive ends? If entrapment results precisely because decision makers become irrationally committed to the pursuit of some goal, then might it be possible—by changing our analysis of the goal itself—to transform a costly into a potentially beneficial process?

Consider here the many situations in which people are determined to better themselves in some way, but are lacking in the emotional wherewithal to stick to their commitments and good intentions. A dieter wishing to stick to a difficult weight loss regimen, a smoker who wishes to give up cigarettes once and for all, a drug abuser, indeed any makers of a resolution designed to improve themselves in some way are candidates for an entrapment procedure that may facilitate efforts to stick to self-improvements. The very acts of effort justification, the sense of having too much invest to quit, may now be used in the service of "screwing one's courage to the sticking place."

For example, consider the plight of the alcoholic who is trying to abstain from drinking. The more time that has elapsed since the individual's last drink, the greater the pressure to "justify the correctness," or at least not undo, the hard work that was needed to avoid drinking. The increasing passage of time of abstinence thus forms the prior commitment from which the alcoholic is unwilling to retreat. Or, the prior commitment can take the form of a "deposit contract," in which the alcoholic (or overeater, or drug abuser) allocates some valuable resources (e.g., money) *prior to* beginning the treatment regimen. If the individual does not comply with the treatment program, then he or she stands to lose all or part of the deposit. Said differently, the prior resource allocation may serve to lock the troubled individual into a more functional behavior pattern, perhaps through similar self-justification and/or commitment processes that mediate the more typically costly versions of entrapment (cf. Christensen-Szalanski & Northcraft, 1984).

If entrapment processes can be employed for more positive or prosocial reasons, how may decision makers go about becoming entrapped by choice? Consistent with other analyses (see Rubin, 1985), we propose the following recommendations:

Avoid limit-setting. If one of the keys to trap avoidance is limit setting (see our description of this research in Chapter 9) then the key to entrapment by choice is not to set limits on one's involvement. Stopping points, opportunities for cool reflection on the costs already incurred, are strictly *verboten* if one wishes to get entrapped in the pursuit of some self-improvement goal.

Avoid people who may weaken resolve. In Chapter 5 it was shown that decision makers' degree of entrapment may be affected by the behavior of a relevant model. If so, then anyone determined to lose weight would be well advised to avoid the company of gourmet diners, and instead to spend as much time as is possible or tolerable with others who are likely to buttress—rather than diminish—one's determination to stick with it. Alcoholics Anonymous, a highly effective organization that has been in business for nearly 50 years now, partly relies for its effectiveness upon the ongoing contact among groups of reformed alcoholics, as well as the contact between reformed alocholics and newcomers who are just beginning to address their problem.

Avoid information about the hard road ahead. We saw in Chapter 4 that the introduction of information that increases the salience of entrapment costs has the effect of decreasing entrapment. It stands to reason, therefore, that if we wish to deliberately induce entrapment, decision makers would be well advised to avoid people, newspaper articles, and so on that may remind them of how costly it may be to stick to their best intentions.

Manifest resolve through public displays of commitment. Entrapment is facilitated by our tendency to behave consistently with public commitments that we make along the way. In an effort to shore up their determination to stop smoking cigarettes, smokers may choose to announce an intention to quit for one and all to hear. Presumably, to renege upon this public commitment would be to experience too great a cost—and not having reneged so far thus becomes the basis for continued abstinence. A public commitment to go without becomes the rationalized basis for continuing to go without. The previously discussed "deposit contract" represents one of several possible public displays of commitment.

Attend to information concerning achievement. We suspect that one of the reasons decision makers become entrapped is that they focus too much on the attainment of some goal up ahead, and this need to achieve blinds them temporarily to the costs that are being incurred along the way. Entrapment by choice, in the service of advancing some self-improvement or self-control regimen, may therefore require decision makers to be as forward looking, self-confident, or ambitious as possible. Anything that can be done to assure the would-be reformers that they have what it takes to reach some objective is likely to be of great service.

The preceding recommendations are by no means an exhaustive listing of the necessary do's and don't of deliberate entrapment. Nevertheless, this listing is suggestive of the kinds of strategies that may be necessary and, perhaps of greater importance, the useful role that entrapment can play. To summarize, then, our third general observation concerns the possibility that the very forces that leads decision makers into a costly, entrapping process may be turned on their ear in the service of promoting entrapment in pursuit of some program for self-improvement or betterment. While some research on the positive consequences of entrapment has been performed (e.g., Sjoberg, 1983), this clearly remains an area for much future scrutiny.

A Broader Trap Backdrop

Although this book has focused on a *particular* process by which people find themselves caught in psychological traps, further analysis in this area would do well to look at the relationship between these kinds of traps and their more distant relatives. Consider, for example, the variety of confidence games that have developed over the years, schemes for entrapping another person in a net that allows subsequent victimization. Or consider the world of animal traps, all those physical devices that exist in the service of imprisoning, maiming, or killing some quarry—be it animal or even human.

A more general analysis of traps than we have chosen to provide in the present data-based excursion might allow the development of a conceptual framework that applies to most traps. Thus, as suggested in an earlier paper (Rubin, 1981) all effective traps seem to share at least three critical properties: first, an ability to lure or distract the trap's victim into behavior that is ultimately quite costly; second, construction in such a way as to permit movement in one direction only—namely, deeper into the trap; and finally, a design that leads efforts at escape to increase the trap's bite. Obviously this threefold listing of key trap features may be partial at best, and a useful area for future exploration concerns the limitations of a simple scheme such as this one. Consider, however, the ways in which these three elements are enacted in traps that range from physical devices to con games to the standard entrapment situations discussed in this book.

Most animal traps work because they contain some form of lure or bait that attracts the quarry's attention, thereby distracting it from the trap's true intentions. A fish sees only the worm dangling on the hook, the mouse its piece of cheese, and the Trojans only the extravagant Greek offering before them. Once the quarry has taken the bait and entered the trap, it soon discovers that the way in is far easier to take than the way out. The cone-shaped net into which a lobster can readily crawl obscures the irreversibility of this move. Finally, notice that the victim's attempts to escape an animal trap often serve only to entrap it all the more. The fish's natural effort to free itself by swimming away from the hook that has caught it has the unfortunate effect of sinking the hook even deeper in its jaw. Efforts to escape quicksand by wriggling about serve only to hasten its terrible effects.

These same three trap characteristics, observable in all animal traps, can also be readily seen in the operation of an effective confidence game. Whether it is a so-called "small con"—played out as a game of three-card monte on a busy urban street corner—or a "big con" of the sort memorialized in the Paul Newman/Robert Redford film, *The Sting*, an effective con requires some initial lure or bait. The con artist's lure or bait is typically based on the mark's greed; the fat wriggling worm is the possibility of getting something for nothing, or perhaps a big killing at the expense of someone else. For a con to work it is also necessary that the mark be induced to cheat another person in order to reap large and easy profits. As a result, the victim's pursuit of the lure tends to obscure the fact that the path taken is not easily reversible. To repeat, it is precisely because the mark's actions are either illegal (as in the con depicted in *The Sting*) or unethical (as in many versions of three-card monte, where the mark is persuaded to "beat the system") that the mere act of participating in the con makes it difficult to get out. Finally, notice that the mark's very efforts to escape—typically by attempting to make a glorious and final big killing before quitting once and for all—only lead to deeper entrapment. The more money that the quarry is persuaded to put up in this effort, the more carefully he or she is apt to guard the investment, and to justify it through the commitment of additional resources. What was once a small lie and a minor bit of deception has now grown to such magnitude that the possibility of escape is seriously diminished.

Animal traps and con games are devices for capturing others. In psychological traps the trapper and the victim are one and the same, and we manage to con ourselves into an entrapping course of action. We are lured or distracted by the objective up ahead—the repair of the old car, victory in Vietnam, and so on. Our full-blown pursuit of a goal manages to obscure the fact that it is costing us something to engage in this quixotic quest, and when we at last turn around and acknowledge the history of increasing expenditure behind us, it now seems easier to continue on than to reverse course or abandon ship. Finally, as we contemplate whether to continue on or quit the situation, costs continue to increase (particularly in situations where the passage of time is at stake), and our efforts to engage in close analysis of our predicament may only serve to deepen the bite of entrapment.

In summary, by broadening our conceptual backdrop to include consideration of all kinds of traps—and not only those described in great detail in this book—it should be possible for future work to develop a more general framework for understanding the nature of all traps. By simultaneously considering the common properties of a wide-ranging assortment of physical and psychological traps, it becomes possible to develop a set of principles—of which the three already described are but initial examples—that may help move explorations in this area beyond their current confines.

Understanding the Cause of Escalating Conflict

In Chapter 7 we noted that decision makers' thoughts, feelings, and behaviors change as they escalate their commitment to a failing course of action. Among other things tactics tend to become more heavyhanded, the number of issues in and the number of parties to the conflict tend to increase, and motivations may shift from doing well to damaging the adversary in some way. In short, in escalating conflicts things seem to move unidirectionally from bad to worse. An interesting question for further study is why it is, exactly, that these kinds of changes take place during conflict escalation. Stated more generally, why do conflicts escalate?

One of several possible answers to this important question is offered by the phenomenon of entrapment. As conflicts escalate between individuals, groups, or nations, each side pours resources into the task of dominating the other. Once these resources have been expended, the protagonists—like the players in the Dollar Auction game—may feel increasingly compelled to justify all they have already spent by spending even more. Thus, quite apart from the disputants' motivation in escalating conflict to outwit or dominate the other side, the tendency toward continued escalation may be governed in good measure by the forces of entrapment.

Clearly, entrapment is not the sole explanation of conflict escalation. Indeed, in their analysis of conflict escalation, impasse, and settlement, Pruitt and Rubin (in press) point to the causal role in escalation of the following processes:

Structural change. Like a rubber band that is stretched too far, and as a result loses some elasticity and can no longer return to its original configuration, the escalation of some conflicts is associated with structural change. Thus, two people in the throes of a heated exchange may say or do such destructive things to each other that even after the conflict appears to have been settled, a residue of resentment remains; things have changed between the two people, and can never (or at least only with very great difficulty) return to the way they once were.

Selective perception. People in the midst of escalating conflict tend to pay attention only to information that confirms their worst fears and fantasies about their adversary; they hear only what they want to hear. Moreover, if information is in fact processed, it is often distorted in the service of confirming one's hypotheses and discounting input that may be disconfirmatory.

Self-fulfilling prophecy. Selective perception often influences behavior, and such behavior may have consequences for the other side that confirm the initial perceptions. Thus, if A expects B to be an angry, defensive person, and A therefore acts in angry, defensive ways in order to ward off the expected attacks of B, B may be provoked into the angry behavior which serves only to confirm A's initial perception; in this way, one party's prophecy for the other is fulfilled in escalating conflict.

These processes, described in one form or other by numerous scholars over the years, combine to drive escalating conflict along a unidirectional pathway. What has not been described in any detail to date, however, is the potentially important role of entrapment in understanding how and why it is that conflicts escalate. Thus, to the preceding listing of major determinants of conflict escalation, we would add the psychology of feeling that one has too much invested to quit.

In the last analysis, when all of the experimental studies of entrapment have been done, and the last word has been spoken on the various ways into and out of psychological traps, we suspect that the study of entrapment will be subsumed—as indeed it should—within the broader study of conflict escalation. It is only fitting, therefore, that we close this book by foreshadowing the end of this particular intellectual pathway, understanding that our joint work over the last decade—as personally and professionally important as it has been—is but one small part of a larger intellectual puzzle. It would never do, would it, for us to have become so invested in the study of entrapment, per se, and the related aspirations and career ambitions to which it might give rise, that we simply do not know how or when to give up? Good entrapment researchers—like the very decision makers who have been the object of our experimental study—must know how to evaluate their actions in the larger scheme of things.

References

Abramson, L., Seligman, M., & Teasdale, J. (1978). Learned helplessness in humans: Critique and reformulation. *Journal of Abnormal Psychology, 87,* 49–74.

Ankuta, G. (1981). *Public and private self-consciousness, models, and entrapment.* Unpublished manuscript, Tufts University.

Arkes, H.R., & Hackett, C. (1984). *The psychology of sunk costs.* Unpublished manuscript, Ohio University.

Aronson, E. (1980). *The social animal* (3rd ed.). San Francisco: W.H. Freeman.

Asch, S.E. (1951). Effects of group pressure upon the modification and distortion of judgment. In H. Guetzkow (Ed.), *Groups, leadership, and men.* Pittsburgh: Carnegie.

Bandura, A. (1973). *Aggression: A social learning analysis.* Englewood Cliffs, New Jersey: Prentice-Hall.

Bandura, A. (1977). *Social learning theory.* Englewood Cliffs, New Jersey: Prentice-Hall.

Baron, R.A., & Byrne, D. (1981). *Social psychology: Understanding human interaction* (3rd ed.). Boston: Allyn & Bacon.

Baumeister, R. (1982). A self-presentational view of social phenomena. *Psychological Bulletin, 91,* 3–26.

Bazerman, M.H. (1983). Negotiator judgment: A critical look at the rationality assumption. *American Behavioral Scientist, 27,* 211–228.

Bazerman, M.H., Beekum, R.I., & Schoorman, F.D. (1982). Performance evaluation in a dynamic context: A laboratory study of the impact of a prior commitment to the ratee. *Journal of Applied Psychology, 67,* 873–876.

Bazerman, M.H., Giuliano, T., & Appelman, A. (in press). Escalation in individual and group decision making. *Organizational Behavior and Human Performance.*

Bazerman, M.H., Schoorman, F.D., & Goodman, P. (1980). *A cognitive evaluation of escalation processes in managerial decision making.* Unpublished manuscript, Boston University.

Beck, A. (1967). *Depression: Clinical, experimental, and theoretical aspects.* New York: Harper & Row.

Bem, D.J., (1972). Self-perception theory. In L. Berkowitz (Ed.), *Advances in experimental social psychology* (Vol. 6). New York: Academic Press.

Bem, S. (1974). The measurement of psychological androgyny. *Journal of Consulting and Clinical Psychology, 42,* 155–162.

Bem, S., & Lenney, E. (1976). Sex and the avoidance of cross-sex behavior. *Journal of Personality and Social Psychology, 33,* 48–54.

Berkowitz, L., & LePage, A. (1967). Weapons as aggression-eliciting stimuli. *Journal of Personality and Social Psychology, 7,* 202–207.

Brockner, J. (1977). *The social psychology of entrapment in escalating conflicts.* Unpublished doctoral dissertation, Tufts University.

Brockner, J. (1983). Low self-esteem and behavioral plasticity: Some implications. In L. Wheeler & P.R. Shaver (Eds.), *Review of personality and social psychology* (Vol. 4). Beverly Hills, California: Sage Publications.

Brockner, J., Bazerman, M.H., & Rubin, J.Z. (1984). [Framing and entrapment]. Unpublished data, Tufts University.

Brockner, J., Gardner, A.M., Bierman, J., Mahan, T., Thomas, B., Weiss, W., Winters, L., & Mitchell, A. (1983). The roles of self-esteem and self-consciousness in the Wortman—Brehm model of reactance and learned helplessness. *Journal of Personality and Social Psychology, 45,* 199–209.

Brockner, J., Houser, R.F., Lloyd, K. Nathanson, S., Deitcher, J., Birnbaum, G., & Rubin, J.Z. (1985). *Self-diagnosticity and the escalation of commitment to a failing course of action.* Manuscript under editorial review.

Brockner, J., & Hulton, A.J.B. (1978). How to reverse the vicious cycle of low self-esteem: The importance of attentional focus. *Journal of Experimental Social Psychology, 14,* 564–578.

Brockner, J., & Mazel, L. (1981). *Decision making and El Salvador: Another case of psychological entrapment?* Unpublished manuscript, Tufts University.

Brockner, J., Nathanson, S., Friend, A., Harbeck, J., Samuelson, C., Houser, R., Bazerman, M.H., & Rubin, J.Z. (1984). The role of modeling processes in the 'knee deep in the big muddy' phenomenon. *Organizational Behavior and Human Performance, 33,* 77–99.

Brockner, J., Rubin, J.Z., Fine, J., Hamilton, T., Thomas, B., & Turetsky, B. (1982). Factors affecting entrapment in escalating conflicts: The importance of timing. *Journal of Research in Personality, 16,* 247–266.

Brockner, J., Rubin, J.Z., & Lang, E. (1981). Face-saving and entrapment. *Journal of Experimental Social Psychology, 17,* 68–79.

Brockner, J., Shaw, M.C., & Rubin, J.Z. (1979). Factors affecting withdrawal from an escalating conflict: Quitting before it's too late. *Journal of Experimental Social Psychology, 15,* 492–503.

Brockner, J., & Wallnau, L.B. (1981). Self-esteem, anxiety, and the avoidance of self-focused attention. *Journal of Research in Personality, 15,* 277–291.

Brown, B.R. (1968). The effects of need to maintain face on interpersonal bargaining. *Journal of Experimental Social Psychology, 4,* 107–122.

Buss, A.H. (1980). *Self-consciousness and social anxiety.* San Francisco: W.H. Freeman.

Byrne, D. (1971).. *The attraction paradigm.* New York: Academic Press.

Caldwell, D.F., & O'Reilly, C.A. (1982). Response to failure: The effects of choice and responsibility on impression management. *Academy of Management Journal, 25,* 121–136.

Campbell, D.T. (1969). Reforms as experiments. *American Psychologist, 24,* 409–429.

Campbell, D.T. (1977). Keeping the data honest in the experimenting society. In H.W. Melton & D.J. Watson (Eds.), *Interdisciplinary dimensions of accounting for social goals and social organizations.* Columbia, Ohio: Grid.

Carlsmith, J.M., Ellsworth, P., & Aronson, E. (1976). *Methods of research in social psychology.* Reading, Mass: Addison-Wesley.

Carver, C.S. (1974). Facilitation of physical aggression through objective self-awareness. *Journal of Experimental Social Psychology, 10,* 365–370.

Carver, C.S. (1975). Physical aggression as a function of objective self-awareness and attitudes toward punishment. *Journal of Experimental Social Psychology, 11,* 510–519.

Carver, C.S. (1979). A cybernetic model of self-attention processes. *Journal of Personality and Social Psychology, 37*, 1251–1281.

Christensen-Szalanski, J.J.J., & Northcraft, G.B. (1984). *Patient compliance behavior: The effects of time on patients' values of treatment regimens.* Manuscript under editorial review, University of Arizona.

Christie, R., & Geis, F.L. (1970). *Studies in machiavellianism.* New York: Academic Press.

Cialdini, R.B., Cacioppo, J.T., Bassett, R., & Miller, J. (1978). Low-ball procedure for producing compliance: Commitment then cost. *Journal of Personality and Social Psychology, 36*, 463–476.

Conlon, E.J., & Wolf, G. (1980). The moderating effects of strategy, visibility, and involvement on allocation behavior: An extension of Staw's escalation paradigm. *Organizational Behavior and Human Performance, 26*, 172–192.

Darley, J.M., & Latané, B. (1968), Bystander intervention in emergencies: Diffusion of responsibility. *Journal of Personality and Social Psychology, 8*, 377–383.

Deaux, K. (1976). *The behavior of men and women.* Belmont, California: Brooks/Cole.

Deci, E.L. (1975). *Intrinsic motivation.* New York: Plenum.

Deutsch, M. (1973). *The resolution of conflict.* New Haven: Yale University Press.

Dion, K., Baron, R.S., & Miller, N. (1970). Why do groups make riskier decisions than individuals? In L. Berkowitz (Ed.), *Advances in experimental social psychology* (Vol. 5). New York: Academic Press.

Duval, S., & Wicklund, R.A. (1972). *A theory of objective self-awareness.* New York: Academic Press.

Dweck, C.S., & Gilliard, D. (1975). Expectancy statements as determinants of reactions to failure: Sex differences in persistence and expectancy change. *Journal of Personality and Social Psychology, 32*, 1077–1084.

Eagly, A. (1967). Involvement as a determinant of response to favorable and unfavorable information. *Journal of Personality and Social Psychology, 7*, 1–15 (Monograph).

Easterbrook, J.A., (1959). The effect of emotion on cue utilization and the organization of behavior. *Psychological Review, 66*, 183–201.

Farrell, D., & Rusbult, C.E. (1981). Exchange variables as predictors of job satisfaction, job commitment, and turnover: The impact of rewards, costs, alternatives, and investments. *Organizational Behavior and Human Performance, 27*, 78–95.

Fenigstein, A., Scheier, M., & Buss, A. (1975). Public and private self-consciousness: Assessment and theory, *Journal of Consulting and Clinical Psychology, 43*, 522–527.

Festinger, L. (1954). A theory of social comparison processes. *Human Relations, 7*, 117–140.

Festinger, L. (1957). *A theory of cognitive dissonance.* Evanston, Ill.: Row, Peterson.

Festinger, L. (1964). *Conflict, decision, and dissonance.* Stanford, Calif: Stanford University Press.

Festinger, L., Riecken, H.W., & Schachter, S. (1956). *When prophecy fails.* Minneapolis: University of Minnesota Press.

Fischhoff, B. (1975). Hindsight ≠ foresight: The effect of outcome knowledge on judgment under uncertainty. *Journal of Experimental Psychology: Human Perception and Performance, 1*, 288–299.

Fischhoff, B. (1982). Debiasing. In D. Kahneman, P. Slovic, & A. Tversky (Eds.), *Judgment under uncertainty: Heuristics and biases.* New York: Cambridge University Press.

Fox, F.V., & Straw, B.M. (1979). The trapped administrator: Effects of job insecurity and policy resistance upon commitment to a course of action. *Administrative Science Quarterly, 24*, 449–471.

Frost, J.H., & Wilmot, W.W. (1978). *Interpersonal conflict*. Dubuque, Iowa: Wm. C. Brown.

Gaes, G.G., Kalle, R.J., & Tedeschi, J.T. (1978). Impression management in the forced compliance situation: Two studies using the bogus pipeline. *Journal of Experimental Social Psychology, 14*, 493–510.

Gallup, G. (1978). *The Gallup opinion index*. Princeton, New Jersey: American Institute of Public Opinion.

Geen, R.G., & Gange, J.J. (1977). Drive theory of social facilitation: Twelve years of theory and research. *Psychological Bulletin, 84*, 1267–1288.

Gerard, H.B., & Rabbie, J.M. (1961). Fear and social comparison. *Journal of Abnormal and Social Psychology, 62*, 586–592.

Gibbons, F.X. (1978). Sexual standards and reactions to pornography: Enhancing behavioral consistency through self-focused attention. *Journal of Personality and Social Psychology, 36*, 976–987.

Gibbons, F.X., & Wicklund, R.A. (1976). Selective exposure to the self. *Journal of Research in Personality, 10*, 98–106.

Goffman, E. (1959). *The presentation of self in everyday life*. New York: Doubleday-Anchor.

Halberstam, D. (1969). *The best and the brightest*. Greenwich, Connecticut: Fawcett.

Harrison, S., & Nathanson, S. (1982). [Toward the development of an individual difference measure of entrapment-proneness]. Unpublished data. Tufts University.

Heider, F. (1958). *The psychology of interpersonal relations*. New York: Wiley.

Hirschman, A.O. (1970). *Exit, voice, and loyalty: Responses to decline in firms, organizations, and states*. Cambridge, Massachusetts: Harvard University Press.

Holmes, D.S., & Bennett, D.H. (1974). Experiments to answer the question raised by the use of deception in psychological research. *Journal of Personality and Social Psychology, 29*, 358–367.

Hornstein, H. (1970). The influence of social models on helping. In J. Macauley & L. Berkowitz (Eds.), *Altruism and helping behavior*. New York: Academic Press.

Hornstein, H., Fisch, E , and Holmes, M. (1968). Influence of a model's feelings about his behavior and his relevance as comparison other on observers' helping behavior. *Journal of Personality and Social Psychology, 10*, 222–226.

Hottes, J.H., & Kahn, A. (1974). Sex differences in a mixed-motive conflict situation. *Journal of Personality, 42*, 260–275.

Houser, R.F. (1982). *The effects of self-esteem, self-consciousness, and performance attribution on psychological entrapment*. Unpublished master's thesis, Tufts University.

James, W. (1890/1952). The principles of psychology. In R.M. Hutchinson (Ed.), *Great books of the Western World*. Chicago: Encyclopedia Brittanica, 1952. (Originally published, 1890).

Janis, I.L. (1982). *Groupthink* (2nd Ed.). Boston: Houghton-Mifflin.

Janis, I.L., & King, B. (1954). The influence of role-playing on opinion change. *Journal of Abnormal and Social Psychology, 49*, 211–218.

Janis, I.L., & Mann, L. (1977). *Decision making: A psychological analysis of conflict, choice, and commitment*. New York: Free Press.

Janoff-Bulman, R. & Brickman, P. (1980). Expectations and what people learn from failure. In N.T. Feather (Ed.), *Expectancy, incentive, and action*. Hillsdale, New Jersey: Erlbaum.

Jones, E.E., & Davis, K.E. (1965). From acts to dispositions: The attribution process in person perception. In L. Berkowitz (Ed.), *Advances in experimental social psychology* (Vol. 2). New York: Academic Press, 1965.

Kahn, A., Hottes, J., & Davis, W.L. (1971). Cooperation and optimal responding in the prisoner's dilemma game: Effects of sex and physical attractiveness. *Journal of Personality and Social Psychology, 17*, 267–279.

Kahneman, D., Slovic, P., & Tversky, A. (1982). *Judgment under uncertainty: Heuristics and biases*. New York: Cambridge University Press.

Kahneman, D., & Tversky, A. (1979). Prospect theory: An analysis of decisions under risk. *Econometrica, 47*, 263–291.

Kelley, H.H. (1967). Attribution theory in social psychology. In D. Levine (Ed.), *Nebraska symposium on motivation*. Lincoln: University of Nebraska Press.

Kiesler, C.A. (1971). *The psychology of commitment*. New York: Academic Press.

Lamm, H., & Myers, D.G. (1978). Group-induced polarization of attitudes and behavior. In L. Berkowitz (Ed.), *Advances in experimental social psychology*. New York: Academic Press, 1978.

Latané, B., & Darley, J.M. (1970). *The unresponsive bystander: Why doesn't he help?* New York: Appleton-Century-Crofts.

Latham, G.P., Wexley, K.N., & Pursell, E.D., (1975). Training managers to minimize rating errors in the observation of behavior. *Journal of Applied Psychology, 60*, 550–555.

Levi, A. (1982). *Escalating commitment and risk taking in dynamic decision behavior*. Unpublished doctoral dissertation, Yale University.

Levitin, T.E. (1979). Children of divorce. *Journal of Social Issues, 35*, 1–25.

Lewicki, R.J. (1980). *"Bad loan psychology": Entrapment and commitment in financial lending*. Unpublished manuscript, Duke University.

Lewin, K. (1938). The conceptual representation and measurement of psychological forces. *Contributions to Psychological Theory*, 1.

Lewin, K. (1947). Group decision and social change. In T. Newcomb & E. Hartley (Eds.), *Readings in social psychology*. New York: Holt.

Lingle, J.H., Brock, T.C., & Cialdini, R.B. (1977). Surveillance instigates entrapment when violations are observed, when personal involvement is high, and when sanctions are severe. *Journal of Personality and Social Psychology, 35*, 419–429.

Louis, M.R. (1980). Surprise and sense making: What newcomers experience in entering unfamiliar organizational settings. *Administrative Science Quarterly, 25*, 226–251.

Maccoby, E.E., & Jacklin, C.N. (1974). *The psychology of sex differences*. Stanford: Stanford University Press.

Mann, L. (1971). Effects of a commitment warning on children's decision behavior. *Journal of Personality and Social Psychology, 17*, 74–80.

Mann, L., & Taylor, V. (1970). The effects of commitment and choice difficulty on predecision processes. *Journal of Social Psychology, 82*, 221–230.

Manz, C.C., & Sims, H.P. (1981). Vicarious learning: The influence of modeling on organizational behavior. *Academy of Management Review, 6*, 105–113.

McFarlin, D.B., Baumeister, R.F., & Blascovich, J. (in press). On knowing when to quit: Task failure, self-esteem, advice, and nonproductive persistence. *Journal of Personality*.

Milgram, S. (1974). *Obedience to authority*. New York: Harper.

Miller, I.W., & Norman, W.H. (1979). Learned helplessness in humans: A review and attribution-theory model. *Psychological Bulletin, 86*, 93–118.

Mischel, W. (1968). *Personality assessment*. New York: Wiley.

Mischel, W. (1973). Toward a cognitive social learning reconceptualization of personality. *Psychological Review, 80*, 252–283.

Myers, D.G. (1978). Polarizing effects of social comparison. *Journal of Experimental Social Psychology, 14*, 554–563.

Mynatt, C., & Sherman, S.J. (1975). Responsibility attribution in groups and individuals: A direct test of the diffusion of responsibility hypothesis. *Journal of Personality and Social Psychology, 32*, 1111–1118.

Nathanson, S., Brockner, J., Brenner, D., Samuelson, C., Countryman, M., Lloyd, M., & Rubin, J.Z. (1982). Toward the reduction of entrapment. *Journal of Applied Social Psychology, 12*, 193–208.

Northcraft, G.B., & Wolf, G. (1984). Dollars, sense, and sunk costs: A life cycle model of resource allocation decisions. *Academy of Management Review, 9*, 225–234.

Orne, M. (1962). On the social psychology of the psychological experiment. *American Psychologist, 17*, 776–783.

Platt, J. (1973). Social traps. *American Psychologist, 28*, 641–651.

Porter, L.W., Crampon, W.J., & Smith, F.J. (1976). Organizational commitment and managerial turnover: A longitudinal study. *Organizational Behavior and Human Performance, 15*, 87–98.

Pruitt, D.G., & Johnson, D.F. (1970). Mediation as an aid to face saving in negotiation. *Journal of Personality and Social Psychology, 14*, 239–246.

Pruitt, D.G., & Rubin, J.Z. (in press). *Conflict: Processes of escalation and de-escalation*. Reading, Mass: Addison-Wesley.

Regan, D.T., & Fazio, R. (1977). On the consistency between attitudes and behavior: Look to the method of attitude formation. *Journal of Experimental Social Psychology, 13*, 28–45.

Reibstein, O.J., Youngblood, S.A., & Fromkin, H.L. (1975). Number of choices and perceived decision freedom as determinants of satisfaction and consumer behavior. *Journal of Applied Psychology, 60*, 434–437.

Rosenberg, M. (1965). *Society and the adolescent self-image*. Princeton, New Jersey: Princeton University Press.

Rosenthal, R., & Jacobson, L. (1968). *Pygmalion in the classroom*. New York: Holt, Rinehart, & Winston.

Rotter, J.B. (1966). Generalized expectancies for internal versus external control of reinforcement. *Psychological Monographs, 80*, (1, Whole No. 609).

Rubin, J.Z. (1978a). [Magnitude of incentive and entrapment]. Unpublished data, Tufts University.

Rubin, J.Z. (1978b). [Effect of income source on entrapment]. Unpublished data, Tufts University.

Rubin, J.Z. (1981). Psychological traps. *Psychology Today*, March, 52–63.

Rubin, J.Z. (1985). *The book of traps*. Unpublished manuscript.

Rubin, J.Z., & Brockner, J. (1975). Factors affecting entrapment in waiting situations: The rosencrantz and guildenstern effect. *Journal of Personality and Social Psychology, 31*, 1054–1063.

Rubin, J.Z., Brockner, J., Small-Weil, S., & Nathanson, S. (1980). Factors affecting entry into psychological traps. *Journal of Conflict Resolution, 24*, 405–426.

Rubin, J.Z., & Brown, B.R. (1975). *The social psychology of bargaining and negotiation*. New York: Academic Press.

Rubin, J.Z., & Samuelson, C. (1980). [Effect of perceived attractiveness on entrapment]. Unpublished data, Tufts University.

Rusbult, C.E. (1980). Commitment and satisfaction in romantic associations: A test of the investment model. *Journal of Experimental Social Psychology, 16*, 172–186.

Rusbult, C.E., & Farrell, D. (1983). A longitudinal test of the investment model: The impact on job satisfaction, job committment, and turnover of variations in rewards, costs, alternatives, and investments. *Journal of Applied Psychology, 68*, 429–438.

Rusbult, C.E., Zembrodt, I.M., & Gunn, L.K. (1982). Exit, voice, loyalty, and neglect: Responses to dissatisfaction in romantic involvements. *Journal of Personality and Social Psychology, 43*, 1230–1242.

Salancik, G.R. (1977). Commitment and the control of organizational behavior and belief. In B.M. Staw & G.R. Salanick (Eds.), *New directions in organizational behavior*. Malabar, Florida: Robert E. Krieger.

Sarason, I.G., Smith, R.E., & Diener, E. (1975). Personality research: Components of variance attributable to the person and the situation. *Journal of Personality and Social Psychology, 32*, 199–204.

Scheier, M.F., (1976). Self-awareness, self-consciousness, and angry aggression. *Journal of Personality, 44*, 627–644.

Scheier, M.F., Buss, A.H., & Buss, D.M. (1978). Self-consciousness, self-report of aggressiveness, and aggression. *Journal of Research in Personality, 12,* 133–140.

Scheier, M.F., & Carver, C.S. (1977). Self-focused attention and the experience of emotion: Attraction, repulsion, elation, and depression. *Journal of Personality and Social Psychology, 35,* 625–636.

Schelling, T.C. (1960). *The strategy of conflict.* New York: Oxford Press.

Schlenker, B.R. (1980). *Impression management: The self-concept, social identity, and interpersonal relations.* Monterey, California: Brooks/Cole.

Schoorman, F.D. (1984). *The escalation bias in performance appraisal judgments.* Unpublished manuscript, University of Maryland.

Seligman, M.E.P. (1975). *Helplessness: On depression, development, and death.* San Francisco: Freeman.

Shaw, M.E. (1976). *Group dynamics: The psychology of small group behavior* (2nd ed.). New York: McGraw-Hill.

Shubik, M. (1971). The dollar auction game: A paradox in noncooperative behavior and escalation. *Journal of Conflict Resolution, 15,* 109–111.

Sjoberg, L. (1983). Value change and relapse following a decision to quit or reduce smoking. *Scandinavian Journal of Psychology, 24,* 137–148.

Skinner, B.F. (1953). *Science and human behavior.* New York: Macmillan.

Snyder, M. (1981). Impression management: The self in social interaction. In L. Wrightsman & K. Deaux, *Social psychology in the 80s* (3rd ed.). Monterey, California: Brooks/Cole.

Spence, J.T., & Helmreich, R. (1972). The attitudes toward women scale. *Journal Supplement Abstract Service Catalog of Selected Documents in Psychology, 2,* 66–67.

Staw, B.M. (1976). Knee-deep in the big muddy: A study of escalating commitment to a chosen course of action. *Organizational Behavior and Human Performance, 16,* 27–44.

Staw, B.M. (1979). Rationality and justification in organizational life. In B.M. Staw & L.L. Cummings (eds.), *Research in organizational behavior* (Vol. 2). Greenwich, Connecticut: JAI Press.

Staw, B.M. (1982). Counterforces to change: Escalation and commitment as sources of administrative inflexibility. In P. Goodman (Ed.), *Change in organizations.* Jossey-Bass.

Staw, B.M., (1984). *Escalation at the credit window: Bank decisions on non-performing loans.* Unpublished manuscript, University of California.

Staw, B.M., & Ross, J. (1978). Commitment to a policy decision: A multitheoretical perspective. *Administratice Science Quarterly, 23,* 40–64.

Staw, B.M., & Ross, J. (1980). Commitment in an experimenting society: An experiment on the attribution of leadership from administrative scenarios. *Journal of Applied Psychology, 65,* 249–260.

Staw, B.M., Sandelands, L.E., & Dutton, J.E. (1981). Threat-rigidity effects in organizational behavior. A multi-level analysis. *Administrative Science Quarterly, 26,* 501–524.

Stoner, J.A.F. (1962). *A comparison of individual and group decisions involving risk.* Unpublished master's thesis, Massachusets Institute of Technology.

Strodtbeck, F., & Mann, R. (1956). Sex-role differentiation in jury deliberations. *Sociometry, 19,* 3–11.

Swap, W.C., & Rubin, J.Z. (1983). Measurement of interpersonal orientation. *Journal of Personality and Social Psychology, 44,* 208–219.

Tedeschi, J.T., Schlenker, B.R., & Bonoma, T.V. (1971). Cognitive dissonance: Private ratiocination or public spectacle? *American Psychologist, 26,* 685–695.

Teger, A. (1980). *Too much invested to quit.* New York: Pergamon Press.

Tesser, A., & Rosen, S. (1975). The reluctance to transmit bad news. In L. Berkowitz (Ed.), *Advances in experimental social psychology* (Vol. 8). New York: Academic Press.

Tropper, R. (1972). *The effects of conflict structure and relative strength on escalation.* Unpublished manuscript, Boston University.

Turner, R.G. (1977). Self-consciousness and anticipatory belief change. *Personality and Social Psychology Bulletin, 3,* 438–441.

Tyler, T.R., & Sears, D.O. (1977). Coming to like obnoxious people when we must live with them. *Journal of Personality and Social Psychology, 35,* 200–211.

Vandivier, K. (1972). Why should my conscience bother me. In A. Heilbroner (ed.), *In the name of profit.* Garden City, N.Y.: Doubleday.

Vroom, V. (1964). *Work and motivation.* New York: Wiley.

Wanous, J. (1980). *Organizational entry: Recruitment, selection, and socialization of newcomers.* Reading, Mass.: Addison-Wesley.

Weiner, B. (1974). *Achievement motivation and attribution theory.* Morristown, New Jersey: General Learning Press.

Weiss, H.M. (1977). Subordinate imitation of supervisory behavior. *Organizational Behavior and Human Performance, 19,* 89–105.

Wicklund, R.A. (1975). Objective self-awareness. In L. Berkowitz (Ed.), *Advances in experimental social psychology* (Vol. 8). New York: Academic Press.

Wicklund, R.A., & Frey, D. (1980). Self-awareness theory: When the self makes a difference. In D.M. Wegner & R.R. Vallacher (Eds.), *The self in social psychology.* New York: Oxford.

Winer, B.J. (1971). *Statistical principles in experimental design* (2nd ed.). New York: McGraw-Hill.

Wolf, G., & Conlon, E.J. (1984). *The ecology of sunk cost problems.* Unpublished manuscript, University of Arizona.

Wortman, C.B., & Brehm, J.W. (1975). Responses to uncontrollable outcomes: An integration of reactance theory and the learned helplessness model. In L. Berkowitz (Ed.), *Advances in experimental social psychology* (Vol. 8). New York: Academic Press.

Wortman, C.B., & Dintzer, L. (1978). Is an attributional analysis of the learned helplessness phenomenon viable? A critique of the Abramson–Seligman–Teasdale reformulation. *Journal of Abnormal Psychology, 87,* 75–90.

Younger, J.C., & Doob, A. (1978). Attribution and aggression: The misattribution of anger. *Journal of Research in Personality, 12,* 164–171.

Zajonc, R.B. (1965). Social facilitation. *Science, 149,* 269–274.

Zanna, M.P., & Pack, S.J. (1975). On the self-fulfilling nature of apparent sex differences in behavior. *Journal of Experimental Social Psychology, 11,* 583–591.

Zimbardo, P.G. (1970). The human choice: Individuation, reason, and order versus deindividuation, impulse, and chaos. In W.J. Arnold & D. Levine (Eds.), *Nebraska symposium on motivation* (Vol. 17). Lincoln, Nebraska: University of Nebraska Press.

Zimbardo, P.G. (1972). Pathology of imprisonment. *Society, 9,* 4–8.

Author Index

Subject Index

Springer Series in Social Psychology (Recent Titles)